D1542025

Bach Studies

This volume of essays reflects the increasing breadth and scope of current Bach research. The fifteen essays by American and European scholars address a wide range of topics and issues: Magnificat, Cantata, and Passion; Parody and Genre; The *Well-Tempered Clavier*; and Transmission and Reception. Many of the authors focus on works which – due to the new Bach chronology – can now be examined in a new light. Seen as a whole, the essays combine source-critical and analytic methods with historical and theological interpretation to consider problems of genesis and style, as well as questions of transmission and reception.

In the first part of the collection, the authors use new approaches to examine Bach's working methods and compositional procedures in a variety of vocal genres, including the Magnificat and the St John Passion, as well as the cantata ritornello and accompanied recitative. The second section is concerned with broader issues. Transcription and parody, and stylistic and notational conventions are discussed in a variety of works, including the French overtures for keyboard, three transcriptions for organ, the Chromatic Fantasia and Fugue, and the Lutheran masses. In the third section, the authors draw on primary source-materials along with musical evidence to identify Bach's compositional procedures in the *Well-Tempered Clavier*, and to reconstruct the "four conceptual stages" of the Fugue in C Minor from Book I. The final part of the volume, devoted to *Rezeptionsgeschichte*, traces the ways in which Bach's works were transmitted during his lifetime – up until the time of Mozart. In documenting the Bach-reception in the twentieth century, several newly discovered chorale harmonizations by Anton Webern are transcribed and analyzed.

This collection of essays will be of great importance to all those involved in the music of J. S. Bach, whether as scholars or students, performers or listeners. The work contained here represents the state of Bach scholarship in the 1980s and charts the course of Bach studies in the decades ahead.

Bach Studies

Edited by
Don O. Franklin

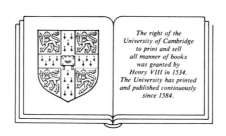

The right of the
University of Cambridge
to print and sell
all manner of books
was granted by
Henry VIII in 1534.
The University has printed
and published continuously
since 1584.

Cambridge University Press

Cambridge
New York   New Rochelle
Melbourne   Sydney

Published by the Press Syndicate of the University of Cambridge
The Pitt Building, Trumpington Street, Cambridge CB2 1RP
32 East 57th Street, New York, NY 10022, USA
10 Stamford Road, Oakleigh, Melbourne 3166, Australia

© Cambridge University Press 1989

First published 1989

Printed in Great Britain at the University Press, Cambridge

British Library cataloguing in publication data
Bach studies.
1. German music. Bach, Johann Sebastian –
Critical studies
I. Franklin, Don O.
780′.92′4

Library of Congress cataloguing in publication data
Bach studies / edited by Don O. Franklin.
p.   cm.
Includes index.
ISBN 0–521–34105–1
1. Bach, Johann Sebastian, 1685–1750 – Criticism and
interpretation. I. Franklin, Don O.
ML410.B13B18   1989
780′.92′4 – dc19   88–15961   CIP

ISBN 0 521 34105 1

DISCARDED
WIDENER UNIVERSITY
WIDENER
WOLFGRAM
LIBRARY
CHESTER, PA.

ME

Contents

v

Plates

Part 4   Transmission and reception

*Reproduced by permission of the following: private owner (Plates 1 and 2);
the Robert Owen Lehman Collection, on deposit at the Pierpont Morgan
Library (Plate 3); the Gertrude Whittall Collection, Music Division,
The Library of Congress (Plate 4); the Paul Sacher Foundation,
Basel (Plate 5); Riemenschneider Bach Institute, Berea, Ohio (Plate 6);
Stanford University Library (Plate 7); Concordia Seminary, St Louis,
Missouri (Plates 9 and 11); Gerhard Herz, Louisville, Kentucky
(Plate 10); the Music Library of Yale University (Plate 12); Music
Division, the Library of Congress (Plate 13); collection of William
H. Scheide, Princeton, (Plates 8, 14 and 16); and the Hans Moldenhauer
Archives, Spokane, Washington (Plate 15).*

Preface

The present volume of essays, the first in what is hoped will be a continuing series, reflects the increasing breadth and scope of current research on J. S. Bach. The essays are based on papers read at an international conference held at the University of Michigan-Flint in April of 1985. To mark the Bach tercentenary, the university invited fifteen American and European scholars to contribute papers which, while representative of traditional Bach scholarship, are indicative of the changing profile of Bach studies in the 1980s.

The *Spiritus Rector* of the conference (even though not in attendance) was Hans-Joachim Schulze, whose *Studien zur Bach-Überlieferung im 18. Jahrhundert* appeared in 1984. Schulze, in the introduction to his epoch-making study, calls for a more broadly based and synthetic approach to Bach's music – "a productive *Wechselwirkung* between philological research, on the one hand, and new aesthetic, analytic, and stylistic approaches, on the other." He states that specialized studies, such as those included in this volume, may prove more useful than large-scale works in achieving this synthesis. "Only bold questioning, controversial hypotheses, and unconventional methods," he concludes, "will be able to open up new paths of inquiry in Bach studies in the decades ahead."

The fifteen papers in this collection combine source-critical and analytic methods with historical and theological interpretation to address a wide range of issues. Arranged by topic – Magnificat, Cantata and Passion, Parody and Genre, The *Well-Tempered Clavier*, and Transmission and Reception – the majority of the essays focus on Bach's working methods and compositional procedures. Several authors, drawing on a variety of primary source materials, offer detailed descriptions of Bach's music-writing procedures; others attempt to reconstruct the "precompositional" steps in the design of a fugue, the composition of instrumental ritornelli, and the overall plan of the Magnificat – in order to recapture the "inner dialogue of the compositional process", in Robert Marshall's words. In some cases, as with the study of the composing score for the C major fugue from Book II, an historical–analytical approach is used; in others, as in the discussion of the accompanied recitative in Cantata 163, the approach is primarily analytical.

Many of the essays examine repertories and genre which – due to the new Bach chronology – can now be considered in a new light. This is particularly true for the Leipzig *Jahrgang* and the St John Passion, as well as for the Chromatic Fantasia and Fugue, and *WTC* II, two of the more problematic instrumental works. In the papers concerned with broader issues – transcription and parody, and stylistic and notational conventions – the authors examine a variety of vocal and instrumental works, including the Lutheran masses, the French Overtures for keyboard, and three transcriptions for organ.

The final part of the volume is devoted to *Rezeptionsgeschichte* – a branch of study relatively new to Bach scholarship, as Ludwig Finscher makes clear at the outset of his essay. In describing the current state of international Bach research and the role of *Rezeptionsgeschichte* in particular, he writes: "Only now, I think, and only due to Schulze's monumental achievement [*Studien* and *Bach Dokumente*] can we start to ask the questions that should have been asked in the beginning: What did Bach's contemporaries know about the composer and his music? Which of his works did they know? Who were the people who knew this music?" Finscher's essay is both historical and historiographical, providing an overview of the critical methodologies used by early twentieth-century Bach scholars, as well as a detailed account of the reception of Bach's music by his students and other contemporaries in the late eighteenth century. The essay which follows focuses on Webern's "creative confrontation" with Bach, providing transcriptions of newly-discovered chorale harmonizations and other examples of Bach's influence on Webern's compositional technique. The final essay, a close examination of several important American Bach sources, sheds new light on Bach's copying-out procedures, as well as on his relationship with Wilhelm Friedemann.

Seen as a whole, the essays represent the state of Bach scholarship in the 1980s. More diverse in scope and methodology than the "new Bach research" initiated by the philological studies of Dürr and Dadelsen in the early 1950s (Dürr's *Studien über die frühen Kantaten Johann Sebastian Bachs* was published in 1951), the papers address questions of transmission and reception, as well as problems of genesis and style. It is our hope that, in published form, they will provide an impetus for new directions in Bach research and contribute toward establishing – in Hans-Joachim Schulze's words – "the basis for a new understanding of Bach's music."

The 1985 Bach conference and the publication of this volume would not have been possible without the generous support of the Cabinet of the University of Michigan-Flint, under the leadership of the Acting Chancellor Dr Marvin J. Roberson, the University of Michigan-Flint Endowment Fund, the Committee on Special Events, the University of Michigan-Flint Music Department, and the Office of Research and Development of the University of Pittsburgh. The collaboration of Professor Douglas Miller, (University of Michigan-Flint (in translating the Siegele essay), and of Sharon Saunders (in preparing the indexes), is also gratefully acknowledged.

DON O. FRANKLIN
University of Pittsburgh

JOHANNES TALL
University of Michigan-Flint

Part I
Magnificat, Cantata and Passion

On the origin of Bach's Magnificat: a Lutheran composer's challenge

ROBERT L. MARSHALL

How do we cope with masterpieces? There is probably a branch of psychology that deals with this – if not, there should be. For our encounter with a great work of art is undeniably a powerful experience, indeed an unsettling one – an experience that, for the moment, at least, leaves us emotionally and intellectually transformed. Moreover, our responses to the momentary "trauma" of great art are not only strong but quite complex. As with other traumatic experiences, we seem, after our exposure to the great work, to pass through a series of stages in our more or less conscious, more or less "rational" efforts to come to terms with what we have read or seen or heard or performed.

Our initial reaction is surely mostly an emotional one. It is an amalgam of strongly felt "affects" consisting most immediately of those feelings directly (and, we may presume, deliberately) generated by the content of the particular work and broadly describable as "happy" or "sad." But this, as it were, "directed" response is accompanied by an "uplifting" feeling, best described, perhaps, as one of elation – often approaching euphoria. From the creator's point of view, this is of course a most desirable and flattering result, but one which he could hardly have counted on. But there is also the admixture of yet another affect in this initial emotional response: it is the not altogether comfortable feeling of awe, that is, boundless admiration subtly blended with a touch of envy!

It is clear that most of us never have the opportunity or the inclination to pass beyond this multi-layered, and ultimately ambivalent, emotional stage in our experience of the great work. This calls to mind the following remark by Albert Einstein: "This is what I have to say about Bach's life work: listen, play, love, revere – and keep your mouth shut." Very well. Perhaps that is good, eminently wise advice. But there is a further stage, one of which

3

Einstein himself was quite well aware in other realms of experience: a stage of reflection. In art, the existence of this stage is of course a testimony to the fact that the masterpiece challenges our minds as much as it excites our feelings. We are moved not just to respond to it but to try to understand it: to try to discover the sources of its remarkable power by subjecting it to rational examination – that is, to an analysis aimed at uncovering the principles of its construction, at identifying the elements of its style, and at recognizing the terms of its expressive vocabulary. We also hope to understand the work by considering it historically – setting it against larger cultural contexts of time, place, genre, and tradition. This "analytical" stage, this attempt to grasp the work with our intellect, surely represents an attempt to master its power over us, and testifies to our need to assert some kind of control over great works of art – putting it crudely, to cut them down to manageable size.

Inevitably, though, we continue – even after such intellectual efforts – to remain spellbound and bewildered in the presence of great works; and we may, accordingly, find ourselves progressing to yet a further stage of confrontation: a stage that may be described as an attempt at de-mystification. In this last stage we seek to gain control, to master the masterpiece, and its hold over us, by remembering that it is, after all, not some natural phenomenon, the work of a supernatural God, but the artifact of someone not altogether unlike ourselves – some flesh-and-blood mortal. Therefore, we now address our questions to the maker of the masterpiece – the artist – rather than the work itself and begin to learn as much as we can about him in order, finally, to obtain some sort of answer to a new question: how he did it. This question may be irreverent – even, in some sense, an indiscreet invasion of privacy. (It may in fact be such a consideration that moved Einstein to offer his sobering advice.) But the issue of origins, of genesis, is one of the eternal questions we ask of all mysteries – and so it is almost invariably raised with respect to great works of art as well; for answering this question seems to hold out the prospect of illuminating the masterpiece from an altogether different and promising direction: from within.

What this pursuit implies is nothing less than the attempt to enter into the mind of the creator: in the case of music, to try, with a leap of the imagination, to "become the composer composing" – to reconstruct, as far as possible, what he must have perceived as the options and choices available to him in matters large and small, as he was absorbed in the act of creation; in other words, we try to recreate the inner dialogue of the compositional process.

The following, admittedly, is such a self-indulgent exercise in demystification, if that indeed is the correct word – or perhaps even, as

Einstein implied, an inexcusable act of hubris. It will have as its object one of the greatest masterpieces of church music: Johann Sebastian Bach's Magnificat.

In attempting a reconstruction of the "inner dialogue of the compositional process," it is crucial to realize that much, if not in fact most, of the creative act is actually done internally: in the mind, and not on paper.[1] The written notation at any moment may represent a rather advanced stage in the weighing of alternatives, any number of which may have been already generated, evaluated, and rejected in the composer's mind before he set down what he thought – at least for the moment – was the solution he was seeking. He might then reconsider his choice once again, and make a visible correction on the page. What might appear to us, then, when we examine a composer's working score or sketch, to be his first and last (that is, his second) thoughts, may in reality be the penultimate and final choices in a considerably longer succession of options that never had to be written down. In fact it turns out to be the case with the Magnificat that the most important decisions were made before the composer ever put pen to paper. To gain insight into these it is necessary to record other kinds of evidence – and also to engage in speculation of the kind that, depending on one's intellectual disposition, can be described either as "unfounded" or "imaginative."

In contrast to the vast majority of his vocal music, which was written within a three-year period at the breathtaking rate of approximately one composition per week, Bach had considerably more time at his disposal for the composition of the Magnificat. For it was to be performed on Christmas Day 1723; and, in Leipzig, Bach was not obliged to compose and perform cantatas during the preceding Advent season. Specifically, from 29 November, the day following the performance of his cantata for the first Sunday of Advent, and the Magnificat performance on 25 December, Bach was freed of the obligation of performing regular Sunday cantatas. Actually, Bach's last *new* composition before the Magnificat was composed earlier still: during the week preceding Sunday 14 November; for both his Advent cantata (Cantata 61, performed on 28 November), and his cantata for the 26th Sunday past Trinity (Cantata 70, performed a week earlier on 21 November) had been composed years before, in Weimar.[2]

---

[1] This point was emphasized by Hugo Riemann as early as 1909. See his "Spontane Phantasietätigkeit und verstandesmässige Arbeit in der tonkünstlerischen Produktion," *Jahrbuch der Musikbibliothek Peters für 1909*, 16 (1910), pp. 33–46.

[2] See Alfred Dürr, *Zur Chronologie der Leipziger Vokalwerke J. S. Bachs*, 2nd ed. (Kassel, 1976), p. 63.

In short, Bach had the luxury of almost six *weeks* (from 15 November to 24 December), rather than the usual six (or even three) *days* for the composition of the Magnificat.[3] And he obviously was intent on taking advantage of the extra time. The Magnificat was by far Bach's most ambitious vocal composition since his assumption six months earlier of the position of Thomaskantor and Director of Church Music for the city of Leipzig. With its twelve movements (sixteen, counting four interpolations about which there will be more to say), the Magnificat is easily twice as long as the normal six-movement cantata.

Moreover, the Magnificat contains no "easy" movements, such as *secco* recitatives or plain four-part chorale harmonizations – forms which, after all, pose far fewer compositional problems on the whole than do elaborate arias and choruses. Indeed, in the Magnificat there is not just one full-scale choral movement, as in the usual Sunday cantata, but no fewer than five. It is also necessary to recall that for the same day – Christmas Day 1723 – for which Bach composed the Magnificat, he also composed a second new work, a sanctus setting for chorus and orchestra, BWV 238. Finally, he revised for performance yet a third work, the quite extensive cantata, *Christen ätzet diesen Tag*, BWV 63, which had, however, been *composed* ten years earlier, in Weimar.[4] All things considered, then, six weeks' time could not have been that much of a luxury, after all, for the composition of the Magnificat.

But composing at breakneck speed was simply a fact of life for a composer in the early eighteenth century. And it was this fact, of course, that dictated how composers of the time approached the act of composition in the first place and molded their attitude towards the question of originality. Originality, as a conscious concern, could hardly have existed for Bach and his contemporaries. Quite the contrary: they were far more interested in drawing on the accumulated experience and the techniques developed by their predecessors and contemporaries, for doing so obviously facilitated their task. Therefore, in setting out to compose a sacred work like the Magnificat Bach had at his disposal, and was willing to adopt virtually without reservation, a broad array of time-tested (that is, "conventional") formal and stylistic procedures that governed the typical arias and choruses

---

[3] That Bach in Leipzig most likely had only three or four days for the actual composition of a regular Sunday cantata is demonstrated in my *The Compositional Process of J. S. Bach* (Princeton, 1972), Vol. 1, p. 235.

[4] See Dürr, *Zur Chronologie*, p. 64.

of the late Baroque era and that included rhythmic and melodic figures, harmonic groundplans, and fairly standardized formal patterns of repetition.[5]

As is well known, the Magnificat is preserved in two distinct versions. The first, in the key of E flat, BWV 243a, was the one written for Christmas Day 1723 – Bach's first Christmas in Leipzig as Thomaskantor. The far more familiar second version in D major, BWV 243, is now known to have been prepared some time between 1732 and 1735 – very likely just about ten years after the first – for a performance on 2 July 1733: the feast of the Visitation of Mary, and, most significantly, the day decreed to mark the official end of the five-month period of national mourning that followed upon the death of the Saxon Elector Friedrich August I the previous February.[6] For both versions, the only surviving original sources are the autograph scores, documents that serve as perfect examples of the two extremes found among Bach's musical manuscripts: the working or composing score on the one hand, and the fair copy on the other. (Both scores are housed in the Deutsche Staatsbibliothek, East Berlin: Mus. MS autograph Bach P 38 (E flat version) and P 39 (D major version) respectively.[7])

It is not surprising that the autograph of the D major version is by far the more handsome of the two, whereas that of the E flat version is vastly more informative as to the formation of the work. But it too represents a relatively advanced stage in the composition's genesis. Accordingly, it will be necessary not so much to examine the autograph evidence – the marginal sketches and the fairly numerous corrections of relatively minor details (an issue treated elsewhere)[8] – as to attempt to trace the process of composition back to an even more embryonic stage, its *pre-history*: the stage where the planning of the work had not yet reached the point where Bach was prepared even to take up a sheet of manuscript paper and rule lines on it, the stage where the piece was still being formulated in general terms in the composer's mind, a stage, as it were, "before genesis."

---

[5] The most extensive discussion of Bach's use of the traditional figures in the Magnificat appears in Ulrich Meyer, "Musikalisch-rhetorische Figuren in J. S. Bachs Magnificat," *Musik und Kirche*, 43 (1973), pp. 172–81.

[6] See the editor's commentary in Johann Sebastian Bach, *Magnificat, BWV 243: Faksimile des Autographs*, ed. Hans-Joachim Schulze. *Faksimile-Reihe Bachscher Werke und Schriftstücke*, 21 (Leipzig, 1985), pp. 7–9.

[7] For a closer description of the manuscripts see *Neue Bach Ausgabe* (NBA), II/3, *Kritischer Bericht (KB)*, pp. 10–15, pp. 18–21 and Marshall, *The Compositional Process*, especially Vol. 1, pp. 47–53, 54–56.

[8] See Marshall, *The Compositional Process*, and, especially, Alfred Dürr's critical report, *NBA*, II/3, *KB*, pp. 37–51.

It is clear that before the first musical notations could be set down they had to be preceded by what may be called "pre-compositional" planning. During this stage Bach considered his "given" material, the text, in order, first, to uncover its various implications for the musical setting and then, once uncovered, essentially to implement them directly. For example, the general design and structure of the text were allowed to dictate the general design and structure of the music: that is, the number of text verses largely determined the number of movements, while the accentual patterns of the text, its prosody, obviously influenced the choice of meter as well as specific decisions regarding the rhythm of thematic ideas and even the choice of pitches.

But there were considerations even more "preliminary" and fundamental than these. Bach had to take into account local conditions and traditions and also the particular purpose of the pending performance of the Magnificat. Like countless settings of the work extending back to the early Middle Ages, Bach's Magnificat was to be performed as part of a Vespers service; but it was to be part, specifically, of a Lutheran Vespers service – in eighteenth-century Leipzig, and for Christmas Day. According to the liturgical usage in Leipzig at the time, the Magnificat was to be sung on high feasts of the church year not, as was the case on regular Sundays, in German and in a simple unaccompanied motet or *a cappella* style, or as an even simpler harmonized congregational hymn; rather, it was to be performed as a full-scale concert piece for voices and instruments, and in Latin. Furthermore, for the specific high feast of Christmas, a long-standing Leipzig custom called for the inclusion, within the performance of the Magnificat proper, of a series of hymn texts (both in German and in Latin) which were completely independent of the Magnificat text. They provided something like a miniature summary of the Christmas story. But, as we shall see, they also presented a German Lutheran composer of the early eighteenth century with a unique compositional challenge.[9]

Bach's 1723 version of the Magnificat contained four such hymns, or *Laudes*, as they were called at the time. They are designated in the Bach literature as movements A to D. The first is a setting of Martin Luther's chorale "Vom Himmel hoch"; the second is a setting of an anonymous text, "Freut euch und jubiliert"; the third, movement C, is based on the first lines of the greater doxology, "Gloria in excelsis Deo"; movement D, finally, is a

---

[9] The most recent and most comprehensive survey of the Leipzig traditions bearing on Bach's setting is presented in Robert M. Cammarota, "The Sources of the Christmas Interpolations in J. S. Bach's Magnificat in E-flat Major (BWV 243a)," *Current Musicology*, 36 (1983), pp. 79–99.

strophe from a Christmas hymn dating back to the late sixteenth century, "Virga Jesse floruit."

In addition to Bach's autograph there is a manuscript, of Leipzig provenance, containing exactly the same four hymns in exactly the same order. They were presumably composed by Johann Kuhnau; the only source, however, is an anonymous set of parts.[10] The existence of this setting underlines the fact that Bach, in planning his Magnificat composition, found his artistic freedom circumscribed not only by the requirements of the Leipzig liturgy but also by the precedents established by his musical predecessors.

Indeed, Bach's *Laudes* are particularly fascinating in that they seem to survey in almost systematic fashion the various historical styles of vocal music. "Vom Himmel hoch" is an *a cappella* chorale cantus firmus motet in the strict *stile antico*. "Freut euch und jubiliert" is still basically polyphonic but considerably lighter in texture and with an independent basso continuo; its copious voice-pairings in parallel motion are obviously indebted to early Baroque practice. (The movement has been shown in fact to bear a strong similarity to a setting of the same text by Sethus Calvisius, himself a Thomaskantor in Leipzig in the early seventeenth century. It was published in 1603, along with Calvisius's settings of other Christmas *Laudes* including "Vom Himmel hoch" and "Gloria in excelsis Deo.")[11] "Gloria in excelsis Deo" is characterized by more fundamentally chordal, more declamatory writing reminiscent perhaps of the later seventeenth-century Venetian tradition as cultivated in Germany by the Thomaskantors Johann Schelle, Johann Kuhnau and others. The "Virga Jesse" movement, finally, is set in the very latest operatic style as a modern duet for soprano, bass and continuo.

The musical influences to which Bach was subjected, however, were not limited to those connected with strictly local customs such as the Leipzig Christmas hymns but inevitably extended to the vast repertory of earlier settings of the venerable Magnificat text itself. Bach was not only familiar with many Magnificat settings: he copied out several himself and performed them in Leipzig. In fact, a number of remarkable formal details in his setting were apparently gleaned from earlier models. The universal Christian musical heritage, then, along with the particular musical and liturgical traditions of Lutheran Leipzig, necessarily shaped the direction of Bach's

---

[10] Musikbibliothek der Stadt Leipzig, Sammlung Becker III.2.124.

[11] See Albrecht Tunger, "Johann Sebastian Bachs Einlagesätze zum Magnificat: Beobachtungen und Überlegungen zu ihrer Herkunft," *Bachstunden: Festschrift für Helmut Walcha zum 70. Geburtstag*, ed. Walther Dehnhard and Gottlob Ritter (Frankfurt, 1978), pp. 22–35.

thinking as he turned his attention to the traditional twelve-verse text of the Magnificat, consisting of the ten verses of the Gospel according to St Luke, 1:46–55, augmented by the two additional verses of the lesser doxology "Gloria Patri et Filio."

Now, in formulating his general plan Bach was obliged to observe the contemporary musical conventions that dictated that each of the twelve verses of the Magnificat was to be set as a separate movement – with effective contrast insured by the juxtaposition and alternation of solo and choral numbers. The work would begin and end with choral movements which thus provided an exterior frame. In addition there were perhaps one or more further internal choruses that served to punctuate a series of solo numbers: arias, and possibly duets and other vocal combinations.

There was also an extra-musical constraint impinging on the composer's artistic autonomy, one that critically affected the temporal dimensions of the work. For there were time limitations imposed by the overall duration and full schedule of the Leipzig Vespers service as a whole. The Magnificat setting, after all, was to be only one item on a long agenda.[12] These limitations of time, together with the stylistic convention that fairly dictated that just about every verse of the Magnificat text was to be set as a separate movement, conspired to assure that the individual movements of Bach's setting were kept short. In fact no single movement of Bach's Magnificat is more than 100 measures long, and the entire twelve-movement work (that is, not counting the extra hymns) fills less than 600 measures. This is most untypical for an obviously ambitious composition from the pen of Johann Sebastian Bach.

Bach may have made some jottings as to the succession and alternation of movement types on a separate piece of paper, but it is just as possible that he worked this out entirely in his head. In any event, the overall design of the work, as well as the tonal relationships for the whole work – that is, the order of keys for the individual movements – was evidently firmly decided upon well before Bach began to write down any musical notation in the surviving composing score: the autograph simply contains no corrections that bear on these fundamental matters. Therefore, we may conclude that Bach decided before he began what may be called the stage of "formal

---

[12] See the order of service in C. S. Terry, *Bach: The Magnificat, Lutheran Masses and Motets* (London, 1929; reprinted New York, 1972), p. 5. A slightly different and even longer program appears in Terry's *Joh. Seb. Bach Cantata Texts Sacred and Secular* (London, 1925; reprinted 1964), pp. 66–7.

composition," the writing down, that the work would have the following design (see Figure 1).[13]

Movement	Type	Key
1 Magnificat	Chorus	I
2 Et exultavit	Solo	I
3 Quia respexit	• Solo	vi
4 Omnes generationes	Chorus	iii
5 Quia fecit mihi magna	Solo	V
6 Et misericordia	• Duet	ii
7 Fecit potentiam	Chorus	IV–I
8 Deposuit	Solo	iii
9 Esurientes	Solo	II♯
10 Suscepit Israel	• Trio	vi
11 Sicut locutus est	Chorus	I
12 Gloria Patri	Chorus	I

Figure 1 The order of movements and keys

The outline calls for five choral and seven solo movements: the choruses appearing as structural pillars after every two (or three) solo numbers, with the final choral pillar reinfored and doubly anchored, as it were. There is in addition a progressive increase in the number of vocal soloists in the movements just *preceding* each successive chorus: movement 3 ("Quia respexit") is a solo aria (for soprano), movement 6 ("Et misericordia") a duet (for alto and tenor), movement 10 ("Suscepit Israel") a trio (for two sopranos and alto). (Incidentally, assuming this interpretation of the rationale of Bach's scheme is correct – that is, that it systematically observes such a principle of successive increase in the number of soloists – then it would settle a troubling question of performance practice regarding this work by indicating that the 'Suscepit Israel' movement was conceived not as a chorus but as a trio, and should be performed accordingly.) The tonal plan of the work is largely symmetrical as well (see Figure 2).[14]

[13] Since the same tonal plan underlies both the E♭ and D major versions, the keys are indicated here by Roman numerals rather than pitch names (capitals=major mode; lower case= minor mode).

[14] Open noteheads represent movements in the major, filled-in noteheads movements in the minor mode. D major, as the key of the more familiar version, has been selected for the diagram.

Figure 2 The tonal plan

The tonic is doubly presented at both the beginning and end (movements 1–2, 11–12); these tonic pillars enclose at each end movements in the key of the relative minor (movements 3 and 10). The next two movements in the first half of the composition (4 and 5) are on the third and fifth degrees, respectively: that is, together with the two opening movements in the home key, they outline the tonic chord. The keys of the movements in the second half of the work do not arpeggiate a triad but rather descend by step from the dominant back to the tonic, with the fifth and fourth degrees in effect "shadowed" by *their* own dominants, that is, the second and tonic degrees of the home key. In the case of the chorus "Fecit potentiam," the centerpiece of the composition (movement 7), this "shadow" relationship is expressed within the movement itself. It begins in the subdominant and ends a fifth higher on the tonic. In this way Bach has managed to reintroduce the home key of the Magnificat most strategically at the mid-point of the work.

To repeat the main point: Bach's composing score contains no corrections testifying to any changes of mind bearing on these fundamental matters of movement type and tonal design. These issues were settled and decided before Bach wrote down a single note.

The autograph also reveals – again by virtue of the absence of any pertinent changes – that Bach had reached his basic decisions concerning style, scoring and form with respect to the individual movements during the pre-compositional stage. This applies not only to such matters as tempo, meter, thematic character and compositional technique but also to the most striking formal refinements of Bach's setting: the decision to detach the words "omnes generationes" from the third verse of the Magnificat text (the "Quia respexit") and to set them as an independent chorus; the decision to conclude the central "Fecit potentiam" chorus with a sudden tempo shift to adagio and a change from polyphonic to chordal texture at the final words of the verse, "mente cordis sui;" and, finally, to repeat the music of the first movement at the words "sicut erat in principio" at the end of the final chorus.

Of course, none of these formal effects was original with Bach. They can all be found in Magnificat settings by Bach's forerunners and contemporaries. For example, as Terry was apparently the first to observe, a Magnificat attributed to Albinoni manifests the same treatment of the "omnes generationes" and the "mente cordis sui" passages as that found in Bach.[15] And Monteverdi, as early as 1610, brought back the opening material of the first chorus at the words "sicut erat in principio." But all this is only further evidence that Bach used the planning stage of the compositional process not only to ponder the musical implications of the particular liturgical constraints attached to the task, but also to survey – and indeed to exploit – the rich artistic tradition which he had inherited and to which of course he himself belonged.

We have yet to address the basic issue bearing on the origin and conception of the Magnificat which is raised by the fact that the work exists in two versions (and two manuscripts). It is clear from the autograph score of the E♭ version that Bach entered, and accordingly composed, the movements in the normal order. As the score is laid out movement 2 follows movement 1, movement 3 follows movement 2, and so on up to the end of the work. This is typical of Bach's practice. There is, in fact, only one unambiguous exception to the rule that Bach normally composed the movements of a vocal work in the sequence in which they were to be performed, and that exception, paradoxically enough, is the score of the same E♭ version of the Magnificat. The autograph reveals that the four supplementary movements were not composed (that is, written down) until the entire standard Latin text had been set. Verbal directions in the score indicate at what points in the work the *Laudes* are to be performed.

It is difficult to know exactly what to make of the fact that the Christmas interpolations appear at the very end of the composing score. It may mean that Bach was not yet aware or informed, when he began to set down the Magnificat, that the local Leipzig Christmas tradition called for these interpolations – or it had simply slipped his mind for the moment. If this was the case (and it may have been), then we would have a true, but trivial, instance in which Bach indeed composed the movements of a work out of their expected sounding order – trivial, because it would have been the consequence of mere ignorance, not choice. But it is also possible that Bach well knew about the four interpolations when he began writing but intended at first to make use of some pre-existent setting, such as Kuhnau's,[16] and that

[15] See Terry, *Bach: The Magnificat*, pp. 17, 19. The score is published as Edition Eulenburg No. 1074, ed. Felix Schröder (Zurich, 1968). According to Michael Talbot (*The New Grove*, Vol. 1, pp. 216ff.), the ascription to Albinoni is "of dubious authenticity."

[16] Hans-Joachim Schulze raises this possibility, too. See the *Nachwort* to his edition of the D major version published as Edition Peters No. 9850 (Leipzig, 1979), pp. 76ff.

in any case he preferred to approach the Latin Magnificat as an integral work that should maintain its formal integrity and self-sufficiency and should be readily performable without the supplemental items. There would also have been a practical advantage to that; for Bach would surely have been interested in insuring that his composition was usable on those high feasts other than Christmas when the elaborate Magnificat settings were performed in Leipzig – but without the Christmas movements.[17] And, again, Bach did in fact remove them when he prepared the score for the D major version around ten years later.

It would seem, then, that the four interpolated movements were not – and were not intended to be – an integral part of Bach's conception of the work. And we have seen the logical plan that underlies the organization of the twelve movements of the Latin composition (Figures 1 and 2). The four additional movements, then, must have constituted a considerable problem for Bach: namely, how to insert these foreign bodies into the carefully designed order in a way that not only caused minimal disruption but, if possible, managed to produce a logical, even compelling, formal organization of its own. This, I submit, was this Lutheran composer's particular challenge.

It will come as no surprise to learn that Bach solved the problem both effectively and economically. He indicated that the four hymns were to follow after movements 2, 5, 7 and 9. This particular placement was not pre-ordained. It differs, for example from that found in a recently recovered, anonymous Magnificat, of Leipzig provenance, into which Kuhnau's *Laudes* were evidently inserted.[18] The result of Bach's disposition is that the sixteen movements of the E♭ version are so ordered that the work falls into two large parts or sections (Figure 3).

It is now a bipartite work in a way that it was not (and is not) when the hymns are absent. The first part consists of movements 1 to 7, along with movements A and B: nine movements in all. The second part consists of movements 8 to 12, along with movements C and D: seven in all. The nine movements of the first part present a strict alternation of choruses and solo numbers that culminate in the *tutti* chorus "Fecit potentiam."

The second part is based not on the alternation of choral and solo movements but rather on a different principle of organization, one consisting of choruses only at the beginning and end. Moreover, both the opening

---

[17] There were at least fourteen such occasions, besides Christmas. See Günther Stiller, *Johann Sebastian Bach und das Leipziger gottesdienstliche Leben seiner Zeit* (Kassel, 1970), pp. 65, 80–1.

[18] See Cammarota, "The Sources," pp. 87–9.

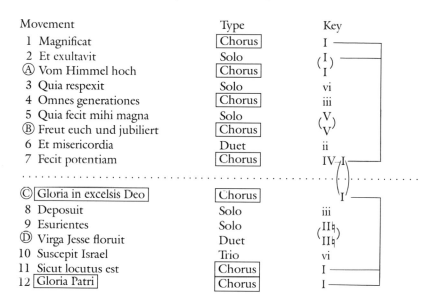

Figure 3 The Christmas Magnificat (BWV 243a): order of movements and keys

and final movements of Part II, movements C and 12, are set to "Gloria" texts: the greater and lesser doxologies, "Gloria in excelsis" and "Gloria Patri," respectively. These framing choruses enclose a succession of five movements that observe a principle of increasing textural density: movement 8, "Deposuit," is a solo aria (for tenor) and unison strings; movement 9, "Esurientes," is again a solo aria (for alto) but this time with two obbligato instrumental parts (two recorders); movement D, "Virga Jesse floruit," calls for a vocal duet; movement 10, "Suscepit Israel," is a vocal trio; and movement 11, "Sicut locutus est," is a five-part, *a cappella* chorus with basso continuo. Bach also insured that the four interpolated movements did not disturb the careful tonal design by simply having each of them duplicate and reinforce the key of the preceding number.[19]

There can be little doubt, however, that Bach regarded this solution, resourceful and even elegant as it is, as less than ideal from the aesthetic, and perhaps even from a theological or Christian, point of view. For the E flat Magnificat is, after all, in the final analysis, a hybrid both musically and textually, and even constitutes a questionable violation of a sacred

[19] Schulze, on the contrary, believes that the inclusion of the hymns "had undesirable consequences for the tonal organization of the whole." See the facsimile edition, pp. 6, 12; and Edition Peters, pp. 76, 79.

biblical text. (This is probably also the reason that the Leipzig town council had attempted to ban the singing of *Laudes* as early as 1702.)[20] One suspects, therefore, that Bach must have been eager for the opportunity to recast it – and did so, as we now know, some ten years later, around 1733: that is at about the same time that he began to compose the Mass in B Minor and in general began to display increased interest in the composition of Latin sacred texts.[21]

What has this attempt to imagine how Johann Sebastian Bach approached the composition of his Magnificat accomplished? It has demonstrated that Bach must have arrived at just about all of the fundamental decisions bearing on the design and the dimensions of one of his most majestic works before he had written a single note on paper. As Philipp Spitta once declared:

In general the creative act [for Bach] was an internal one . . . Despite the great complexity of his music we know of few cases where the layout of a piece was rejected once it had been worked out. Nor did he often falter while working out the details. Some times he made changes when he took up a work again at a later date; but for an understanding of the way it was formed in the beginning, the evidence provided by such changes tells us nothing.[22]

It is easy to imagine that Spitta was thinking of the Magnificat when he wrote these words. The composing-score certainly does contain a great number of corrections of detail, and Bach certainly made changes when he took up the work again and penned the D major version. But, as Spitta said, they tell us virtually nothing of the way the work was formed "in the beginning." In order to come closer to that mystery it turned out to be necessary to get behind the written record and, in effect, to stand the usual method for investigating the compositional process on its head. Instead of analyzing sketches and autograph corrections, it proved more fruitful to ascertain what aspects of the work underwent no visible changes and to assess the implications of such negative evidence. The results necessarily are conjectural: they amount virtually to an attempt to read Bach's mind. But since the conclusions do after all derive from objective observations of "hard" manuscript evidence, buttressed with historically verifiable information bearing on the religious and musical traditions to which the work belongs,

[20] See Martin Geck, "J. S. Bachs Weihnachts-Magnificat und sein Traditionszusammenhang," *Musik und Kirche*, 31 (1961), pp. 257–66, especially p. 264.
[21] On this point see Schulze, foreword to the facsimile edition, pp. 8ff.
[22] Philipp Spitta, "Beethoveniana," *Zur Musik: Sechzehn Aufsätze* (Berlin, 1892), p. 181.

there is reason to think that they are not just idle guesses, but to some (unfortunately unknowable) extent resemble what really must have been Bach's earliest reflections and decisions as he embarked on the creation of one of the grandest masterpieces in the history of sacred music.

Expressivity in the accompanied recitatives of Bach's cantatas

GEORGE J. BUELOW

Many of the distinguishing characteristics of Bach's music have been well-documented and analyzed over the course of some 100 years of Bach scholarship. Yet, surprisingly, still poorly defined are several key facets of an integral style that will need to be established before his music can be fully evaluated in a context of Baroque music history. More attention has been focused on the instrumental music, both solo and ensemble, than on the vocal works. While the Passions, the B minor Mass and a few of the church cantatas have received considerable and varied analyses, most of the cantatas began to attract musicological attention only in the 1950s. For these we continue to lack comprehensive stylistic analyses to pinpoint important distinctions in Bach's changing and evolving musical style between the early Mühlhausen compositions and the masterworks of the Leipzig years.

When we examine only one aspect of that vocal repertory, the recitatives, we confront the perplexing situation that they are seldom discussed in the Bach literature.[1] Nevertheless, Bach's recitatives in their richness of musical ideas and their somewhat idiosyncratic stylistic details are as important to an overall conception of Bach's musical achievements in his sacred works as any other component of that style.

Looking beyond Bach's music for a moment, one finds that in general the subject of the recitative has been largely ignored by musical scholarship.

---

[1] Three German dissertations have studied aspects of Bach's recitatives: F. Graupner, *Die Rezitativbehandlung des Evangelisten in der Matthäuspassion von J. S. Bach* (Göttingen, 1951); H. Melchert, *Das Rezitativ der Kirchenkantaten J. S. Bachs* (Frankfurt/Main, 1958); and W. Spindler, *Das Verhältnis zwischen Wort und Ton in den Kantaten Johann Sebastian Bachs: die musikalische Umsetzung der Rezitativ-texte* (Erlangen-Nürnberg, 1973). Spindler's dissertation was not available to this author. A lengthy extract from Melchert's dissertation appeared in the *Bach-Jahrbuch* 45 (1958), pp. 5–83.

There is little written about the recitative styles of most Baroque composers,[2] and as yet no history of the recitative as it quickly became a major feature of music in the seventeenth and eighteenth centuries. And although the theory of recitative as found in the writings of Baroque theorists has been examined in the literature on Baroque music, these same concepts have with few exceptions not been related to the recitative practice of various Baroque composers. Even more problematical is the failure to trace what seems to be a cross-fertilization between operatic and various styles of sacred music, as this process already affected the recitative in North Europe in the seventeenth century. This is a particularly serious gap in the history of the recitative, hampering all attempts to identify the origins of Bach's own recitative style.

For Bach's recitatives we find both general errors and specific confusion in the literature. In the recent general article on the recitative in *The New Grove Dictionary*, Jack Westrup stated incorrectly that "Bach's recitatives, though perfectly geared to the German language, are basically an adaptation of the idioms of Italian opera; and there is no difference in style between his use of it in his sacred and his secular works."[3] Martin Ruhnke, one of the few writers to contribute informed observations about the recitative, states in an article discussing the Italian recitative style in German music:

> Bach writes an individual recitative style. The melody is not fully subservient to the text as practiced by Italian composers and as promulgated by German theorists. It is more independent and richer, but also more excited and dramatic. Sometimes the dramatic expression will be achieved at the cost of correct declamation. Undoubtedly Bach had known true Italian recitative, but he had not restricted himself to this norm.[4]

Some of the confusion about and even the disinterest in Bach's recitatives may be traced back to Philipp Spitta. Although he describes in some detail (for his time) many of Bach's cantatas in his monumental biography, and although he often singles out important expressive passages in the recitatives, he is unable to explain Bach's method of composition or his remarkable achievements in this area. One reads his descriptions of the recitatives with some disappointment, as, for example, Spitta's explanation of Bach's "unique recitative style":

[2] For an exceptional case, see the important study by Dale E. Monson, "*'Recitativo semplice' in the 'Opera Serie' of G. B. Pergolesi and his Contemporaries*" (unpublished Ph.D. diss., Columbia University, 1983).

[3] *The New Grove Dictionary of Music and Musicians*, ed. Stanley Sadie (London, 1980), Vol. 15, p. 645.

[4] Martin Ruhnke, "Das italienische Rezitativ bei den deutschen Komponisten des Spätbarock", in *Analecta musicologica*, 17 (Cologne, 1976), p. 108.

Bach is the only one who even here borrowed nothing from outside, but created much that was new. Expressive declamation was by no means all he aimed at. A general principle of music governs his compositions for recitative, a law above and beyond those which rule over mere declamation, which sometimes is identical with them, but not unfrequently defies them and forces them to give way; and it is precisely this which fits his recitatives to the style of church music. We instantly feel that the arbitrary subjective feeling is subdued to a sublime artistic conception, which confines it within invisible limits. The stream of melody in Bach's recitative is sometimes so full and equable that we can unhesitatingly disjoin it entirely from the words of the text.[5]

Later Spitta returns to the subject of Bach's recitatives and makes the following even more surprising explanation:

Bach's recitative. . .has in it something of the character of a prelude or an independent fantasia. The composer wanders through the realm of musical imagery and gives himself up to realising it, now in one way and now in another – prompted to do so now by some important factor, and now by something wholly unimportant, and without even renouncing his right to absolute free-will.[6]

Spitta's rather romanticized view of Bach's recitative technique was the result of his own musical and cultural background. While as an able scholar he may have understood the theoretical basis of recitative style, that is, as a form of sung rhetoric, as an oration in musical tones, or any of the other similar explanations found in various treatises, Spitta apparently could not transfer this same conceptual basis to Bach's unique achievements in his recitatives. Spitta was therefore wrong, but to his credit was his attempt to understand Bach's recitative style, something most recent Bach scholars have failed to achieve.

The first question to ask about Bach's accompanied recitatives is why he used this particular style when he did. In an analysis of some 120 accompanied recitatives as compared with about 425 simple recitatives, this study found nothing to illuminate specific reasons for Bach's choice of the accompanied recitative style. In individual instances, of course, one finds certain dramatic aspects of a cantata text demanding the distinction of a colorful instrumental accompaniment. One reason why Bach undoubtedly employed the accompanied style was because it required the singer to be less free and more measured in the expression of a particular text. One contemporary theorist and composer, Bach's nemesis Johann Adolph Scheibe, supported this theory, and he was one of the few to suggest a specific affec-

[5] Philipp Spitta, *Johann Sebastian Bach*, translated by Clara Bell and J. A. Fuller-Maitland (Leipzig, 1873–80; English trans., London, 1889; repr. New York, 1951), Vol. 1, pp. 495–6.
[6] *Ibid.*, Vol. 2, p. 531.

tive character for the accompanied recitative. In his *Critischer Musikus* he observed the following:

The singer shall in such a recitative speak out with greater gravity and more slowly; therefore he must be guided more by the beat of the measure than in the previous forms of recitative. For the most part this type of recitative is used in the church. And certainly it is more suited to rousing and increasing devotion than when a recitative is sung freely and without an accompaniment [of instruments]. It moves one more and penetrates deeper into the heart. Since also the words are sung more slowly and thus are pronounced more clearly, so will they be better understood in a church. And lastly, I have discovered through experience that no form of recitative better promotes edification than this, and thus it is also the least objectionable form.[7]

Table 1 gives a chronology of Bach's Weimar cantatas based on the work of Alfred Dürr. An indication is given of the number and types of recitatives in each cantata. A question-mark indicates an uncertainty in the dating of a cantata. The problem of dating in some instances and the probability of lost cantatas makes it difficult to establish the stylistic development of the recitative style and usage in the Weimar period. But certain facts seem clear. In the 23 cantatas (of which only one is secular), 44 recitatives are included. These are of three types: simple (often erroneously called *secco*), simple with *arioso* segments; and those accompanied with instruments that may or may not have *arioso* sections. Just nine cantatas employ only the simple form, but in these nine, half of the recitatives (some ten of the twenty) include some kind of *arioso* passage or passages. In eleven of the cantatas there are fifteen accompanied recitatives.[8]

Assuming Dürr's dating of before 1714 for the secular hunting cantata BWV 208, *Was mir behagt, ist nur die muntre Jagd*, will remain uncontested, then it must contain the earliest preserved recitatives by Bach, and, as the chronology shows, it is rich in recitatives. All six are short and in a rather simple style with little harmonic tension, few chord changes, rather conjunct melodies, and a few typical "operatic" note repetitions in the vocal line. Three of them include some form of a concluding melismatic, *arioso* passage, a stylistic feature that Bach develops considerably in his later recitatives.

---

[7] Johann A. Scheibe, *Critischer Musikus* (Leipzig, 1745), pp. 747–8.

[8] Table 1 suggests one anomaly among these earlier Weimar cantatas. The three cantatas from the text *Jahrgang* of 1717 by Franck for which the Weimar version of the cantata is lost, i.e., BWV 70a, 186a and 147a, were without recitatives if they were true to the published form of the text. It would seem unlikely that these lost cantatas did not contain recitatives when every other cantata written by Bach for Weimar included at least one, and usually more than one.

Table 1 *Bach's earliest cantatas with recitatives arranged chronologically* *

Cantata	Mvt. no.
1713	
? 1 BWV 208: Was mir behagt	I Simple/*arioso*
	III Simple/*arioso*
	V Simple+aria duet
	VI Simple
	VIII Simple/*arioso*
	X Simple
1714	
? 2 BWV 18 (or February 1715): Gleich wie der Regen	II Simple/*arioso*
	III Acc. (with *arioso* and choral Litany)
3 BWV 182: Himmelskönig sei willkommen	III Simple/*arioso*
4 BWV 12: Weinen, klagen	III Acc.
5 BWV 172: Erschallet ihr Lieder	II Simple/*arioso*
? 6 BWV 21 (or December 1713?): Ich hatte viel Bekümmernis	IV Acc.
	VII Acc. (duet)
? 7 BWV 54: Widerstehe doch der Sünde	II Simple/brief *arioso*
8 BWV 199: Mein Herze schwimmt im Blut	I Acc.
	III Acc.
	V Simple
	VII Acc.
9 BWV 61: Nun komm, der Heiden Heiland	II Simple/*arioso*
	IV Acc.
10 BWV 152: Tritt auf die Glaubensbahn	III Simple *arioso*
	V Simple
? 11 BWV 63 (or 1715): Christen, ätzet diesen Tag	II Acc.
	IV Simple/*arioso*
	VI Acc.
1715	
12 BWV 80a: Alles, was von Gott geboren	II Simple/*arioso*
	IV Simple/*arioso*
13 BWV 31: Der Himmel lacht	III Simple/*arioso*
	V Simple
	VII Simple
14 BWV 165: O heiliges Geist– und Wasserbad	II Simple
	IV Acc.
15 BWV 185: Barmherziges Herze	II Acc.
	IV Simple
16 BWV 161: Komm, du süsse Todesstunde	II Simple/*arioso*
	IV Acc.

Table 1 (*cont.*)

17 BWV 162: Ach, ich sehe itzt, da ich zur Hochzeit gehe	II Simple IV Simple
18 BWV 163: Nur jedem das Seine	II Simple IV Simple/*arioso* (duet)
19 BWV 132: Bereitet die Wege	II Simple/*arioso* IV Acc.

1716

20 BWV 155: Mein Gott, wie lang	I Acc. III Simple/*arioso*
21 BWV 70a: Wachet, betet!	No recitatives?
22 BWV 186a: Ärgre dich, O Seele nicht	No recitatives?
23 BWV 147a: Herz und Mund	No recitatives?

* Chronology according to Alfred Dürr, *Studien über die frühen Kantaten Johann Sebastian Bachs*, 2nd ed. (Wiesbaden, 1977).

The accompanied recitatives found in the Weimar cantatas largely utilize the simple style, with the chordal accompaniment, normally realized by the continuo player, given to a string ensemble. There are, however, notable exceptions in Cantatas 18, 21, 199, 165, 161, and especially Cantata 63. The fact that two of the earliest of the works with unusually expressive accompanied recitatives are Cantatas 18 and 21 points again to the problem of an accurate chronology, and forces some restraint in drawing conclusions about the development of Bach's conscious dramatizing of his recitatives. Dürr himself is uncertain as to the dating of Cantata 18; he places it early in 1714, as is shown in Table 1, but believes it may have been first performed (or repeated from an earlier performance) on 24 February 1715.[9]

Even though the date of composition is uncertain, clearly Cantata 18 contains Bach's most complex and highly organized accompanied recitative from this early period. There is no precedent in any other cantata from 1714 for its length, complex vocal melismas, and the provocative troping of portions of the German litany – perhaps a model for Bach's use of chorales in recitatives for a number of Leipzig cantatas. The striking harmonic coloring of *Des Teufels Trug verkehre*, with its passage of tritone-related chords, is a fine example of Bach's remarkable sensitivity to harmonic expressiveness, and the several long *arioso* passages are good examples of a style that had already become characteristic of Bach's recitatives. Finally, the extensive melismatic

[9] See Alfred Dürr, *Studien über die frühen Kantaten Johann Sebastian Bachs*, 2nd ed. (Wiesbaden, 1977), pp. 65 and 221, for conflicting datings.

passages on words such as "berauben", "fallen ab", "Verfolgen", and particularly "irregehen," while perhaps inspired by briefer melismatic treatment of words found in the recitatives of contemporary North German opera – for example in Keiser's works – are contradictory to all Baroque theory of recitative and unlike the Italian opera recitatives composed during the first part of the eighteenth century. Table 2 gives this recitative text with indications where Bach emphasized specific words or lines of text with particular musical expressivity.

Table 2 *BWV 18/3, Mein Gott, hier wird mein Herze sein, recitative for tenor, bass, Choral Litany, 4 violas, 2 flutes and basso continuo*

(Capital letters indicate Choral Litany; italics indicate *arioso* passages; bold face indicates melismatic passage.)

1 *TENOR*
Mein Gott, hier wird mein Herze sein:
Ich öffne dir's in meines Jesu Namen!
So streue deinen Samen
Als in ein gutes Land hinein.
Mein Gott, hier wird mein Herze sein:
Lass solches Frucht, und hundertfältig bringen.
O Herr, Herr, hilf! O Herr, lass wohlgelingen.
DU WOLLEST DEINEN GEIST UND KRAFT ZUM WORTE GEBEN.
ERHÖR UNS, LIEBER HERRE GOTT!

2 *BASS*
Nur wehre, treuer Vater, wehre,
Das mich und keinen Christen nicht
Des Teufels Trug verkehre.
Sein Sinn ist ganz dahin gericht',
Uns deines Wortes zu **berauben**
Mit aller Seligkeit.
DEN SATAN UNTER UNSRE FÜSSE TRETEN.
ERHÖR UNS, LIEBER HERRE GOTT!

3 *TENOR*
Ach! viel' verleugnen Wort und Glauben
Und **fallen ab** wie faules Obst,
Wenn sie **Verfolgung** *sollen leiden.*
So stürzen sie in ewig Herzeleid,
Da sie ein zeitlich Weh vermeiden.
UND UNS FÜR DES TÜRKEN UND DES PAPSTS GRAUSAMEN MORD UND
LÄSTERUNGEN,

Table 2 (*cont.*)

WÜTEN UND TOBEN VÄTERLICH BEHÜTEN.
ERHÖR UNS, LIEBER HERRE GOTT!

4 *BASS*

Ein andrer sorgt nur für den Bauch;
Inzwischen wird der Seele ganz vergessen;
Der Mammon auch
Hat vieler Herz besessen.
So kann das Wort zu keiner Kraft gelangen.
Und wieviel Seelen hält
Die Wollust nicht gefangen?
So sehr verführet sie die Welt,
Die Welt, die ihnen muss anstatt des Himmels stehen,
Darüber sie vom Himmel **irregehen.**
ALLE IRRIGE UND VERFÜHRTE WIEDERBRINGEN,
ERHÖR UNS, LIEBER HERRE GOTT.

However, none of the accompanied recitatives composed before Bach arrived in Leipzig displays such remarkably sophisticated compositional techniques as the first one in Cantata 63. This too is a work of uncertain dating, probably composed for Christmas 1714, but also perhaps for the same festival in 1715.[10] The exact year of composition is largely irrelevant, for among all of the Weimar cantatas no other accompanied recitative achieves such a stunning standard of oratorical expressivity. Table 3 gives the text together with an English translation; for the music to the complete recitative, see Example 1.

Baroque theorists, when describing the recitative, confirm that it was based on a concept of sung speech, and that it should be thought of as an oration in tones, a free style of singing more declaimed than sung. That Bach considered himself a skilled rhetorician is clear from Birnbaum, when he says of him:

The parts and advantages which the working out of a musical composition has in common with rhetorical art, he [Bach] knows so fully, that one hears him not only with satisfying pleasure when he turns his well-versed conversations to the similarity and correspondence of both, but one marvels also at the skilled application of the same in his work.[11]

---

[10] *Ibid.*, pp. 174–5. Dürr corrects here the tentative dating of this cantata which he gave in the first edition as 1713. Based on a study of the manuscript, he concludes that Cantata 63 was probably composed for Christmas of 1714 or possibly 1715.

[11] Scheibe, *Critischer Musikus*, p. 997.

Table 3 *BWV 63/2, text of recitative, O selger Tag!*

O selger Tag! O ungemeines Heute,	O blessed day! O extraordinary present,
An dem das Heil der Welt,	on which the salvation of the world,
Der Schilo, den Gott schon im Paradies	The hero, which God already in
dem menschlichen Geschlecht	Paradise promised to the human
verhiess,	race,
Nunmehro sich vollkommen dargestellt,	Now fully presents himself and seeks to
Und suchet Israel von der	rescue Israel from captivity and the
Gefangenschaft und Sklavenketten	chains of slavery
Des Satans zu erretten.	Of Satan.
Du liebster Gott, was sind wir arme	Thou dearest God, but still what are
doch?	we wretches?
Ein abgefallnes Volk, so dich verlassen;	A renegade people which abandons
Und dennoch willst du uns nicht	Thee;
hassen;	And yet you will not hate us;
Denn eh wir sollen noch nach dem	For before we shall ever, according to
Verdienst zu Boden liegen,	merit, be laid in a grave,
Eh muss die Gottheit sich bequemen,	Must the Godhead first submit
Die menschliche Natur an sich zu	To take the nature of Man upon
nehmen,	Himself,
Und auf der Erden im Hirtenstall zu	And on earth in a shepherd's stable
einem Kinde werden	become a child.
O unbegreifliches, doch seliges	O incomprehensible, yet blessed
Verfügen!	arrangement!

Bach's knowledge of rhetoric came from the humanistic basis of all education in Germany before the end of the eighteenth century. And yet it is one of the distinctions of Bach's recitative style, especially his accompanied recitatives, that he is unusually sensitive to words and finds such a variety of musical and rhetorical means to express them. His achievement in his recitatives, as is true for so many other aspects of his music, is atypical for the late stages of the musical Baroque.

The first recitative in Cantata 63 illustrates numerous approaches by Bach to musical and rhetorical expressivity. The text concerns the birth of Christ, and the unknown poet has written a moving exegesis on this event, culminating in the memorable response of the Christian witness: "O unbegreifliches, doch seliges Verfügen" ("O incomprehensible but blessed arrangement"). The total effect results from a number of expressive devices, but any attempt to separate them somewhat defeats an understanding of

Example 1 BWV 63/2, "O selger Tag!", alto recitative (from *NBA* I, 2)

Example 1 (*cont.*)

Example 1 (*cont.*)

Example 1 (*cont.*)

Example 1 (*cont.*)

Bach's total musical statement. With this understood, my analysis of the recitative will be limited to a discussion of four categories of techniques.

I First, there is the quality of overall mood resulting from the vocal and instrumental ranges. In keeping with the feeling of subdued amazement, one feels a sense of awe. Bach arranges the alto voice to be supported largely by lower string harmonies. Only in a few instances, for particular word emphases, does the voice part fall below the first violin line and penetrate the string texture, as for example in measure 10, for "Satan," measure 11 with the melisma on "erretten," in measure 14 for "arme doch," in measure 16 on "uns," in measure 18, for "zu Boden liegen," and in measure 25, for "unbegreifliches."

II Second, the voice part often emphasizes words by means of dissonant intervallic leaps, through dissonant relationships with the accompanying parts, and through melismatic gestures. (Harmony, of course, plays a major role in these devices, but for reportorial clarity the harmonic element will be discussed in a separate category.) Bach's detailed emphasis of words in this manner occurs in almost every measure. The following are the most striking examples:

m.1: "O selger Tag," set to a melisma that includes a highly expressive *Bb* set against the *Bα* of the violin 2 – an effective coloring of the melisma with a sound almost suggesting to us the "blue notes" found in vocal and instrumental jazz.

m.2: "O ungemeines," a leap of a seventh into the tritone with the continuo bass and violin 1.

m.4: "Welt," with a leap into a seventh and a tritone.

m.5: "Paradies," a second against the violin 1, and the auxiliary tone *F* as a seventh against the bass and viola part.

m.6: "Geschlecht," a seventh with violin 1, tritone with the bass.

mm.9–12: "Gefangenschaft und Sklavenketten des Satans zu erretten." These three highly complex measures include a variety of musical devices to add expressive and symbolic weight to the words: a tritone and seventh on "Ge-FANGEN-schaft," as well as a tritone relationship within the melodic fragment itself. In addition, in measure 10, a series of suspensions, capturing the voice part in the chain of sixteenths, first with the "chains" of the continuo line, and then with the parts inverted, the suspension of a seventh becomes a ninth. In measure 11, the voice part cadences with every tone dissonant to its context until released in the E minor triad.

m.13: "Liebster." Again, a melismatic gesture, recalling the opening of the recitative, but in this instance with the expressive dissonances against the bass, viola and violin II.

m.14: "Arme doch," with a leap into a tritone, and the coloring of the auxiliary turn by a second.

m.15: A leap to a seventh on "AB-gefallnes"; a tritone and seventh on "Volk."

m.16: Minor second on "uns."

m.17: To be noted is the absence of dissonances on the word "hassen," although customarily one would expect such an expressive treatment in a Bach recitative. Here, of course, the consonant setting underscores the words "nicht hassen."

m.18: Tritone and seventh on "noch"; leap into a second on "Verdienst zu."

m.19: Leap to a ninth on "liegen."

m.20: Seventh and tritone on "be-QUE-men."

m.21: A leap to a tritone and seventh on "sich."

m.22: Minor and major second on "auf DER Erden."

m.23: Leap to a tritone and seventh on "Hirtenstall."

m.24: An especially affecting seventh and tritone E♭ for the exclamation "O."

A sub-class of expressive intervallic leaps includes those of the consonant sixth. This form of melodic leap is often referred to in Baroque theoretical descriptions of the *Figuren*, and sometimes has the label of *Exclamatio*.[12] While usually given as a leap up by a minor sixth, in Bach's works as well as other Baroque composers the leap of a major or minor sixth in either direction often suggests a heightening of the expressive impact of a vocal line. In this recitative we see, for example:

m.1: The use of a minor sixth, descending, on "O selger Tag" in ornamented form.

m.13: A similar use of an ornamented minor sixth, but ascending for "Du liebster Gott," contributing an element of formal coherence to the recitative.

mm.3–4: A leap down by a major sixth on "Welt," and immediately back up again on "der Schilo."

mm.10–11: The ornamented melodic movement by a minor sixth in the continuo is followed in the voice part for the "erretten" melisma.

m.23: A leap up by a major sixth on "zu El-nem."

mm.26,27,28: The effective use of minor sixths within the "Verfügen" melisma, and the major sixth leap for "un-BEGREIFLICHES."

III A third means of expressivity in recitatives is the more obvious types of melodic figures which serve to illustrate the text in various ways – most especially by the range of an individual part and by disjunct melodic movement. This certainly explains the sixteenth-note passage representing Satan's chains in both the continuo and the voice part in measure 10. Also to be considered are:

m.15: "abgefallnes."

m.18: "zu Boden liegen," already cited for the progression of the voice part beneath the violin 1 line.

m.20: the leap to "GOTT-heit."

---

[12] See my article, "Rhetoric and Music," in *The New Grove Dictionary of Music and Musicians*, Vol. 15, p. 798.

m.22: The same low tones for "Erden" that were employed for "Boden" in measure
   18. Especially effective are the rhetorically inspired rests, for example, preceding
   each of the exclamations of "O." In the most dramatic of these, Bach places rests
   before and after the final "O" in measure 24, preceding the climatic line of
   the text.

IV A fourth means of expressivity depends on the role of harmony,
harmonic progression, and the often resulting unusual bass movement. The
tonal structure of this recitative moves through two cycles of largely
dominant-oriented modulations from C through A to the first sectional
cadence in E minor. Then, a new progression begins in measure 12, but is
interrupted in measure 19 on the words "zu Boden liegen" ("to be laid in
earth [in a grave]"), where the seventh chord on E resolves deceptively to a
seventh chord on C, with the bass having proceeded by a diminished third.
This pivotal measure moves the recitative into the flat keys of the tonal
spectrum and allows Bach to resolve the passage in F major in measure 24,
for the line: "in Hirtenstall zu einem Kinde werden" ("to become a child in
a shepherd's stable") – F major chosen more than likely for its affective
association with the pastoral nature of the Nativity. There are also, of
course, a number of highly expressive dissonant relationships between
chord progressions, with the following being especially poignant:

mm.6–7: The C♮ to C♯ for "nunmehro sich vollkommen."
mm.12–13: The striking change from G♮ in the viola to G♯ in the violin 1 for
   "Du liebster."
mm.18–19: The B♮ to B♭, as well as G♯ to G♮, for "zu Boden liegen."
m.23: Although not a cross-relationship, there is the harmonic tension produced
   between the A♮ and B♭ in the bass for the line "zu einem Kinde," which abruptly
   stops on the verb "werden."

Finally, the climax of the recitative occurs in the last eight measures –
an *arioso* passage that stands as one of Bach's superb achievements – with a
number of expressive devices brought together to emphasize the text,
"*O unbegreifliches, doch seliges Verfügen*" ("O incomprehensible, though
blessed arrangement"). Having begun with the E♭ exclamation on "O," the
voice leaps a tritone and then another tritone for "unbegreifliches." A rhetorically expressive rest occurs before "doch seliges"; a leap of an octave to
"seliges" is followed by a melisma on "Verfügen." This is repeated first at the
interval of a fourth by the continuo while the violin I intensifies the harmonic background with a strangely beautiful motive fluctuating diatoni-
cally and chromatically around A.

The voice part restates the text, this time with a powerful leap of a major
sixth on "unbegreifliches," as the continuo part begins a restatement of the

head motive of the previous measure. But the bass stops abruptly, only to continue with a repetition of the entire vocal passage a fourth lower. Once again the continuo returns to the motive which appeared earlier in the voice part, was then imitated in the bass line, and now is restated a third time. Is it too poetical to see and hear in this passage the constant reflection and amazement for this "blessed arrangement" of God, which repeats itself over and over in the minds of all who think upon its significance? As if the sublime expressivity of this passage were insufficient, Bach closes the recitative in an extended half cadence on E, in which the cadential half-step A–$G\sharp$ sounds over and over in what seems a reflective, hushed – might we say awed? – tonal ending that fades away but never concludes.

Most of the expressive devices reviewed in this recitative could be labelled using the terminology of musical rhetoric that had been established by German music theorists of the seventeenth and eighteenth centuries. We do not know if Bach thought of his compositional procedures in these terms, or whether he would have given labels to these examples of melodic and harmonic expressivity. But that he understood the principles of rhetorical stress available to him in music, and especially in the recitatives, and that he used his unique craft as a composer to speak in musical tones, cannot be doubted. It seems strange that Spitta found such complex and yet uniquely expressive recitatives as "improvisatory" or totally unrelated to the text.

Such examples of Bach's music place before us that great mystery which lies at the basis of much of his art. This recitative provides a glimpse into that still indefinable balance of musical genius, all-encompassing craft, and the indestructable faith and zeal of the German Protestant. As Bach scholarship enters a new century of research, it needs to examine more closely the elements of the expressive and the rhetorical, but also the religious and clearly mystical underpinnings of so much of his sacred music. Musical analysis has brought us far in comprehending Bach's craftsmanship, but Bach's mind and the way in which that mind reflects his soul still often elude us. The recitatives in themselves may provide an important if still largely ignored resource for enriching our understanding of those most personal concomitants of Bach's sacred music.

Aria forms in the Cantatas from Bach's first Leipzig *Jahrgang*

STEPHEN A. CRIST

As is well known, the aria form in the first half of the eighteenth century was standardized almost to the point of stereotype. Most arias begin and end with an instrumental ritornello which contains much of the thematic material for the entire movement. In *Der vollkommene Capellmeister*, Mattheson gives a concise description of other salient features of the form:[1]

The aria is. . .correctly described as a well-composed song, which has its own particular key and meter, is usually divided into two parts, and concisely expresses a great affection. Occasionally it closes with a repetition of the first part, occasionally without it. In the first instance it is called *Da capo*, i.e., from the top, or actually from the head. . .   (Part II, Chapter 13, Paragraph 10)

The most important formal characteristic of the aria is the presence of two contrasting vocal sections. More often than not in early eighteenth-century arias, the first vocal section returns at the conclusion of the movement.

Bach's arias are extraordinarily diverse, in contrast to those of his contemporaries. In fact, it seems that Bach deliberately and systematically varied the elements of aria composition throughout his career, in order to create as many different forms as possible – much as he did for other genres, such as the chorale prelude in the *Orgelbüchlein*, the prelude and fugue in the *Well-Tempered Clavier*, and the concerto grosso in the Brandenburg Concerti.[2]

---

[1] Ernest C. Harriss, *Johann Mattheson's Der vollkommene Capellmeister: A Revised Translation with Critical Commentary* (Ann Arbor, 1981), p. 432.

[2] Spitta noted over 100 years ago "the fact, which may be observed throughout Bach's works, that when he essays the employment of a new form, he never contents himself with a single attempt, but endeavors to exhaust it as far as possible by repeating the experiment." Philipp Spitta, *Johann Sebastian Bach*, translated by Clara Bell and J. A. Fuller-Maitland (Leipzig, 1873–80; English trans., London, 1889, repr. New York, 1951), Vol. 1, p. 434.

The present study is based upon examination of the arias in the cantatas composed during Bach's first year in Leipzig (1723–4). This segment of Bach's *œuvre* was chosen because *Jahrgang* I contains a sizeable but manageable group of approximately 80 new arias that is delimited by natural chronological boundaries.[3] Moreover, this set of movements seems fairly representative of the Leipzig arias as a whole (at least, so far as I have sampled them). Finally, since the cantatas of *Jahrgang* I were composed at the rate of approximately one per week, they offer a glimpse of Bach's spontaneous compositional activity that is not readily observable in other collections such as the *Well-Tempered Clavier*, the *Musical Offering*, and the *Art of Fugue*, which were produced over a longer span of time.[4]

About two-thirds of the 78 new arias in the *Jahrgang* I cantatas are in *da capo* form, while the others are in a variety of non-repeating forms, in which each portion of the text is set just once. There are actually two different types of *da capo* arias; they are referred to in the Bach literature as "strict" and "free" *da capo* arias.[5] In both, the opening text returns at the end. The decisive difference between the two is purely musical. The A section of a strict *da capo* aria always ends in the tonic and is repeated intact at the conclusion, giving it an ABA form. In free *da capo* arias, however, the A section modulates and ends in a key other than the tonic (usually the dominant).[6] Consequently, some recomposition of the *da capo* return is necessary, and the resultant form is A B A'.

The non-*da capo* arias in *Jahrgang* I manifest a variety of forms. The most common is the binary form (about seventeen movements), which usually has the following structure:

---

[3] The arias in the Magnificat and the St John Passion, which also date from this period, have been excluded from present consideration.

[4] Given Bach's hectic schedule, it seems unlikely that he could have devoted more than a few hours to the composition of any given aria.

[5] The terms "reine Dacapoarien" and "freie Dacapoarien" appear in Alfred Dürr's *Studien über die frühen Kantaten Johann Sebastian Bachs* (Leipzig, 1951; revised edn, Wiesbaden, 1977), pp. 152ff. The term "freies Da-capo" is also used in Werner Neumann's *Handbuch der Kantaten Johann Sebastian Bachs*, 4th edn (Leipzig, 1971). The English equivalents, "strict" and "free" *da capo*, are found in William H. Scheide's unpublished monograph, "Bach Achieves His Goal. His First Year of Regular Church Music Following the Leipzig Lutheran Calendar."

[6] All ten of the *Jahrgang* I free *da capo* arias in major keys and seven of the twelve in minor keys modulate to the dominant. Of the remaining free *da capos* in minor keys, three modulate to the mediant (BWV 22/2, 75/10, and 76/12) and two to the subdominant (BWV 179/5 and 81/1).

Rit. –	A –	Rit. –	B –	Rit.
I	modulation away from tonic (usually to dominant)	new key	modulation back to tonic	I

A related form that appears seven times in *Jahrgang* I is the tripartite (ABC) form. This is essentially an expansion of the binary form, with a second modulatory section before the return to the tonic:

Rit. –	A –	Rit. –	B –	Rit. –	C –	Rit.
I	modulation away from tonic (usually to dominant)	new key	further modulation	new key	modulation back to tonic	I

The remaining five *Jahrgang* I arias (BWV 119/3, 73/4, 181/1, 181/3, and 67/6) belong to none of the formal categories described thus far.

It is not possible here to provide detailed analyses of all the *Jahrgang* I arias; indeed, a separate study could be devoted to the non-repeating forms alone. Instead we will concentrate on the general factors that determined the forms of the arias, and examine just a few of the more unusual *da capo* arias in *Jahrgang* I.[7]

One of the chief determinants of the forms of Bach's arias was the libretto.[8] The libretto sources are of two types: volumes of sacred poetry by well-known contemporary poets, and printed libretti which were distributed to members of the congregation for their use during the cantata performances and at home. Despite the fact that text prints survive for only about a third of the *Jahrgang* I cantatas, the available evidence (summarized in Table 1) shows that the musical forms of the arias almost always agree with the forms found in the libretti.

This observation is particularly significant because the relationship between cantatas and their libretti was different in the first half of the eighteenth century from what it is today. We fully expect libretti to agree with the musical settings because nowadays they are normally published *after* a vocal work has been composed. But the texts of all the movements in Table 1 were in existence *before* Bach composed these cantatas.

---

[7] For a fuller discussion of much of the material in this essay, see my Ph.D. dissertation, "Aria Forms in the Vocal Works of J. S. Bach, 1714–24" (Brandeis University, 1988).

[8] *Da capo* form was indicated in eighteenth-century libretti either by the repetition of the opening portion of the text or by the printing of the words "Da Capo" at the end of the aria text.

Table 1 *Textual and musical forms of Jahrgang I arias with printed libretti*

| BWV | Da capo indication in libretto | | | Form of musical setting |
	Yes	No		
59/4		X	=	binary
24/1		X	≠	free *da capo*
24/5		X	=	tripartite
69a/3	X		=	strict *da capo*
69a/5	X		≠	binary
77/3	X		≠	binary
77/5	X		=	strict *da capo*
64/5	X		=	strict *da capo*
64/7	X		=	strict *da capo*
73/2	X		=	strict *da capo*
73/4		X	=	strophic
81/1	X		=	free *da capo*
81/3	X		=	free *da capo*
81/5	X		=	strict *da capo*
83/1		X	≠	strict *da capo*
83/3	X		=	strict *da capo*
144/2	X		=	strict *da capo*
144/5		X	=	tripartite
181/1		X	≡	A B A′ B′
181/3		X	=	Hälftige Form
22/2	X		=	free *da capo*
22/4		X	≠	free *da capo*
67/2		X	=	binary
67/6		X	=	strophic
104/3	X		=	free *da capo*
104/5	X		=	strict *da capo*

In several instances, a printed volume clearly served as the composer's textual source. For example, the libretti for Cantatas 59 and 24 are from a collection of texts entitled *Fünfffache Kirchen-Andachten* by the Hamburg cleric Erdmann Neumeister. Since this publication appeared in Leipzig in 1717, it seems likely that Bach worked directly from it when he composed Cantatas 59 and 24 some six years later.[9]

[9] Facsimiles of the texts of Cantatas 59 and 24 may be found in Werner Neumann, *Sämtliche von Johann Sebastian Bach vertonte Texte* (Leipzig, 1974), pp. 296–7. These two libretti also appeared earlier in a collection entitled *Geistliche Poesien mit untermischten Biblischen Sprüchen und Choralen auf alle Sonn- und Fest-Tage durchs gantze Jahr* (Eisenach, 1714; 2nd ed., 1717). It is worth mentioning also that only four of the seven movements in Neumeister's text for Cantata 59 were set by Bach, and that there is some uncertainty about the correct order of

Bach probably also used a printed source in composing Cantatas 69a, 77, and 64. Helmut K. Krausse has recently shown that the libretti of these cantatas are reworkings of texts from Johann Knauer's *Gott-geheiligtes Singen und Spielen des Friedensteinischen Zions* (Gotha, 1720–1).[10] Since there are substantial differences between the cantata texts and those in the Knauer print, it seems unlikely that the print itself served as Bach's text exemplar. But these texts may have been revised by Bach or by an assistant under his supervision.

Unfortunately, very little is known about the texts of the other eight cantatas in Table 1 (BWV 73, 81, 83, 144, 181, 22, 67, and 104) are all contained in two prints, entitled *Texte zur Leipziger Kirchem-Music* (Leipzig, 1724), in the Saltykow-Stschedrin State Public Library in Leningrad.[11] The prints offer no clue as to the authorship of these libretti; all we know is that they are among the few surviving exemplars of the collections of cantata texts which were printed in Leipzig by Immanuel Tietzen, and which were distributed to church members upon payment of a fee.

In his article on the Leipzig text prints, William H. Scheide has convincingly argued that these printed libretti did not serve as Bach's text exemplars for this group of cantatas. Rather, Scheide believes that, in these instances, Bach worked from manuscript sources of the texts, most of which are lost.[12] It may be that Bach's librettist prepared two manuscript copies of each text, one for the composer and the other for the printer. In any case, it seems reasonable to assume that the text sources used by Bach contained the same formal indications as the published libretti.

In sum, although the prints represented in Table 1 stand in varying relationships to Bach's cantatas, the similarities and differences between the textual and musical forms of the arias provide evidence of Bach's formal preferences.

Another factor which played a role in determining the forms of Bach's arias is the structure of the texts. Table 2 provides a tabulation of the textual and musical forms of all 78 arias in the *Jahrgang* I cantatas.[13]

the third and fourth movements. See Dietrich Kilian, *Kritischer Bericht* (1960) to *Johann Sebastian Bach. Neue Ausgabe sämtliche Werke* (NBA), I/13, pp. 74–7.

[10] Helmut K. Krausse, "Eine neue Quelle zu drei Kantatentexten Johann Sebastian Bachs," *Bach-Jahrbuch*, 67 (1981), pp. 7–22. Facsimiles of the relevant portions of the print are included at the end of the article.

[11] Facsimiles of these prints are in Neumann, *Texte*, pp. 422–31. For a full account of their discovery, see Wolf Hobohm, "Neue 'Texte zur Leipziger Kirchen-Music'," *Bach-Jahrbuch*, 59 (1973), pp. 5–32.

[12] William H. Scheide, "Zum Verhältnis von Textdrucken und musikalischen Quellen der Kirchenkantaten Johann Sebastian Bachs," *Bach-Jahrbuch*, 62 (1976), pp. 83ff, 88.

[13] A period marks the end of a sentence, italicized letters indicate repetition of a line, and the letter "x" represents an unrhymed line.

Table 2 *Text structures and musical forms of the Jahrgang I arias*

Rhyme Scheme	Strict Da capo	Free Da capo	Binary	Other
4 lines				
1 a. abab				181/3 ("Hälftige Form")
b. ab.ab	83/1			
2 a. a.bba	75/5	75/10, 76/5, 76/12, 81/1		
b. ab.ba	105/5			
3 aa.bb		76/10	48/4	
5 lines				
4 ab.aab	37/2			
5 aa.bba	166/5			
6 aba.bb		136/3		
7 a.bbba	75/3	75/12		
8 xa.bba	77/5, 95/5, 109/3, 109/5, 64/7, 73/2, 44/3, 44/6	90/3	136/5, 69a/5, 77/3, 57/2	181/1 (ABA'B'), 119/5 (tripartite)
9 a. xa.bab	76/3, 90/1			
b. x.a.bab	81/5			
10 xa.abb			25/5	
11 ax.bba	104/5	89/3		

Table 2 (*cont.*)

Rhyme Scheme	Strict *Da capo*	Free *Da capo*	Binary	Other
12 ab.xab	148/4			
13 aa.xbb	166/2			
14 abb.xa			86/5	
6 lines				
15 a. ababcc			46/5	37/5 (tripartite)
b. ab.abcc		167/1,		65/6 (tripartite)
c. aba.bcc		179/5	153/8	
d. aba.b.cc				65/4 (tripartite)
e. ababcc			179/3, 190/5	24/5 (tripartite)
16 a. a.abccb		40/7		
b. aa.bccb	86/2		40/4	
c. aab.ccb	64/5	22/2, 24/1, 148/2, 104/3		
17 a. aab.bcc	69a/3		105/3	60/3 (tripartite)
b. aabb.cc		22/4	25/3	
18 a. a.bba.cc			89/5	
b. a.bb.a.cc				
19 aa.bcbc	167/3	46/3		
20 abbcca		48/6, 81/3		
21 ab.ccba				119/3 (unique)

22 a.	abccab	83/3		190/3	
b.	ab.ccab	144/2			
23	abaccb				
7 lines					
24	xa.bb.cca		138/5		
25	ax.bbcca		23/1	153/6	
26	aabb.ccx				
8–12 lines					
27	*a*bba*a*.cc*a*				144/5 (tripartite)
28	aab.ccb.ddb				67/6 (strophic)
29	ababcc.ddee	59/4			
30	*a*bba.*a*cca.*a*dda				73/4 (strophic)

As a rule, arias with relatively short texts tend to be in *da capo* form while those with longer texts are more often in non-repeating or other forms. For instance, about three-quarters of the 39 *Jahrgang* I arias with four- or five-line texts are in strict or free *da capo* form. On the other hand, all but two of the seven arias with more than six lines are in non-*da capo* forms.[14]

Moreover, the length of the opening sentence seems to have influenced the forms of the arias. When the first sentence contains two or three lines, as is the case for the majority of the *Jahrgang* I arias, it is difficult to predict whether the movement will be in *da capo* or non-repeating form.[15] However, if the first sentence of an aria text is shorter or longer than usual, definite formal preferences are observable. For instance, every two-sentence aria text in which the first sentence contains just one line (BWV 75/5, 75/10, 76/5, 76/12, 81/1, 75/3, 75/12, 40/7) is set in *da capo* form. On the other hand, if the first sentence contains more than three lines, the musical setting is almost always in a non-repeating form (BWV 179/3, 190/5, 24/5, 105/3, 60/3, 144/5, 59/4). (The only exceptions are BWV 23/1 and 22/4, which will be discussed presently.) It is not difficult to find an explanation for these patterns. It seems obvious that the longer an opening sentence is, the less well it lends itself to repetition at the end of the movement. Yet an unusually short opening sentence practically demands repetition, in order to achieve formal balance with the rest of the text.

It is hardly coincidental that the only two *da capo* arias in which the first sentence has more than three lines, "Du wahrer Gott und Davids Sohn," BWV 23/1, and "Mein alles in allem, mein ewiges Gut," BWV 22/4, are from the two cantatas composed for Bach's audition for the Leipzig cantorate on 7 February 1723.[16] Ferdinand Zander convincingly argues that the texts of these two works were penned by the same (anonymous) author.[17] The fact that two of the three aria texts in these cantatas have unusually long first sentences is surely an idiosyncrasy of this particular librettist. An obvious consequence of the presence of four lines in the A sections of these movements is that there is less repetition of individual

---

[14] The arias with six-line texts are divided about equally between *da capo* and non-repeating forms.

[15] About three-quarters of this group of arias are in *da capo* form, while the others are in non-repeating forms.

[16] Regarding the origins of these two cantatas, see Christoph Wolff, "Bachs Leipziger Kantorats-probe und die Aufführungsgeschichte der Kantate 'Du wahrer Gott und Davids Sohn' BWV 23," *Bach-Jahrbuch*, 64 (1978), pp. 78–94.

[17] Ferdinand Zander, "Die Dichter der Kantatentexte Johann Sebastian Bachs: Untersuchungen zu ihrer Bestimmung," *Bach-Jahrbuch*, 54 (1968), pp. 28–9.

textual units (words, lines, phrases) than is usual in the Bach arias. In other respects, though, BWV 23/1 is a typical *da capo* aria: lines 1–4 are set in the A and A′ sections, and lines 5–7 in the B section. The first two vocal sections of BWV 22/4 are also quite normal: lines 1–4 are set in the A section and lines 5–6 in the B section. But the allocation of text in the *da capo* return (A′) is unusual: it contains just the first line instead of all four. Perhaps Bach departed from the convention of repeating the entire first sentence at the end of a *da capo* aria because he considered the opening sentence of BWV 22/4 to have been an inappropriate conclusion with its list of petitions:

> Mein alles in allem, mein ewiges Gut,
> Verbessre das Herze, verändre den Mut;
> Schlag alles darnieder,
> Was dieser Entsagung des Fleisches zuwider!
> Doch wenn ich nun geistlich ertötet da bin,
> So ziehe mich nach dir in Friede dahin!

In any case, another peculiarity of this aria suggests that Bach decided fairly early on to handle the text this way. At the end of the A section (mm. 41–4), after lines 1–4 had been set, the second half of line 1 ("mein ewiges Gut") is set again. Since the repetition of this phrase does not enhance the meaning of the text, it must have been repeated purely for formal reasons: to enable the A and A′ sections to end with the same words.

Let us now turn briefly to five other movements which deviate from the norm: the arias in Table 1 whose musical forms contradict those in the text prints. Bach set two of them ("Mein Erlöser und Erhalter," BWV 69a/5, and "Mein Gott, ich liebe dich von Herzen," BWV 77/3) in binary form, even though *da capo* form is indicated in Knauer's libretti. Almost all of the aria texts in the Knauer print are in *da capo* form, and there is no reason why Bach's settings of these two could not also have been. But evidently the forms of BWV 69a/5 and 77/3 were altered so that they would conform to a rotating cycle of forms.

As Table 3 shows, each of the cantatas from the Eighth through to the Thirteenth Sunday after Trinity has two arias, one of which is in *da capo* form and the other in a non-repeating form.

Furthermore, the form of the first aria in each cantata matches the form of the last aria of the preceding cantata. In order for this scheme to work, it was necessary that the second aria in Cantata 69a and the first aria in Cantata 77 have non-repeating forms, despite the *da capo* indications in the libretti. For this segment of *Jahrgang* I, then, it seems that this rotational system was an important determinant of the forms of the arias, and that the forms

Table 3 *Chronology and forms of the arias in Jahrgang I cantatas,*
8–13 post Trin.

Occasion	BWV	*da capo* form	non-repeating form
8 post Trin. (18 July 1723)	136/3	X	
	136/5		X
9 post Trin. (25 July)	105/3		X
	105/5	X	
10 post Trin. (1 August)	46/3	X	
	46/5		X
11 post Trin. (8 August)	179/3		X
	179/5	X	
12 post Trin. (15 August)	69a/3	X	
	69a/5		X
13 post Trin. (22 August)	77/3		X
	77/5	X	

required by the system took precedence even when they conflicted with other factors.

On three other occasions (BWV 24/1, 83/1, 22/4) the opposite situation is found: Bach chose *da capo* form although it was not indicated in the libretti. The text of "Ein ungefärbt Gemüte," BWV 24/1, with the common form aab.ccb (rhyme scheme 16c), could easily have been set in a non-repeating form.[18] But during his first year in Leipzig, Bach consistently set aria texts with this structure in *da capo* form, regardless of the form given in the libretto. Similarly, there is no reason why he could not have chosen a non-repeating form for "Erfreute Zeit im neuen Bunde," BWV 83/1 (rhyme scheme 1b–ab.ab). But during this period Bach seems to have preferred *da capo* form for four-line aria texts.[19] The brevity of these texts surely sug-

[18] In fact, five of the Weimar arias with this text structure (BWV 150/5, 31/6, 165/3, 186a/3, 186a/5) were set in non-repeating forms, while only two (BWV 208/4 and 199/2) were set in *da capo* form.

[19] Seven of the nine *Jahrgang* I arias with four-line texts are in *da capo* form. The two exceptions are BWV 48/4 (binary) and BWV 181/3, which is in a modified binary form in which all four lines are set in each of the two vocal sections ("Hälftige Form").

gested the possibility of repeating the opening sentence at the end of the movement, even when a *da capo* return was not present in the libretto. The structural weight of a *da capo* return was especially necessary in BWV 83/1, a lengthy movement with one of the largest ensembles ever assembled by Bach for an aria, including pairs of horns and oboes, strings, continuo, and a virtuoso solo violin.[20] The expanded structure of *da capo* form seems particularly appropriate since this aria (which expresses the joy of the "Erfreute Zeit im neuen Bunde") is the opening movement of the cantata, substituting for the usual large-scale choral movement. By contrast with BWV 24/1 and 83/1, it is unclear why *da capo* form should have been preferred in "Mein alles in allem, mein ewiges Gut," BWV 22/4. Bach chose, none the less, to set all three arias in Cantatas 22 and 23 (which, as was mentioned earlier, were performed on the same day) in *da capo* form.

Several other patterns emerge from Table 2; they demonstrate that certain text structures were associated with either strict or free *da capo* form. For instance, free *da capo* form was favored for texts with the forms a.bba (rhyme scheme 2a) and aab.ccb (rhyme scheme 16c). On the other hand, all but one of the nine *da capo* arias with the text form xa.bba (rhyme scheme 8) are in strict *da capo* form. (Six other movements with this text form are in a variety of non-repeating forms.)

Another striking phenomenon in *Jahrgang* I concerns the distribution of *da capo* forms. Although there is no discernible change in the forms of the aria texts over the course of the year, one finds, if one divides the *Jahrgang* in two, using the Advent *tempus clausum* as a mid-point, that the density of free *da capo* arias is much higher in the first half of the *Jahrgang* than in the second (see Table 4). Moreover, at the end of the *Jahrgang* there is an especially high concentration of strict *da capo* arias: all but three of the ten arias in the last five new cantatas (BWV 104, 166, 86, 37, 44) have this form.

The shift from free to strict *da capo* arias may reveal a change in Bach's outlook during his first year in Leipzig. When he first assumed his duties as Thomaskantor, he was probably eager to explore the possibilities of the aria,

---

[20] Regarding Cantata 83, Spitta writes:

The music for the festival of the Purification has assumed the form of a complete Italian concerto; and, as if Bach was resolved to force this on the hearer's consciousness, he adds a violin part *concertante* to both the first and third movements, one being an aria for the alto and the other for the tenor. The resemblance to an instrumental concerto is indeed so conspicuous that we might almost be tempted to think it had been founded on one, and remodelled from its first form for church purposes. This, however, is not the case.

Spitta, Vol. 2, p. 390.

Table 4 *Distribution of aria forms in Jahrgang I*

Segment 1 1 post Trin. (30 May 1723)–25 post Trin. (14 November 1723):
    strict *da capo* = 12/41 (29%)
    free *da capo* = 15/41 (37%)
    non-repeating and other forms = 14/41 (34%)

Segment 2 2 Christmas (26 December 1723)–1 post Asc. (21 May 1724):
    strict *da capo* = 14/33 (42%)
    free *da capo* = 4/33 (12%)
    non-repeating and other forms = 15/33 (45%)

---

especially the relatively new and unusual free *da capo* form.[21] But after a year of extraordinarily intense compositional activity – including about one cantata per week, plus the Magnificat, the St John Passion and several other works – Bach may have found it necessary to lighten the load by relying more heavily on the conventional strict *da capo* form.

Space limitations do not permit detailed consideration here of the *Jahrgang* I arias in strict *da capo* form. Most of them have the same overall design:

Rit. – A – Rit. – B –   *da capo*
I   I   I   modulation (usually to mediant or dominant)

Often the opening lines are set twice, and there is a modulation in the A section:

Rit. –   A1 –   Rit. –   A2 –   Rit.
I   modulation (usually   new key   modulation back   I
       to dominant)   to tonic

However, one interesting exception is "Mein Jesus soll mein alles sein," BWV 75/3, an early example of the *dal segno* aria, a form which did not come into widespread use until the second half of the century.[22] This movement

---

[21] Bach had previously composed only a handful of free *da capo* arias. He did not invent this form, however; it is found as early as the end of the seventeenth century in operas by Alessandro Scarlatti and Carlo Pallavicino. See Malcolm Boyd, *Bach* (London and Melbourne, 1983), pp. 131–2.

[22] According to *The New Harvard Dictionary of Music*,

In the second half of the eighteenth century, a number of alternative forms for the aria emerged. One possibility was an abridgment of the da capo – the dal segno aria, in which the return was not to the beginning of the aria but to a point marked by a sign after the ritornello, often the beginning of the second full statement of the first strophe.

See Don Randel, ed., *The New Harvard Dictionary of Music* (Cambridge, Massachusetts and London, 1986), p. 49. *Cf.* also Charles Rosen, *Sonata Forms* (New York and London, 1980), p. 43, and Michael Robinson, "The Aria in Opera Seria, 1725–1780," *Proceedings of the Royal Musical Association*, 88 (1961–2), p. 40.

follows the usual pattern for strict *da capo* arias until the end of the B section
(mm. 110ff). Ordinarily a full statement of the ritornello in the tonic is
heard at this point. In BWV 75/3, however, the line of demarcation
between the end of the B section and the beginning of the *da capo* return is
blurred by the omission of the ritornello and an unusual recomposition of
the A section. The head motive of the ritornello reappears with the last
line of the text ("mein allersüsssten Freudenwein") in measures 111–12 (see
Example 1). Immediately thereafter the second half of the A section is

Example 1 BWV 75/3, Tenor aria, "Mein Jesus soll mein alles sein"

(a) Head motive of ritornello: oboe/violin I, mm. 1–2

(b) Tenor, mm. 26–7

mein Je - sus soll mein   al - les sein

(c) Tenor, mm. 111–12

mein al - ler-süss-ster   Freu-den-wein

quoted in a staggered fashion: the literal restatement begins in the tenor part
at measure 115 (mm. 115ff=mm. 54ff), in the continuo part at measure
118 (mm. 118ff=mm. 57ff), and in the string and oboe parts at measure
121 (mm. 121ff=mm. 60ff). The result of this procedure is that one gains
the impression of a full *da capo* return, whereas an entire statement of the
ritornello and the first half of the A section have actually been omitted.
Presumably Bach recomposed the *da capo* return on account of the excessive
length of the A section. If he had not adjusted it, the movement would have
run to 194 measures, making this aria one of the longest in the *Jahrgang*.
And Bach was certainly aware that Cantata 75, with fourteen movements,
would be long enough without a full *da capo* return in the first aria.[23]

[23] Ironically, BWV 75/3 is even shorter in the *Bach-Gesellschaft* edition. Marshall has pointed
out that Wilhelm Rust, the editor of Cantata 75, inadvertently omitted measures 112–25 of
this movement. See Robert L. Marshall, "Zur Vollständigkeit der Arie 'Mein Jesus soll mein
alles sein' aus Kantate BWV 75," *Bach-Jahrbuch*, 51 (1965), pp. 144–7.

Of greater formal interest are the free *da capo* arias. Most of them have the following form:

Rit. –	A –	Rit. –	B –	Rit. –	A′ –	Rit.
I	modulation away from tonic (usually to dominant; see footnote 6)	new key	modulation	sudden return or modulation back to tonic	I	I

Occasionally, one of the internal ritornelli is omitted or the return to the tonic is delayed until well into the A′ section. I will draw attention here to just a few unusual movements.

The alto arias "Jesus macht mich geistlich reich," BWV 75/10, and "Jesus schläft, was soll ich hoffen?" BWV 81/1, exhibit many of the characteristics of free *da capo* form. But in neither movement is the text (a.bba=rhyme scheme 2a) set according to its sentence structure (line 1 = A and A′ sections, lines 2–4 = B section). In BWV 75/10, all four lines are present in each of the first two vocal sections, and line 1 alone in the third:

> mm. 1–16   = ritornello (i)
> mm. 17–35 = lines 1–4 (i–III)
> mm. 36–44 = ritornello (III)
> mm. 45–69 = lines 1–4 (III–v)
> mm. 70–87 = ritornello (v–i)
> mm. 88–102 = line 1 (i)
> mm. 103–19 = ritornello (i)

The form of BWV 81/1 is also unusual:

> mm. 1–8   = ritornello (i)
> mm. 9–26 = lines 1–4 (i–iv)
> mm. 27–31 = ritornello (iv)
> mm. 32–6 = line 1 (iv–i)
> mm. 37–44 = line 1 (i)
> mm. 45–53 = ritornello (i)

In this movement, the entire text is set in the first vocal section, while the other two contain just the opening line. Furthermore, the customary ritornello between the second and third vocal sections is omitted, and the target key of the modulation is the subdominant instead of the dominant or mediant. However, the most striking feature of this aria is the extremely brief B section (just five measures); the A′ section clearly begins in measure 37 with the return of the opening material in the tonic.

The formal peculiarities of BWV 75/10 and 81/1 are attributable to an important feature of their texts: there is a closer connection between the two sentences than is usual. In other *Jahrgang* I arias with the same text structure (BWV 75/5, 76/5, 76/12), there is a degree of discontinuity between the first and second sentences. The first sentence of BWV 75/5 is a personal statement of Christian experience ("Ich nehme mein Leiden mit Freuden auf mich"); the second merely summarizes a general doctrinal principle ("Wer Lazarus' Plagen/Geduldig ertragen,/Den nehmen die Engel zu sich"). The other two texts open with imperatives (BWV 76/5: "Fahr hin, abgöttische Zunft!"; BWV 76/12: "Liebt, ihr Christen, in der Tat!"), and are followed by reflections occasioned by the content of the first sentence (BWV 76/5: "Sollt sich die Welt gleich verkehren,/Will ich doch Christum verehren,/Er ist das Licht der Venunft;" BWV 76/12: "Jesus stirbet für die Brüder,/Und sie sterben für sich wieder,/Weil er sich verbunden hat"). In BWV 75/10 and 81/1, however, the two sentences form a single unit; therefore Bach avoided dividing the text.

BWV 75/10	BWV 81/1
Jesus macht mich geistlich reich.	Jesus schläft, was soll ich hoffen?
Kann ich seinen Geist empfangen,	Seh ich nicht
Will ich weiter nichts verlangen;	Mit erblasstem Angesicht
Denn mein Leben wächst zugleich.	Schon des Todes Abgrund offen?

The unconventional form of the bass aria "Auf Gott steht meine Zuversicht," BWV 138/5, suggests that Bach was experimenting with the idea of a rondo–aria hybrid late in the summer of 1723.[24] Since the text is unusually long (seven lines), and it is the only aria in Cantata 138,[25] Bach took the opportunity to compose a movement in an expanded version of the free *da capo* form:

mm. 1–20	= ritornello (I)
mm. 21–45	= A, lines 1–2 (I–V)
mm. 46–57	= ritornello (V)
mm. 58–73	= B, lines 3–4 (V–vi)
mm. 74–81	= ritornello (vi)
mm. 82–90	= beginning of A, line 1 (I)
mm. 91–118	= C, lines 5–7 (vi–iii)
mm. 119–44	= A', lines 1–2 (I)
mm. 145–65	= ritornello (I)

[24] Cantata 138 was first performed on the Fifteenth Sunday after Trinity, 5 September 1723.

[25] The cantata for the following Sunday (Sixteenth Sunday after Trinity, 12 September 1723), "Christus, der ist mein Leben," BWV 95, also has just one aria.

The key to this aria is the short quotation of the beginning of the A section just before the second contrasting section. Without it, the middle third of the movement would sound like a subdivided B section (such as is found in BWV 179/5, for instance). But this fragment of the A section sets apart the two contrasting sections, and gives the movement a rondo-like quality (A B A' C A'' instead of A B A').

The structure of the text (xa.bb.cca=rhyme scheme 24) did not demand such an unusual form; it could easily have been accommodated within the normal parameters of the *da capo* aria (e.g., lines 1–2=A; lines 3–7=B). Although the presence of three sentences obviously suggested that they be set in three separate sections, this could have been accomplished by simply dividing the B section in two (lines 3–4=B1; lines 5–7=B2).

The notion that Bach was engaged in formal experimentation is strengthened by the observation that just a few days earlier he had composed another movement with a rondo-like form, the tenor aria "Wohl dir, du Volk der Linden," BWV 119/3.[26] As was the case for BWV 138/5, the text of BWV 119/3 did not demand the invention of the musical form. (Indeed, two other *Jahrgang* I arias, BWV 48/6 and 81/3, with the same text structure (ab.ccba=rhyme scheme 21) are both in free *da capo* form.) But instead of the expected *da capo* design, Bach created a unique form for this aria:

mm. 1–12   =ritornello (I)
mm. 12–17a =lines 1–2 (I–V)
mm. 17b–20=ritornello (V)
mm. 21–6a =lines 3–6 (I–vi)
mm. 26b–8a =ritornello (vi)
mm. 28b–34=lines 1–2 (vi–iii)
mm. 35–7   =ritornello (iii)
mm. 38–50 =lines 3–6, 1–2 (iii–I)
mm. 51–63 =ritornello (I)

BWV 119/3 diverges from the normal *da capo* form in several respects. It has no clearly delineated A and B sections; rather the entire text is set twice in four sections punctuated by ritornelli. The tonal plan is also unusual: there is an unexpected return to the tonic at the beginning of the second vocal section (mm. 21ff), yet the section which occupies the position of the *da capo* return (mm. 28ff) is modulatory. Furthermore, all six lines of text are set (in reverse order) in the final vocal segment. The result of these features is a rondo-like form which is characterized by the repetition

---

[26] Cantata 119 was premiered at the ceremony for the installation of the town council on 30 August 1723.

of lines 1–2. We do not know what sparked Bach's interest in the possibility of combining the rondo and aria forms. But that he composed two such movements in chronologically adjacent cantatas is striking indeed.

The last free *da capo* aria I will consider is "Es kömmt ein Tag, so das Verborgne richtet," BWV 136/3, which has the following form:

mm. 1–10 = ritornello (i)
mm. 11–26 = A (i–v)
mm. 27–8 = ritornello (v)
mm. 29–37 = B (v)
mm. 38–9 = ritornello (v)
mm. 40–9 = A′ (v–i)
mm. 50–60 = ritornello (i)

Several unusual features of this movement support the notion that it was originally in binary form.[27] First, it seems strange that the B section begins and ends in the same key, whereas in most other arias it is highly modulatory. Moreover, the tonal plan of the A′ section (v–i) is opposite that of A (i–v). Finally, the *da capo* return does not conform to the usual pattern for free *da capo* arias: ordinarily the A′ section is a recomposition of A, but in this movement the two sections are entirely different. These difficulties vanish at once, however, if one accepts the hypothesis that BWV 136/3 is simply an expansion of an aria in the following binary form:

mm. 1–10 = ritornello (i)
mm. 11–26 = A (i–v)
mm. 27–8 = ritornello (v)
mm. 40–9 = B (v–i)
mm. 50–60 = ritornello (i)

We have seen that the forms of the Bach arias were influenced by a variety of factors, including the libretti, the structures of the texts, and more abstract considerations such as formal experimentation. But this brief encounter with the arias in *Jahrgang* I has also made us aware that Bach treated the aria form differently from most of his contemporaries: he viewed it as a limitless network of possibilities rather than an inflexible mold. By bringing his prodigious imagination to bear upon the aria, Bach transformed it from the banal to the sublime.[28]

---

[27] Marshall traces this idea back to Rust, who first set forth his hypothesis about the origins of the aria in the preface to the *Bach-Gesellschaft* edition of Cantata 136 (Vol. 28, p. xxx). See Robert L. Marshall, *The Compositional Process of J. S. Bach* (Princeton, 1972), pp. 209–10, and especially fn. 56.

[28] This study has benefitted greatly from a careful reading by Robert L. Marshall, to whom I should like to express my gratitude.

The regulative and generative roles of verse in Bach's "thematic" invention

PAUL BRAINARD

Hermann Abert wrote in 1922:

There is one aspect of Bach's cantatas and passions about which even today no agreement seems to have been reached – namely concerning his relationship to vocal music [*Gesang*] in general. Some regard him as the greatest master of declamation German music has ever had; others maintain that, like Beethoven, he merely treated voices like instruments and therefore does not deserve to be called a vocal composer at all.[1]

Abert might seem at first to share the second of these opinions. He readily concedes the "unvocal quality" (*Ungesanglichkeit*) of many of Bach's arias. It does not however follow from this (he continues) that Bach's melodic invention could be validly described as "instrumental." Indeed the whole thrust of Abert's argument is to deny the genuine relevance of the "vocal/instrumental" dichotomy altogether. With Bach, he writes, "only the musical line matters, completely irrespective of whether it is carried by a human voice or by an instrument." Bach's is "a completely abstract music, which disregards all external, material sound and admits only music as such to be valid."

Though debatable as a general proposition (for Bach was anything but unconcerned with "material sound"), Abert's point lacks neither interest nor merit. It harks back, albeit with quite different overtones, to the famous passage from Johann Adolph Scheibe's *Critischer Musicus* in which Bach is taken to task for demanding "that singers and instrumentalists should be able to do with their throats and instruments whatever he can play on the

---

[1] This and the following quotations in this paragraph are taken from Hermann Abert, "Bach und wir," *Gesammelte Schriften und Vorträge*, ed. Friedrich Blume (Halle, 1929), pp. 137–8 (my translation).

clavier."[2] Now that Scheibe has been rehabilitated from his one-time role as "Philistine" *vis-à-vis* Bach (an Artusi of the eighteenth century, as it were),[3] we may I think take his observation more nearly at face value and acknowledge the considerable truth it contains. To argue about separate "vocal" and "instrumental" domains in the cantatas and oratorios of Bach comes close, as Abert recognized, to missing the point. At the very least it distracts our attention from the much larger objective of understanding the thought-processes and the external as well as the self-imposed constraints that shaped Bach's vocal music.

As one aspect of that larger question, I have been investigating some very elementary matters affecting our view of Bach the *musicien–poète* (to misappropriate slightly the title of Schweitzer's famous 1905 study). That the composer was thoroughly grounded in the workings of prosody and versification has never been questioned; indeed for a long time he was thought to be the author of more than a few of the unattributed texts of his own cantatas. Though that no longer seems so likely, a command of the craft of poetry was surely, as the theorists of his time proclaimed it had to be, part and parcel of his command of the craft of composition itself.

The nature of Bach's response, as a composer, to the texts with which he had to deal has been investigated – usually rather haphazardly – from a number of points of view, but never (so far as I know) from the standpoint of versification itself. It has occurred to me that it might be of interest, and perhaps of considerable value, to examine Bach's vocal settings in relation to their verse categories, and thus to explore more systematically the extent to which poetic structure itself acts as a determinant of his musical invention.

As those familiar with the cantata texts will immediately realize, the task of establishing such poetic classes is in itself potentially very problematic: varying rhyme schemes, numbers of lines, line lengths, internal changes of meter, etc. all constitute complicating factors. I propose to sidestep that issue for the present by confining myself to first lines alone, which of course lend themselves more readily to an objective classification. That this is not so simplistic or unfruitful a procedure as might be supposed, will I hope emerge as we proceed.

[2] *Der Critischer Musicus. Erster Theil* (Hamburg, 1738), *Sechstes Stück. Dienstags den 14 May, 1737*, p. 46; translation from *The Bach Reader*, ed. Hans T. David and Arthur Mendel (New York 1945, revised ed. 1966), p. 238.

[3] George J. Buelow, "In Defence of J. A. Scheibe against J. S. Bach," *Proceedings of the Royal Musical Association*, 101 (1974/5), pp. 85–100; Günther Wagner, "J. A. Scheibe – J. S. Bach: Versuch einer Bewertung," *Bach-Jahrbuch*, 68 (1982), pp. 33–49.

To date, the investigation has been arbitrarily limited to the versified arias and duets from all of Bach's sacred cantatas from 1713/14 on, excluding known contrafacts ("parodies") and movements whose first-line settings are based on chorale melodies. For the purposes of the present report, an additional condition was imposed: I shall here consider only those settings that exhibit substantial identity between their vocal openings and ritornellos. (The reasons for this limitation are related to my opening remarks; they will be clarified farther on.) The resulting sample of slightly more than 300 movements is, I believe, large enough to permit general conclusions. The table below summarizes some results of an initial phase of the inquiry, involving a reductive analysis of first-line settings in the two overwhelmingly largest verse categories within the sample, trochaic and iambic tetrameter. The objective was to discover patterns of correlation between poetic and musical meter – that is, of stress-placement within the measure, under each of the several varieties of musical meter found within my sample.

Some basic schemata in settings of four-foot trochaic (total instances = 118) and iambic (total = 94) first lines

---

A in quaternary (binary) meter   No. of instances

  1 The four stresses on alternate (strong) beats of ¢ or equivalent:

  troch. ¢ ♩ ♩ ♩ ♩ | ♩ ♩ ♩ [♩]   13
          X – X –   X – X [-]

  iamb. ¢ ♪| ♩ ♩ ♩ ♩ | ♩ ♩ ♩ [♩]   20
          – X – X –   X – X [-]

  2 The four stresses on successive beats of ¢ or equivalent (first stress prevailingly on a weak beat):

  troch. ¢ ⅊ ♪♪♪♪♪♪| ♪ [♪♪]   28
           X – X – X – X [-]

  iamb. ¢ ⅊ ♪♪♪♪♪♪♪| ♪ [♪]   12
          – X – X – X – X [-]

B in ternary or compound meter, but related to A 1 by virtue of quaternary organization:

  1 The four stresses on the first beats of four bars of ⅜ or (rarer) ¾ :

troch. [reversal common] 20

X - X - X - X -

iamb. [rare] 11

- X - X - X - X [-]

2 Variants apparently peculiar to iambic settings (first bar invariably trisyllabic):

a. 8

'-' X - X - X - X [-]

b. 3

'-' X - X '-' X - X [-]

C in ternary meter:

1 The four stresses on the first and third beats of each of a pair of ¾ bars, with anacrusis:

troch. 4

X - X - X - X -

iamb. 7

- X - X - X - X [-]

iamb. [final stress on beat 2] 4

- X - X - X - X

2 The four stresses on alternate beats of triple time:

troch. [the cæsura is the only invariant] 3

X - 'X' - X - X -

iamb. ["hæmiola" effect] 5

- X - X - X - X -

3 The four stresses on successive beats of triple time, first stress on downbeat:

troch. 4

X - X - X - X [-]

iamb. 4

- X - X - X - X -

Some commentary on the table is in order. Note first that it encompasses only a little more than two-thirds of the set in question (the remaining third offering no discernible basis for classification – which is surely a significant fact in itself). Second, the alert reader may already have noticed, from the bracketing of final syllables in a number of cases, that hypercatalectic (nine-syllable) iambic and catalectic (seven-syllable) trochaic lines have been grouped together with their "normal" acatalectic (eight-syllable) counter-parts. This reflects a conclusion reached only after an exhaustive comparison (reported on in the original version of this paper delivered at the 1985 Flint meeting) between eight- and nine-syllable iambic settings, from which it emerged that although the two groups indeed differed (in part, predictably) from one another, such differences were primarily the result of factors other than the syllable-count. Within this set, in other words, the distinction between "masculine" and "feminine" line-endings appeared to be of secondary formative importance.

In a related vein, it has sometimes been argued in the theory of German prosody, and might well be argued in music, that the iambic and trochaic versions of (in particular) tetrameter are in effect two forms of the same thing, distinguishable only by an entirely secondary criterion: the presence or absence of an initial unstressed syllable or musical upbeat. This is at least superficially borne out by several categories in the Table, notably group A 1. Here we can adduce numerous instances in which the simple addition of an upbeat to a line of trochaic tetrameter would render it functionally indistin-guishable from an iambic one. Compare, for instance, musical Examples 1a and 1b with one another. Neglecting (for the moment) their differing melodic shapes and the slight rhythmic modification found in Example 1b, they show the same placement of metrical stresses.

A comparable degree of metrical similarity exists between the iambic set-ting of Example 2a and the trochaic one of Example 2b. But if we were to try to interchange the verse lines of this second pair with those of the first (Example 1a/b), we would immediately run into insuperable obstacles: the stress-placements coincide, but the word-boundaries do not, so that

Example 1 a BWV 13/5, mm. 1–2, 9–10
b BWV 104/3, mm. 1–2, 7–8

Example 1 (*cont.*)

Example 2 a BWV 58/3, mm. 1–2, 13–14
b BWV 82/3, mm. 1–2, 10–11

(among other things) the musical cæsuras of Example 2 would make text transferral from Example 1 impossible – all this of course quite apart from the wide differences of sense and affective import between the individual lines as well as their settings.

The obvious moral is that the constraints imposed by verse upon music go well beyond those of stress-placement alone. To begin with, syntax and internal line-divisions are limiting factors at least as significant as those of stress and non-stress. For a further instance of the role played by syntax, consider Example 3, whose voice-line and harmony in the second measure of the theme are predicated on a continuation and resolution yet to come:

> Gott, dem der Erdenkreis zu klein,
> Den weder Welt noch Himmel fassen,
> Will in der engen Krippe sein.

Example 3 BWV 91/3, mm. 1–2, 9–10

Only at this point in the text is the rhetorical period complete; the open-endedness of Bach's first phrase is a direct translation of this circumstance into music. In this web of constraints – stress placement, syntax, word- and line-division and others – we of course have the reason why Bach, when faced with the task of adapting an existing vocal composition to a new text, apparently strongly preferred, whenever it was feasible, to commission the writing of new poetry modelled as closely as possible after the old in every detail of line structure, rhyme scheme, etc., as well as affect and imagery.[4]

In category A 2 of the Table, the trochaic and iambic versions of the basic tetrameter pattern are again seen to be identical in all respects save the initial syllable. One of the principal variants of the trochaic scheme given here is one in which the opening quarter-rest is replaced by a note, thus prolonging the first stress. Comparison shows that this almost invariably

---

[4] For this procedure Werner Neuman coined the term "dichterische Parodie" in his valuable study "Über Ausmaß und Wesen des Bachschen Parodieverfahrens," *Bach-Jahrbuch*, 51 (1965), pp. 63–85.

corresponds to the syntactical importance and *sense*-stress of the first word. See for instance Example 4, in which the name "Jesus" is prolonged, whereas in the rhythmically analogous Example 5 no such word-extension would have been appropriate; here the basic scheme A 2 appears without substantial alteration.

Example 4 BWV 113/5, mm. 1–2, 13–15

Example 5 BWV 123/3, mm. 1–2, 5–6

The matter of sense-stress, as distinct from the abstract or schematic stress-patterns of prosody, was interestingly dealt with by Johann Mattheson:

What matters here is that one should know how to judge properly just which words are actually to be stressed. And here there is no better advice than that one should examine all sorts of utterances, especially in prose, and should endeavor to find the right word, perhaps through the following means.

If I for example would want to know where the word-stress would be in this sentence: "**Unser** Leben ist eine Wanderschafft"; then I would only need to present the proposition in question and answer form, namely: "**Was** ist unser Leben? Eine Wanderschafft." Thus this reveals that the emphasis would rest upon the word "**Wanderschafft**"; and if the composer makes such a word prominent in one or another unconstrained way with his tones, he will be "**clear**".[5]

Although the applicability of Mattheson's "rhetorical question" method to Bach's texts turns out to be quite limited, their settings bear out the extraordinary degree to which Bach subscribed to the spirit of Mattheson's remarks.

Category B 2 of the Table involves foot-substitution at the beginning of the verse line: that is, the nominally unstressed initial syllable of the iamb is placed on a downbeat in triple (and more seldom in binary) meter.[6] This subtle counterpoint between musical and poetic stresses frequently reflects characteristics of the verse in question. In Example 6, for instance, it corresponds to the apostrophe: "*Ihr*, die ihr euch von Christo nennet"; in Example 7 it interprets: *I* will carry the cross. (A further instance of the same phenomenon occurs in the earlier Example 3, a variant of the iambic pattern of category C 3.) But this rule is not invariable, as we see in Example 8, where poetry and music appear less well matched, in that the durational stresses of the melody partially contradict, or at least neutralize, the metrical ones. Here it seems we must concede the predominance of factors other than those of either prosody or sense-stress in Bach's conception.

Example 6 BWV 164/1, mm. 1–2, 9–12

---

[5] *Der vollkommene Capellmeister* (Hamburg, 1739), Chapter 5, paragraphs 96-7 (Ernest Harriss's translation).

[6] In the Table these syllables are designated by the symbol: "-".

Example 7 BWV 56/1, mm. 1–4, 17–20

Ich will den Kreuz - stab_____ ger - ne tra - - (gen)

Example 8 BWV 109/5, mm. 1–2, 17 20

Der Hei - land ken - net____ ja die Sei - nen

This last example, whose dubious declamatory qualities are rare but by no means unique in Bach, raises a further question of a more general sort. The high preponderance of tetrameter verse in the cantata texts correlates, in purely statistical terms, with a general preference on Bach's part for metrically regular, "quadratic" phrase structure in (especially) the initial statements of first lines. Are these two facts meaningfully related? That seems to me extremely doubtful. Although it is true that the four-stress line happens to have been most frequently set by direct musical analogy (as in groups A 1, A 2 and B 1 of the Table), "regular" musical phrasing tends to prevail under so many different prosodic conditions that a "cause and effect" relationship seems ruled out.

Category A 2, for instance, offers evidence in point. In both the iambic and trochaic forms of this pattern, the remainder of the incomplete second measure is almost invariably filled out either by rests (Example 9), by beginning a restatement of the first text line (as seen above in Example 4), or – most frequently of all – by continuing immediately with the second line (Example 10). In at least these instances, then, binary or "quadratic" phras-

Example 9 BWV 18/4, mm. 1–2, 9–10

Example 10 BWV 93/6, mm. 1–2, 9–10

ing would seem to reflect a musical preference rather than any particular property of the poetic model.

Similar conclusions can be drawn from Bach's settings of trimeter verse (of which 43 instances were tabulated, all but four of them iambic). Here, despite the shorter line, the prevailing tendency is again to arrive at four-unit phrasing, often by one of the following means:

a extending the length of one of the three stresses (frequently the third), thus achieving the durational equivalent of four (Example 11);

b linking the first line directly with the second, producing the near-equivalent of an Alexandrine (likewise illustrated by Example 11);

c repeating the first line;

d repeating individual words (a very frequent expedient: Example 12);

e using "longanacruses" (Example 13) or concluding rests (in analogy to Example 9 above).

Example 11 BWV 154/4, mm. 1–2, 7–8

Je - su, laß dich fin - den, laß doch mei - ne Sün - den

Example 12 BWV 5/5, mm. 1 2, 13–14

Ver - stum-me, ver-stum-me, ver - stumme, Höl - len heer

Example 13 BWV 152/2, mm. 1–2, 11–12

Tritt auf die Glau - bens - bahn

Particularly interesting, though (regrettably, for our purposes) few in number, are Bach's musical realizations of iambic pentameter, of which there are eight instances within the sample. Together they supply a valuable corrective to any tendency we might have to over-simplify from the sorts of evidence just considered. Throughout this small group, the impact of verse-meter upon musical invention seems especially clear and, in several cases, beyond question – notably from the irregular phrase-length that results from straightforward projection of the five iambs (or five iambs plus one syllable) upon either binary (Example 14) or ternary (Example 15) meter. In both cases three-bar phrases are the inevitable outcome. In Example 16, along with several other features that make this aria an almost motet-like model of declamation, we note that the pentameter line occupies six beats in a ¼ context – surely not fortuitously.

Of all the settings within the total sample, those of dactyllic verse are by far the most uniform, as is the verse-category itself. Of the 35 instances encountered, all have "binary" line structure (tetrameter or dimeter), and in all but three the initial dactyllic foot is preceded by an unstressed syllable ("upbeat"). Bach's treatment follows suit. All feet within the line tend with great regularity to follow the scheme ♪♪♪ in ternary or compound, ♩♪♪ in binary meter. The further verse-types encountered – iambic dimeter (eight instances), trochaic dimeter (six), and Alexandrines (four) – contribute nothing new to the discussion.

What has emerged thus far, then, is that the several categories of verse can indeed be seen to correlate meaningfully with certain metrical and rhythmic configurations in Bach's arias, but that there are several degrees and many kinds of textual input, as well as certain compositional elements (like phrase length) that show clear links to prosody only on occasion. We have seen, too, that irrespective of verse-class, differences of syntax, line-division, sense-stress, and the like exert an influence upon Bach that frequently transcends the rudimentary constraints posed by the nominal arrangement of poetic feet, or by (say) the differences between iambic and trochaic, or catalectic and acatalectic verse.

That brings us to the crux of the matter: where does the merely regulative role of prosody overlap with, or give way to, a *generative* role? Can it be shown that the poetic model induces musical responses that go beyond mere conformity with line-structure to a state in which music embodies qualities of the verse that are unique to a particular exemplar, and hence not attributable merely to a generalized set of prosodic constraints?

The range in degree of verse-responsiveness in Bach is, as we have seen, quite large. It is not overly hard to find settings in which he seems to defy all

Example 14 BWV 41/2, mm. 1–2, 16–18

Laß uns, o höch-ster Gott, das Jahr_ voll-brin-gen,

piano

Example 15 BWV 147/7, mm. 1–2, 6–8

Hilf, Je-su, hilf, daß ich auch dich be-ken-ne,

Example 16 BWV 105/5, mm. 1–2, 9–10

Kann ich nur Je-sum mir zum Freunde machen,

but the bare mechanical attributes of a given verse-type.[7] In other cases, however (such as the earlier Examples 3, 4, 6, and 7), it is precisely such departures from prosodic conformity, from the "norms" of abstract schemes, that provide some of our strongest evidence that Bach was not merely scanning his texts perfunctorily, not merely imposing independently conceived melodies upon unresisting textual partners. I will limit myself to but one additional illustration of this point: Example 17 (a variant of the iambic

Example 17 BWV 38/3, mm. 1–2, 13–14

pattern of category A 2), where we note how the nominally unstressed initial "ich" is accented musically as a downbeat; but the following syllable overtops it in pitch and is further stressed through elongation as well as syncopation, producing a subtle equilibrium of emphasis that seems to capture the quintessence of the line.

By far the most conclusive evidence for text-generated musical invention comes, however, from Bach's use of musical figures in response to certain image-evoking or emotionally laden words. We have already passed over several notable instances of this; Examples 1a, 2b, 5 and 7 are among the more obvious ones. This particular path of investigation is of course well worn[8] and needs no lengthy re-traversal here despite its manifest bearing on our understanding of Bach as a vocal composer. Of the large vocabulary of musical–rhetorical figures as a whole, I would venture the opinion that it will not take us very far in the present context, because although the figures can supply names for a whole variety of compositional devices, proof that they *generated* musical ideas is in most cases very hard to come by. With pictorial and affective figures, however, we are on relatively safe ground. Best known among them are fairly self-evident devices such as chromatic inflections for terms of sadness or distress, melismas for words like "Freude" or

[7] It may or may not be significant that almost all such instances depart substantially from the "standard" patterns given in the Table.

[8] Still among the very best studies of its kind is André Pirro's *L'Esthétique de Jean-Sébastien Bach* (Paris, 1907).

"eilen," sustained notes for "harren," "Ruhe," and the like, and the musical counterparts for directional or spatial concepts (high/low, rising/falling, etc.). Others are more subtle. Consider in our earlier Example 2a, for instance, how Bach has overlaid the word "vergnügt" (contented) with the "sigh" motive that properly derives from "Leiden" (suffering): a precise musical analogy of the paradox that underlies the text.

The penchant of most Baroque composers for literal pictorialism is often dismissed – unjustifiably in my view – as simplistic and superficial, having little or nothing to do with the deeper and more "legitimate" domains of musical expression. One of the usages that particularly courts the ridicule of the literal-minded – in Bach no less than in the madrigalists of the sixteenth century – is that of pictorial figures in the context of a negative statement.[9] As Bach's younger contemporary Christian Gottfried Krause observed,[10] music offers no way of rendering the sense of words like "never" or "not." Krause lays the responsibility upon the poet to couch aria texts wherever possible in the affirmative. "Instead of 'Mein Herz ist nicht betrübt'," he writes, "the poet should preferably say 'Mein Herz ist voller Freuden'; instead of 'Mein Geist ist ohne Freuden' let him set 'Mein Geist ist voller Trauren'." And so on.

Bach's poets (who of course belonged to the two generations preceding that of Krause) were not so considerate of the composer's problems in observing strict logic – a fact for which, on balance, I think we can only be grateful. Bach, for his part, flung himself into the portrayal of negatively framed affects and images with every bit as much enthusiasm as with affirmatively stated ones. We can just possibly infer his consciousness of the potential irony of this practice from Example 18, where he first clearly mirrors the trembling uncertainty of "Erschüttre dich," then cries out the countermanding "nicht" with every stress at his disposal. But far more often the injunction *not* to do something is all but lost in the musical depiction of precisely that which is being forbidden. I cannot resist quoting the beginning of an aria from Cantata 111 (Example 19) which plays off the negative "nicht" against one of the more elaborate musical puns in all of Bach. It consists of his taking the verb "entsetzen" in its original lexical meaning, "aus dem Sitz kommen oder bringen" (to displace or be displaced), with devastatingly graphic results. In my view this aria also constitutes a compelling refutation of the notion that Bach's figural language is a mere surface detail.

[9] On pp. 246ff of his study (see note 8) Pirro cites a number of criticisms of this practice by Bach's contemporaries, adding several trenchant observations of his own.

[10] *Von der Musikalischen Poesie* (Berlin, 1753), pp. 262–4.

Example 18 BWV 99/3, mm. 1–4, 13–16

Example 19 BWV 111/2, mm. 1, 5–7

And now, harking back to the beginning of this essay, we can also note that because that figural language is word-based, its advance appearance in a ritornello decisively over-rules any supposition that vocal and instrumental writing constitute neatly separable categories, let alone that the theme in question could be said to be specifically "instrumental" in nature.

The scholar who has carried the theory of "instrumental dominance" in Bach to its farthest extreme to date is Werner Neumann. He has recently argued, indeed, that the time may have come

gradually to dismantle the hegemony of *text* in our æsthetic of Bach. It has given us that tiresome multiplicity of text-interpretive studies that doggedly track down pictorial, symbolic, affective, rhetorical illustrative figures while studiously ignoring the countless declamatory anomalies and crudenesses in view of which one can only speak of a spirit of proud disdain of text [*den Geist stolzer Textmißachtung*].[11]

This is of course written in the context of Neumann's long-standing argument that a large share of Bach's vocal music (excluding recitatives, motets, and other "genuinely vocal" settings) is inherently instrumental in conception. In cantata choruses and arias, that argument is heavily based on the relationship between instrumental ritornelli and the body of the settings they precede. Having discussed it at length elsewhere,[12] I will confine myself here to a restatement of the point that wherever the melody of an aria's ritornello is substantially identical to that of its voice-line, this by itself constitutes virtual proof of an at least nominal observance of the prosody of its text in the devising of the ritornello theme, and that the presence of affective or pictorial figures in that theme further documents the dependence on the poetic model. It is true that such identity is often disguised by an overlay of ornamentation in the ritornello, in comparison to which a simpler, skeletal voice-line can give the appearance of being a reduction; yet this interpretation is in most cases no more provable than is the converse. One of the more elaborately ornamented ritornelli of this kind is that of BWV 169/3 (Example 20); here it seems almost beyond dispute that it is the vocal version of the first two measures that constitutes the true *inventio*, the

Example 20 BWV 169/3, mm. 1, 9–10

---

[11] Werner Neumann, "Das Problem 'vokal–instrumental' in seiner Bedeutung für ein neues Bach-Verständnis," in *Bachforschung und Bachinterpretation heute*, ed. Reinhold Brinkmann (Leipzig, 1981), p. 83.

[12] "The Aria and its Ritornello: The Question of 'Dominance' in Bach," in *Bachiana et alia musicologica. Festschrift Alfred Dürr zum 65. Geburtstag*, ed. Wolfgang Rehm (Kassel, 1983), pp. 39–51.

ritornello being merely the *elaboratio* of a textually-generated musical idea. The utter relativity of the vocal/instrumental distinction *per se* is further underscored by the occasional instances (like Example 21) where it is the voice that elaborates on the instrumental tune rather than *vice versa*. Here as elsewhere, the subtle interplay of textual and musical factors in Bach far exceeds the "vocal *vs.* instrumental" issue in both interest and importance.

Example 21 BWV 133/4, mm. 1–3, 9–11

An obvious limitation of the approach taken here is that it leaves un-touched the question of the role (if any) of poetry in shaping larger musical contexts. Günther Wagner, in reviewing the various positions taken by twentieth-century scholars concerning the text–music relationship in Bach, goes so far as to claim that text and its interpretation, occupying an at best "incidental" layer in the "Vielschichtigkeit" of Bach's music, are "in any case incapable of establishing contexts over longer stretches."[13]

My disagreement with the first part of this claim will be self-evident. Concerning the second, I would like to suggest a few qualifications. First, it is undeniable that the majority of poetic aria forms in the texts of Bach's cantatas and oratorios are shaped by musical conventions, rather than the other way around. Their musical settings, considered purely as formal struc-tures, owe everything to tonal considerations and to standard procedures of statement, restatement, and elaboration; in most cases they owe virtually nothing to their texts. It does not therefore follow that poetry is "incapable" of determining musical form; the main reason it often does not do so is simply that the concept of a continuously word-generated music conflicts

[13] Wagner, "J. A. Scheibe – J. S. Bach," p. 40.

directly with another ideal of the later Baroque: that of unity of affect and hence of motivic content. From the moment when he first adopted Neumeister's importation of Italian vocal forms into music for the German Church, Bach knowingly relinquished the declamatory and text-interpretive advantages (and the text-determined structures) of the motet in favor of the competing tendencies of the newer aria: singleness of affect and drastic limitation of the motivic vocabulary of a given piece. Uniquely among his contemporaries, however, Bach largely resolved this conflict by transforming the ritornello from a mere introduction or "setting in motion" into a distillation of affect and thought-content that both subsumed the whole, and could at the same time be used to generate internal contexts, particularly by means of the device (often termed *Einbau*) of embedding the vocal line(s) into integral instrumental restatements of the ritornello.[14] To date we know of no other composer who used it in the same way, or to anything like the same extent, as Bach. In his arias, the recurrent presence (and sometimes virtual omnipresence) of the ritornello – not just as a boundary-articulation, but as a co-determinant of the interior "course of events" – bespeaks, in my view, a wholly original *Formwille* that we have only just begun to understand.

Finally, we should remind ourselves that Bach well knew the limitations of stereotyped models, and was ready and willing to let poetic structure determine not only local contexts, but overall movement layout, whenever the principles of musical unity threatened to conflict intolerably with either prosody or poetic content. Among the most striking of the numerous available illustrations of this point is the bass aria from Cantata 139 (too space-consuming to be reproduced here). Its poetry embodies the familiar progression from a negative premise to a positive turn of events, together with the customary didactic conclusion:

> Das Unglück schlägt auf allen Seiten
> Um mich ein zentnerschweres Band.
> Doch plötzlich erscheinet die helfende Hand.
> Mir scheint des Trostes Licht von weiten;
> Da lern ich erst, daß Gott allein
> Der Menschen bester Freund muß sein.

Bach's setting of the first sentence seems to take "schlagen" both literally (to judge from the "percussive" rhythm and angularity of the vocal opening) as well as in its "proper" contextual meaning: "Misfortune binds [schlägt]

---

[14] See my essay "Aria and Ritornello: New Aspects of the Comparison Handel/Bach," in *Bach, Handel, Scarlatti: Tercentenary Essays*, ed. Peter Williams (Cambridge, 1985), pp. 21–33.

about me on every side a heavy band" (the imagery is roughly that of a barrel-hoop, the "surrounding on every side" being clearly mirrored in the interaction between the solo violin and the oboes d'amore).

The third line, however, brings an abrupt shift not only of content, but also of versification (from iambs to dactyls); and Bach accordingly introduces a new segment in $\frac{6}{8}$. A portion of the ritornello intervenes, but is twice succeeded by a wholly new *andante* section devoted to the final three text lines. Thereafter the opening music returns intact. Almost needless to say, the aria does not end with this restatement of its "pessimistic" initial ideas. Bach has chosen instead a modified rondo, with the "helping hand" music forming the vocal conclusion. A conventional *da capo* treatment of this particular text would have been, for Bach the *musicien–poète*, little short of unthinkable.

The St John Passion:
theology and musical structure

ERIC T. CHAFE

Ever since Friedrich Smend's ground-breaking 1926 study of Bach's St John Passion, musical scholarship has recognized that the structure of the Passion – far from being in any sense the result of hurried preparation, as once believed – was carefully designed with a great deal of musico-theological intent.[1] In order to interpret the meaning of even the most obvious instances of structural patterning in this as in many another work of Bach's, a considerable degree of involvement in theological aspects of the Passion is necessary. Our understanding of the St John Passion is immeasurably enriched the more we recognize how closely Bach's compositional intent intertwines the two disparate elements of sound and extra-musical meaning, as if on a higher level of contrapuntal interaction. And much that we are concerned with when we compare Bach's two Passions is traceable to the composer's musical realization of a set of quite different theological intentions from the one work to the other. This insight is very important to their criticism; for the theological intent of the St John Passion is less involved with allegorizing the sphere of human feelings than that of the St Matthew Passion. The St John Passion cannot be considered a lesser work than its successor on that account; and, in fact, the piece lacks nothing in the intensity and, one might say, the virtuosity of its musico-allegorical aspects, which is truly astonishing at times.

Recent years have seen an increasing – although still not sufficiently widespread – awareness that the "special" character that marks the St John

Certain material from this article will appear in my full study of the Passion in *Tonal Allegory in the Music of J. S. Bach* (University of California Press, 1989), forthcoming.

[1] Friedrich Smend, "Die Johannes-Passion von Bach. Auf ihren Bau untersucht," *Bach-Jahrbuch*, 23 (1926), pp. 105–28, reprinted in *Friedrich Smend Bach-Studien*, ed. Christoph Wolff (Kassel, 1969), pp. 11–23.

Passion as different from the St Matthew Passion is owing considerably to the highly individual nature of John's gospel.[2] This feature of Bach's setting is noteworthy in itself, because in the seventeenth and early eighteenth centuries the distinguishing characteristics of the different gospels did not constitute a major interest of theology. Rather the reverse, as the "synoptic" character of the major Passion poems makes clear – for example, the Brockes text. In this respect, therefore, the St John Passion is unique for its time. The work seems modern in its giving Johannine characteristics equality with, and even precedence over, Lutheran ones; and we can, as a result, use modern commentaries on John to illuminate it, rather than Luther's writings on the Passion (the latter are vastly more important in the case of the St Matthew Passion). While several of the particular emphases that emerge in Bach's setting, such as christology and the view that John's overall goal is "trust," can be traced to Luther's interpretations of John, much of the remainder – especially the structural aspects – can only be attributed to Bach's direct interaction with the gospel itself.[3]

In light of this last remark the several stages of revisions that the St John Passion underwent during the course of two decades (and several performances in Leipzig) may be considered to reflect the fact that Bach's first Leipzig Passion might not have fallen perfectly in line with the requirements of the local theological authorities, whose outlook was certainly dominated by the dogmatic concerns of Lutheranism. As we know, when Bach was notified in 1739 that the Passion performance that year was to be cancelled, his answer indicated unmistakably that he anticipated objection to the text and had met with such a situation before.[4] The likeliest candidate for the 1739 performance, on the basis of philological evidence, is the St John Passion.[5] The St Matthew Passion underwent none of the textual revisions

---

[2] See Eric Chafe, "Key Structure and Tonal Allegory in the Passions of J. S. Bach: An Introduction," *Current Musicology*, 31 (1981), pp. 41–5; Elke Axmacher, *"Aus Liebe will mein Heyland sterben": Untersuchungen zum Wandel des Passionsverständnisses im frühen 18. Jahrhundert*, Beiträge zur theologischen Bachforschung 2 (Neuhausen-Stuttgart, 1984), pp. 149–65.

[3] On Luther's indebtedness to John see Walther von Loewenich, *Luther und das Johanneische Christentum*, Forschungen zur Geschichte und Lehre des Protestantismus, ed. Paul Althaus, Karl Barth and Karl Heim, Siebente Reihe, Band IV (Munich, 1935).

[4] Werner Neumann and Hans-Joachim Schulze, eds., *Bach-Dokumente II: Fremdschriftliche und gedruckte Dokumente zur Lebensgeschichte Johann Sebastian Bachs 1685–1750* (Leipzig, 1969), pp. 338–9; *The Bach Reader*, ed. Hans T. David and Arthur Mendel, revised ed. (New York, 1966), pp. 162–3.

[5] As is well known, the Leipzig passion performance alternated annually between the Thomaskirche and the Nikolaikirche; in 1739 it would have taken place in the Nikolaikirche, which could not accommodate a presentation of the St Matthew Passion. The

of its predecessor; and its theological character is Lutheran from the ground up, so to speak.[6] The St John Passion, however, has another textual background entirely – one that is much less overtly "theological" in character – and the revisions to some six of its texts can be seen as an attempt to bring the theology of the work closer to that articulated in the St Matthew Passion.[7] It is tempting, therefore, to think that Bach arrived at the particular character of the earlier work on his own, before the Leipzig theological establishment exerted its influence. In any case, the work projects a strong Johannine character that is far less mediated by orthodox Lutheran influences than its successor; and this aspect must constitute the starting point for comprehensive interpretation of the work.

I: The Passion as "Trost": glorification and "realized eschatology"

Since the characters of Bach's two Passions depend greatly on theological factors, it is necessary to delineate some of the major differences in musico-theological intent between the two. Most striking of all the Johannine characteristics that Bach's work exhibits is the viewpoint on the Passion as Jesus's glorification, the crucifixion as a triumphant event, the "lifting up" of Jesus that links the crucifixion with the resurrection and ascension and

St Mark Passion might have been intended for re-performance there in 1739; but there is no evidence for that, and Bach's statement that the work in question had already been performed a few times fits best with what we know of the St John Passion. There is no set of parts for the work from around the year 1739; but the autograph pages of the score were copied some time during the late 1730s or early 1740s, and the most probable datings for performances of the work around that time are "one before and one after 1742" (see Alfred Dürr, "Zur Chronologie der Leipziger Vokalwerke J. S. Bachs," *Bach-Jahrbuch*, 44 (1957), pp. 114–15; Georg von Dadelsen, *Beiträge zur Chronologie der Werke Johann Sebastian Bachs*, Tübinger Bach-Studien, Heft 4/5 (Trossingen, 1958), pp. 132–3).

[6] Elke Axmacher, "Ein Quellenfund zum Text der Matthäus-Passion," *Bach-Jahrbuch*, 64 (1978), pp. 181–91; *"Aus Liebe,"* pp. 28–52, 170–85.

[7] Details of the revisions are given in Arthur Mendel, *Kritischer Bericht* to NBA II/4 (Kassel, 1974), pp. 168–72. Commentary on the revisions has tended towards the rather unlikely criterion of poetic quality as the prime motivating factor for the changes (see also Rudolf Wustmann, "Zu Bachs Texten der Johannes- und der Matthäus-Passion," *Monatsschrift für Gottesdienst und kirchliche Kunst*, Jahrgang 15 (1910), pp. 126–31). Mendel suggests at one point that "it is conceivable that objections in terms of spirituality played a role [in the text revisions]" (p. 168). In fact, on the basis of examination of the theological differences between the original and revised texts, it emerges that there is an unmistakable appearance of the theme of man's guilt and sin in several of the revised passages; and this theme, otherwise very little in evidence in the St John Passion, is central to the St Matthew Passion text. These points are explored in detail in my forthcoming book on Bach's vocal music (University of California Press).

makes the Passion a part of John's "Book of Glory."[8] Bach is careful to make
his intentions clear in the two choral prologues, and the text of "Herr, unser
Herrscher" states the theme of glorification in the most explicit terms:

> Herr, unser Herrscher,
> dessen Ruhm in allen Landen herrlich ist!
> Zeig' uns durch deine Passion,
> dass du, der wahre Gottessohn,
> zu aller Zeit,
> auch in der grössten Niedrigkeit,
> verherrlicht worden bist.
>   Da Capo

The meaning of "Herr, unser Herrscher" is illuminated by Luther's commentary on Psalm 8, from which the opening lines of the chorus are drawn.
Luther noted a dualism between the eternal and worldly aspects of majesty
that are presented in the words "Herr" (the divine name of God) and
"Herrscher" (a ruler in the purely earthly sense).[9] In Bach's prologue the
words "herrlich" (ending the main section) and "verherrlicht worden bist"
(ending the middle section) suggest, in the first instance, the eternal pre-
existent and unchanging God of John's prologue, and in the second, the
process of glorification that God become mortal undergoes on earth in the
Passion.[10] This process for John was initiated by the crucifixion, which
represented, on the one hand, the adverse response of the "world" to the
question of Jesus's kingship, and, on the other, the triumphant "lifting up"
of Jesus. This dualistic sense – rooted in the opposition between worldly
and spiritual meanings – is very characteristic of John's conceptual world,
and, as we will see, lies at the heart of Bach's intention for the St John
Passion.

Jesus's glorification in abasement is announced in "Herr, unser Herrscher"
as the theme of the Passion. And Bach shows that all the traditional external
signs of worldly suffering, lamentation and abasement – dissonance, chromaticism, the minor key – cannot be allowed to dictate our interpretation
of the affect of this movement. The idea of glorification cannot, of course,
be fully manifested at this point; (its message will be completed only in
the arias "Es ist vollbracht" and "Mein teurer Heiland"). But "Herr, unser

---

[8] This theme is emphasized in virtually every commentary on John's gospel; see, for example,
Raymond Brown, *The Gospel According to John XIII–XXI*, The Anchor Bible (New York,
1970), Vol. 29a, pp. 541–2.

[9] *D. Martin Luthers Werke*, Kritische Gesamtausgabe, 45. Band (Weimar, 1911), pp. 207–11;
English translation in *Luther's Works*, ed. Jaroslav Pelikan (St Louis, 1955) Vol. 12 (Selected
Psalms 1), pp. 99–101.

[10] Axmacher, "*Aus Liebe*," p. 163.

Herrscher" projects an impressive dramatic grandeur, nevertheless, a tone that is certainly not dominated by lamentation. Although the opening choruses of Bach's two Passions both begin from the framework of Jesus's suffering – throbbing pedal tones with overlayered dissonances – the entry of the chorus in "Herr, unser Herrscher" is block-like, sudden and dramatic, its "off-the-beat" shouts of the divine name, "Herr," followed by continually rising 16th-note passages set in opposition to the lamenting features. In "Kommt, ihr Töchter," however, the undramatic, imitative entry of the voices suggests rather that the affect arises directly from the suffering. The relatively cool "show us" ("Zeig' uns") that constitutes the central petition to the deity in "Herr, unser Herrscher" sets up a considerably different role for the Passion from the paranetic "Kommt . . . hilft . . . seht ihn . . . seht die Geduld . . . seht auf unsere Schuld" of the St Matthew Passion. It is related to the representation of awe in the presence of the deity rather than to the notion of mankind's "conformity" to Christ's sufferings. The urging of mankind to acknowledgment of sin and guilt, repentance and love is the point from which the St Matthew Passion sets forth, whereas in its dealing with the "showing" and the "drawing" of mankind by an all-powerful God whose very sufferings and death are triumphant events, the St John Passion emphasizes the benefit of faith, but not the "Gewissensangst" that belongs to the stages of earthly tribulation and guilt. The "visual" quality suggested in the words "Zeig' uns" can be considered a conceptual correlative of the well-known emphasis on symmetry in the earlier Passion. And in the sense that its structure is to a large extent pre-planned, "imposed" from without, rather than arising from the human events and emotions of the narrative, the St John Passion can be said to center around the particularly elevated theme of the glorification of the Messiah–king.

In John there is one place above all where a "showing" of the paradoxical "glorification in abasement" occurs: the so-called "royal inscription" – "Jesus of Nazareth, King of the Jews" – that is placed over the cross in Hebrew, Latin and Greek. Thus Raymond Brown, author of one of the foremost English-language commentaries on John:

The "lifting up" of the Son of Man which will draw all men to him (predicted in xii 32) begins on the cross where Jesus is physically lifted up from the earth. For other men crucifixion would have been an abasement; but because Jesus lays down his life with power to take it up again (x 18), there is a triumphant element in the Johannine concept of crucifixion. It is a death that achieves glorification, and the crucified Jesus is proclaimed as king in the principal languages of the world (xix 19–20).[11]

[11] Brown, *The Gospel According to John XIII–XXI*, p. 541.

The "royal inscription" is, of course, a famous example of Johannine irony, admitting of both worldly and spiritual interpretations. Bach uses this scene and its concluding chorale "In meines Herzens Grunde" as the culmination of his symmetrical centerpiece for the Passion, the so-called "Herzstück." Preceding it are the events of John's trial, dominated by antithesis, the strife over the worldly/spiritual dualism as embodied in the issue of Jesus's kingship. Following the "Herzstück," the "showing" demanded in "Herr, unser Herrscher" takes place; it is completed in the scene of Jesus's death in the two arias "Es ist vollbracht" and "Mein teurer Heiland." The G minor hortatory dialogue "Eilt, ihr angefocht'nen Seelen," introducing the final scene of the "Herzstück" and the third division of the Passion (see section IIb below), urges faith as the route to understanding the meaning of the Passion; the chorale "In meines Herzens Grunde" expresses the internalizing of the meaning of the crucifixion and the "royal inscription", and, finally, "Es ist vollbracht" presents the *direct* sense of Jesus's glorification in abasement and "Mein teurer Heiland" its beneficial meaning for mankind: the Passion as "Trost," or, in the viewpoint that is widely associated with John, "realized eschatology." Underlying the meaning of the two arias are the words of John that meant so much to Luther: "In der Welt ihr habt Angst; aber seid getrost, ich habe die Welt überwunden" (16:33).[12] A text such as this shows the extent of Luther's indebtedness to John, which he ranked among the highest of the books of the Bible.[13] "Herr, unser Herrscher" was created to announce the paradox of Jesus's glorification in abasement, and the events of the Passion from the trial to Jesus's death were intended to indicate how it becomes a reality through faith.

Between Bach's prologue and the public proclamation of Jesus's kingship in the "royal inscription," the St John Passion brings out the idea of the inversion of meaning that the physical events of the trial, punishments, crucifixion, death and burial of Christ, undergo in John. John's dualistic world view involves an array of literary devices – irony, misunderstanding, double, inverted and hidden meanings, antithesis and the like – and, as if in awareness of this aspect of the gospel, many of Bach's madrigal texts utilize antithesis. Whereas the St Matthew Passion stresses Luther's demand that mankind recognize its guilt and become "conformable to Christ in His sufferings," the St John Passion treats virtually every adverse event of the

---

[12] Walther von Loewenich, *Luther und das Johanneische Christentum*, pp. 15–22.
[13] Martin Luther, *Selected Biblical Prefaces*, in John Dillenberger, *Martin Luther: Selections from his Writings edited and with an Introduction* (New York, 1961), pp. 18–19.

Johannine narrative in terms of its benefit for mankind.[14] The various arias, choruses and chorales describe Jesus's imprisonment as setting us free (chorale, "Durch dein Gefängnis"), His wounds as healing us, His bondage as loosening our bondage to sin (aria, "Von den Strikken"), the scourging in terms of the congealing of the blood on Jesus's back into rainbow patterns as a sign of God's grace (aria, "Erwäge"), and so on. There is no emphasis on the struggle and tribulation of faith; man is the direct and, it seems, the immediate, passive beneficiary of the victorious death of the Messiah–king. The key idea is the "Trost" that overcomes worldly "Angst." This idea appears in two key places: "Erschein' mir in dem Bilde zu Trost in meiner Not" (from the chorale that ends the "Herzstück" in which the anticipation of inner benefit is voiced: "drauf kann ich fröhlich sein") and "O Trost für die gekränkten Seelen" (from "Es ist vollbracht"). And it is underscored in related expressions throughout the Passion. The emphasis on "Trost" marks a turn to the idea of faith "realized in experience"; that is, faith in its subjective, affective aspect. In Walther von Loewenich's words, "In trust we have the point at which faith and experience intersect."[15] Whereas in Bach's treatment of John's trial the severe idea of faith "in opposition to experience" is emphasized (in the "hidden" meanings that underlie the *turbae*, as we will see), in the final "scene" of the "Herzstück" – dealing with the crucifixion and inscription – the idea of faith "realized in experience" begins to emerge.

The scenes of the trial and inscription set the stage, as it were, for the scene of Jesus's death, to which Bach assigns an overtly triumphant character that is perfectly in keeping with the victorious meaning of Jesus's last words in John.[16] The middle section of "Es ist vollbracht" erupts into the militant *stile concitato* on the words, "Der Held aus Juda siegt mit macht und schliesst den Kampf"; here John's sense of victory is so vividly projected as to become a palpable reality. The words "und schliesst den Kampf" indicate as well that the sense of conflict that permeates John's gospel and is manifested in his well-known literary devices is transcended by those who believe. Although Bach's musical treatment of the crucifixion in the St Matthew Passion also

[14] Luther's view of the purpose and nature of meditation on the Passion appears in several places in his writings; the most succinct is his *A Meditation on Christ's Passion* (translation of *Ein Sermon von der Betrachtung des heiligen Leidens Christi* (1519)), *Luther's Works*, ed. Jaroslav Pelikan (Philadelphia, 1969), vol. 42, pp. 7–14.

[15] Walther von Loewenich, *Luther's Theology of the Cross*, trans. Herbert J. S. Bouman (Minneapolis, 1976), pp. 77–88.

[16] The words usually translated as "Es ist vollbracht" or "It is accomplished" are, in John's Greek, a cry of triumph, *tetelestai*.

places Jesus's death clearly within the perspective of the resurrection, the
tone of the latter work is, fittingly, not one of triumph. In this respect the
St Matthew Passion holds to the emphasis on guilt that characterizes the
first stages of Luther's meditative "program" for the Passion as well as to
Matthew's christological portrait of Jesus as the "Man of Sorrows."[17] Bach's
treatment of Jesus's last words in the St John Passion must be compared to
the bleak anguish of the Eb minor recitative of the St Matthew Passion,
"My God, My God, why has thou forsaken me," in order to appreciate fully
the difference between a theology that directly emphasizes the Passion as
Jesus's glorification *versus* one that reserves the overt expression of victory
for Easter.

At the point where the sense of glorification is most prominent in the
Passion Bach utilizes a sequence of two movements to represent Jesus's
glorification in abasement, then its benefit for mankind. "Es ist vollbracht"
is separated by the briefest of recitatives – "Und neigte das Haupt und
verschied" (two measures) – from the bass dialogue-with-chorale, "Mein
teurer Heiland." "Es ist vollbracht" deals with the dualistic aspect of Jesus's
death – elegaic, descending lines for solo gamba in the minor key sections
versus ascending D major arpeggios and triumphant flourishes in the central
segment – while "Mein teurer Heiland" presents a sense of reconciliation
rather than of contrasted extremes. Its D major tonality is an affirmation of
the key of the middle section of "Es ist vollbracht"; and its pastorale character and chorale verse underscore the message that Jesus's suffering and
triumph have become the source of consolation for man. Here John's
well-known emphasis on "realized eschatology" comes to the fore; the
believer is redeemed *already in this life*.[18]

Bach's text articulates this last idea in terms of the particular idea –
freedom – that is given a foremost place in both Luther's and John's theolo-
gies. The question of freedom for John – in a famous passage such as "the
truth shall make you free" – is closely bound up with John's emphasis on
dualism, manifested above all in the evangelist's frequent reference to two
worlds, above and below, the attributes of the former of which are light, life,
truth, freedom, and the like, while their opposites belong "below." Faith is

---

[17] See note 14.

[18] See, for example, Brown, *The Gospel according to John I–XII* (New York, 1966), pp. cxvi–cxxi,
on realized eschatology in John. On Luther's interpretation see Von Loewenich, *Luther und
das Johanneische Christentum*, pp. 15–22. And Renate Steiger ("Die Welt ist euch ein
Himmelreich: Zu J. S. Bachs Deutung des Pastoralen," *Musik und Kirche*, 41 (1971),
pp. 1–8, 69–79) shows that in movements such as "Mein teurer Heiland" Bach represents
the idea of realized eschatology by means of the pastorale style.

the only gateway to the world above; but John's emphasis on "realized eschatology" affirms that through faith that world can be present here and now.
Luther's theology as set forth in his tract on Christian Freedom also views
faith in terms of the freedom it brings for man.[19] Freedom is placed at the
center of Bach's structure – in the E major chorale, "Durch dein Gefängnis"
– where it presents the general gospel message of the benefit of Jesus's sufferings for mankind. At the culmination of the "Herzstück" the chorale
"In meines Herzens Grunde" replaces the collective "uns" of "Durch dein
Gefängnis" by the personal "meines" and "ich." Then, "Mein teurer
Heiland," in a series of questions put to the dying Jesus, combines both
the personal element ("Bin ich vom Sterben frei gemacht?" and "Kann ich
durch deine Pein und Sterben das Himmelreich ererben?") and the general
theological concern of the Passion ("Ist aller Welt Erlösung da?"). Jesus's
silent answer, "Yes," is the simple interpretation given to the words of the
narrative, "Und neigte das Haupt and verschied." This is the point in the
Passion at which the petition of the opening chorus is fulfilled, where,
following the completion of Jesus's glorification in humiliation, we are
shown in dialogue with the dying but victorious Christ that the "seeing" of
its meaning comes with the acceptance of its personal relevance for the
individual, the "hearing" of the word of promise, spoken in silence.
Whereas "Durch dein Gefängnis" represents an "objective" and collective
theological message, "In meines Herzens Grunde" represents the ability of
faith to perceive the identity of the Messiah in His lowest, earthly estate. In
relation to this, "Mein teurer Heiland" gives the other side of faith, the side
particularly to be found in John: its ability not merely to see beyond adverse
worldly events, but to anticipate, and thus to experience now ("foretaste"
in the Lutheran tradition), the benefits of Jesus's glorification. The freedom
that is announced "theologically" in "Durch dein Gefängnis" and the inner
experience of "In meines Herzens Grunde" are joined in "Mein teurer
Heiland," which completes the emphasis on "realized eschatology" in
the Passion.

II: Structure

The tonal plan of "signs"

We have spoken of a "visual" component in the structure of the St John
Passion that is linked to the idea of symmetry in the work. The words "Zeig'

[19] Martin Luther, *The Freedom of a Christian* (1520), in Dillenberger, *Martin Luther: Selections*,
pp. 42–85; see especially pp. 58–9.

uns, durch deine Passion" in the prologue suggest that from this standpoint
the Passion as a whole may in some sense be considered a "sign." Since the
topic of signs has such strong Johannine associations that were important to
Luther and can be demonstrated to have been known by Bach, we will
consider it in relation to the allegorical tonal plan of the work, where its
resonance is greatest.

First the Johannine–Lutheran background. As is well known the first part
of John's gospel (the narrative before the Passion) is called the Book of Signs,
and the remainder the Book of Glory (the Passion, resurrection and ascension taken together). Luther's preferring John to the other gospels was
bound up with the fact that John's treatment of Jesus's "works" – that is, the
miracles or Signs – reduced their number and gave them a subordinate place
to the teachings (the Johannine discourses).[20] In fact, the miracles possess a
highly symbolic character that is linked to Jesus's discourses: the changing of
water into wine is associated with the saying "I am the true vine" and a
corresponding discourse, the feeding of the five thousand with "I am the
bread of life," the raising of Lazarus with "I am the resurrection and the life,"
and so on.[21] Jesus's identifying Himself in a saying that begins with the
words "I am" as part of a discourse on the meaning of the sign confirms the
role of the signs not merely as catalysts to faith, but as manifestations in the
realm of flesh of the higher, spiritual meaning that was offered to man in
Jesus's speeches. Hence the often sacramental nature of the symbols: bread,
water, wine. Commentators on John often consider that the evangelist
intensified the symbolic character of the miracles by giving them a numerological significance as well: there are seven signs, seven discourses and seven
"I am" sayings.[22] Yet, while the miraculous character of the signs is "evidence" of higher power, faith cannot be dependent on such outward occur-
rences. Luther continually emphasized that signs were always accompanied
by a "word" of promise, and without the hearing of that word the sign
remained hollow; faith that remained bound to signs was of a lower degree
than faith that expressed a perfect inner readiness to do God's will.[23]

Although the arrangement and number of the signs is clearly circumscribed within the so-called Book of Signs, it must be emphasized that in no
way are the signs thereby separated conceptually from the rest of the gospel.

---

[20] Dillenberger, *Martin Luther: Selections*, pp. 18–19; for a discussion of this characteristic of
John see Brown, *The Gospel according to John I–XII*, pp. 525–32.
[21] Brown, *The Gospel according to John I–XII*, The Anchor Bible, Vol. 29, pp. cxxxix–cxliv.
[22] *Ibid.*, pp. cxxxix–cxlii.
[23] Von Loewenich, *Luther's Theology of the Cross*, p. 96.

The Passion, in fact, may be considered to represent the greatest of all Jesus's signs, that of the cross, the symbol for inversion of the outward meaning of physical events and the agent of the "lifting up." The cross was, of course, the center of Luther's work, the *theologia crucis* the only true definition of theology.[24] And the fact that for both Luther and John faith and the theology of the cross are central is one of the strongest links between them. In Luther's view John's reducing the signs and concentrating on their symbolic meaning links them all to faith in the identity of Jesus as the Messiah revealed in the cross, a theme that is echoed throughout Bach's work (in Cantata 12, on the theology of the cross, for example, the cross is called the "Zeichen Jesu").

Bach's means of realizing the idea of signs in the St John Passion arises from the fact that the word for cross in German is the same as that for the sharp sign – "Kreuz" – a symbolism that is known from a number of his works. And we know from the chorale cantata, "Aus tiefer Not" (BWV 38), based on Luther's paraphrase of Psalm 130, that Bach made the association between signs in the theological and musical senses. In his setting Bach added to the sequence of chorale-derived texts a recitative based on one of John's "signs" passages. In this, the fourth of six movements, Bach placed the chorale melody in the basso continuo, beneath a recitative that refers to Jesus's words to the king whose son had been healed, as recounted in the gospel for the day:[25]

Ah! that my faith is still so weak, and that I must build my trust on unsafe ground! How often must new signs soften my heart! What? don't you know your helper, who but speaks a single word of trust and right away, before your weakness could imagine, the hour of rescue appears. Trust only the hand of the Almighty and his mouth of truth.

This passage makes clear that the "word" is more important than the outward sign; yet the sign has an important role in the earlier stages of the process of faith as a means of preparing the individual for the granting of true faith. In the recitative Bach represents the idea of the insecurity of the earlier stages of faith by means of modulation down a fifth within the bass *cantus firmus* (the "unsafe ground") so that from the beginning of the

[24] *Ibid.*, p. 21.
[25] "Ach! dass mein Glaube noch so schwach, und dass ich mein Vertrauen auf seichtem Grunde muss erbauen! Wie ofte müssen neue Zeichen mein Herz erweichen! Wie? kennst du deinen Helfer nicht, der nur ein einzig Trostwort spricht, und gleich erscheint, eh deine Schwachheit es vermeint, die Rettungsstunde. Vertraue nur der Allmachtshand und seiner Wahrheit Munde" (my translation in text).

second *Stollen* ("Wie ofte müssen neue Zeichen. . .") the chorale appears in D Phrygian rather than A Phrygian, the only instance in all his music of a chorale cantus firmus that does not hold to its original transposition level. As part of the confirmation of the new key, he then sets the word "Zeichen" (signs) to a diminished seventh chord, three tones of which – E♭, F♯ and C♮ – are new to the mode (see Example 1).[26] Cantata 38 uses a tonal plan of

Example la Cantata 38/4 (*Recitativo a battuta*), mm. 1–7

b Pitch content of Phrygian scales on *A* and *D* compared

[26] That is, the Phrygian mode in the one-flat "system" (the F hexachord) comprises the tones *A*, *B♭*, *C*, *D*, *E*, *F*, *G*; but because of the normal sharpening of the third of the final chord *C♯* is introduced, so that in practice the pitch-content of the mode resembles the harmonic minor scale of its "subdominant" (in this case D minor). Thus Athanasius Kircher (*Musurgia Universalis* (Rome, 1650), p. 51), for example, calls the scale of A harmonic minor (in our terms) Phrygian and places it in cantus durus; and he names the sequence *E, F, G♯,*

descending fifths between its successive movements to represent the idea of sinking into the depths of spiritual humiliation as indicated in the text "Aus tiefer Not," before returning to its original key in analogy to the message of redemption that is given in the last movement.[27] In this respect the modulation associated with the word "signs" initiates the key that represents the "nadir," so to speak; Bach's focus on the word "Zeichen" thus provides an unmistakably graphic sense of the catalytic role of signs in faith, that of humbling man, of pushing him to awareness of his finite, human estate and his need for God's aid.[28] The structure of a Lutheran art work could aspire to no higher theological goal than the form of dialectic of spiritual humiliation and hope that is represented in "Aus tiefer Not" as in countless others of Bach's works.[29]

In the St John Passion the symbolism of the tonal plan has the same basis: the work is organized into nine key areas – flat, sharp, natural, flat, sharp, flat, natural, sharp, flat – that form a huge symmetrical array of the musical

---

A, Bb (!), C, D, E, Hypophrygian (also cantus durus). This strange usage arises from the interpretation of semitonal chord relationships at cadences – what we would call VI–V or iv⁶–V, as well as the Neapolitan sixth relationship – as indications of the Phrygian or Hypophrygian modes. Kircher thus describes the famous tonal shift that takes place in Carissimi's *Jephte* (where all the aforementioned relationships occur) as a move to the Hypophrygian mode mixed with the Phrygian (p. 603); mode is in these terms almost a harmonic style rather than an ordered set of pitches. Bach was, of course, aware of the sense that the Phrygian mode resembled the harmonic minor scale a fifth below, and that the Phrygian cadence contained an ambiguity of incompleteness (a half-close in the subdominant) and completeness (the archaic modal association according to which the major chord is the final and the semitone drop in the bass is the main distinguishing characteristic of the Phrygian mode); he exploits this ambiguity in the many cases where the Phrygian cadence is associated with rhetorical questions (e.g., the final line of Cantata 161: "How then can death harm me?"). In the case of the recitative in Example 1 the tones E, F and C# belong to the Phrygian scale on A, while the Eb, F# and C♮ belong to that on D. The word "Zeichen" is thus a focal point for the shift down a fifth.

[27] See Luther's commentary on Psalm 130 in *Luther's Works*, ed. Jaroslav Pelikan (St. Louis, 1958), Vol. 14 (Selected Psalms III), pp. 189–94.

[28] Luther's commentary on Psalm 130 (*Ibid.*, p. 194) makes this point clear; and Bach's return to the original key of E Phrygian in the final chorale (which sums up the Lutheran meaning) is made in a manner that suggests redemption from without: the low D of the D minor ending of the preceding movement is retained as the bass of an E major $^4_2$ chord, a striking tonal juxtaposition that produces an immediate "miraculous" or non-causal sense of shift.

[29] A substantial number of the Bach cantatas – nos. 106, 9, 20, 87, 95, and so on – use the plan of tonal descent (modulation in the flat direction) followed by ascent (the sharp direction) to represent this dialectic, which is always clearly expressed in the texts. I have treated this idea in terms of Luther's *analogy of faith* in "Luther's 'Analogy of Faith' in Bach's Church Music," *dialog*, 24 (Spring 1985), pp. 96–101.

signs, with the sharps (crosses in German) at the center. All six permutations of the ordering of signs are used to create a highly abstract arrangement of key areas (see Figure 1).[30] In addition, many of the modulations between key areas are carefully placed so as to underscore the sense that the shift from one sign to another – associated three times with the "Kreuz"/sharp symbolism – is a significant event.[31] Although the primary dimension of key structure in the St John Passion is its symmetrical array of key areas according to their sharp or flat signatures, the work also presents three large-scale progressions from flats to sharps that span two or more flat/ [natural]/sharp segments and are associated with the general direction of redemption: two of these involve an emphasis on freedom ("Durch dein Gefängnis" and "Mein teurer Heiland"), while the third – the overall tonal dynamic of Part I from G minor to A major – is associated with Peter's repentance. (As suggested below, these rising progressions are a means by which Bach represents the "drawing" of mankind through the "lifting up" of the cross.) Even the brief dialogue on truth between Jesus and Pilate modulates to sharps, culminating with Jesus's words, "He who is of the truth hears my voice," before Pilate's cynical "What is truth," his return to the crowd, the release of Barabbas and the scourging of Christ turn the tonality step by step towards the flats that constitute the next key area. There is, in fact, a strong sense that "tonal allegory" in the St John Passion creates the association of flats for the world below and sharps for the world above. The narratives of the crucifixion and the "royal inscription" take place in the flattest keys of the Passion, Bb minor and Db, while the interpretation of their *meaning* in terms of the ability of faith to liberate man from the present world is presented in the sharpest keys. The key plan of the entire Passion is firmly set within the flats as boundaries of the here and now with the sharps as regions of transcendence.

At a significant point in the Passion the expression "Gnadenzeichen" (sign of grace) is used: the aria "Erwäge," paired with the *arioso* "Betrachte, meine Seel" at the beginning of the "Herzstück." This "Gnadenzeichen," described in the text of "Erwäge," is the forming of the pattern of blood on Jesus's back into the shape of the rainbow, sign of God's covenant with

---

[30] Chafe, "Key Structure," pp. 41–5.

[31] The modulation to sharps for the fifth segment appears on the line "Weissest du nicht, dass ich Macht habe, dich zu *kreuzigen?*"; the modulation back to flats for the sixth segment is made on the line "Und er trug sein *Kreuz*, und ging hinaus zur Stätte, die da heisset Schädelstätt'; welche heisset auf Ebräisch: Golgotha!"; and the modulation to sharps for the eighth segment is made on the line "Es stund aber bei dem *Kreuze* Jesu seine Mutter und seine Mutter Schwester." More complete details on these and the other "structural" modulations of the Passion will be found in my forthcoming book.

Noah after the flood. Throughout his writing Luther had much to say about
the Old Testament signs and their being bound to a "word" of promise from
God.[32] In the St Matthew Passion the *arioso* "Am Abend, da es kühle war"
reaches back through the scriptures to join Adam's fall with that of Christ
in Gethsemane as well as the first reconciliation with Noah to that of the
cross. The rainbow, sign of the old covenant, is in this sense the Old Testament counterpart of the cross, sign of the new covenant. It is interesting,
in this light, that the "Herzstück" of the St John Passion modulates from the
Eb/C minor key area in which it begins ("Betrachte" and "Erwäge") "up"
to the E major chorale "Durch dein Gefängnis," where the theological
message of freedom is centered in the Passion, then returns to end in Eb
with the chorale "In meines Herzens Grunde," in which the joining of
Jesus's name and cross is indicated. If the antithesis of sharp and flat keys in
the "Herzstück" can be taken to allegorize the worlds above and below,
the upward/downward curve of the "Herzstück" is, perhaps, a realization of
the two "signs" that join the two worlds: the rainbow and the cross.

   The idea of symmetry is one that is all too easily overworked in Bach.
But of all his works the St John Passion is the one in which it is not only
indisputably in evidence in several different forms, but in which it constitutes a vital part of Bach's penetration of the text and its significance. In
the St John Passion the grouping of repeated choruses gives a palpable
sense of symmetrical order in several places, while in a number of madrigal-
texted movements – 'Herr, unser Herrscher," "Erwäge" and "Es ist vollbracht" above all – symmetry correlates with the idea of glorification in
abasement. Symmetry, as is well known, appears in Bach's music as a means
of representing divine majesty (the theme of "Gott ist mein König," Cantata
71) and glorification (the "Et resurrexit" theme of the Mass in B Minor).[33]
Besides the classically Johannine associations of glorification and predetermined order, it may now be suggested that the overall plan of key areas in
the Passion represents the identity of the name of Christ and the cross sign
by means of the "chiastic" or cruciform symmetry that Smend linked to the
visual identity of the letter "Chi" (standing for Christus) and the abbrevia-
tion for the word "Kreuz," as Bach used them on the score of the St Matthew Passion.[34] Smend, it may be remembered, saw the symmetrical array

---

[32] Heinrich Bornkamm, *Luther and the Old Testament*, trans. Eric W. and Ruth C. Gritsch, ed.
      Victor I. Gruhn (Philadelphia, 1974), pp. 179–87.

[33] Walter Blankenburg, "Die Symmetrieform in Bachs Werken und ihre Bedeutung," *Bach-
      Jahrbuch*, 38 (1949–50), pp. 24–39.

[34] Friedrich Smend, "Luther und Bach," pp. 169–70. In the score of the St Matthew Passion
      Bach uses abbreviations of the following kinds: "Weissage uns, Xste," "Komm, süsses X,"
      "so steig herab vom X."

90

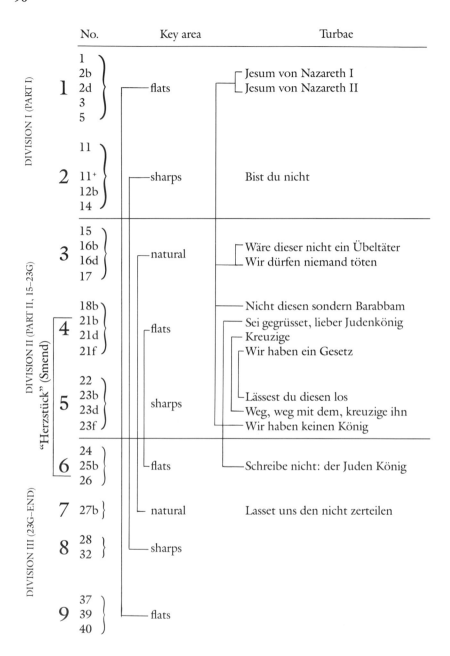

Figure 1 St John Passion: Structure

Chorales	Choruses and Dialogues

HERR, UNSER HERRSCHER

─O grosse Lieb
Dein Will gescheh'

Wer hat dich so geschlagen
─[HIMMEL, REISSE/
Jesu, deine Passion]

─Petrus, der nicht denkt zurück

─Christus, der uns selig macht

─Ach, grosser König

Durch dein Gefängnis

EILT, IHR ANGEFOCHT'NEN SEELEN

In meines Herzens Grunde

─Er nahm alles wohl in acht
MEIN TEURER HEILAND/
─Jesu, der du warest tot
─O hilf, Christe, Gottes Sohn

RUHT WOHL

Ach Herr, lass dein lieb Engelein

of repeated choruses and the culmination of his "Herzstück" in the chorale "In meines Herzens Grunde, dein Nam' und Kreuz allein" ("In the depths of my heart, thy name and cross alone"), as a realization in the structure of the work of this identity of Name and Cross.[35] The recognition of a symmetrical arrangement of the tonal areas of the Passion extends this idea to the entire oratorio (see Figure 1). Bach's symmetrical plan of key areas with the sharpest keys at the center thus seems unmistakably to join the name and cross of Christ in a huge sign whose ultimate meaning is the inseparability of Christology and the theology of the cross; this is, of course, the theology behind what is announced in the opening chorus, and it is one of the great cornerstones of Lutheran belief, derived to a considerable extent from John.[36]

The dualistic plan: faith

The dualism of adverse physical events (Jesus's trial, suffering and death) and their spiritual meaning (Jesus's glorification and His redemption of the world), announced as the theme of the Passion in "Herr, unser Herrscher" and brought to completion in "Es ist vollbracht" and "Mein teurer Heiland," provides one of the most important keys to Bach's conception of the structure of the Passion. This idea is realized brilliantly in a plan comprising, from one standpoint, a structure that follows the main divisions and dramatic emphases of the physical narrative, and, from another, an "abstract" symmetrical design that is allied to the theological meaning of the Passion (primarily the key scheme, centered on the so-called "Herzstück" and the chorale "Durch dein Gefängnis"). This form of simultaneous "double planning" can be found in other works of Bach;[37] it may

[35] Friedrich Smend, *Joh. Seb. Bach. Kirchen-Kantaten* (Berlin, 1948–9), Heft VI, pp. 49–50.

[36] Von Loewenich, *Luther und das Johanneische Christentum*, pp. 39–40.

[37] For example, although Friedrich Smend's well-known delineation of the Credo of the Mass in B Minor as a symmetrical structure is widely accepted, there is another aspect to the groundplan of the "Credo" that is both more easily audible and more readily justified according to Luther's own divisions of the Nicene Creed (Friedrich Smend, "Luther and Bach," *Bach-Jahrbuch*, 34 (1937), p. 37; new edition in Smend, *Bach-Studien*, pp. 169–70). In both the small and large catechisms, Luther divides the creed into three articles – creation, redemption and sanctification – corresponding to the three persons of the Trinity (*The Book of Concord*, trans. and ed. Theodore G. Tappert (Philadelphia, 1959), pp. 344–5, 411–20). Instead of a 3×3 grouping of the nine movements of the "Credo," the Lutheran division is an "asymmetrical" 2+4+3. And each of these three divisions forms a clearly audible "crescendo" in instrumentation that ends with a tutti. In relation to this "dynamic" arrangement Smend's is a more abstract, visual plan that corresponds to the "script" rather than to the "sound" pole.

be considered to provide a representation of the "religious dialectic" that lies behind Baroque allegorical expression.[38]

Presumably one of Bach's earliest ideas for the structure of the St John Passion was the icon-like tonal plan of musical signs that serves as a focus for the more "abstract," signific aspects of the work. But it had to go hand in hand with a quite different plan that arose from a profound understanding not only of the structure of John's account of the Passion, but of the very *reason* that John developed his structure in the first place. John's Passion narrative falls into three main divisions, as indicated in Figure 2: (1) the arrest and interrogation of Jesus (Part I); (2) the trial before Pilate; and (3) the crucifixion, death and burial.[39] John himself, as modern scholarship believes, made several manipulations in the sequence of events as presented in the synoptic gospels in order to arrive at his structure and its symbolic purposes: for example, he places the crucifixion a day earlier than the other gospels, so that the last supper is no longer the passover meal, this in order to make Jesus's death take place at the time that the passover lambs were killed, thereby strengthening the sacrificial aspect of Jesus as "Lamb of God"; he places the scourging at the center of the trial instead of after Jesus is delivered over for crucifixion, and so on. But easily the most striking change is the structure of the trial itself, which John arranges into a seven-fold shifting of locale back and forth between an inner room of the praetorium, where the dialogues between Jesus and Pilate take place, and the outside, where the crowd is gathered. The dialogues inside are confined, in Bach's setting, to recitative, and take up something closer to the elevated themes of the Johannine discourses – power, truth, the Kingdom above – while the latter – primarily *turbae* – constitute the sheer visceral demand for blood. The dualism of the physical and the spiritual thus resides at the heart of both Bach's and John's thinking and their structural patterning. John's gospel is famous for what Brown calls its "typical chiastic patterns," and of these the trial is the best known and the most conspicuous: episode one resembles episode seven, episodes two and six and three and five are similar, while John's shifting of the scourging was done to place it at the center of the trial (episode four), for it is the only scene that involves the "Kriegsknechte" rather than Pilate or the crowd.[40] Whether or not John intended the idea of his chiastic trial scene as a form of "sign," as Bach undoubtedly did, is uncertain; but both John's and Bach's structures have a

---

[38] Walter Benjamin, *The Origin of German Tragic Drama*, trans. John Osborne (London, 1977), p. 175.

[39] Brown, *The Gospel according to John XIII–XXI*, pp. 785–6.

[40] *Ibid.*, pp. 857–9.

strong numerological component that is "signific" in character. The seven
episodes of John's trial are sometimes related conceptually to John's seven
signs, seven discourses and "I am" sayings; while Bach's "Herzstück" and
overall structure of signs are based on division into three. The structure and
symbolic nature of John's trial must be considered as having provided the
spiritual impetus for Bach's creating his symmetrical "Herzstück," even
though, as we will see, the two do not coincide. John's trial culminates in
the judgment of crucifixion, whereas Bach's "Herzstück" extends intention-
ally beyond that point (see Figure 2).

John's dramatic and independent structure for the trial is based on the
antithesis of inside/outside locations and of dialogues between Jesus and
Pilate *versus* shouts from the crowd for a particular reason. The trial is the
natural climax of what John has been emphasizing throughout the gospel:
the question of the identity of Christ and what the criteria are for establishing His identity. In the trial this issue has come to center more and more
upon the title "king" (of the Jews), the one christological title that has the
possibility of interpretation in both worldly and spiritual senses, and that
therefore raises the sense of conflict between the two kinds of values.
Throughout the gospel John uses forensic expressions – witnesses, law,
testimony, signs, advocate, and the like – to the extent that some commentaries have suggested that the entire gospel was conceived as a form of symbolic trial. As we will see, the christological question enters so prominently
into all the symbolic aspects of Bach's structure that we may conclude that
he, too, was attempting to expand the idea of the trial to the entire Passion.
In his making the most antagonistic and dramatic element of the narrative –
the *turbae* – into the mainstay of his symmetrical tonal plan and its transcen-
dent meaning, Bach makes an important statement concerning the inverted
significance of physical events and objects, one that expresses much of the
spiritual basis for musical allegory: the theological vision of the world as a
trial, or – as Bach's cantata texts tell us – a hospital for the spiritually sick, a
place where meaning, or healing of the spiritual sense, comes only with the
ability to see the truth of the world above.[41]

Bach's structural equivalent to John's symmetrical trial – the "Herzstück"
(see Figure 2) – comprises a flat/sharp/flat tonal grouping in which two
choruses of the first segment – "Kreuzige ihn" and "Wir haben ein Gesetz"
– are transposed into sharps and heard in reverse order with new texts in
the second segment: now "Lässest du diesen los" and "Weg mit dem, kreu-

---

[41] On the Lutheran view of life as trial within the context of the *theologia crucis* see Von Loewenich, *Luther's Theology of the Cross*, pp. 134–9.

zige ihn"; a third chorus from the first segment, "Sei gegrüsset, lieber Judenkönig," is repeated in the original key after the return to flats in segment three of the "Herzstück," to the text "Schreibe nicht: der Juden König." The pivotal modulation from flats to sharps has the effect of "centralizing" the chorale "Durch dein Gefängnis," in which appears the antithesis of Jesus's imprisonment and the freedom it brings to man. Bach, too, bases his structure on antithesis (realized in terms of sharp/flat transposition); but he shifts what we might call his "symbolic trial" further along, so that it begins with the scourging – the center of John's trial; its center deals with the climactic ending of John's trial, the final rejection of Jesus in "Wir haben keinen König" and the judgment of crucifixion; and its final segment extends beyond John's trial and into division three, ending with the narrative of the "royal inscription" and the chorale response, "In meines Herzens Grunde," thereby effecting a sense of resolution at the end of the "Herzstück." The inscription itself was an addition of John's to the Passion narrative; it is generally considered a classic example of Johannine irony, for the sign is intended to mock Jesus, but from John's perspective, that of faith, it tells the truth. Bach's extension of his version of the trial to culminate with the narrative of the crucifixion *itself* and the royal inscription – rather than the *judgment* of crucifixion – actually brings out a traditional interpretation of John's meaning that is less clearly articulated in the gospel itself: namely, that the trial has two judgments, both made by Pilate – the first the judgment of death made under pressure from the crowd and culminating the segment in sharps (the trial proper, the judgment of the world, expressed in the physical structure), and the second the spiritual, faith judgment of Christ as "King of the Jews," the theme that has run through the entire trial; this now culminates the "Herzstück" in the flat key area in which it began (representing the appearance of the "truth" in the world "below"). Bach's shift removes the conception of the trial from dependence on exact correspondence to the physical events of the narrative, giving it a more symbolic character, which is itself a very Johannine characteristic.

But in order to bring out the message of the royal inscription as the final, the true judgment, Bach had to overlap the "Herzstück" with John's division three. His solution was to make the beginning of division three return to flats, thereby enabling the repeat of the music of "Sei gegrüsset, lieber Judenkönig" as "Schreibe nicht: der Juden König" *in its original key*, B♭, and the tonal closure of the "Herzstück" in E♭ (the other *turbae*, we remember, were transposed down a semitone from their original flats to sharps, creating the sense of antithesis). The "Herzstück" thus begins in E♭ with meditation on the scourging ("Betrachte, meine Seele") and ends in the same key with

Key areas	Passion Nos.	Textual Structure in John (chapter and verse nos.)
	A. xviii 1–27	**Division 1: THE ARREST AND INTERROGATION OF JESUS**
flats	(1–3)	*Unit 1:* The arrest of Jesus
		1–3: Setting of the scene in the garden
		4–8: Jesus meets the arresting party and shows His power
		(9): Parenthetical explanatory addition.
		10–11: Peter reacts to the arrest by striking at the servant
	(4–9)	Change of scene, closing the first unit and opening the second, as Jesus is taken from the garden to Annas.
modulatory	(10)	*Unit 2:* The interrogation of Jesus.
		(14): Parenthetical explanatory addition.
sharps	(11–14)	15–18: Introduction of Peter into high priest's palace; first denial
		19–23: Annas interrogates Jesus who protests his innocence
		(24): Insertion to prepare for Pilate trial: Jesus sent to Caiaphas
		25–27: Peter's second and third denials

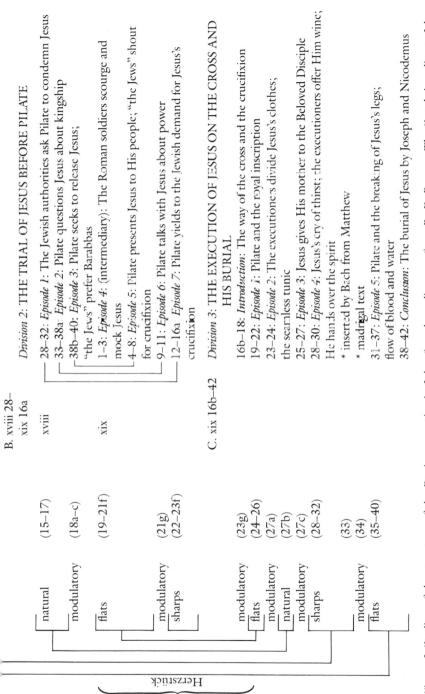

Figure 2 Outline of the structure of the Passion narrative in John (based on diagrams from R. E. Brown, *The Gospel According to John XIII–XXI*, pp. 875–6 and 859), with bracketing to indicate the symmetrical key structure of the St. John Passion

meditation on the crucifixion and royal inscription ("In meines Herzens
Grunde"). After the close of the central sharp segment with the B minor
chorus "Wir haben keinen König denn den Kaiser" and the D major narrative of the judgment of crucifixion, Bach makes the "crossover" modulation
from sharps on the phrase "Und er trug sein *Kreuz*" (just as he had modulated *into* this segment with a conspicuous sharp on the word "kreuzigen,"
both places seeming to affirm the cross as the central "sign" of the Passion).[42] The word "Golgatha" then marks the move to flats; the recitative
ends in G minor with the arrival at Golgotha, and Bach articulates the
beginning of John's division three and the change of physical location with
a dialogue of introductory, hortatory character, "Eilt, ihr angefocht'nen
Seelen" ("Hasten, ye deeply troubled spirits"), thereby interrupting the
pattern of repeated choruses. "Schreibe nicht: der Juden König" not only
returns to its original key; it is separated by "Eilt, ihr angefocht'nen Seelen"
from the *turbae* that were transposed to sharps. The third "scene" of the
"Herzstück" thus provides simultaneously a sense of reconciliation and that
of a new beginning, by virtue of its roles in the "symbolic" and physical
structures that it overlaps. "Eilt, ihr angefocht'nen Seelen" is set in G minor
like the opening chorus of the Passion; and it is a chorus that served perhaps
as the conceptual model for several opening choruses of hortatory character
in other Bach works: "Kommt, ihr Töchter" (opening chorus of the
St Matthew Passion), "Kommt, eilet und laufet" (opening chorus of the
Easter Oratorio), "Kommet, ihr verworf'nen Sünder" (Bach's new text for
the first movement of Handel's Brockes Passion).[43] So we can be sure that
Bach was fully aware of the physical structure of three divisions (which he
observes in the St Matthew Passion as well) and knowingly superimposed
the "Herzstück" and the symmetrical plan of musical signs on it, probably
as a means of emphasizing the split between worldly and spiritual values.

  Following the new beginning at Golgotha – now identified in the text of
"Eilt, ihr angefocht'nen Seelen" as the place where the "pilgrimage" of faith
is completed – the return of "Sei gegrüsset" as "Schreibe nicht" – the only
turba to be repeated in its original key – provides an additional association
with the idea of completion. Both "Sei gegrüsset" and "Schreibe nicht"
resemble the beginning of the soprano aria "Ich folge dir gleichfalls," also in
Bb (see Example 2). This is a meaningful association, for the next of "Ich
folge dir gleichfalls" has a pronounced Johannine character in its description

---

[42] See note 31.
[43] On Bach's new text for Handel's Brockes Passion see Andreas Glöckner, "Johann Sebastian
Bachs Aufführungen zeitgenössischer Passionsmusiken," *Bach-Jahrbuch*, 63 (1977), p. 105.

Example 2 St John Passion, interconnections between recitative (8), aria
"Ich folge dir gleichfalls" (9) and chorus "Sei gegrüsset,
lieber Judenkönig" (21b)

of Jesus as "mein Leben, mein Licht," and in its reference in the verb
"ziehen" ("an mir zu ziehen, zu schieben, zu bitten") to Jesus's "drawing" all
men to Him through the "lifting up." Presumably Bach intended the return
to flats in this scene to signify the actualization of the "following" of Christ
in terms of the inner acceptance of His identity, the spiritual meaning
behind the physical motion urged in "Eilt, ihr angefocht'nen Seelen." The
span between the two bass dialogues, "Eilt, ihr angefocht'nen Seelen" and
"Mein teurer Heiland" exhibits, as mentioned earlier, a general overall
"dynamic" of tonal ascent from G minor to D major that is closely analogous
to that from the opening scene of the Passion to the end of Part I (G minor
to A major). This sense of tonal ascent was no doubt intended in both
places to suggest the "drawing" of humanity by Christ. The culminating
segment of the "Herzstück," in its presentation of the faith acceptance of
the true meaning of the "royal inscription" ("In meines Herzens Grunde"),
thus marks the beginning of man's ascent to salvation as the freedom from
death ("Mein teurer Heiland") that is the outcome of Jesus's glorification
("Es ist vollbracht").

III: Christology – the "Jesus of Nazareth" choruses

As suggested above, Bach's use of the *turbae* of the St John Passion as the mainstay of his symmetrical centerpiece is a means of subordinating their literal dramatic meaning in the narrative to their larger theological significance. Meaning in the allegorical art work is supplied from without; and the actions and events of the physical narrative of the Passion are not those of man's free will but the agents of a higher order. As shown in Figure 1, twelve of the fourteen *turba* choruses of the Passion – excepting only the two that do not deal with the issue of the trial ("Bist du nicht," addressed to Peter, and "Lasset uns den nicht zerteilen," the chorus of soldiers casting lots over the robe) – involve correspondences with others of the set. This aspect, which adds a dimension of musical integration to the work, also has a theological purpose. The first nine *turbae* of Part II belong to the "real" trial scene whose extension by Bach to include the tenth chorus – "Schreibe nicht: der Juden König" – may no doubt be considered an additional reference to the law *via* the number associated with the ten commandments, as it is in the St Matthew Passion.[44] In the St John Passion, more than its successor, the "series" of *turbae* projects a sense of antithesis with the christological meaning of the Passion; for the choruses of the earlier work not only emphasize antagonism to Christ in their tendency towards violent, agitated affects – chromaticism, the obsessive "Kreuzige" rhythm, and the like – their very inter-relatedness and the lesser number of meditative movements make the crowd of persecutors into a presence of great dramatic intensity. All the more, then, we must consider Bach's dealing with the idea of the ability of faith to perceive the true identity of Christ even within the *turbae* themselves. For recognition that the adverse events of the trial have another, spiritual meaning is the means by which the prayer of the opening chorus is answered.

This brings us to a second great Johannine christological *locus* that, like the "royal inscription," appears in the Passion narrative and is given special treatment by Bach: the famous "ego eimi" ("I am") expression that Jesus uses in several places in the gospel without a predicate and in the emphatic construction that, if translated literally, would mean something like "I myself am"; the expression is frequently interpreted as standing for the name of God – that is, it represents self-revelation on the part of the deity. Although not so obviously a "sign" as the "royal inscription," in the Passion narrative

---

[44] Martin Jansen, "Bachs Zahlensymbolik, an seinen Passionen untersucht," *Bach-Jahrbuch*, 34 (1937), pp. 96–117; Friedrich Smend, "Bach's Matthäus-Passion," *Buch-Jahrbuch*, 25 (1928), pp. 1–95, reprinted in Smend, *Bach-Studien*, pp. 24–83.

the "I am" is used in conjunction with the two short choruses set to the name "Jesus of Nazareth," and when it is spoken – in Jesus's identifying Himself with the words "ich bin's" – the arresting party draws back and falls to the ground.[45] John presumably wants us to attribute to Jesus's words the miraculous character of a sign. In this place, prefaced with a characteristically Johannine reference to Jesus's foreknowledge of the events of the Passion ("Als nun Jesus wusste alles, was ihm begegnen sollten"), we have a sense of the intrinsic majesty and divinity of Christ set up at the beginning of the narrative, before the adverse events of the Passion attempt to deny them by such means as the restatement of the music of the "Jesus of Nazareth" choruses to new, antagonistic texts and the initiating of the pivotal modulation from flats to sharps in Part I on Peter's "Ich bin's *nicht*." Like the "royal inscription," the "I am" saying connects up with the text of the opening chorus with its references to God's name and its message of the Messiah king who is glorified in humiliation.

The strikingly individual character of John's language and concerns, when compared with those of the synoptic gospels, can be readily recognized by anyone with a modicum of sensitivity to literary style. In this respect the gospel is apt to inspire an interest in the hidden significance of ordinary events, a sense that meaning is deeper than surface appearances, even antithetical to them. This idea is presented by Bach in the series of choruses sung initially to the words "Jesus of Nazareth." They are associated, as we saw, with one of John's "I am" sayings, which appears in the recitative between them ("Ich bin's"); and they are musically characterized by their active flute part and circle-of-fifths harmony with Phrygian cadence ending (see Example 3). The harmonic content of each chorus encompasses the full span of chords that comprise what the theorist Johann David Heinichen called the "ambitus" of the key: the progression V i iv VII–III–VI in minor, while the Phrygian cadence (iv⁶–V) was a traditional means of signalling the "ambitus" of either a major or a minor key by means of the juxtaposition of its flattest and sharpest harmonies.[46] Perhaps, then, Bach intended the circular, all-encompassing harmonic character of the chorus to signify something like John's image of Jesus, who remains apart from the adverse circumstances in which He is placed. The minor-key tonality of the

[45] Brown, *The Gospel according to John I–XII*, pp. 533–8.

[46] Johann David Heinichen, *Neu erfundene und Gründliche Anweisung* (Hamburg, 1711), pp. 261–3; on the background for the taking over of the old "mi/fa" idea of solmization into the harmonic tonality of the early seventeenth century as the Phrygian cadence, see Carl Dahlhaus, *Untersuchungen über die Entstehung der harmonischen Tonalität* (Kassel, 1968), pp. 260–2.

Example 3 St John Passion 2b and 2d, the "Jesus of Nazareth" choruses

Example 3 (*cont.*)

choruses, as of Jesus's "Ich bin's," makes, like "Herr, unser Herrscher," the important statement of the incarnation, that God is to be revealed in His shame and humiliation rather than His glory. The very brevity and distinctness of the "Jesus of Nazareth" choruses aids in their recall by the listener, for later in the Passion the music of these choruses will reappear three more times all with different texts – making five in all. But only two of these later appearances have been fully recognized as such by Bach scholars: the fourth, "Nicht diesen, sondern Barrabam" (in answer to Pilate's question "Shall I release unto you the King of the Jews?"), and the fifth, "Wir haben keinen König denn den Kaiser" (in response to Pilate's "Shall I crucify your king?"). The associations with the idea of kingship are obvious (see Example 4).

The one remaining occurrence of the "Jesus of Nazareth" music – the third in order of appearance within the Passion – is more remarkable because the four-measure chorus is now grafted on to the beginning and ending of a longer chorus, "Wir dürfen niemand töten," that is itself a repetition of the first section of a chorus heard shortly before without the "Jesus of Nazareth" music. (That is, the basis of "Wir dürfen niemand töten" (thirteen of its seventeen measures) is the opening section of the chorus "Wäre dieser nicht ein Übeltäter" (thirteen measures); the latter continues with "wir hätten dir ihn nicht überantwortet" (fifteen measures combining the chromatic fugue theme of the first section with a new one); in "Wir dürfen niemand töten" the thirteen repeated measures are preceded by a half-measure from the beginning of "Jesus of Nazareth" and followed by the final three measures of that chorus.) In addition, Bach has the flute pattern from "Jesus of Nazareth" run through the whole of "Wir dürfen niemand töten," a detail that has often been mentioned in commentary on the Passion[47] (see Example 5). In this way "Wir dürfen niemand töten" is literally embedded within "Jesus of Nazareth," an occurrence that projects such a striking sense of intent that we are compelled to seek its explanation in a theological interpretation.[48]

---

[47] Since completing this study I have received an article from Werner Breig, "Zu den Turba-Chören von Bachs Johannes-Passion," in *Geistliche Musik: Studien zu ihrer Geschichte und Funktion im 18. und 19. Jahrhundert*, Hamburger Jahrbuch für Musikwissenschaft, Bd. 8, ed. Constantin Floros, Hans Joachim Marx and Peter Petersen (Laaber, 1985), pp. 65–96; Breig, too, notices the appearance of the "Jesus of Nazareth" music in "Wir dürfen niemand töten" and explains it differently (pp. 80–5).

[48] It is possible, of course, that as Breig suggests (*ibid.*, p. 83), Bach might have originally planned a four-bar chorus for "Wir dürfen niemand töten," and the link to "Wäre dieser nicht ein Übeltäter" came later; this aspect of the *Entstehungsgeschichte* of the Passion does not, of course, lessen the sense of theological intent – rather the reverse.

Example 4 St John Passion 18b, "Nicht diesen, sondern Barrabam" and 23f,
"Wir haben keinen König"

Example 4 (*cont.*)

Example 5 St John Passion 16d, "Wir dürfen niemand töten," first and last three measures

According to its literal meaning as the response of the crowd to Pilate's words, "Then take him and try him according to your laws," "Wir dürfen niemand töten" refers to the fact that under Roman rule the power of execution had been taken away from the Jews. Later in the trial the crowd demands Jesus's death in accordance with Jewish law: "Wir haben ein

Gesetz und nach dem Gesetz soll er sterben." Jesus dies to satisfy Jewish law,
but His execution is carried out by the Romans, whose method was
crucifixion. The recitative following "Wir dürfen niemand töten" explains
the significance of this occurrence: "Auf dass erfüllet würde das Wort Jesu,
welches er sagte, da er deutete, welches Todes er sterben würde." Jesus's
prediction of the means of His death occurred in John, 12:32 with the
words, "When I am lifted up from the earth, I will draw all men unto me,"
where it is followed by much the same phrase as follows 'Wir dürfen
niemand töten." "Wir dürfen niemand töten" thus points ahead to the
crucifixion and its special Johannine association of Jesus's glorification. The
chorus joins symbolically the cross and the name of Jesus, the latter added
to its music in the form of the "Jesus of Nazareth" reference. It may be possible, therefore, to read into the text the Lutheran view that the law, whose
ultimate purpose – God's "alien work" – was an expression of death as the
judgment for sin, lost its efficacy in Jesus's death; it would now be replaced
by the cross as symbol of the gospel of forgiveness of sin and resurrection.
But the context of this first reappearance of the "Jesus of Nazareth" music
makes clear also that a major part of the motive for repeating the music was,
as in the case of "Nicht diesen, sondern Barabbam" and "Wir haben keinen
König," the issue of Jesus's identity as King of the Jews; for the ensuing
recitative continues with a dialogue between Jesus and Pilate on the question of Jesus's kingship, then the scene as a whole culminates with two
verses of the chorale "Herzliebster Jesu," the first beginning "Ach, grosser
König."[49]

What becomes clear as these five "Jesus of Nazareth" choruses thread
through the trial in a pattern of transposition that alternately rises a fourth
and falls a third (or falls a fifth and rises a sixth) – G minor, C minor, A minor,
D minor, B minor – is that they lead towards the final ironic inscription over
the cross, "Jesus of Nazareth, King of the Jews," the message of the Passion
that is denied openly in "Wir haben keinen König." The pattern of transposition suggests that the *immediate* meaning of the choruses – which is apparent in the first two – is represented by the tonal shift down a fifth (humiliation), while the ultimate meaning is represented by the motion of the
entire series from flats to sharps (analagous to the "lifting up"). The "zig-

---

[49] And "Ach, grosser König" is set apart from the other chorales of the Passion in that it has a
running-eighth-note bass line. The opening "scenes" of Parts I and II both end with verses
of the chorale "Herzliebster Jesu" in G minor and A minor, respectively; and the two scenes
both begin with christological choruses ("Herr, unser Herrscher" and "Christus, der uns
selig macht") and contain inter-related *turbae*.

zag" pattern is a perfect representation of the dialectical character of faith in Lutheranism: that is, the law brings man down, humiliates him, and Christ raises him again. There is a sense that "Wir dürfen niemand töten" echoes the fifth commandment ("Thou shalt not kill"), distorts it into a worldly meaning, just as "Wir haben keinen König denn den Kaiser" appears to blaspheme against the first commandment; and this sense of worldly *versus* spiritual meanings underlies all the "Jesus of Nazareth" choruses. The last of the series, "Wir haben keinen König denn den Kaiser," culminates the central sharp-key segment of the Passion and is followed immediately by the judgment of crucifixion – the ending of John's trial – before the turn to flats. In short, the continued references to the music that originally accompanied the name "Jesus of Nazareth" suggest that Jesus's name constitutes a "hidden" meaning carried over from the first two choruses, and used thereafter in the trial as a response to questions concerning the King of the Jews. That is, we are intended to understand all repetitions of the chorus as reiterations of the name "Jesus of Nazareth" in situations where the identity of the King of the Jews is called into question. The "hidden" significance of the chorus seems to invite our perception of its meaning as an allegory of faith. The name "Jesus of Nazareth" is, of course, an affirmation, associated with a famous Johannine *locus* of divine self-revelation, while the repetitions of its music all emphasize negatives: "Wir dürfen *niemand* töten," "*Nicht* diesen, sondern Barabbam," and "Wir haben *keinen* König." Bach's device, therefore, suggests Luther's description of Jesus as the "Yes" that is hidden behind the "No" of the law (that is, the *turbae*).[50]

And Bach, as if in confirmation of the association of the "Jesus of Nazareth" music to recognition of Jesus's kingship, uses practically the same music yet a sixth time, now in B minor, varied somewhat, and without the flute part, in the Christmas Oratorio to the text "Wo ist der neugeborne König der Juden?" (see Example 6). For many years this latter chorus has been generally accepted on the basis of a 1916 article by Gerhard Freiesleben as a parody of the chorus "Pfui dich" from the lost St Mark Passion;[51] the correspondence to the "Jesus of Nazareth" choruses was not mentioned by Freiesleben although he refers to other choruses from the two surviving Passions to support his thesis of the Passion-like character of "Wo ist der neugeborne König der Juden?" The recognition of Jesus's kingship by the Magi signified, of course, the initial spread of the "Word" to the gentiles as

[50] Althaus, *The Theology of Martin Luther*, pp. 58, 407.
[51] Gerhard Freiesleben, "Ein neuer Beitrag zur Entstehungsgeschichte von J. S. Bachs Weihnachtsoratorium," *Neue Zeitschrift für Musik*, 83: 29/30 (1916), pp. 237–8.

Example 6 Christmas Oratorio, "Wo ist der neugeborne König der Jüden?"

well. The meaning of this device of repetition with a different text, at least in the St John Passion, is the recognition of Jesus's identity as the Messiah by those with faith; we are not far from Luther's idea of the "hidden God" who is revealed through faith in the cross of Christ, the point to which the "Jesus of Nazareth" series of choruses leads, nor from the foundation of Luther's Christology in John's assertion of the identity of Jesus and the Father.[52]

[52] Paul Althaus, *The Theology of Martin Luther*, pp. 181–93 (see especially p. 182); Walther von Loewenich, *Luther und das Johanneische Christentum*, pp. 20, 35–41.

In summary, Bach, in the St John Passion, shows an uncanny penetration of the structure of John's Passion account and, even more important, of its highly symbolic presentation of the crux of faith in the recognition of the identity of the man Jesus of Nazareth as the Messiah and the crucifixion as the primary means by which this identity is proclaimed to the world. The inseparability of these theological issues is a particular attribute of John's gospel that is realized in a profound manner in Bach's structure. Along the way to this realization Bach developed a groundplan for the St John Passion that exhibits a dualistic character formed of abstract, signific aspects as well as a respecting of the divisions and character of the physical narrative. This dualism is one that is fundamental to the sphere of theology, on the one hand – with its emphasis on the divided worlds of the physically present, the here and now (or the world "below" in John's scheme), *versus* the world of the future fulfillment (John's world "above") – and, on the other, to the Baroque antithetical "Lebensgefühl," which is directly owing to such theological beliefs. The particular language, structure, dramatic antagonisms and theological concerns of John's gospel are rooted in the idea of worlds "above" and "below," and the ability of faith to see beyond the physically present and into the other world. In the twentieth century Walter Benjamin's so-called "philosophical criticism" or "aesthetics of redemption" has given us a sense of the centrality of inner antinomy – "sound" *versus* "script" in written language, and the like – to the Baroque impulse to allegorical expression, viewing allegory as the aesthetic correlative of the "devaluation" of physical life and its meaning under the Lutheran doctrine of justification by faith.[53] In this light the dualistic dimension of the ground plan of the St John Passion (and of other works, such as the "Credo" of the Mass in B Minor), and in a larger sense the dualism of the very existence of elaborate planning *versus* the sense of contingency and exaggerated expressive antithesis that is most evident here in the *turbae* can be seen as a mirror of the "allegorical expression heightened to the utmost" that Theodor Adorno, following Benjamin, saw as fundamental to Bach's work.[54] That is, the plan of the St John Passion is concerned with the question of significance itself, an emphasis that seems particularly appropriate in light of Bach's creative interaction with a gospel that exhibits the same concerns. In its own way, one very different from that of the St Matthew Passion, Bach's first Leipzig Passion is a virtuoso piece in the musical allegorizing of theological themes.

---

[53] Benjamin, *The Origin*, pp. 138–48.

[54] Theodor Adorno, "Bach defended against his devotees," in *Prisms*, trans. Samuel and Shierry Weber (Cambridge, 1981), p. 141.

That it could have been perceived as such at the time is more than doubtful; and there are, as I indicated earlier, suggestions that several layers of later revision to the work were prompted by an endeavor to bring it in line with a theological viewpoint closer to that of the second Passion produced by Bach in Leipzig. When all is said and done, however, the St John Passion projects a sense of theological intent that is surpassed by no other work; and on that account it makes an impressive claim to be considered theology as well as music. The primary basis of Bach's achievement in this work, more than in its successor, is the composer's direct interaction – unmediated so far as we know by extensive theological material – with the gospel itself.

Part 2
Parody and genre

Bach's parody technique and its frontiers

ALFRED MANN

The waves of moral indignation that the discoveries of Handel's extensive use of existing material caused in the nineteenth and early twentieth centuries have receded, and modern scholarship – guided by the realization that Bach's working procedure did not essentially differ from that of Handel or any other composer of his time – has soberly replaced plagiarism and *Entlehnungen* ("appropriations") with the time-honored term parody. But this term, like its counterpart "paraphrase," now in turn needs to be washed clear of negative connotations: paraphrase denotes a work created on the basis of existing prose, as parody denotes a work created on the basis of existing music. There is no need to remind the reader of the proliferation of the great works emanating from the *cantus Romanus*, of the cantus firmus technique in later periods, or of Classical examples of the contrafactum. One might, rather, summarize the present argument in the single question: are we justified in considering parody a separate issue in the work of a composer whose writing is so overwhelmingly focused upon chorale melodies which are not his own?

Bach's wondrous craftsmanship is so concentrated that ever new creative impulses arise in the process of composition, but our accepted vocabulary is too pale to reflect the wider implications of this process. As an example we might quote the Triple Concerto in A Minor, BWV 1044, in which Bach again takes up the concertino scoring of the Fifth Brandenburg Concerto. The Schmieder catalogue states laconically: "All three movements can be traced to earlier compositions." ("Alle drei Sätze gehen auf frühere Kompositionen Bachs zurück.") One is apt to accept the bibliographic entry as the whole story: that the concerto is not an original work but merely a series of transcriptions. Yet transcription is a broad term, and, when applied to Bach's music, its meaning becomes elusive indeed.

115

Unlike Bach's other keyboard concertos, this work is derived from an earlier keyboard work. The *sujet* is the Prelude and Fugue in A Minor, BWV 894, an extraordinarily intense manifestation of Bach's keyboard virtuosity. The relentless triplet rhythm of the prelude continues in the fugue, so that the entire work becomes a veritable exercise in triplet figuration. It may have been a problem of structure that prompted Bach's return to the earlier composition. In the concerto, the lively textures of the Prelude and Fugue are separated by a middle movement of great lyrical repose. Bach chose the Adagio from the organ trio BWV 527, possibly with a view towards a specific challenge posed by the new genre of the keyboard concerto: extended *cantabile* writing appears in the solo part of the harpsichord, whose detached tone is placed in juxtaposition to the sustained tone of the other solo instruments. The design of the organ scoring with its parallel thirds and sixths as well as canonic figuration was particularly well suited to a juxtaposition of melodic lines, but Bach's transcription results in far greater complexity of texture.

Philipp Emanuel relates in the first of his extensive letters to Forkel that Bach took a delight in converting trios "on the spur of the moment" ("aus dem Stegereif") into complete quartets. The middle movement bears witness to such achievement. Though the fourth voice, inserted into ingenious transpositions of the existing material, is deliberately kept accompanimental, it assumes a thematic importance of a special kind: it is a pizzicato figure with which the violin part emulates the tone of the harpsichord. Its function is crucial to balancing the instruments, for while the figure passes from violin to flute, it never appears in the harpsichord part. What eludes this summary description is the infinitely fine detail of melodic intensification, as well as the modulatory coda – placing the C major Adagio in the context of the A minor work through an elaboration of the new thematic material – an ending such as only Bach could write.

But what about the A minor work itself? The opening diatonic progression in the prelude, immediately reappearing in rhythmic augmentation over which the melodic line breaks into triplet patterns, imparts to the concerto movement a ritornello that produces a triplet figuration of its own, distinct from the model. The parody is limited to the solo part, so that a clear concerto effect is established at the outset. Yet what detail of description could ever account for the bold cuts, elongations, and unending wealth of transformation?

In the final movement, the transcription process nevertheless gains new dimensions. In ostensibly stark contrast to the model, a tutti framework is newly designed, yet with thematic material carved from its inherent components – the ritornello emerging as a double fugue that turns the original work into a triple fugue. The idea of the accompanying pizzicato is totally transformed, here as well as in the opening movement. The solo part ends with a cadenza which, like that of the Fifth Brandenburg Concerto, recalls the works of the young organ virtuoso. But the integration of elements is different. The blending of solo and orchestra produces an entity that carries the keyboard concerto beyond the typical sonorities of the Baroque. Thus it becomes difficult indeed to speak of a work that is not original. In Bach's age, originality of execution might have taken precedence over originality of invention, but where is the fine line between such execution and invention?

The term *Choreinbau* might, again, be regarded as too insufficient. Nothing could be further removed from the somewhat mechanical process that this term implies than the opening chorus of Cantata 146, which Bach based on the slow movement from the harpsichord concerto BWV 1052. How independent the choral writing is in its conception is demonstrated by the singular fact that a new fugal exposition begins in the vocal parts where the melodic line of the original obbligato part ends. The case of the concerto BWV 1052, as such, illustrates the problem of parody in a very curious manner, for it involves a premise to which modern scholarship has been apt to be too readily committed – the "transcription from a model that must have been lost." The typically violinistic figures contained in the solo parts of this concerto, forming what might be called pedal-points on the tones of the open violin strings, seem to be an unmistakable guide. But are we on secure ground in assuming that all of Bach's keyboard concertos must be transcriptions?

The question becomes more complex when a documented pattern, such as the transformation of violin concertos to harpsichord concertos, is absent. The opening of the Gloria from Bach's A Major Mass, BWV 234, is a parody of the last movement of Cantata 67, a highly dramatic representation of the vision of Christ's reappearance amidst the disciples. But the Gloria is thematically related to the Kyrie, for which no model is to be found in the cantata. Can we be sure that it is based on another model, now lost, because of the fair-copy appearance of the autograph or because parody seems to be the usual procedure in the Lutheran Masses of Bach? And how can the thematic connection between Gloria and Kyrie be explained other than to surmise that the latter must have been newly composed to fit the former? (See Examples 1a–c.)

A similar question arises in the case of the Gloria of the F Major Mass, BWV 233. Its concluding chorus is based on the first movement of Cantata 40, but its opening chorus seems to be independent and to suggest a lost

Example 1a BWV 67/6 (bass aria), mm. 10–17

b BWV 234 Gloria, mm. 37–41

c BWV 234, Kyrie, mm. 1–4

model in the style of the first or third of the Brandenburg Concertos. Yet it also bears a certain resemblance to the tenor aria ("Christenkinder, freuet euch") from the same cantata. The movements are alike in their scoring – both include oboes and horns – as well as in their general rhythmic, harmonic, and melodic conformation. And the argument that Bach might have used the same cantata for fashioning the opening and concluding sections of the Gloria is persuasive. But if Bach did use the same cantata, we would be able to arrive at no more definite a conclusion than to state that the cantata movement *resembles* the opening of the movement from the mass – for a comparison of the two shows new invention in every detail (see Examples 2a and b).

Example 2a BWV 233, Gloria, mm. 1–10

b BWV 40/7 (tenor aria), mm. 1–4

Thus we must include an additional concept in our deliberations – namely, that of "reminiscence." That it has to be considered seriously is borne out by another work whose provenance is problematic: the second movement from the Prelude, Fugue and Allegro in E♭ Major, BWV 998. Though the fugue is preserved in Bach's autograph, its authenticity has been doubted. It suggests the sectional structure of the old keyboard canzona, since the opening exposition is followed by elaborations of two new themes that are again and again linked to the principal subject in a manner approaching the pattern of a triple fugue (see Examples 3a and b). The latter

Example 3a BWV 998, Fugue, mm. 1–8

b BWV 998, Fugue, mm. 65–70

two themes, however, do not appear contrapuntally combined but rather are juxtaposed, and their succession shows a similarity to the F minor prelude from the second book of the *Well-Tempered Clavier*, BWV 881/1, that seems too strong to be overlooked.

Taken in its many guises then, what is the parody process in Bach's work? How far do its frontiers extend? It is, above all, a manifestation of Bach's own unending power of invention. Existing works generate new works, and the composer reaches again and again into the wealth of material he himself has created. It is evident that the creative process does not cease when Bach begins to "copy" – that is, when he turns to an old score in order to modify it for a new purpose. Transcription leads to revision and revision to the expression of totally new ideas. It is composition in the original meaning of the word: Bach produces new works, as did the medieval masters of the motet and the renaissance masters of the parody mass. What guided him in the process must have been a keen awareness of parts of his past *œuvre* – what in particular he remembered and what, to his mind, held special promise for further elaboration. The composer's memory of his own works extends from the obvious to the remote – and practical necessity merges with critical choice, "borrowing" with abiding inspiration.

Three organ-trio transcriptions from the Bach circle: keys to a lost Bach chamber work

RUSSELL STINSON

J. S. Bach's organ trios, as listed in the Schmieder catalogue,[1] fall into three categories: free works, including the six trio sonatas, BWV 525–30; chorale settings; and transcriptions. Whereas Bach's authorship of the pieces from the first two categories cannot be questioned, doubts have been raised, on musical as well as text-critical grounds, about the authenticity of each of the organ trio transcriptions attributed to him.[2] Despite their *opera dubia* status, however, these works shed light on transcription practice during and after Bach's time, and in certain cases their significance extends to other domains. For example, the Trio in G Minor, BWV 584, a piece evidently of nineteenth-century origin, preserves readings from the tenor aria of Cantata 166, *Wo gehest du hin*, found in none of the work's sources; by comparing the trio with the cantata's original performing parts, Alfred Dürr has been able to reconstruct a second obbligato part for the movement.[3]

This study will focus on three transcriptions of similar value: the Trio in G Major, BWV 1027a, and two trios not listed in the Schmieder catalogue. The transcriptions represent versions of the first, second, and fourth movements of the "work-complex" that includes two of Bach's most

---

[1] See Wolfgang Schmieder, *Thematisch-systematisches Verzeichnis der musikalischen Werke von Johann Sebastian Bach* (Leipzig, 1950).

[2] This includes the three trios published in the *Neue Bach-Ausgabe* volume of the organ transcriptions of works by other composers, as the volume's editor freely admits. See Karl Heller, ed., *Johann Sebastian Bach: Neue Ausgabe sämtlicher Werke*, Serie IV, Band 8, *Bearbeitungen fremder Werke* (Kassel and Leipzig, 1979) (hereafter cited as *NBA* IV/8), p. vi; and *NBA* IV/8, *Kritischer Bericht* (1980) (hereafter *KB*), p. 11.

[3] See Alfred Dürr, ed., *NBA* I/12, *Kantaten zum Sonntag Cantate bis zum Sonntag Exaudi* (1960), pp. 5–8; and *NBA* I/12, *KB* (1960), pp. 18–22.

familiar chamber compositions: the Sonata in G Major for Viola da gamba and Obbligato Harpsichord, BWV 1027, and the Sonata in G Major for Two Flutes and Continuo, BWV 1039. (These two works are different versions of the same composition.) Scholars have demonstrated that BWV 1027 and 1039 must be derived from a lost composition, and have succeeded in partially reconstructing this work. But because only one of the organ transcriptions, BWV 1027a, has been studied in any detail, some fairly obvious clues about the lost original have thus far been overlooked.[4] Furthermore, as of yet there have been no attempts to determine who might have prepared the two transcriptions not listed in Schmieder. I hope to show that a detailed investigation of all three can substantially improve our picture of the lost original and can allow plausible arguments to be made regarding their authorship.

Any discussion of the organ transcriptions must begin by considering the relationship between BWV 1027 and BWV 1039 and addressing the question of an original version. It will be helpful to start by summarizing the source situation. Apparently the only pre-1750 source for the BWV 1039 is St 431, a set of parts prepared by two anonymous scribes and whose watermark suggests a date of 1735–45.[5] The scribe for the flute parts may also be responsible for the entry of the chorale, *Gib dich zufrieden und sei stille*, BWV 510, in the second *Clavierbüchlein* for Anna Magdalena Bach; the

---

[4] Not only is BWV 1027a the only one of the three included in the Schmieder catalogue; it is also the only transcription which has been published. See Vol. 9 of the Peters edition, *Johann Sebastian Bachs Kompositionen für die Orgel*, ed. Max Seiffert (Leipzig, 1904), and Vol. 6 of the Breitkopf & Härtel edition, *Johann Sebastian Bach: Sämtliche Orgelwerke*, ed. Heinz Lohmann (Wiesbaden, 1968). All three transcriptions will be included in my forthcoming edition, "Keyboard Transcriptions from the Bach Circle," to be published by A-R Editions (Madison, Wisconsin).

The most substantial discussion of the unpublished transcriptions to date is a two-paragraph commentary in Peter Williams, *The Organ Music of J. S. Bach* (Cambridge, 1980–4), Vol. 1, pp. 331–2. Williams also devotes space to two other trio transcriptions of Bach works not included in Schmieder: an arrangement of the Sinfonia in D Minor (BWV 790), which will be mentioned later in this essay, and a transcription of the final movement of what is evidently another lost Bach chamber or orchestral work, a work that apparently is the model for the G minor gamba/harpsichord sonata (BWV 1029). See Vol. 1, pp. 320 and 329–31. For an edition of the latter trio, see Walter Emery, ed., *J. S. Bach: Prelude, Trio, and Fugue in B Flat for Organ* (London, 1958).

[5] This manuscript is housed in the Deutsche Staatsbibliothek, East Berlin. For a description, see Hans-Peter Schmitz, ed., *NBA* VI/3 (*Werke für Flöte*), *KB* (1963), pp. 48–9. *NBA* VI/3 (1963), p. x, contains a facsimile of one page. For data on its watermark, see Wisso Weiss and Yoshitake Kobayashi, *Katalog der Wasserzeichen in Bachs Originalhandschriften* (*NBA* IX/1) (1985), *Textband*, p. 57.

copyist of the continuo part, who appears in the Bach scores only in this instance, displays a hand very similar to Bach's. It is thus possible that both copyists were members of Bach's immediate circle. The principal source for BWV 1027 – P 226/2 – is an autograph fair copy which, on the basis of handwriting and watermark evidence, can be assigned to the 1740s.[6]

The traditional view of the relationship between the two works, proposed by Rust[7] and Spitta,[8] is that BWV 1039 represents an original version from which BWV 1027 was adapted. This notion was first questioned by Friedrich Blume in an article published in the late 1920s.[9] He argued that since both works consist of three distinct voices and are in effect trio sonatas, it would be amiss to consider BWV 1027 as a "true" transcription. The only difference he noted between the two is the necessary octave discrepancy between the gamba and second flute parts. He concluded that it is impossible to ascertain which work is the original and which is the arrangement.

The reasons Blume gave for his opinions are hardly compelling. To begin with, there are numerous discrepancies between the two works in terms of ornamentation and articulation markings, as well as several passages where the bass lines are completely different. BWV 1027 has, in this respect, all the earmarks of a "revised version," since it contains considerably more ornaments and articulation indications than BWV 1039.[10] The bass-line discrepancies are even more telling, since the left-hand harpsichord part of BWV 1027, with its higher proportion of small note values (sixteenths and eighths), is essentially an ornamented version of BWV 1039's continuo. It was these differences, presumably, which led Rust and Spitta to their conclusions.

About 30 years after Blume's article appeared, Ulrich Siegele, in an important study of Bach's transcription practices in his instrumental music, maintained that the original is neither BWV 1039 nor BWV 1027, but rather a

---

[6] This manuscript is also the property of the Deutsche Staatsbibliothek. On its dating, see Hans Eppstein, ed., *NBA* VI/4, *Drei Sonaten für Viola da gamba und Cembalo* (1984), p. v, and *NBA* IX/1, *Textband*, p. 60. *NBA* VI/4, pp. vi–viii, contains facsimiles of three pages.

[7] See Wilhelm Rust, ed., *Johann Sebastian Bachs Werke* (*Bach-Gesellschaft* edition), Vol. 9, *Joh. Seb. Bachs Kammermusik: Erster Band* (Leipzig, *ca.* 1860), pp. xxii and xxv.

[8] See Philipp Spitta, *Johann Sebastian Bach* (Leipzig, 1873–80; London, 1889, New York, 1951), Vol. 1, p. 725.

[9] See Friedrich Blume, "Eine unbekannte Violinsonate von J. S. Bach," *Bach-Jahrbuch*, 25 (1928), pp. 96–118, esp. pp. 115–16.

[10] From what is known about Bach's compositional process, it is far more likely that he would have added ornaments and articulation markings during the course of a revision than that he would have removed them.

lost sonata in B♭ major for two recorders and continuo.[11] Three notes in
BWV 1039's continuo are lower than *C*, and Siegele took these unusually
low pitches as the first clue that the tonality of the original was higher than
G major. He then went on to contend that certain features of St 431 suggest
that its scribes were transposing from a source in B♭ major. For example,
there is one instance in the continuo part (second movement, m. 103, last
note) where a pitch is apparently given a minor third too high. He also
observed a peculiarity in the second flute part (first movement, m. 17).
While the first *f♯″* in this measure is altered to *f″* by a natural sign, the
second one is altered by a flat: *F♯* in G major, of course, equates to an *A* in
B♭ major. Since the two notes in question would have been flattened in
B♭ major, Siegele reasoned that the scribe inadvertently copied the flat from
his exemplar on the second *f″*, instead of changing it to a natural as he had
done on the first one.

A transposition from B♭ to G major, Siegele realized, would have been
greatly expedited if the transposition were also from French violin clef
(a G clef on the bottom line) to treble clef, the clef used for the flute parts of
St 431. Such a transposition requires changing only clefs and accidentals.
Bach's practice of using the French violin clef primarily for the recorder led
Siegele to his choice of instrumentation. As additional evidence for his
recorder-sonata hypothesis, he mentioned that over half the pitches of the
flute parts of BWV 1039 lie in the octave *d′* to *d″*, which he claimed to be an
"uncomfortable" range for the eighteenth-century flute. He maintained that
it is far less awkward for a recorder to play in the octave *f′–f″*. Siegele
believed that the St 431 copyists did not simply transpose the recorder
sonata, but that they altered its musical substance as well. He concluded
that BWV 1039 is not an authentic Bach work, but a transcription by two
of his pupils. This, he argued, would explain its odd figured bass.[12]

Siegele did not question the authenticity of BWV 1027. He did assert,
though, that Bach arranged it from the lost recorder sonata and not
BWV 1039. He maintained that it is not necessary to assume a direct
relationship between BWV 1039 and BWV 1027 just because of their
common tonality, especially when there are such important compositional

---

[11] Ulrich Siegele, "Kompositionsweise und Bearbeitungstechnik in der Instrumentalmusik
Johann Sebastian Bachs" (unpublished diss., University of Tübingen, 1957), published by
Hänssler-Verlag (Stuttgart) in 1975. See pp. 52–74 of the published version.

[12] Although Siegele was the first to challenge the authenticity of BWV 1039, it was Ludwig
Landshoff who first pointed to the spurious nature of its figured bass. See the preface to the
first volume of *J. S. Bach: Trio-Sonaten*, ed. Ludwig Landshoff (Leipzig, 1936–7).

differences between the two as the octave discrepancies in the bass parts.[13] Siegele was apparently aware only of the organ transcription of the fourth movement, BWV 1027a. He concluded that, since it has more in common with BWV 1039 than BWV 1027, it must have been arranged from the former. He also dismissed it as a Bach work because of some glaring structural defects (to be discussed later).

In an article published in the mid-1960s, Hans Eppstein offered yet another hypothesis.[14] He posited, like Siegele, that BWV 1039 is not an original version, but argued that the lost original was probably a sonata for two violins and continuo in G major.[15] Eppstein, too, mentioned the low tessitura of the flute parts and he pointed out passages which are modified apparently to avoid notes lower than d', the lowest pitch on the eighteenth-century flute.[16] But he demonstrated as well that all of these passages would have fallen within the violin's compass without any alteration. And he cited instances in BWV 1027 and the organ transcriptions of the first and fourth movements where they appear to be preserved in their original state. Eppstein also noted that there are other passages in BWV 1027 which are altered exactly as they are in BWV 1039. Since such modifications are unnecessary with the instrumentation of BWV 1027, he contended that Bach must have adapted it from BWV 1039. Consequently, he concluded that BWV 1039 is an authentic Bach work. To account for those cases where BWV 1027 seems to preserve passages in their original state which are altered in BWV 1039, Eppstein postulated that Bach occasionally drew from the lost violin sonata, even though the only "source" of the work available to him at the time was his memory of it.

Although Eppstein considered BWV 1039 to be an authentic Bach arrangement of the lost violin sonata, he maintained that its figured bass (which, among other things, contains a seventh chord at the very con-

---

[13] See first movements, mm. 4, 6–7, 20–22; second movements, mm. 6–10, 12–14, 84 5, 96–7; and fourth movements, mm. 46–7, 90–3, 115–19.

[14] See Hans Eppstein, "J. S. Bachs Triosonate G-dur (BWV 1039) und ihre Beziehung zur Sonate für Gambe und Cembalo G-dur (BWV 1027)," *Die Musikforschung*, 18 (1965), pp. 126–37. Material from this article also appears in Eppstein's monograph, *Studien über J. S. Bachs Sonaten für ein Melodieinstrument und obligates Cembalo* (Uppsala, 1966), pp. 71–5.

[15] In a recent edition of BWV 1039, Eppstein has published a reconstruction of this work, based almost exclusively on his 1965 article. See Hans Eppstein, ed., *J. S. Bach: Triosonate für zwei Flöten und Continuo mit Rekonstruktion der vermutlichen Urfassung für zwei Violinen* (Munich, 1980).

[16] Siegele also mentioned these alterations, but not in conjunction with his recorder-sonata hypothesis.

clusion of the third movement) could hardly have been fashioned by him. He made no comment on whether Bach might have prepared the organ transcriptions, but he did contend that at least the transcriptions of the outer two movements may be somehow related to the violin sonata, since they appear to render passages in their original form which are altered in BWV 1039 and BWV 1027. (Although he was aware of all three organ transcriptions, he evidently had access to only these two.)

Eppstein's accounting of the various aspects of this "work-complex" is the most cogent on all counts, even though his theory about the preparation of BWV 1027 might seem far-fetched. As for BWV 1039, there is really no evidence whatever against Bach's authorship, primarily because St 431 shows no signs of being the working score for a transcription. There is reason, though, to doubt the authenticity of its figured bass. Perhaps Bach instructed the scribe of St 431's continuo part, possibly a student of his, to invent the figured bass symbols as a sort of composition exercise.[17] More important, the peculiarities in St 431 which Siegele saw as evidence of a transposition could be more readily construed as simple copying mistakes.[18] And clearly, the low continuo notes do not suggest that BWV 1039 was transposed from a higher key.[19] Nor is there any evidence of a

[17] This would have been in no way incongruous with what Bach's pedagogical methods seem to have been. For instance, Siegele has argued convincingly that Bach instructed C. P. E. Bach to invent the upper parts to a given bass in the case of the Sonata in G Major for Flute, Violin and Continuo (BWV 1038). See *Kompositionsweise*, pp. 31–46. It appears that the son's assignment was just the opposite with the Flute Sonata in C Major (BWV 1033). Robert Marshall has presented the attractive hypothesis that this work represents Emanuel's attempt at composing a continuo line to a pre-existing unaccompanied flute sonata by his father. See Robert L. Marshall, "J. S. Bach's Compositions for Solo Flute: A Reconsideration of their Authenticity and Chronology," *Journal of the American Musicological Society*, 32 (1979), pp. 463–98, esp. pp. 465–71. More specifically related to our concerns, Marshall also maintains that the scribe of "Gib dich zufrieden und sei stille," BWV 510, in the second *Clavierbüchlein* for Anna Magdalena, was "obviously a young pupil who was assigned the exercise of fitting a bass to a given melody." See Marshall's notes to the Nonesuch recording, *The Notebook of Anna Magdalena Bach* (DB–79020) (New York, 1981). (This copyist may be identical to the scribe of the flute parts of St 431.)

[18] For example, the scribe for the flute parts may have been accustomed to canceling sharps with flats (a fairly common practice, even as late as the eighteenth century) and may have accidentally reverted to this technique in one instance, even though his exemplar used the more modern natural sign.

[19] Eppstein attacked this argument of Siegele's by enumerating other instances in Bach's instrumental music where the continuo descends below c. One such case occurs in the E minor flute sonata, BWV 1034, which contains a BB. Its highest flute pitch is a stratospheric g''', rendering the possibility of its having been transposed from a higher key very unlikely.

transposition in the sources for BWV 1027 or the organ transcriptions. Furthermore, the fact that all the surviving versions of the "work-complex" are in G major would alone seem to imply that key as the tonality of the original. Concerning the instrumentation of the original version, the modifications made to accommodate the flute's range in BWV 1039 constitute the strongest evidence in Eppstein's favor. That the overwhelmingly predominant scoring for trio sonatas in the Baroque era was two violins, plus continuo, lends further credibility to his hypothesis.

Eppstein also appears to have been on the right track with regard to the organ transcriptions. They obviously *are* transcriptions (numerous passages in all three are altered in ways that can only be explained as a transcriber's modifications), and it seems impossible that they were arranged from either BWV 1039 or BWV 1027. Generally, their readings correspond to those of BWV 1039, instead of the embellished readings from BWV 1027. But all three transcriptions appear to preserve passages in their original state which are altered in BWV 1039 and BWV 1027. It would seem, therefore, that the only logical conclusion one can draw about the organ transcriptions and their model(s) is that all three were arranged either directly or indirectly – it is possible that the fourth-movement transcription is an arrangement of another (lost) organ trio transcription – from the lost original, the same work which evidently served as the model for BWV 1039.

At first glance, the organ transcriptions would seem to imply that this lost original was scored for violin, gamba and continuo: the middle voices of all three are generally in the same octave as the gamba part of BWV 1027 rather than Flute 2 of BWV 1039. Consider, however, the impracticality of transcribing Eppstein's violin sonata for two manuals and pedals without transposing the second violin part down an octave; the result would be prolonged periods during which the player's hands are crossed. Organ trios do frequently require hand-crossings, but not even remotely close to the degree that would have been the case if both obbligato voices of the organ transcriptions were treble parts. This format would have posed formidable technical difficulties indeed, especially in the fast second- and fourth-movement transcriptions, which are problematic enough to perform with the upper parts an octave apart. Thus, it appears that the only feasible way of preparing organ transcriptions of movements from Eppstein's violin sonata would have been to transpose the second violin part down an octave. In light of all the evidence which supports Eppstein's hypothesis about a lost original version, it seems quite plausible that the organ transcriptions were fashioned in precisely this manner. The ensuing discussion of the organ transcriptions, then, proceeds from the premise that the original version of

BWV 1039/1027 is a lost sonata for two violins and continuo in G major, and that BWV 1039 was arranged from this work by Bach himself.

Each organ transcription survives in just one source. That of the first movement transcription is a manuscript in the hand of the Gräfenroda cantor, Johann Peter Kellner (1705–72), which now comprises the twelfth fascicle of the voluminous miscellany, P 804[20] (see Plate 1). Kellner, who was renowned by his contemporaries as an organ virtuoso, is remembered today primarily for his large collection of Bach manuscripts. He is unquestionably one of the most important copyists in the sources for Bach's instrumental music, especially keyboard works. Besides being personally acquainted with Bach, he was an extremely prolific copyist of his music. Whether he was also a Bach pupil is open to conjecture. Handwriting and watermark evidence suggest that his copy of the organ transcription originated sometime after 1730.[21] Its title page reads: *Trio in G♮./Adagio*. The source consists of a single bifolio: folio 1r serves as the title page; folios 1v and 2r contain musical text; folio 2v is blank. At the end of folio 2r Kellner wrote "Sequi allegro," surely meaning that he intended for a transcription of the second movement to follow. We will return to this inscription during the discussion of the second-movement transcription. (Folios 1v and 2r are reproduced in Plate 1.)

There is only one instance where the first-movement transcription seems to preserve a passage in its original state which was subsequently altered in BWV 1039 and BWV 1027.[22] Beginning on the tenth beats of measure 6 in Flute 1 of BWV 1039, and the seventh and tenth beat of measure 18 of Flutes 1 and 2, respectively, a figure is presented which commences with a syncopated octave leap. This figure is also stated by Flute 2 in measure 6, but with one important exception: the octave leap is replaced by repeated notes (see Example 1). The leap was omitted apparently to accommodate the flute's range. Flute 2 seems to have been transposed up an octave in measures 4–6 to avoid the *c♯'* which Violin 2 of the original played on the sixth beat of measure 6. Measures 16–18 of Flute 1 represent an analogous spot where the transposition was unnecessary. A similar alteration was made in the gamba part of BWV 1027. In the middle voice of the organ transcription,

---

[20] Housed in the Staatsbibliothek Preussischer Kulturbesitz, West Berlin. For an inventory, see Wolfgang Plath, ed., *NBA* V/5 (*Klavierbüchlein für Wilhelm Friedemann Bach*), *KB* (1963), pp. 24–35. A comprehensive description is found in Russell Stinson, "The Bach Manuscripts of Johann Peter Kellner and his Circle" (unpublished Ph.D. diss., University of Chicago, 1985), pp. 17–37. The present essay is a revised version of a chapter from this study.

[21] See Stinson, pp. 145, 155–61, and 164.

[22] See Eppstein, "J. S. Bachs Triosonate G-dur," pp. 131–2.

Example 1 First movement: mm. 3–6

however, the interval between the last note of measure 3 and the first note of measure 4 is only a perfect fifth, as compared to a twelfth in BWV 1039 and BWV 1027. As a result, the octave leap in measure 6 is maintained.

This issue aside, the organ transcription should be discussed in its own right. Its most interesting aspect is how the continuo of the lost original was adapted as a pedal part. While the range of the continuo was *BB–d'* (assuming that it looked no different from the continuo of BWV 1039), the transcriber's pedalboard evidently had only the standard two-octave compass, *C–c'*.[23] This discrepancy posed difficulties which he was able to resolve only partially. The three-bar continuo figure which accompanies the principal theme (see mm. 1–3, 4–6, 13–15 and 16–18) was inherently problematic for the transcriber in this regard, since it frequently involves *d'*. Except in the first half of measure 13, where a modulation occurs, the statements of this figure in BWV 1039 and BWV 1027 are virtually identical. But in the organ transcription it appears in no less than four different versions, owing more to the transcriber's inconsistency, though, than the limitations of the pedal range (see Example 2).

The transcriber's use of the figure would seem to provide a clue as to the transcription's authenticity, for it is most unlikely that Bach would have presented the figure so carelessly, while stating it with such consistency in other versions of the movement. One does not need to look beyond its only source for a candidate, for the evidence points only to Kellner. Kellner

---

[23] All notes lower than *C* and higher than *c'* are avoided. See also *NBA* VI/3, *KB*, p. 50, n. 13.

Plate 1 Trio in G major: *Adagio* (first-movement transcription),
copy by J. P. Kellner, P 804/12, fo. 1v and fo. 2r

Example 2 First movement: mm. 1–2; 4–5, 13–14 and 16–17

appears to have had an unusually keen interest in keyboard transcription. A large number of the Kellner-circle Bach copies are devoted to keyboard transcriptions, and Kellner may have copied out Bach's unaccompanied violin and cello works to arrange some of them for keyboard.[24] Moreover, we know that Kellner's pupil, Leonhard Frischmuth (?–1764), arranged six of Tartini's violin concertos for harpsichord, suggesting that Kellner used transcription as a pedagogical tool or, at least, that Frischmuth was influenced by his teacher in this respect.[25]

Kellner's interest in the organ trio is documented as well. Among his extant organ compositions are two such works.[26] It is also significant that Johann Anton Gottfried Wechmar (1727–99), evidently a member of Kellner's immediate circle and possibly one of his students, made copies of three of the six trio sonatas, BWV 525–30, since his exemplars were

[24] See Russell Stinson, "J. P. Kellner's copy of Bach's sonatas and partitas for violin solo," *Early Music*, 13 (1985), pp. 199–211, esp. pp. 200–2.

[25] Frischmuth published these transcriptions as his Op. 4 under the title *VI Concerti del Sig' Tartini accommodati per il Cembalo da L. Frischmuth in Amsterdamo* (n.d.). See Otto E. Albrecht and Karlheinz Schlager, eds., Répertoire International des Sources Musicales: *Einzeldrucke vor 1800* (Kassel, 1971–81), Vol. 3, p. 123; and Minos Dounias, *Die Violinkonzerte Giuseppe Tartinis* (Wolfenbüttel, 1935), p. 198.

[26] See Georg Feder, ed., *Johann Peter Kellner: Ausgewählte Orgelwerke* (Lippstadt, 1958).

probably lost copies by Kellner.[27] More important, the only source for
another organ trio transcription of a Bach work, that of the Sinfonia in
D minor, BWV 790, happens to be in Frischmuth's hand.[28] And the only
source for what is surely an organ trio transcription of a Telemann trio
sonata ("Trio 9" from *Essercizi i Musici*) was owned by Wechmar.[29] Considering the evidence presented above, it seems likely that both of these trios
are products of the Kellner circle too.

There is also reason to view Kellner's copy of the first-movement transcription as the working score for his own transcription. Preparing an organ
arrangement of the first movement of the lost violin sonata would have been
a fairly straightforward task as far as the obbligato parts are concerned.
Kellner would have needed only to copy Violin 1 note for note and transpose Violin 2 down an octave (so there is no cause to doubt that he was
transcribing as he copied, merely because of the neat appearance of his
obbligato voices). The only correction in either obbligato voice occurs at
the very beginning of the score, where a treble clef is changed to an alto
clef in the middle staff. If Kellner were transcribing from a source with
two violin parts (both of which, of course, would have been notated in

---

[27] Wechmar's copies are housed in the Musikbibliothek der Stadt Leipzig. See Peter Krause,
   Handschriften der Werke Johann Sebastian Bachs in der Musikbibliothek der Stadt Leipzig (Leipzig,
   1964), pp. 23–8; and Stinson, "The Bach Manuscripts," pp. 61–6.

[28] This manuscript is also owned by the Musikbibliothek der Stadt Leipzig. See Krause, p. 25;
   and Stinson, pp. 68–9.

[29] This manuscript is also among the holdings of the Musikbibliothek der Stadt Leipzig. See
   Dietrich Kilian, ed., *NBA* IV/5–6 (*Präludien, Toccaten, Fantasien und Fugen für Orgel*), *KB*
   (1978–9), pp. 116–17. According to Williams, *The Organ Works*, Vol. 1, pp. 14–15, it is not
   known which of the two versions of the Telemann sonata represents the original and which
   is the transcription. But it seems obvious that the organ trio must have been prepared from
   the chamber version (scored for flute, violin and continuo). First of all, it would be virtually
   unheard of in Germany during the eighteenth century for a chamber work to be arranged
   from an organ or keyboard composition, rather than *vice versa*. Secondly, even though the
   organ trio contains no modified readings which would indicate that it is a transcription – its
   readings are practically identical to those in the chamber trio – it is in D major, whereas the
   chamber version is in E major. The continuo of the chamber trio often ascends to $d\sharp'$ and e',
   pitches generally unavailable on German pedalboards at this time. The pedal part of the
   organ trio, on the other hand, never goes higher than d'. The advantages in transposing the
   chamber trio down a step to prepare an organ version, therefore, are clear. There is no conceivable reason why a transcriber would have transposed the organ trio up a step to fashion
   a version for flute, violin and continuo. The organ trio is included in Traugott Fedtke, ed.,
   Georg Philipp Telemann: Orgelwerke, (Kassel, 1964) Vol. 2. It is listed as TWV Anh. 33:4 in
   Martin Ruhnke, *Georg Philipp Telemann: Thematisch–Systematisches Verzeichnis seiner Werke*,
   Instrumental Werke 1 (Kassel, 1984).

treble clef), he easily could have copied down the treble clef either inadvertently or because he had not yet realized that Violin 2 would have to be transposed down an octave.

Fortunately, the pedal part is far more suggestive of a working score, for the passages shown in Example 2 imply that Kellner was constantly experimenting with ways of transferring the continuo figure, discussed above, as he prepared the manuscript. Noteworthy too, they form an evolutionary chain of sorts, adhering ever more closely to the continuo of BWV 1039 as the transcription progresses. Kellner's primary consideration at the outset seems to have been to modify the figure so that it could easily be played on a pedalboard (note the substitution of quarters for eighths), while his main concern from measure 5 on evidently was to produce a faithful rendition of his model.

The source for the second-movement transcription seems to have been prepared at some point during the second half of the eighteenth century by a scribe who evidently appears in the Bach sources only in this instance.[30] This manuscript now forms a fascicle of the miscellany, P 288.[31] It consists of a bifolio, all four pages of which are taken up by a musical text. Folio 1r contains the title: *Trio ex G dur. – J. S. Bach*.

The organ transcription differs from BWV 1039 and BWV 1027 in a number of interesting ways. To begin with, there seem to be two instances where it preserves in their original state passages which are altered in the other versions of the movement. In all three versions, measures 22–8 are permeated by a sixteenth-note motive characterized by an arpeggiated descending seventh. But in the statement in BWV 1039 by Flute 2 beginning on the third beat of measure 27, the descending seventh is replaced by an ascending perfect fourth (see Example 3). A b' is given on the downbeat of measure 28, instead of a b, presumably because a flute could not have played the latter. The same alteration occurs in Flute 2 on the downbeat of measure 106, with c'' being substituted for c', but this measure is not included in the organ transcription (see below). Interestingly, this change resulted in parallel fifths between Flute 2 and the continuo (note the progression from $f'\sharp$ and B at the conclusion of measure 27 to b' and e on the downbeat of measure 28). An analogous passage where the substitution was unnecessary is found in Flute 1 at measures 58–9. The first note of the middle voice of the organ transcription in measure 27 is a B, apparently reflecting the b of Violin II of

---

[30] See *NBA* IV/5–6, *KB*, p. 60.

[31] Located at the Staatsbiliothek Preussischer Kulturbesitz. For a description and inventory, see *NBA* IV/5–6, *KB*, pp. 59–62; and Stinson, "The Bach Manuscripts," pp. 41–3.

Example 3 Second movement: mm. 27–8

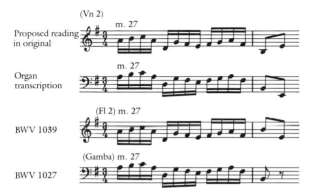

the original. BWV 1027 agrees with the organ transcription here, as far as the *B* is concerned; what is unexplainable, however, is the *E* which follows. Obviously, a violin could not have played *e*, and one assumes the original read *b–e'* here. Perhaps the copyist or transcriber wrote the note an octave too low.

The second instance also involves this descending seventh motive. In measures 57–62 Flute 2 was again presumably transposed up an octave, beginning with the first note of measure 57, to avoid *b* and *c'♯* (see Example 4). This transposition was unnecessary in Flute 1 at measures 26–31 and measures 104–5. Flute 2 returns to the correct octave in measure 63 by descending to *c"♯* rather than ascending to *c"'♯*. The organ transcription seems to reflect the original by beginning on *B* in measure 57. (At this point BWV 1027 agrees with BWV 1039.)

It is significant as well that the organ transcription contains six fewer measures than BWV 1039/1027: measures 100–6 and the first beat of measure 107 of BWV 1039/1027 are missing from the organ transcription; measure 100 and the first beat of measure 101 of the organ transcription, conversely, are comprised in part of material not found in either BWV 1039 or BWV 1027 (see Examples 5 and 6).

All indications are that the transcriber excised the missing measures and composed a transitional passage in their place. For instance, it is odd that in measures 96–104 the middle voice presents two statements of the subject at the same pitch level without any intervening material whatsoever. This happens nowhere else in the organ transcription and occurs in neither

Example 4 Second movement: mm. 56–7 and 62–3

BWV 1039 nor BWV 1027.[32] (Actually, no Bach fugue comes to mind that employs this device.) The statements themselves are also anomalous. The first one concludes with three eighths (see the first three notes of measure 100); the second one starts on the wrong pitch (*a* instead of *d*), adds a sixteenth to the end of the next beat, and sounds two notes simultaneously on the beat immediately following. No other statements in the organ transcription vary the subject by these means, and the same is true for all the statements in BWV 1039 and BWV 1027.

The transcriber's possible motives for omitting measures 100–6 of the violin sonata are by no means clear. Assuming that these bars differed from BWV 1039 only on the downbeat of measure 106, where Violin 2 presumably played *c'*, they would not have been particularly difficult to incorporate. (And, in this regard, it is worth noting that this same seven-bar passage had already been transcribed in mm. 22–28 and mm. 53–59.) One can more easily speculate about why the statements in measures 96–104 were modified as they were. It would appear that two of the modifications in measure 100 were made to fit the middle voice to the pedal part. The only plausible reason for concluding the first statement with descending eighths instead of the descending ♩♩♩ motive used throughout the movement would have been to avoid an *e/f♯* dissonance on the second half

---

[32] The statements in the right-hand part of the organ transcription, Flute 1 of BWV 1039, and the upper harpsichord voice in BWV 1027 at measures 28–35 are in no way analogous. They are separated by cadential material (unrelated to the subject) at measures 32–3. Furthermore, the statement which begins in measure 33 inverts the subject and presents only its first half.

Example 5 Second movement: organ transcription, mm. 93–107

Example 6 Second movement: BWV 1039, mm. 91–113 (from *NBA* VI/3)

Example 6 (*cont.*)

of the first beat. Likewise, what reason other than maintaining this motion in parallel thirds could the transcriber have had for starting the second statement on *a* rather than *d*? The implication here, of course, is that the pedal line of measure 100 was the first of the two to be composed. The alterations of the third beat of measure 100 and the downbeat of measure 101 could be explained by postulating that the transcriber realized the monotonous effect inherent in "back to back" statements at the same pitch level, and that he embellished the opening beats of the second statement to achieve some variety.

The organ transcription also differs from BWV 1039/1027 at measures 90–3 (see Example 7). Whereas the obbligato parts of the organ transcription use tied notes in measures 90–2, those of BWV 1039 and BWV 1027 employ a figure borrowed from their bass lines at measures 22–4: ♪♪♪♪♪ | ♪ . The reading in the organ transcription, to be sure, is unimaginative when compared to that in BWV 1039/1027. But there really is no cause to doubt that it reflects the lost violin sonata.

Example 7 Second movement: organ transcription and BWV 1039, mm. 89–93

In fact, the reading bears a certain similarity to a passage from the fugue of the Passacaglia in C minor, BWV 582 (see Example 8). The two passages exhibit some obvious common traits: ¾ time, three-voice texture, bass parts which contain sequentially descending sixteenth-note figures; and two upper voices comprised chiefly of tied dotted half-notes. In addition, both supply these half-notes with trills, probably meant to be employed for the

Example 8 Passacaglia in C Minor, BWV 582, mm. 269–71 (from *NBA* IV/7)

duration of the passage in all three instances. (And, in this connection, it is possible that the scribe of the organ transcription omitted a trill on e′; if so, a further parallel would exist.) They also play similar structural roles within their respective movements (the Passacaglia can be viewed as a two-movement work, a set of variations followed by a fugue). Both conclude with episodes consisting of constant sixteenth-note motion in every measure; more importantly, these episodes appear near the end of the movements and they are immediately followed by tonic statements of subjects which produce recapitulation-like effects.

Measures 90–2 are the only bars in BWV 1039 in which the continuo is assigned nothing but sixteenths, the smallest note value in the part. One might argue, therefore, that the transcriber simplified the violin parts so that he could devote his full attention to performing the continuo, which he chose to incorporate without modification. Despite its rapid motion, though, this passage could not be more idiomatically suited to the pedalboard, since it can be played throughout with alternating feet that are never more than a seventh apart. Several of the eighth-note passages, which involve awkward, wide leaps a good deal of the time, are far more difficult to perform. The organ transcription would seem to reveal that Bach revised measures 90–3 of the second movement of the violin sonata when he prepared BWV 1039. Evidently, this was the only alteration in the entire composition not made out of concern for the flute's range.

Whoever prepared the organ transcription was faced with two fundamental problems in adapting the continuo. His pedalboard must have also had a compass of *C–c′*, whereas the range of the continuo was *BB–e′* (assuming, again, that it was identical to that of BWV 1039).[33] But this was a minor

[33] All notes lower than *C* and higher than *c′* are avoided in the pedal part of the organ transcription.

matter compared to the continuo's frequent sixteenth-note scalar passages, which are next to impossible to pedal at a fast tempo. The transcriber resolved the latter problem by systematically reducing chains of sixteenths to eighths, while still preserving their melodic character (this is clearly illustrated in the pedal part of Example 5).

The altogether admirable manner in which the continuo is transcribed in P 288, plus the absence of errors that might be construed as "conceptual" mistakes (like those in P 804), lead one to believe that the scribe was copying from an existing transcription. And this transcription does not appear to be the work of J. S. Bach, since it apparently represents a corruption of a Bach composition, a corruption not carried out in a particularly ingenious or successful manner. The transcriber would have better disguised the corruption and created a more convincing reading in measure 100 had he subordinated the pedal part to the middle voice – instead, he did just the opposite – for the obvious reason that the latter carries the subject.

Several factors suggest that Kellner is again the transcriber. The evidence supporting his authorship is, fortunately, not restricted to the "Sequi Allegro" notation at the conclusion of his copy of the first-movement transcription, which strongly suggests that he prepared a transcription of the second movement as well. To begin with, both transcriptions were conceived for an instrument with a pedal compass of C–c'. More significant, both were prepared according to the same method: Violin 1 is assigned to the right hand; Violin 2 is transferred to the left hand and consistently transposed down an octave; and the continuo, with appropriate modifications, is given to the feet.

In addition, the mere fact that the only source for the second movement transcription is a fascicle from P 288 implies ties to Kellner. P 288 and its sister volumes P 286 and P 287 (both miscellanies too) are the only manuscripts from the extensive *Sammlung Voss* which contain Bach copies by members of the Kellner circle.[34] Kellner, who is the principal copyist of the three sources, appears in twelve fascicles, and an anonymous scribe who was in his charge appears in one of these along with him. And it seems that no less than eight other fascicles containing Bach copies by anonymous scribes who were evidently not in Kellner's immediate circle were prepared from either extant or lost Kellner copies.[35] Does it not seem very likely that the

[34] P 286 and P 287 are also the property of the Staatsbibliothek Preussischer Kulturbesitz. See *NBA* IV/5–6, *KB*, pp. 53–9 and Stinson, "The Bach Manuscripts," pp. 39–41, for details.

[35] See *NBA* IV/5–6, *KB*, pp. 54, 372, 397, 437, and 539; and *NBA* IV/8, *KB*, pp. 35, 46, and 75.

scribe of the second movement transcription was also working from a source in Kellner's hand?

Finally, the apparent excision of six measures is not inconsistent with Kellner's scribal habits. To judge from some of his Bach copies which transmit corrupt versions of works due to the omission of sizeable sections of material,[36] he would not have been above shortening the second movement of the violin sonata to fit his needs (whatever they might have been). To summarize, there is considerable internal and external evidence to support Kellner's authorship of this transcription, and he is the only person for whom any such evidence exists.

The source for the fourth-movement transcription, BWV 1027a, also forms a fascicle of a miscellany, MS 7 from the *Sammlung Mempell-Preller*.[37] It was copied out by an anonymous scribe who was in the charge of Johann Nicolaus Mempell (1713–47), and it seems to date from the 1730s.[38] Little is known about Mempell other than that he worked as a cantor and organist in the village of Apolda from 1740 until his death. Numerous copies of Bach keyboard works by Mempell and his scribe have survived. The title page of the MS 7 copy reads: *Trio ex G.♯./2. Clavier/et/Pedal./di/Bach/Possess:/ J. N. Mempell*. This source also consists of a single bifolio: folio 1r serves as the title page; the remaining three pages are taken up by musical text.

There are three instances where this transcription appears to preserve passages in their original state which are altered in BWV 1039 and BWV 1027.[39] This movement is another fugue whose subject contains an octave leap in its sixth measure. The statement in BWV 1039 by Flute 2 at measures 89–97, however, employs repeated notes on c'' in measure 95 instead (see Example 9). Flute 2 was evidently transposed up an octave for this statement so that notes below d' would be avoided. The substitution of c'' for c''' enabled it to return to the correct octave. Both the organ transcription and BWV 1027 preserve the leap.

A figure is introduced at measure 49 which also contains an octave leap. But the statement by Flute 2 in measures 51–4 again omits it; instead the e'' in measure 51 is repeated (see Example 10). The reason for the omission seems to be that Flute 2 was again transposed up an octave in measures

---

[36] See Stinson, "J. P. Kellner's Copy of Bach's Sonatas and Partitas."

[37] Located at the Musikbibliothek der Stadt Leipzig. See Krause, pp. 29–36; and *NBA* IV/5–6, *KB*, pp. 120–1 and 192–4.

[38] According to Hans-Joachim Schulze. See his "Wie entstand die Bach-Sammlung Mempell-Preller?", *Bach-Jahrbuch*, 60 (1974), pp. 104–22, esp. p. 120; and *Studien zur Bach-Überlieferung im 18. Jahrhundert* (Leipzig-Dresden, 1984), p. 87.

[39] See Eppstein, "J. S. Bachs Triosonate G-dur," pp. 129 and 132–3.

Example 9 Fourth movement: mm. 89–96

Example 10 Fourth movement: mm. 45–51

Example 10 (*cont.*)

46–51. The interval between the last note of measure 45 and the first note of measure 46 in the organ transcription is a descending second, whereas in BWV 1039 and BWV 1027 it is an ascending seventh. The repetition on *e″* in measure 51 of BWV 1039 allowed Flute 2 to return to the correct octave. The organ transcription again preserves the leap.

The same material transposed up an octave in measures 46–51 was apparently transposed up an octave in Flute 2 at measures 139–42 as well. The interval between the last note of measure 138 and the first note of measure 139 in Flute 2 is an ascending seventh, while the interval between the last note of measure 127 and the first note of measure 128 in the organ transcription is an descending second (see Example 11). BWV 1027 again agrees

Example 11 Fourth movement: mm. 127–31; mm. 138–42

with BWV 1039. (The four passages given in Example 11 are totally analogous; the reason for the measure number discrepancy is that the arranger of the organ transcription obviously omitted measures 115–25 of his model. This omission will be discussed shortly.)

There are notable discrepancies, regarding the method of transcription, between the transcription of this movement and the two already considered. First of all, it is the only one in which Violin 2 does not appear to have been consistently transposed down an octave. One assumes that the transcriber chose not to use transposition in measures 8–16 and 89–97 because Violin 2 presumably never went any higher than Violin 1 here (if the flute parts of BWV 1039 can be taken as any indication); consequently, there would have been no need for using octave transposition to avoid hand-crossings. That Violin 2 was evidently transposed down two octaves in measures 76–8 is puzzling since it only needed to be transposed down one octave to keep it consistently lower than Violin 1. Measures 30–4 will be discussed momentarily.

Another difference between this transcription and the other two is the transfer of continuo material to the left hand instead of the feet in measures 16–22 and 97–102, resulting in "hybrid" statements of the subject (which begin in the left hand and are then transferred to the pedals) in measures 16–24 and 97–105. Measures 16–24 and 97–105 of BWV 1039 represent the only passages where the subject is stated in the continuo part, and it can scarcely be coincidental that here and only here continuo material is assigned to a manual part in the organ transcription. A logical conclusion would be that the transcriber did not feel capable of playing the initial portion of the subject on the pedals (the section prior to the first pair of tied quarters), because of its fast eighths and awkward leaps. (The remainder of the subject, on the other hand, moves for the most part in stepwise half-note motion.) But this does not explain why the subject is simplified in both measures 16–22 and 97–102 of the left-hand part of the organ transcription or why the initial segment of the subject is simplified only in these two passages. All the simplifications involve the substitution of a quarter for two eighths – the most common modification made to the continuo part in adapting it to the pedals throughout the transcription (see m. 18,2; m. 97,4; m. 99,2; and m. 101,4). The only remotely plausible explanation for the simplifications is that the present transcription is actually an arrangement of another (lost) transcription in which the subject was assigned to the pedals in measures 16–22 and 97–102 with the quarter-note simplifications enumerated above. And it would follow that the arranger of the present transcription did not care to attempt a pedal performance of the opening segment of the subject even with the simplifications. To pursue this hypothesis a step further, he transferred both passages to a manual part without bothering to restore the missing eighths.

In any event, assigning these bars to the left hand created a void in the pedal part which the transcriber filled with material presumably composed by himself (see Example 12) and possibly derived from measures 44–7 and

Example 12 Fourth movement: BWV 1027a, mm. 17–23 and 98–104

61–3 of the continuo. Whereas the upper two parts of the organ transcription and all parts of BWV 1039 and BWV 1027 are virtually identical in measures 17–19 and 98–100, the pedal offers distinctly different readings. Beginning with the first pair of tied quarters in the subject, the transcriber opted to transfer the continuo back to the pedals (see measures 22–4 and 103–5), apparently because the tied quarters, the subsequent half-note, and the tied quarters which follow pose no difficulties for pedal performance. At the first point of transfer (m. 22), the subject is passed from the left hand to the pedals without incident; in measure 103, however, it drops out altogether for three beats, before being reinstated on the fourth beat.

Measures 17–22 and 98–103 of the organ transcription also differ with respect to which of the obbligato parts of the original is retained and which is omitted. In the first passage Violin 2 is assigned to the right hand and Violin 1 is omitted, in the second passage Violin 1 is assigned to the right hand and Violin 2 is omitted. It is not clear why the transcriber chose Violin 2 over Violin 1 in measures 17–22, but in so doing he supplied both passages with the same material for the upper obbligato part (to judge from BWV 1039, measures 17–22 of Violin 2 were essentially the same as measures 98–103 of Violin 1).

A further discrepancy between the fourth-movement transcription and those of the other two movements appears in measures 30–4 and 111–14: the fourth-movement transcription inverts the violin parts (see Examples 13 and 14). The transcriber evidently took this liberty because he preferred to play the eighth-note figures here – which contain more leaps than any

Example 13 Fourth movement: BWV 1039 and BWV 1027a, mm. 26–34

Example 14 Fourth movement: BWV 1039, mm. 107–14 and 126–7;
BWV 1027a, mm. 107–16

eighth-note figures in the movement – with his right hand only. It is perhaps possible that he wrote down exactly what the original contained, but it is difficult to imagine that it did not incorporate the invertible counterpoint that BWV 1039 and BWV 1027 make use of in measures 26–33 and 107–14. The discrepancy becomes more significant still when one realizes that in the second-movement transcription the left hand is given several passages that are at least as technically demanding as those which were apparently transferred to the right hand in the present transcription (see mm. 26–7, 39–40 and 55–6 of the second-movement transcription).

Measures 30–4 deserve further comment. As a result of the inversion of the violin parts, the transcriber evidently was forced to transpose Violin 1 down an octave (this happens nowhere in the other two transcriptions) in measures 30–3. Consequently, it was not necessary to transpose Violin 2 down an octave here. (This transposition pattern was not followed in measures 111–14 because of the comparatively low tessitura of the Violin 1 part.) For the first two beats of measure 34 Violin 1 drops out, being replaced by filler composed by the transcriber. He appears to have preferred his two quarters (on *a* and *e*) to a half-note on *e* or *e'*, even though either half-note would have enabled Violin 1 to proceed with little interruption (the only interruption being an octave or two-octave jump between the obbligato parts on the third beat).

That Bach prepared this transcription seems impossible. To begin with, the decision to transfer continuo passages to the left hand and to invert the obbligato parts was surely made to make the transcription easier to play. Judging from Bach's authenticated organ trios, he would not have found it necessary to make such alterations. The simplification of the continuo is executed in such a way that it also supports the case against Bach's authorship. The transcriber was obviously unconcerned about consistency in this regard, as measures 49–56 and 66–81 reveal most clearly, and the simplification is functional at best. (Example 15 illustrates the simplification technique in measures 49–56.)

But the unbalanced form of the organ transcription supplies the strongest evidence that Bach is not responsible for it. The formal design of the movement as it stands in BWV 1039 and BWV 1027 is symmetrically conceived, as Siegele pointed out in his discussion of the organ transcription.[40] It is a fugue which contains four different episodes, labelled A, B, C, and D in Figure 1; S designates statements of the subject. All the episodes except D are stated twice, once in the first half of the movement and once in the second half. The statements in the second half invert the obbligato parts; in

[40] See *Kompositionsweise*, pp. 69–74.

Example 15 Fourth movement: BWV 1039 and BWV 1027a, mm. 49–56

the statement of A in the second half the phrase sequence is inverted as well. D, the longest episode, is presented only once, forming the centerpiece. Each half is framed by a 25-bar exposition and a single statement of the subject. With C practically omitted altogether in the second half of the organ transcription, the symmetric shape – as Siegele observed – is indeed destroyed.

It is of course conceivable that the fourth movement of the violin sonata contained just one statement of C and that when Bach prepared BWV 1039, he added a statement in the second half, realizing the symmetrical design which would result. Certain peculiarities in the organ transcription – illustrated in Example 14 – strongly suggest, however, that the transcriber knowingly excised a sizeable portion of his model.

These peculiarities take several forms, the first of which involves octave transposition. The bass figure of A^1 in BWV 1039, BWV 1027, and measures 26–9 of the organ transcription begins with three half-notes, which are followed by three quarters. In the first statement of A^1 in each of the three surviving versions of the movement (mm. 26–9), the first two half-notes of the bass figure are at the same pitch, and the remaining notes are either a half-step or minor sixth (in BWV 1027) above or a minor third below. In the second statement (mm. 111–14) the second half-note is an octave lower than the first, and the remaining notes are either a half-step or minor sixth above or a minor third below the second half-note. Bach seems to have transposed the figure down an octave (beginning with the second half-note) so that it would lie in the same low register as the first bars of C's bass line. There was no need for a transposition in measures 26–9 since the first note of the bass line of A^2 is in the same register as that of A^1.

mm. 1–25	26–33	34–41	42–8	49–58	59–65	66–81	82–106	107–14	115–26	127–34	135–42
Expo.	A¹ A²	B	S	C	S	D	Expo.	A² A¹	C*	B	S
(25 mm.)	(8)	(8)	(7)	(10)	(7)	(16)	(25)	(8)	(12)	(8)	(8)
								(obbligato parts inverted)			

BWV 1039 and 1027:	65	+	16	+	61
BWV 1027a:	65	+	16	+	50

* Eleven bars of this section omitted in the organ transcription.

Figure 1 The form of the fourth movement of BWV 1039/1027

The fact that the transposition was made in the organ transcription automatically raises doubts as to its authenticity. The final note of the A^1 bass line in measure 114, E, is immediately followed by an a, instead of the A which BWV 1039 and BWV 1027 use. It simply does not make any sense that Bach would have transposed the figure down an octave, only to return immediately to the same register in which it began. The E half-note in measure 114 is even more peculiar. Although not melodically identical, the bass lines of A^1 and A^2 in BWV 1039 and BWV 1027 have the same rhythm. It is hard to see Bach replacing the ♩ ♩ ♩ ♩ of the figure with something as motivically incoherent as this half-note. Another oddity is the abrupt and awkward tonal shift from A minor to G major in measures 115–16. There is also a modulation to G major in measure 115 of BWV 1039 and BWV 1027 (the tonic cadence is arrived at a bar later), but it is followed by a circle-of-fifths progression which ultimately leads to E minor (mm. 122–3), resulting in a smooth transition to the G major tonality of the final bars. Again, that Bach would have modulated to G major here with little if any preparation seems highly unlikely. A final peculiarity is that measure 115 of the organ transcription is its only measure which is not a component of a larger unit. It merely provides a one-bar interlude between A and B.

What the transcriber appears to have done is quite obvious. He evidently decided to omit measures 115–25 of the original altogether, probably because of the problems in adapting the continuo to a pedalboard.[41] Besides being very rapid, the continuo ascends above c' in measures 121–2. The transcriber had already dealt with the same material in measures 49–60 – and not altogether successfully, one might add (see Example 15). Perhaps he did not wish to bother with it a second time. He probably substituted ♩ — for ♩ ♩ ♩ ♩ in measure 114 because a half-rest gives the performer more time to prepare for the abrupt register shift from E to a in measure 115. Had the octave transposition not taken place in measures 112–14, the three quarters could have been incorporated with no problems. It would have been impossible to proceed directly from A^1 to B without some type of transitional material, which is the function of measure 115. Only the lower two voices of the measure seem to have been composed by the transcriber, who may have derived the rhythm of the pedal voice from the continuo at measure 126; the upper obbligato part is evidently a literal transcription of Violin 1 at measure 126 (minus the tie on the first note).[42]

---

[41] This is also Hermann Keller's opinion. See his *Die Orgelwerke Bachs* (Leipzig, 1948), p. 109.

[42] The organ transcription is probably also corrupt in measure 86, where the middle voice uses rests instead of quarter-notes (most likely due to a copying error), and in measure 124, where the middle voice has quarters instead of eighths (evidently another instance of a simplification made by the transcriber to ease technical difficulties).

All of which brings us to the question of who, besides Bach, might have
prepared the transcription. Kellner has to be considered as a candidate, not
only because of the likelihood that he made the other two transcriptions
(which suggests that he may have prepared a transcription of the entire violin sonata), but also because of his ties to Mempell, which are documented
by certain manuscripts. Mempell owned one of Kellner's Bach copies, and
Kellner owned one of Mempell's Bach copies. Moreover, Mempell and his
principal copyist (the scribe of the fourth-movement transcription) prepared copies of Kellner's keyboard music.[43] Kellner and Mempell also lived
within close proximity to one another: Gräfenroda (where Kellner lived)
and Heyda (where Mempell was born and where he presumably lived until
around 1740) are neighboring villages. (These circumstances have given rise
to the belief that Mempell may have been a Kellner pupil.)[44] And since it
cannot be demonstrated from what sources Mempell and his scribe prepared their Bach copies, it seems likely that they used lost Kellner copies as
exemplars, especially considering that Kellner is the only member of the
Bach circle to whom Mempell is known to have had ties. The assumption
that Mempell's scribe made a copy of a Kellner transcription is also supported by the range of the present transcription's pedal part, which shows
that it too was conceived for an instrument with a pedal compass of C–c'.[45]
Finally, the corrupt nature of the transcription – most notably the excision
of several bars near the end – brings the second-movement transcription to
mind.

Despite these factors, however, the discrepancies between the fourth-
movement transcription and those of the first and second movements,
outlined above, are substantial enough to suggest that someone other than

---

[43] For particulars on these sources, see Schulze, "Wie entstand," pp. 115–16; Schulze, *Studien
zur Bach-Überlieferung*, pp. 82–3; *NBA* IV/5–6, *KB*, pp. 94–5 and 192–4; and Stinson,
"The Bach Manuscripts," pp. 67–8. The Kellner copy owned by Mempell contains the
Prelude in C Sharp Major (BWV 848/1) from Book I of the *Well-Tempered Clavier*, and it
currently comprises a fascicle in MS 8 from the *Sammlung Mempell-Preller* (Musikbibliothek
der Stadt Leipzig). Although Schulze assigns this copy to Wolfgang Nicolaus Mey (?–?), a
member of Kellner's circle, it is unquestionably in Kellner's hand. See Stinson, "The Bach
Manuscripts," pp. 47–8, 114, and 166–7.

[44] See Schulze, "Wie entstand," pp. 116–17, and *Studien zur Bach Überlieferung*, pp. 83–4.

[45] Notes below *C* and above *c'* are once again avoided. Both Seiffert and Lohmann (see note 4)
print a $c\sharp'$ for the fourth beat of the pedal part in measure 55 of their editions. The MS 7
copy, however, clearly reads b, and there is no reason to question the reading on musical
grounds. Moreover, if the transcriber's pedalboard had extended to $c\sharp'$, he surely would have
made the second half of measure 51 conform to that of measures 49 and 53 by using four
eighths in the order: b–$c\sharp'$–a–b (see Example 15).

Kellner is involved – someone like Mempell or his copyist. The general carelessness with which the transcription was made suggests that the MS 7 score could represent the copyist's working score for a transcription of his own. Mempell's interest in the organ trio is documented by the inclusion of seven such works in the *Sammlung Mempell-Preller* in copies either by himself or by his scribe.[46] More significant, at least three of these trios are transcriptions.[47] Whether the model for the present transcription was a lost organ transcription – a possibility mentioned above in connection with the transfer of continuo material to the left hand – or the lost violin sonata itself must remain open. If the model were a lost Kellner transcription, one would like to believe that it too consistently assigned Violin 1 to the right hand, Violin 2 (transposed down an octave) to the left hand, and the continuo to the pedal, and that the arranger of the surviving transcription deviated from Kellner's method in order to compensate for his own relatively poor organ technique.[48]

Although we may never know who was responsible for these transcriptions, it is safe to assume that none was prepared by Bach himself. This realization does little to diminish their importance as examples of eighteenth-century transcription practice. Nor does it obscure the fact that all three are crucial to our understanding of a lost Bach chamber work. For this reason alone they deserve to be better known to scholars and performers alike.

[46] See Krause, pp. 29 (entries 1–3), 31 (entry 16) and 33–4 (entries 28 and 32); Schulze, "Wie entstand," p. 112; and Schulze, *Studien zur Bach-Überlieferung*, p. 78, for particulars.

[47] In addition to the fourth-movement transcription, MS 7 contains a copy of the Trio in C Minor (BWV 585), an arrangement of the first two movements of a sonata for two violins and continuo by J. F. Fasch. MS S × 11 (Musikbibliothek der Stadt Leipzig) contains an organ transcription of a trio by Pietro Locatelli, whose original version has not survived. (I would like to thank Dr Hans-Joachim Schulze of the Bach-Archiv, Leipzig, for confirming my suspicion that this organ trio is indeed a transcription.) MS 7 also contains the Trio in G Major (BWV 586), a work which is evidently either a transcription of a Telemann trio or merely based on a theme by Telemann. If the former is the case, the *Sammlung Mempell-Preller* would include not three but four organ trio transcriptions. On BWV 585 and 586, see Williams, *The Organ Works*, Vol. 1, pp. 269–71.

[48] I have been unable to locate any information on the organs Kellner and Mempell had at their disposal which might shed light on the authorship of this transcription or either of the other two trios.

"This fantasia. . .never had its like": on the enigma and chronology of Bach's Chromatic Fantasia and Fugue in D Minor, BWV 903

GEORGE B. STAUFFER

I have taken infinite pains to discover another piece of this kind by Bach, but in vain. This fantasia is unique, and never had its like.

Thus spoke Johann Nicolaus Forkel of the Chromatic Fantasia and Fugue in D Minor, BWV 903, in his ground-breaking Bach biography of 1802.[1] Time has shown Forkel to be correct in his assessment of the piece, for the Fantasia's daring chromatic passage-work, bold harmonic excursions and free recitative, and the Fugue's dramatic unfolding and climactic conclusion, have proven to have no stylistic equal in Bach's *œuvre*.

Yet for music historians, Forkel's comment has taken on a second meaning, for in terms of its genesis, too, the Chromatic Fantasia and Fugue is unique. No other Bach work seems to have undergone such a prolonged evolution. This evolution began with Bach's composition of the piece and continued, presumably at a somewhat later date, with his full-scale revision of the Fantasia and his refinement of numerous details in both the Fantasia and the Fugue. In this altered state, the Chromatic Fantasia and Fugue resembled other Bach keyboard works, which were subjected to a steady

This essay is based on a greatly expanded version of a paper presented at the "Wissenschaftliche Konferenz J. S. Bach," Karl-Marx-Universität, Leipzig. The German version has been published under the title "'Diese Fantasie ist einzig. . .und hat nie ihres gleichen gehabt' – Zur Rätselhaftigkeit und zur Chronologie der Bachschen Chromatischen Fantasie und Fugue BWV 903," in *Bericht über die wissenschaftliche Konferenz "J. S. Bach – Weltbild, Menschenbild, Notenbild, Klangbild"* (Leipzig, 1988). I am indebted to the Research Foundation of CUNY and to the John Simon Guggenheim Memorial Foundation for financial support that facilitated research on the early sources of the Chromatic Fantasia and Fugue.

[1] Johann Nicolaus Forkel, *Über Johann Sebastian Bachs Leben, Kunst und Kunstwerke* (Leipzig, 1802); modern reprint, ed. Walther Vetter (Berlin, 1982), p. 98.

flow of improvements during the composer's lifetime.[2] But unlike other pieces, the Fantasia and Fugue does not seem to have stopped evolving after Bach's death in 1750. On the contrary, it appears to have gained new life. If we are able to trust the earliest surviving sources of the work, the manuscript copies most directly connected with Bach and his circle, the lost autographs (there must have been at least two) of the Fantasia and Fugue were relatively neutral as far as performance indications are concerned. We can hypothesize with reasonable assurance that Bach's personal copies were "clean" manuscripts, much like the well-known autograph of *Well-Tempered Clavier* I, Berlin, DSB, P 415,[3] which is almost devoid of performance indications.[4]

But again to judge from the extant sources, the Chromatic Fantasia and Fugue appears to have acquired accretions in startling number after 1750. Cues for the execution of the *passaggi* were introduced, in the form of "sinistra" and "destra" indications (in Berlin, SPK, P 295 or P 320, for instance), fingering (in Berlin, SPK, P 887, P 1152, or Bologna, CM, DD 78), or broken flags and directed note stems (in Berlin, SPK, P 212, P 228, or the Hoffmeister & Kühnel print of 1802); in the earliest copies of the work (Berlin, DSB, P 803, and Berlin, SPK, P 275, P 421, and P 651), no such aids are to be found (Example 1). Dynamic markings *á la empfindsamer Stil* were written into the Fantasia (in Berlin, SPK, P 577). The "dorian" notation of the Fantasia, that is, D minor notated without a B♭ in the key signature, was modernized (in Berlin, SPK, P 212, P 1083 and other manuscripts). The arpeggios of the Fantasia, most certainly notated as half-note chords in Bach's original manuscripts, were written out in full (in Berlin, SPK, P 551, P 577, and P 1152).[5] Ornaments, too, were presented more specifically (in P 212 or the Hoffmeister print).

[2] On Bach's habit of constant revision see George Stauffer, "J. S. Bach as Reviser of his own Keyboard Works," *Early Music*, 13 (1985), pp. 185–98.

[3] For an explanation of the library sigla used in this article, see note 20.

[4] See the facsimile edition, *Johann Sebastian Bach: Das Wohltemperirte Clavier* (Leipzig, 1971), as well as Walther Dehnhard, "Beobachtungen am Autograph von Bachs Wohltemperierte Klavier I," in *Festschrift für Helmut Walcha zum 70 Geburtstag* (Frankfurt, 1978), pp. 92–106, and Alfred Dürr, *Zur frühgeschichte des Wohltemperierten Klaviers I von Johann Sebastian Bach* (Göttingen, 1984).

[5] The text of the written-out arpeggios found in P 551, P 577, and P 1152 is given in *Bach-Gesamtausgabe* XXXVI (1890), pp. xliii–xliv. In the manuscript Salzburg, DA, MN 104, measure 27 of the Fantasia is written in a manner which implies that each chord in the arpeggio passage is to be rolled twice:

Example 1 Performance indications added to the Chromatic Fantasia, mm. 1–2

a *P 421*, "clean" score, without indications, characteristic of pre-1750 sources

b *P 320*, distribution of notes indicated through "sinistra" (left hand) and "destra" (right hand) markings

c *P 887*, distribution of notes indicated through fingering

d *P 212*, distribution of notes indicated through broken flags and directed note stems

By the nineteenth century, the incrustations coating the Fantasia had become so thick that Conrad Friedrich Griepenkerl found it necessary to add a third staff to accommodate them in his Peters edition of 1819 (see Plate 1, which shows a page from Griepenkerl's edition and a page from the early manuscript copy P 421). Griepenkerl used the auxiliary staff to illustrate the precise manner in which "ambiguously notated" passages were to be played. We cannot reject these posthumous additions as having nothing to do with the composer, however, for Griepenkerl was quick to point out that his edition of the Chromatic Fantasia and Fugue, with its "Indication of a Proper Realization," reflected a performance tradition that ran "from J. S.

Plate 1   Chromatic Fantasia in the manuscript P 421 of 1730 and
the Peters Edition of 1819, edited by Griepenkerl

Bach to Wilhelm Friedemann Bach, from him to Forkel, and from Forkel to his students" – that is, to Griepenkerl himself.[6] Thus the umbilical cord connecting the Fantasia and Fugue with its composer was not severed until 1819, a full 69 years after Bach's mortal remains were laid to earth. This is truly the case of a work living beyond its composer's grave.

And almost needless to say, the additions to the Chromatic Fantasia and Fugue did not cease in 1819. In the Peters Edition of 1839, Griepenkerl's basic text was retained, but new *crescendo* and *diminuendo* signs, *mezzo forte* and *mezzo piano* markings, and metronome indications were added, courtesy of Carl Czerny.[7] In the *Bach-Gesellschaft* edition of 1890 these excesses were eliminated, but Bach's harmonic vocabulary was updated, so that the "Urvater deutscher Harmonie" ("forefather of German harmony"), to use Forkel's apt epithet, now spoke in modern double accidentals (B♭♭ instead of A♮ in measure 50 of the Fantasia, for instance).[8] And in 1910, the final word on Bach's harmonic language in the Chromatic Fantasia and Fugue was uttered by no less than Heinrich Schenker, who based his Universal edition on the *Bach-Gesellschaft* text, but added an extensive introduction in which he analyzed Bach's masterpiece measure by measure.[9]

In retrospect, it is not difficult to understand why the Chromatic Fantasia and Fugue experienced such a prolonged period of gestation. In the second half of the eighteenth century, the Fantasia's expressive recitative writing was quite in step with the vocal ideals espoused by the Enlightenment movement.[10] And the work's rapid changes of emotion and bold harmonic digressions insured its adoption by a generation of composers ruled by *Sturm und Drang* passions. In terms of style, the Chromatic Fantasia and Fugue resembled the progressive free fantasias of Wilhelm Friedemann and

---

[6] *Chromatische Fantasie für das Pianoforte von Johann Sebastian Bach*, ed. Conrad Friedrich Griepenkerl (Leipzig, 1819). The title page includes the remark: "Neue Ausgabe mit einer Bezeichnung ihres wahren Vortrags, wie derselbe von J. S. Bach auf W. Friedemann Bach, von diesem auf Forkel und von Forkel auf seine Schüler gekommen."

[7] *Compositions pour le Piano-Forte sans et avec accompagnement par Jean Sebastien Bach*, ed. Carl Czerny (Leipzig, 1839).

[8] *BG* XXXVI, ed. Ernst Naumann (Leipzig, 1890).

[9] *J. S. Bach: Chromatische Phantasie und Fuge: Kritische Ausgabe*, ed. Heinrich Schenker (Vienna, 1910). Schenker's edition has recently been republished in an annotated English format: *Heinrich Schenker: J. S. Bach's Chromatic Fantasia & Fugue: A Critical Edition and Commentary*, ed. and trans. Hedi Siegel (New York, 1984).

[10] The recitative in the Fantasia is discussed at length in Hans David's classic study, "Die Gestalt von Bachs Chromatischer Fantasie," *Bach-Jahrbuch*, 23 (1926), pp. 23–68, and in Peter Schleuning, "'Diese Fantasie ist einzig. . .': Das Recitativ in Bachs Chromatischer Fantasie und seine Bedeutung für die Ausbildung der Freien Fantasie," in *Bach Interpretationen*, ed. Martin Geck (Göttingen, 1969), pp. 57–73.

Carl Philipp Emanuel Bach, and it is no surprise to see it transmitted side by side with their works in eighteenth-century manuscripts (in P 212, P 275 or Berlin, SPK, P 295, for instance). We know, too, from Forkel and from the source tradition, that both Wilhelm Friedemann and Carl Philipp Emanuel Bach championed the Chromatic Fantasia and Fugue and played a vital role in its dissemination. In a memorable account, Charles Burney described the playing of C. P. E. Bach, as observed in Hamburg in 1770:

After dinner, which was elegantly served, and cheerfully eaten, I prevailed upon him [C. P. E. Bach] to sit down again at the clavichord, and he played, with little inter-mission, till near eleven o'clock at night. During this time he grew so animated and possessed that he not only played, but looked like one inspired. His eyes were fixed, his lower lip fell, and drops of effervescence distilled from his countenance.[11]

Of J. S. Bach's clavier works, only the Chromatic Fantasia and Fugue would have been fully appropriate to Carl Philipp Emanuel's "possessed" manner of performance. The perpetual modernity of the work is under-lined by the gesture of an anonymous Viennese scribe, who after complet-ing a copy of the Fugue around 1800 (in the manuscript Berlin, SPK, Mus. MS 30125), christened Bach's text with the critical judgment: "sehr gut."

Another decisive factor was the suitability of the work for performance on the clavichord and fortepiano, the instruments of the future. There seems to be little doubt that the Chromatic Fantasia and Fugue was written for the harpsichord, since the terms "Cembalo" and "Clavessin" appear regularly in the title of the piece in the earliest sources.[12] But performance on the clavichord or fortepiano was not only *possible* – it seemed to impart even greater animation to the work's theatrical elements. Even before the 1819 Peters Edition appeared with its "für das Pianoforte" label,[13] A. F. C. Kollmann, writing in England, referred to the Fantasia as "a sublime chro-matic sonata for the Piano Forte."[14] And indeed, the work found welcom-ing proponents among the great Romantic pianists. Thus it seems only right that in 1879 Philipp Spitta, whose Bach biography would hold sway almost to the present day, should give the Chromatic Fantasia a final stamp

[11] Charles Burney, *The Present State of Music in Germany, the Netherlands, and the United Provinces* (London, 1773), p. 269.
[12] "Fantasia pour Clavessin" in Darmstadt, HL, Mus. MS 69; "Fantasie chromatique pour le Clavecin" in P 803 (two nearly identical copies); or "Fantasia chromatica pro Cimbalo" in P 421, for example.
[13] See note 6.
[14] A. F. C. Kollmann, *An Essay on Practical Musical Composition* (London, 1799), p. 36.

of nineteenth-century approval by terming it "an emotional *scena*," a phrase drawn from the world of opera.[15]

It is this long, rich, and very complex history that has produced what we might well term the "enigma" of the Chromatic Fantasia and Fugue. We can say with confidence that the work is one of Bach's most important keyboard compositions, but as soon as we pose probing questions about it, we find ourselves enveloped in a mist of uncertainty. Which elements of the Chromatic Fantasia text belong to Bach and which elements to his sons and his students? Which stages of the work's genesis took place during the composer's lifetime? And most critical, perhaps: how does the Chromatic Fantasia fit into Bach's compositional output? A proper response to these questions will surely require a book-length study, and we can hope that some matters, at least, will be resolved in the *Kritischer Bericht* of *Neue Bach-Ausgabe* V/9, when it appears.[16] In the present essay, I should like to explore briefly two aspects that may shed light on the Chromatic Fantasia and Fugue's origin and early evolution. These aspects are the surviving source material and the style of the early variant, BWV 903a.

The source material

The early manuscript and printed sources of the Chromatic Fantasia and Fugue were first outlined in Hans Bischoff's Steingraber edition of 1880.[17] Ten years later, Ernst Naumann presented a more systematic list in his *Bach-Gesellschaft* edition.[18] And in 1926, Hans David reappraised the work of Bischoff and Naumann and drew up the source stemma that has served as the standard down to the present day.[19] With the help of recent studies undertaken in conjunction with the editing of the *NBA*, we can now expand David's list considerably – from seventeen to 37 sources – and we can fill in many details about scribes and dates. David portrayed the manuscripts of the Fantasia as branching out cleanly from three lost auto-

---

[15] Philipp Spitta, *Johann Sebastian Bach* (Leipzig, 1873 and 1879); English edition, trans. Clara Bell and J. A. Fuller-Maitland (London, 1889; reprint, New York, 1952), Vol. 3, p. 182.

[16] Work on Volume V/9 of the *NBA* is currently in progress.

[17] *J. S. Bach: Klavier-Werke*, ed. Hans Bischoff (Leipzig, 1880–8), pp. 110–21.

[18] *BG* XXXVI, pp. xi–xlvii.

[19] David, "Die Gestalt von Bachs Chromatischer Fantasie," p. 59. The source summary in the recently published Henle edition (*Joh. Seb. Bach: Chromatische Fantasie und Fuge*, ed. Georg von Dadelsen and Klaus Rönnau [Munich, 1978]), for instance, is drawn directly from David's findings.

graphs. The addition of nineteen new sources greatly complicates this picture, rendering a stemma tracing the relationship of all the manuscripts back to three autographs highly speculative. It is more useful to group the manuscripts by their probable sphere of origin. Viewed in this fashion, the early sources of the Chromatic Fantasia and Fugue can be listed as follows:

Table 1

Manuscript[20]	Scribe and probable date
BWV 903:	
Krebs circle:	
Berlin, DSB, P 803 (pp. 345–61)	Johann Tobias Krebs (1690–1762) Copying Bach works, *ca*. 1710–at least 1751
Berlin, DSB, P 803 (pp. 185–201)	Samuel Gottlieb Heder[21] (b.1713) Copying for Bach, 1729–31
Leipzig circle:	
Berlin, SPK, P 421 (pp. 2–24)	Anonymous scribe Date: "den 6. December 1730"[22]

---

[20] The library sigla are as follows:
   Berlin, DSB=Berlin-East, Deutsche Staatsbibliothek
   Berlin, HK=Berlin-West, Hochschule der Künste
   Berlin, SPK=Berlin-West, Staatsbibliothek Preussischer Kulturbesitz
   Bologna, CM=Bologna, Civico Museo
   Brussels, CR=Brussels, Conservatoire Royal de Musique
   Copenhagen, KB=Copenhagen, Det kongelige Bibliotek
   Darmstadt, HL=Darmstadt, Hessische Landes- und Hochschulbibliothek
   Dresden, SL=Dresden, Sächsische Landesbibliothek
   Leipzig, BA=Leipzig, Bach-Archiv
   Lubeck, BH=Lubeck, Bibliothek der Hansestadt Lubeck
   New Haven, Ya=New Haven, Music Library of Yale University
   Paris, BA=Paris, Bibliothèque de l'Arsenal
   Salzburg, DA=Salzburg, Domarchiv
   Salzburg, Mo=Salzburg, Mozarteum
   Vienna, GM=Vienna, Gesellschaft der Musikfreunde
[21] Hans-Joachim Schulze, *Studien zur Bach-Überlieferung im 18. Jahrhundert* (Leipzig-Dresden, 1984), p. 120.
[22] The watermark of P 421 is an unusual type, a "Coat of Arms from Schönau," not found in any Bach autograph material (see *NBA* IX/1). Similar Schönau coats of arms appear as watermarks in manuscripts written in the Nuremberg region (information courtesy of Yoshitake Kobayashi).

Table 1 (*cont.*)

Manuscript[20]	Scribe and probable date
Berlin, SPK, P 651	Johann Friedrich Agricola (1720–74) Date: *ca.* 1740.[23] Title in the hand of C. P. E. Bach.
C. P. E. Bach circle:	
Berlin, SPK, P 275 (Fantasia only; pp. 40–1)	Johann Gottfried Müthel (1728–88) With Bach, 1750; with C. P. E. Bach, 1750–3[24]
Berlin, SPK, P 289 (pp. 23–33)	Anonymous 300,[25] a Berlin copyist Date: *ca.* 1755–late 1760s
Berlin, SPK, P 887	Anonymous 300 Date: *ca.* 1755–late 1760s
Leipzig, MB, MS 2a (pp. 159–69)	Anonymous Hamburg copyist Date: after 1802[26]
Connected with the Amalien-Bibliothek:	
Berlin, DSB, AmB 548	Anonymous J. S. Bach I and XIV of the Amalien-Bibliothek[27] Date: between 1758–83. Title in the hand of Johann Philipp Kirnberger.
Berlin, SPK, AmB 56	Anonymous J. S. Bach I of the Amalien-Bibliothek Date: between 1758–83
Berlin, SPK, N.Mus.MS 10487	Anonymous 403[28] Date: between 1758–83
Salzburg, Mo	Anonymous J. S. Bach IX of the Amalien-Bibliothek[29] Date: between 1758–83

---

[23] Alfred Dürr, "Zur Chronologie der Handschrift Johann Christoph Altnickols und Johann Friedrich Agricolas," *Bach-Jahrbuch*, 56 (1970), pp. 44–65.

[24] The watermark of P 275 is a *fleur-de-lis* appearing in Dutch paper that was widely used and widely imitated in Germany (information courtesy of Yoshitake Kobayashi).

[25] So named in the *Tübinger Bach-Studien* series.

[26] The manuscript contains quotations from Forkel's *Über Johann Sebastian Bachs Leben, Kunst und Kunstwerke*, published in 1802.

[27] So named in Eva Renate Blechschmidt, *Die Amalien-Bibliothek* (Berlin, 1965).

[28] So named in the *Tübinger Bach-Studien* series. Anonymous 403 appears to be the same scribe as Anonymous J. S. Bach XIII and Anonymous J. S. Bach III of the Amalien-Bibliothek (information courtesy of Alfred Dürr and Yoshitake Kobayashi).

[29] Anonymous J. S. Bach IX of the Amalien-Bibliothek seems to have also worked as a scribe for the publishing house of Breitkopf.

Table 1 (*cont.*)

Manuscript[20]	Scribe and probable date
Berlin, SPK, P 551 (Fantasia only; pp. 1–6)	"Gebhardt"[30] Date: 2nd half of eighteenth century
Berlin, SPK, P 535 (Fugue only; pp. 4–11)	"Gebhardt" Date: second half of eighteenth century
Berlin, SPK, P 577	"Gebhardt" Date: second half of eighteenth century
Berlin, SPK, P 1152 (pp. 1–15)	"Gebhardt" Date: second half of eighteenth century
Kittel circle:	
Berlin, SPK, P 320 (pp. 12–19)	Johann Nicolaus Gebhardi[31] Date: *ca.* 1800
New Haven, Ya, LM 4838 (pp. 18–30)	Kittel circle scribe Date: *ca.* 1800
W. F. Bach–Forkel circle:[32]	
Berlin, SPK, P 212 (pp. 1–8)	Johann Nicolaus Forkel (1749–1818)
Berlin, SPK, P 1083	Anonymous copyist Date: *ca.* 1800
Hoffmeister & Kühnel print	Edited by Forkel Leipzig and Vienna, 1802
Berlin, SPK, P 228 (pp. 101–15)	Anonymous Berlin copyist Copy of Hoffmeister & Kühnel print
Brussels, CR, U 12.209	Anonymous copyist ("C. Güntersberg"?[33]) Copy of Hoffmeister & Kühnel print

[30] P 551, P 535, P 577, and P 1152 are most certainly written by the same scribe, who signed his name "Gebhardt" (or "Gebhardtti"?) in P 551. The handwriting is not the same as that of J. N. Gebhardi, copyist of P 320.

[31] Yoshitake Kobayashi, *Franz Hauser und seine Bach-Handschriftensammlung* (Göttingen, unpublished dissertation, 1973), p. 92.

[32] According to his own account, Forkel received his copy of the Chromatic Fantasia from Wilhelm Friedemann Bach during the latter's residence in Braunschweig between 1770 and 1774 (*Über Johann Sebastian Bachs Leben, Kunst und Kunstwerke*, p. 98).

[33] Güntersberg's name appears on U 12.209 as "possessor" of the manuscript.

Table 1 (*cont.*)

Manuscript[20]	Scribe and probable date
Peters print	Edited by Griepenkerl Leipzig, 1819. Incorporates several pages from Hoffmeister & Kühnel print.
Lübeck, BH, N 406	Anonymous copyist Copy of Peters print
Vienna:	
Berlin, SPK, Mus. MS 30125 (pp. 2–10)	Anonymous Viennese copyist Date: second half of eighteenth century
Salzburg, DA, MN 104 (pp. 1–16)	Johann Gallus Mederitsch (1752–1835)
Vienna, GM, Q 11732 (Fugue only)	Anonymous Viennese copyist Date: *ca.* 1800
Nuremberg:	
Private collection (Fugue only)	Leonhard Scholz (1720–98)
France:	
Paris, BA, Ms. M.6796 (Fantasia only; fos. 150–1)	Anonymous French copyist[34] Date: second half of eighteenth century
Italy:	
Bologna, CM, DD 78	Anonymous Italian copyist Date: second half of eighteenth century
Provenance unclear:	
Berlin, SPK, P 295 (pp. 302–13)	Anonymous copyist Date: second half of eighteenth century. "Sinistra" and "destra" indications resemble those of *P 320*, but variant readings do not.
Berlin, HK, 6138/20	Ernst Rudorff (1840–1916)
Copenhagen, KB, Weyse Collection	Anonymous copyist Date: second half of eighteenth century
Göttingen/Rosdorf, Eisenberg Collection	Anonymous copyist Date: second half of eighteenth century
Leipzig, BA, *Go.S.26* (Fugue only)	Gustav Hohlstein Date: 1841–5[35]

[34] Mary Cyr, "Bach's Music in France: A New Source," *Early Music*, 13 (1985), pp. 256–9.

[35] Hans-Joachim Schulze, *Sammlung Manfred Gorke* (Leipzig, 1977), p. 19.

Table 1 (*cont.*)

Manuscript[20]	Scribe and probable date
Present whereabouts unknown:	
Dresden, SL, *Mus. 2405-T-48*	Anonymous copyist
(formerly *Mus.c.Ch 52*; Fantasia	Amalien-Bibliothek tradition[36]
only)	Lost since World War II
Munich	Johann Elias Bach
	Lost since 1949–50[37]
BWV 903a.	
Darmstadt:	
Darmstadt, HL, *Mus. MS 69*	Anonymous Darmstadt copyist
	Date: between 1731–5[38]
Present whereabouts unknown:	
Leipzig, Wilhelm Rust Collection	J. L. A. Rust[39]
	Date: 'Bernburg 1757'

This list tells us a number of things about the Chromatic Fantasia and Fugue. First, it attests to the broad dissemination of the work. As might be expected, the Chromatic Fantasia, like many of Bach's other keyboard pieces, was circulated chiefly by the composer's sons and students. We can discern circles centering around Wilhelm Friedemann and Carl Philipp Emanuel Bach well as around the Bach pupils Johann Tobias Krebs, Johann Friedrich Agricola, Johann Philipp Kirnberger (Director of the Amalien-Bibliothek) and Johann Christian Kittel. And it is not altogether surprising to see the Fantasia appearing in manuscripts written in Nuremberg and Darmstadt, for recent investigations of collections from those areas have turned up sizeable deposits of Bach keyboard works.[40] Quite unprecedented, however, are the manuscripts from Vienna, Italy and France. That the Chromatic Fantasia and Fugue was being copied in the eighteenth century in such distant and diverse foreign centers illustrates the truly universal nature of the work's appeal.

[36] According to David, "Die Gestalt von Bachs Chromatischer Fantasie," p. 59.
[37] *Bach-Jahrbuch*, 38 (1949/50), p. 123.
[38] See discussion on p. 175.
[39] *BG* XXXVI, p. xlii.
[40] On the Nuremberg Bach manuscripts see *NBA* IV/5 and 6, *KB*, Vol. 1, pp. 159–60; on the Darmstadt scores, see Schulze, *Studien zur Bach-Überlieferung*, p. 23.

Second, the survey of sources also shows that the Chromatic Fantasia was a piece much in demand by connoisseurs. We can see a good number of professional scribes at work, in C. P. E. Bach's circle (Anonymous 300 and the writer of MS 2a), at the Amalien-Bibliothek (the anonymous copyists of the library as well as "Gebhardt"), and at the Darmstadt court (see comments on the Darmstadt copyist, below). Not only did these vocational writers produce neat, reliable manuscripts (which may account in part for the relative stability of the text of the last version of the Chromatic Fantasia and Fugue); they made copies to order, with the upper staff written in treble or soprano clef,[41] or of the Fantasia or Fugue alone (see the copies by "Gebhardt").

The role of the professional copyists gives a new slant to the controversial *piano* and *forte* markings found solely in P 577. These dynamic markings, adopted by Naumann in the *Bach-Gesamtausgabe*, were rightly criticized by David, who stressed their stylistic inconsistency with Bach's text. David concluded that the indications probably originated with the scribe of P 577 and have no earlier source.[42] If "Gebhardt" was a professional scribe, as he appears to have been, then the impetus for adding the dynamic markings to P 577 becomes clear: rather than slavishly following Bach's text in the manner of a student or disciple, "Gebhardt" undoubtedly strove to please the commissioner of his manuscript. From the viewpoint of marketability, the dynamic markings made P 577 more attractive, more up-to-date. This, too, may account for the written-out arpeggios found in the "Gebhardt" series, first appearing as an insert (P 551) and then penned directly into the text (P 577 and P 1152). The short incipit for the arpeggios found in Salzburg, DA, MN 104,[43] would seem to merit more serious attention.

While the manuscripts reveal much about the Chromatic Fantasia and Fugue's dissemination, they show less about its chronology. Bach's original materials are lost, and no more than five of the extant manuscripts – P 421, Darmstadt Mus. MS 69, P 803 (Krebs and Heder copies) and P 651 – appear to have originated during Bach's lifetime. Of these, only P 421, inscribed "den 6. December 1730," can be dated with certainty. As Spitta pointed out over a century ago, 1730 undoubtedly represents no more than a *terminus post quem non* for the most mature version of the Fantasia and Fugue. The work must go back to an earlier time.

[41] Anonymous 300: treble clef in P 289, soprano clef in P 887; "Gebhardt": treble clef in P 535, P 551, and P 1152, soprano clef in P 577. The Darmstadt scribe generally transferred works written in the treble clef to soprano clef as he copied, to judge from his manuscripts of other Bach pieces.

[42] David, "Die Gestalt von Bachs Chromatischer Fantasie," pp. 56–7.

[43] See note 5.

Although the sources do not tell us *how* early, they provide material for speculation. For one thing, the surviving copies point rather unambiguously to three stages of development. In the first, represented in the early variant BWV 903a found in Darmstadt Mus. MS 69 (and the now-lost J. L. A. Rust manuscript, whose text served as the basis for BWV 903a as printed in the *Bach-Gesellschaft* and elsewhere), the Fantasia had a different incipit, which we will discuss shortly. The Fugue, on the other hand, seems to have been born fully formed, except for a few details that Bach modified later. In the second stage, represented by the Johann Tobias Krebs and Samuel Gottlieb Heder copies in P 803, the opening of the Fantasia was reworked into the form that is generally known today. The single sharply distinctive feature of the second version is the *passaggio* at measures 21–4 of today's standard text, which in P 803 appears as a shorter, two-measure-long variant.[44] In the third and final stage, represented first in the anonymous manuscript P 421 of 1730, the *passaggio* of measures 21–4 (again, of today's standard text) of the Fantasia, which had appeared in BWV 903a, was merged into the P 803 text. This change seems to have been Bach's last major revision of the work, and it is essentially in this third form that the Fantasia and Fugue is passed down in the remaining manuscripts.[45]

Although the general contour of the Fantasia and Fugue remained the same after the second revision, a large number of surface details seem to have changed, especially in the Fantasia. The plethora of small variants suggests that Bach may have owned several autographs with slightly different readings, lending them out intermittently to students for the purpose of copying. Or he may have possessed only one autograph, but verbally passed on recommendations for improvements in the piece as his students wrote it out. Or it may be that Wilhem Friedemann Bach and Johann Christian Kittel willfully introduced the variants that distinguish the manuscripts of their circles from those of others. The lack of pre-1750 source material prevents us from determining which case was true.

The notation of the work also merits scrutiny. Aside from the manuscripts copied by professional scribes, the Chromatic Fantasia and Fugue is consistently transmitted in eighteenth-century sources with a treble clef in the upper staff, and with "dorian" notation in the Fantasia and "modern"

---

[44] The text of the P 803 *passaggio* variant is reproduced in *BG* XXXVI, p. xliii.

[45] Part of the "enigma" of the Chromatic Fantasia and Fugue is the order in which the three versions of the Fantasia were composed. The sequence presented here, also championed by Spitta, David, and others, seems to be the most logical, since BWV 903, in both the P 421 and P 803 forms, is clearly more sophisticated musically than BWV 903a. Nevertheless, one must note the fact that BWV 903a is longer than either version of BWV 903, and Bach very rarely shortened a work when revising it.

D minor in the Fugue. Bach's unusual notation of key has much logic. In the Fantasia, with its rapidly changing harmonic scheme, a B♭ in the key signature would have been as much of a hindrance as a help. In the more tonic- and dominant-oriented Fugue, a B♭ would be more welcome.[46] The consistency of the sources strongly suggests that this "mixed" key signature was Bach's original method of notation, and there is no reason to suppose – as there is for the Fantasia and Fugue in G Minor, BWV 542, for instance – that the Chromatic Fantasia and Fugue originated as two independent pieces.[47]

Given these notational idiosyncrasies, one must ask: at what point in his life did Bach adopt the modern D minor key signature seen in the Fugue and begin to notate keyboard works with the treble clef seen in the entire work? D minor notated with B♭ begins to appear sporadically in Weimar works composed around 1713–14 (Cantatas 208 and 162, for example). By around 1720, Bach seems to have adopted the modern D minor key signature as his standard (in Partita II for Unaccompanied Violin, BWV 1004, or the second movements of Brandenburg Concertos Nos. 1 and 2, for instance), departing from it only for purposes of modal writing. The treble clef also occurs occasionally in pre-Cöthen works, but then seemingly for two specific reasons in keyboard scores: for the right hand of obbligato organ parts in cantatas (Cantata 71) or for the right-hand parts of trios (*Nun komm, der Heiden Heiland*, BWV 660a). Bach does not seem to have used the treble clef with any frequency until the Cöthen period, when it begins to appear in progressive works. One observes it in the harpsichord part to Brandenburg Concerto No. 5, and in dance movements in the *Clavierbüchlein* for Wilhelm Friedemann Bach of 1720. Hence it may be that the Chromatic Fantasia and Fugue originated no earlier than Bach's Cöthen years.

When we turn to style, we also encounter obstacles to evaluation. As Forkel rightly observed, the Chromatic Fantasia *is* unique in terms of its

[46] There is a precedent for this sort of notation in Bach's autographs. In the manuscript Berlin, SPK, P 330, Bach wrote out the first movement of the Concerto in D Minor after Vivaldi, BWV 596, in "dorian" notation. When he reached the *Grave* introduction to the second movement (a fugue), he added B♭ to the key signature and retained it for the rest of the work.

[47] The Fantasia and the Fugue of BWV 542 were widely circulated as two independent pieces during Bach's lifetime and may not have been united in one manuscript until after his death (See George B. Stauffer, *The Organ Preludes of Johann Sebastian Bach* (Ann Arbor, 1980), p. 195). The Fantasia and the Fugue of BWV 903, by contrast, are consistently united in pre-1750 scores.

idiom. We can find traces of keyboard recitative in a number of presumably earlier compositions: the "Capriccio sopra la lontananza del suo fratello dilettissimo," BWV 992, the Toccata in D Minor, BWV 565, the Toccata in D Major, BWV 912, or the Fantasia in G Minor, BWV 542/1. But in none of these works is the keyboard recitative treated with similar mastery. In its bold approach to the *stylus phantasticus*, the mature version of the Chromatic Fantasia is *sui generis*. As such, it evades ready comparison. In its early form, BWV 903a, however, the Fantasia is less individual, and therein lies the opportunity to weigh it against other Bach pieces.

The early variant, BWV 903a

BWV 903a is passed down in Darmstadt Mus. MS 69, whose text agrees in all essentials with the J. L. A. Rust text reprinted in the *Bach-Gesamtausgabe*. The Darmstadt manuscript was written by an anonymous scribe, a professional copyist working in the midst of Johann Christoph Graupner and Johann Samuel Endler at the Darmstadt court (Graupner, of course, had been offered the Thomaskantor position ahead of Bach in 1723; Endler headed the Collegium Musicum in Leipzig just before Bach's arrival there). The watermarks in Mus. MS 69 appear in Darmstadt manuscripts dating from March 1731 to January 1735.[48] Thus it seems unlikely that Mus. MS 69 predates P 421 of 1730. In Mus. MS 69 both the Fantasia and the Fugue are notated with soprano clef in the upper staff and with a modern D minor key signature. But a telling number of superfluous B♭s in the Fantasia and transposition mistakes in the entire work make it clear that the scribe was copying from a manuscript in which the Fantasia was written in "dorian" notation, the Fugue in "modern" notation, and both with the treble clef. Thus if we wish to uphold the hypothesis that the earliest form of the Chromatic Fantasia and Fugue, too, dates after Weimar because of its notation, Mus. MS 69 offers no contradictory evidence.

Stylistically it is the first 23 measures of BWV 903a – the bars that differ from both versions of BWV 903 – that provide material for comparison. Two features of this opening stand out. The first is the triplet figuration, which is presented in a more continuous, uninterrupted form than in BWV 903. The triplets begin in the third measure and run unabated until measure 20, where they become thirty-second notes that flow into an arpeggiated cadence (Example 2). This unusual type of writing, which in

---

[48] For this information I am indebted to Dr Oswald Bill, Director of the Musikabteilung of the Hessische Landes- und Hochschulbibliothek, Darmstadt.

measures 13–22 displays the use of the left-hand voice as both a pedal-point (lower note) and a chromatic line (upper note), has its clearest equal in two other works. The first is the Prelude in D Minor, BWV 875/1, from *Well-Tempered Clavier* II. In the early form of the Prelude, BWV 875a, which goes back at least to the 1720s,[49] one finds the same figurations that appear in BWV 903a, albeit in a slightly more sophisticated, cross-hand guise (Example 3a). In the second example, the first-movement harpsichord cadenza to the early version of Brandenburg Concerto No. 5, BWV 1050a, the connection with BWV 903a is even more striking. Not only the left-hand figuration, but also the broader gestures – the stepwise, regularly shifting harmonies, the tense chromaticism, and the prolonged pedal-point emerging in a concluding cadence (Example 3b)[50] – are very similar. If Bach wrote the early version of Brandenburg Concerto No. 5, with its brilliant obbligato harpsichord part, for the new and presumably grand "harpsichord manufactured in Berlin" that he accompanied home to Cöthen for Prince Leopold in March 1719[51] – an oft-voiced theory – then it is possible that BWV 903a, penned in a similar style, is also somehow related to this instrument.

The second distinctive aspect of BWV 903a points in a similar direction: it is the low note, *AA*, that marks the end of the opening flourish (Example 2, last measure). When Bach revised the Fantasia, he omitted this note and concluded the introductory section four octaves higher, on *a″* (Example 4). The normal compass of German harpsichords in Bach's day was *C* to *c‴*, and the vast majority of Bach's clavier works, indeed most of the pieces in study collections such as the Inventions and Sinfonias, the French and English Suites, and the *Well-Tempered Clavier*, fall within this range. *AA* was a special note, and its presence in BWV 903a suggests that Bach had an unusual instrument at his disposal when he composed BWV 903a. When he reworked the Fantasia, he avoided the low *AA*, probably because it did not exist on the instrument for which he was now writing. Bach's solution, to reverse the direction of the melodic line and replace the low *AA* with an *a″*, reached *via* a dramatic and unexpected leap, improves the score and illustrates well his ability to turn a shortcoming to good advantage.

However, the alteration may also be telling us something about Bach's

---

[49] The earliest source of BWV 875/1 is the manuscript Berlin, SPK, Mus. MS P 1089, written by Bach student Johann Caspar Vogler between 1727–31. See Hans-Joachim Schulze, "'Das Stück in Goldpapier' – Ermittlungen zu einigen Bach-Abschriften des frühen 18. Jahrhunderts," *Bach-Jahrbuch*, 64 (1978), pp. 23–33.

[50] The text of the complete cadenza is given in *NBA* VII/2, Supplement.

[51] See *Bach-Dokumente* II, No. 95.

Example 2 The early variant, BWV 903a, mm. 1–23

Example 2 (*cont.*)

Example 3 Pedal-tone figurations in the early version of the Prelude in D Minor, BWV 875a, and in the harpsichord cadenza to the early version of Brandenburg Concerto No. 5, BWV 1050a

Example 4 Concluding measure of the opening section of
the Chromatic Fantasia, BWV 903 version

personal situation. As Alfred Dürr has shown,[52] trying to match the range
of Bach's clavier pieces with the range of his instruments is a treacherous
business. But in this case, I believe, we can argue convincingly that Bach's
deliberate (though ingenious) avoidance of low *AA* when revising the
Fantasia suggests that an instrument once at his disposal was no longer available. The most obvious instance in which we know this to be true is when
Bach moved from Cöthen to Leipzig in May of 1723, leaving the Cöthen
court's "harpsichord manufactured in Berlin" behind.

What sort of a harpsichord was this instrument? An 1784 "Inventory of
the Princely Instruments in the Music Chamber" from the Cöthen court
tells us. Under No. 32 we read: "The large clavecin. . .with two keyboards,
by Michael Mietke in Berlin, 1719."[53] Although Mietke's name has been
known to historians for some time, examples of his work surfaced only a few
years ago, in the form of two large harpsichords contained in the Schloss
Charlottenburg Collection in Berlin. A feature shared by the Charlottenburg harpsichords is the unusual depth of their original bass range: one
instrument extended down to *FF* (with *FF♯* and *GG♯* missing), the other to
GG (with *GG♯* missing).[54] It is to be admitted that the top note on both
harpsichords was originally *c'''*, which falls one note short of the *d'''* required
by the Chromatic Fantasia and Fugue. But the instrument made for Prince
Leopold would have been custom-designed as far the precise range was
concerned, allowing for the possibility of a high *d'''*. The Schloss Charlottenburg harpsichords demonstrate that Mietke was accustomed to going

---

[52] Alfred Dürr, "Tastenumfang und Chronologie in Bachs Klavierwerken," in *Festschrift Georg von Dadelsen zum 60. Geburtstag*, ed. Thomas Kohlhase and Volker Scherliess (Stuttgart, 1978), pp. 73–88.

[53] *Bach-Dokumente* II, No. 95, Commentary.

[54] See the description of the instruments by William R. Dowd, printed as Appendix C in Sheridan Germann, "The Mietkes, the Margrave and Bach," in *Bach, Handel, Scarlatti: Tercentenary Essays*, ed. Peter Williams (Cambridge, 1985), pp. 119–48.

beyond the standard *C–c'''* compass, especially at the bass end of the keyboard.

The notational and stylistic factors of BWV 903a, then, imply a Cöthen origin for the Chromatic Fantasia and Fugue, with revisions taking place later, in Leipzig (perhaps in 1729, when Bach assumed the directorship of the Collegium Musicum and had call once again for virtuoso clavier pieces?). Ironically, suggesting a possible date of composition of *ca.* 1720 parallels the chronologies proposed by Spitta and David on grounds that can now be discredited. Spitta assigned the Chromatic Fantasia and Fugue to *ca.* 1720 because of its similarity to the Fantasia and Fugue in G Minor, BWV 542, which he presumed to have been composed in the fall of 1720 for Bach's trip to Hamburg.[55] It is now quite certain that BWV 542 stems from an earlier time.[56] David assigned the early version of the Chromatic Fantasia and Fugue (BWV 903a) to *ca.* 1720 on the basis of similarities to toccata figurations occurring in the Prelude in D Minor, BWV 851/1, from *Well-Tempered Clavier* I, a piece that first appeared in the *Clavierbüchlein* for Wilhelm Friedemann Bach of 1720, and to recitative writing occurring in Bonporti's *Concertini e Serenate*, Op. 12, which David dated *ca.* 1720.[57] The Bonporti can now be assigned to a considerably later period, *ca.* 1745.[58]

That we seem to be grasping at straws in order to date the Chromatic Fantasia and Fugue only underlines the fact that we know distressingly little about the evolution of Bach's keyboard style before the appearance of *Well-Tempered Clavier* I in 1723. Between the youthful "Capriccio sopra la lontananza del suo fratello dilettissimo" of Arnstadt and the Inventions and Sinfonias and *Well-Tempered Clavier* I of Cöthen we have no precisely dateable clavier compositions. As a result, we lack a clear picture of Bach's compositional activity during this critical period of growth. Just as Hans-Joachim Schulze recently issued a plea for a full-length book on the transmission of the Bach sources,[59] we must conclude from our examination of the Chromatic Fantasia that there is an equally great need for an encompassing study of the development of Bach's keyboard style.

[55] Spitta, *Johann Sebastian Bach*, Vol. 3, pp. 181–2.

[56] Stauffer, *The Organ Preludes of Johann Sebastian Bach*, pp. 109–10.

[57] David, "Die Gestalt von Bachs Chromatischer Fantasie," pp. 61–3.

[58] L. K. J. Feininger, *Francesco Antonio Bonporti: Catalogus Thematicus Operum Omnium* (Trent, 1975).

[59] Hans-Joachim Schulze, "Die Bach-Überlieferung-Plädoyer für ein notwendiges Buch," *Beiträge zur Musikwissenschaft*, 17 (1975), pp. 45–57.

With regard to the Chromatic Fantasia and Fugue, we would all side with
the well-known doggerel verse that accompanied a copy of the piece sent to
Forkel by Wilhelm Friedemann Bach:

> Anbey kommt an
> Etwas Musik von Sebastian,
> Sonst genannt: *Fantasia chromatica;*
> Bleibt schön in alle *Saecula.*

> (Hereby enclosed, my good man,
> Is a bit of music by Sebastian;
> Otherwise called: *Fantasia chromatica,*
> Will last through all the *saecula.*)[60]

As we puzzle over the enigma and chronology of the Chromatic Fantasia
and Fugue, we can only hope that in time we will learn more about the first
saeculum of those *saecula.*

In memoriam James Sykes

---

[60] Forkel, *Über Johann Sebastian Bachs Leben, Kunst und Kunstwerke*, p. 98; translation adapted
from *The Bach Reader*; ed. Hans T. David and Arthur Mendel (New York, revised edn,
1966), p. 342.

French overture conventions in the hands of the young Bach and Handel

PETER WILLIAMS

I would like to dwell here not on the *diplomatisch* problems – the nature and purpose of early Handel and Bach sources, the copies of French music they knew in their formative years, the dating and pedigree of music in this style that has been attributed to them – but on the *philologisch* ones. I appreciate that *philologisch* points can often be contradicted by *diplomatisch* and that in this particular instance, little is to be gained by speculations about style and its effect on these young composers until one can be sure what pieces of music are indeed theirs.

Clearly, the subject "French Music circulating in central Germany *ca*. 1700–5" is itself a fine topic for a dissertation, and would produce, I fancy, many unexpected facts. Nevertheless, I hope, in the context of the present discussion, that we may take certain things for granted, take on trust what the sources say and examine some purely musical details in two *ouvertures* or *suites de pièces* attributed to our two composers:

Ouverture (Suite) in D Minor HWV 449
All six movements only in a lost MS (Barrett-Lennard Collection) of which two copies were made later: BL Add. MS 31573, fos. 46v–51v (copy made *ca*. 1858 by R. Lacy) and Händel Gesellschaft Vol. 42, pp. 170–5 (ed. F. Chrysander)

Ouverture in F Major BWV 820
Primary source: Lpz MB III.8.4 ("Andreas-Bach-Buch"), pp. 115–18

Of course, whoever it was who composed and/or transcribed these works, the musical details remain; but we have every reason, I think, to trust the ascriptions and believe we are dealing with early, perhaps teenage, works of Bach and Handel.

As we all now know, after three-quarters of a century of books and articles dealing with French rhythms and their notation, one of the most characteristic elements in *ouverture* style comes right at the beginning: the jerky chords of the opening prelude. Perhaps we should rather say: the dotted *figurae* to which a simple series of homophonic harmonies is treated in an arresting, energetic manner by way of preface to a fugue (see Example 1).

Example 1a HWV 449, Ouverture, mm. 1–4

b BWV 820, Ouverture, mm. 1–4

Notice how immediately these two treatments convey two methods used by Lully and his successors: Handel's is more motivic than Bach's, in the sense that the dotted *figurae* pass from voice to voice. (The example from HWV 449 contains no dots, of course, as far as its notation is concerned. Rather than enter the cul-de-sac of argument about dotting motives, I would like to point out that if the motives are *not* dotted, it would be natural therefore to play it much faster. Either way – less fast but dotted, more fast but undotted – this prelude should receive maximum *characterization*.) Bach's, in a manner frequently observed by his particular circle of copyists when they worked in French idioms, preserves characteristic ornaments and relays the explicit dotting.

More important still, notice how both pieces introduce what one might call 'very French' elements in their harmonies. First, the opening section of Handel's *ouverture*, when treated to implicit dotting and ornamentation, produces a fine appoggiatura harmony at the close of the opening Phrygian statement (the old I–VII–VI–V–in D minor, or *clausula primaria ex hypophrygia*; see Example 2). Secondly, although Bach's first accidental

Example 2 HWV 449, Ouverture, mm. 1–4, as performed in a French manner

is characteristically an *Eb* (m. 6), the prelude naturally modulates to the dominant; and – this is a characteristic French touch too – it remains there for an extra measure when it could have returned to the tonic (see Example 3). Both preludes have many such little subtleties and deserve very close scrutiny. Dotted and ornamental, HWV 449 briefly produces passages startlingly full of French flavor (see Example 4). If these two *ouverture*

Example 3 BWV 820, Ouverture, mm. 10–13

Note: written-out ornaments are editorial.

Example 4 HWV 449, Ouverture, mm. 5–12

Note: small notes editorial, as are the dotted rhythms and ornaments; m. 8, the Eb editorial; m. 9, alto has
4 equal quarters in *HG*.

preludes really are the work of two young Germans, one has to attribute to them a precociously clever and musical ability to pick up foreign idioms and stylistic nuance. The fact that the F Major Suite, BWV 820, even reminds one of "presumably" much later Handel pieces (such as the Organ Concerto Op. 4, No. 2)[1] only underlines the grasp of style shown by these "two young Germans."

Let us look at another stylistic detail found in these preludes. The first time the opening section is played, it closes with a full dominant chord; the second time (before the fugue) it invariably does not. BWV 820 has an open fifth, HWV 449, a chord very likely owed to its later copyists (m. 12), but open octaves on the fugue's repeat (m. 54). Later examples by J. S. Bach make this distinction very clear (see Example 5). Now I hope it is not impo-

Example 5a BWV 820, Ouverture, mm. 12–14

b BWV 831a, Ouverture, mm. 18–20

c BWV 988, Var. 16, mm. 15–16

---

[1] We have to say "presumably" to ourselves, since Handel's indebtedness to his earlier music during his later London years has not yet been fully understood.

lite of me to suggest that this is a little detail probably not noticed by most players, and even by some editors in the past who filled in such chords. But after a little consideration, I think we can see the point of the difference: the first time ends with a marked cadence and a big chord, the second time does not but *springs off immediately* with the triple-time fugue-subject. This is why French *ouverture* fugues characteristically begin on the second or third beat of a triple-time measure,[2] giving (as it were) no time to linger on the last strain of the pompous prelude. In an orchestral *ouverture*, the first violins will run off with the fugue-subject whether or not the *ripieno* lingers on a full chord; but there must be many a director who, in Handel's Concerto Grosso Op. 6, No. 10, would prefer to dash off with the fugue and not wait for a whole bar of $\frac{4}{4}$ on the dominant.

The fugue-subjects themselves are both very typical of the genre and may well have the same tempo despite the different notations (see Example 6a and b). Very likely one is to understand BWV 820 as a slurred (*legato*)

Example 6a HWV 449, Ouverture, mm. 12–16

b BWV 820, Ouverture, mm. 14–16

theme, with the ornaments beginning on the main note and the counter-subject played *détaché* (both to preserve the slurring of the subject). The sequences in HWV 449 (see Example 7a), though what we might now call "Handelian," seem to me more French than some of the details in BWV 820, such as the closing measures, whose repetitious tonic is very typical of other early Bach works (see Example 7b), such as the Sonata in D, BWV 963, and the Capriccio in B flat, BWV 992. The rattling, under-worked nature of both fugues is far more true to French style than the later *ouverture* fugues of both composers, such as those in Handel's concertos and oratorios or those in Bach's harpsichord partitas.

A particularly French element in the fugues of BWV 820 and HWV 449 is that fleeting, scurrying quality which is not actually jig-like. Jig-like fugues

---

[2] Assuming that a triple-time measure has three beats and not one.

Example 7a HWV 449, Ouverture, mm. 41–6

b BWV 820, Ouverture, mm. 102–6

($^6_8$, $^9_8$, $^{12}_8$) would have been more directly Italian in association; *louré* fugues ($^6_4$, $^3_4$ with dotted rhythms) have yet another pedigree, a line of development from the halcyon days of Frescobaldi, Louis Couperin and Froberger. The scurrying fugues of BWV 820 and HWV 449 are obviously effective in the *ouverture* context (particularly in the theatre) and the many transcriptions of French *ouvertures* well into the eighteenth century insured the dispersal of this particular fugal type until it lost its association (as in the B minor fugue, from WTC II). Handel seems to be alluding specifically to the strings-and-oboes sound in his subject, as becomes clearer when strings drop out (as it were) and we are left with a trio of two oboes and bassoon (see Example 8). Bach's fugue, though in theory *sui generis* with certain others by his German contemporaries such as Kuhnau and Mattheson, in fact has several "Bach traits" in addition to that final cadence. The sustained length itself[3] or the slight awkwardness at times of the writing for hands – again, not uncommon in early Bach and perhaps a sign that at this period he composed *on paper*, even in tablature? Other points to strike an alert player are both general and specific: general, that the Bach fugue looks or feels much less like a transcription of an orchestral *ouverture* than the Handel; specific, that although both composers made only a passing reference to hemiolas, Bach's are (surprisingly) more subtle than Handel's. Perhaps hemiolas are not very characteristic of French *ouverture* fugues?

---

[3] Judging by, for example, the diffuse Capriccio in E, BWV 993, length itself was an element of interest to the young Bach.

Example 8 HWV 449, Ouverture, mm. 29–41

Note: *f*/*p* and cues are editorial.

How frequently the prelude section of an *ouverture* returned in modified form after the fugue is a statistic I do not know, but as things stand in BWV 820, it is difficult to see how the prelude could have returned after such tonic finality (see Example 7b). Handel's returning prelude mostly leaves out any motivic interest and emphasizes the quarter-note element in the bass (see Example 9). But this too is a kind of "motif" or *figura* characteristic of the *ouverture* style and should be recognized as such. Nor should it be somehow thought to be inferior or less allusive than, for example, the running sixteenth-note motives typical of Bach's later *ouvertures* (orchestral suites, harpsichord works. It is a curious fact that in addition to the famous dotted rhythms, two of the most idiomatic, allusive details in the French *ouverture* style are very plain and "uninteresting": simple quarter-notes and simple sixteenth-notes.

Example 9 HWV 449, Ouverture, mm. 49–52

Note: double dots and ornaments are editorial.

I would like to make a few points about the rest of the two suites that follow these first movements. The chief difference is that HWV 449 proceeds as a keyboard suite with Allemande, Courante and Sarabande, while BWV 820 continues as an orchestral suite with *Entrée*, Menuet and Trio, *Bourrée*. They each end with movements that could be a finale in either tradition, insofar as the traditions were indeed distinct: Chaconne for Handel,[4] Gigue for Bach. As remarked already, however, it is the Handel *ouverture* that sounds more like a transcription than the Bach.

The three regular harpsichord dances of HWV 449 offer no problem, but on the contrary serve to convince us that we are dealing with genuine Handel: they are so like other, more authoritatively preserved, works. Strangely, the second Sarabande begins as if it were a *double* to the first, but continues differently. This rather reminds me of that moment in an early work of Bach in which he too seems at first to be following convention but then (so to speak) changes his mind: the second variation of the organ Passacaglia BWV 582 begins like the first but slides off (*via* a startling seventh chord) in another direction (see Example 10).

Example 10 BWV 582, Passacaglia in C minor, mm. 8–10, 16–18

Handel's Courante, apparently quite simple, is in fact a tissue of hemiola ambiguities such as he exploited in his later music, while the Allemande has a sparseness at its section-beginnings that reminds one of other such dances. Altogether, these movements are very "Handelian"; in comparison, the *Entrée* in BWV 820 is not a bit "Bach-like" and is so shot through with French rhythms and harmonies – though all very simple on the surface – that we may indeed wonder if it was a transcription from something else (see Example 11). Once again, if the young Bach were himself responsible for these details, his grasp of stylistic nuance was very great indeed. So it is in

---

[4] Called *ciacona* in the source, like the Passacaglias for organ by Buxtehude contained in the Andreas-Bach-Buch (BuxWV 159 and 160). I have elsewhere suggested that Bach's putative title for BWV 582 ("Passacaglia" in C Minor for Organ) alludes to the fact that he took the fugue-subject from André Raison's *Passecaille*.

Example 11a BWV 820, Entrée, mm. 3–12

b BWV 820, Entrée, mm. 3–12, notated in the style of a French overture

an interpretation:

the Trio of the Menuet, for not only are both very characteristic of the *ballet* minuet but the Trio is another moment for oboes and bassoon. Note the *basso quasi staccato* effect, reminding one of the slurless bassoon part in the first Trio of the first Brandenburg Concerto, or the *staccato* oboe-basses in that concerto's second Trio (see Example 12). Another interesting detail occurs in the model, textbook-like *Bourrée* of the Suite BWV 820: the

Example 12a BWV 820, Trio, mm. 1–4

Note: all slurs editorial. Tenor *f* in m. 1 copyist's own addition?

b BWV 1046, Trio, mm. 1–5

impression one has here of a rather folksy idiom is confirmed by a passing resemblance to the final *Bourrée* in the very much later "Peasant Cantata" (see Example 13b). The latter may well be a kind of burlesqued chorale, that is, a "chorus" closing a "cantata"; but its pedigree lies in this suite.

Example 13a BWV 820, Bourrée, mm. 8–12

b BWV 212, Final mvt., mm. 1–4

We could find many such points to make in reviewing these two charming suites, and further study might reveal many important lines of inquiry, particularly what musical styles and details impinged on these very gifted young men. For example, discovering in another early Bach work one particular cadence that the Handel scholar Terence Best regards as particularly early Handelian (see Example 14) naturally leads one to wonder if the two

Example 14a HWV 449, Ouverture, mm. 47–8

b BWV 963, Sonata in D Major, mvt. 1, mm. 101–2

young composers picked up this characteristic turn of phrase somewhere in their common legacies. Since their backgrounds had so much that was similar – their early copybooks no doubt concerned with the same Froberger, Pachelbel, Zachow, Strunck, etc. – one might well be struck by how much their early keyboard works already reveal major differences.

I do not know, for instance, why Bach never closed a suite with a chaconne or triple-time variations and/or *ostinato*, as Handel and others did, Buxtehude even in one major organ praeludium (BuxWV 137, contained in the Andreas-Bach-Buch). It was a common enough genre, and we might think that Forkel had some actual evidence for his claim that Bach thought variations an ungrateful medium. Handel's Chaconne in the present suite has a clear sense of shape, whether or not one repeats the *tema* at the end (not in the known source), and one is bound to assume he learnt his French idioms at least in part from Muffat. In this connection, we should also remember that Bach's obituary specifically commented on the young Bach hearing French *musicians* at the Celle court (summer residence?), not merely French *music*. As every student knows, getting to know French styles from notated music can be misleading if he never hears it played by those who understand it.

Part 3
The Well-Tempered Clavier I and II

The four conceptual stages of the Fugue in C Minor, *WTC* I

ULRICH SIEGELE

Introduction

The aim of my analysis – an analysis of compositional technique – is to understand the system of rules according to which a composer writes his music. My purpose is to become familiar enough with the composer's grammar – that is, his repertory of compositional possibilities – so that it is possible to say in a given case what choices a composer made, and, by implication, what possibilities he excluded. In the case of Bach's fugues, I am especially interested in questions of form – form understood in the strictest sense as the arrangement of a work's sections in time – and in questions of thematic structure – that is, the distribution of a work's thematic and non-thematic sections. The realization of a formal and thematic design then leads to questions of contrapuntal technique.

My work does not fall within the tradition of Heinrich Schenker; the genetic stages or conceptual levels presented here have nothing to do with his levels. While I profited, in an earlier phase of my research (the early 1970s) from the formal, more than the substantive, observations of Ludwig Czaczkes,[1] I have since distanced myself from his work. I have also benefited from the insightful observations of August Halm.[2] In a certain sense, however, I am analyzing "at my own risk." To date I have analyzed about 100 compositions by Bach, among them 70 or 80 fugues and fugal pieces, including all the fugues in the *Well-Tempered Clavier*.[3] To show the

---

[1] See Ludwig Czaczkes, *Analyse des Wohltemperierten Klaviers: Form und Aufbau der Fuge bei Bach* (Vienna, 1956–63), Vols. 1 and 2.

[2] See August Halm, *Einführung in die Musik* (Berlin, 1926), pp. 259–70 and 281f.

[3] My study of the *WTC* was carried out during a sabbatical year in 1982–3 with the assistance of the grant awarded by the Deutsche Forschungsgemeinschaft.

results of my work, I have chosen a well-known (perhaps the best-known) fugue from the *Well-Tempered Clavier* as an example. This will make it easier to judge whether my analytical method leads to new results. Rather than describing the steps I took in my analysis, I will describe "the steps Bach took" in composing the work.

The expression "steps Bach took" requires some explanation. When I analyze a piece, I find embedded within it a structural hierarchy, which can be represented as a series of successive stages. These stages lead from the simple to the complex; they begin with basic undifferentiated building blocks, and their step-by-step development yields ever higher levels of differentiation. Of course, it is unlikely that Bach worked out each stage individually as I do here. But I believe that these stages reveal in a temporal sequence the inner structure of Bach's compositional thought, his formal and thematic thinking in composition. Thus when I say "the steps Bach took in composing a work," I mean the probable steps in Bach's compositional thinking. The various genetic stages, however, are mine, not Bach's. In recomposing the piece I am doing what every historian does in his work: he does not reproduce reality; he recreates it. (This is the risk I spoke of earlier.) I realize that my analysis may be criticized because it is based solely on musical evidence rather than on the sources. I hope, however, that through the process of unfolding the inner structure of the work, as seen in four distinct stages, I will contribute to a better understanding of the piece.

The first stage

In composing a fugue, Bach first had to determine the number of fugal entries. For the C minor fugue, he decided on six entries, ordered as two groups of three. He then had to determine the scale degrees for each of these entries. He chose to give the first group of entries the scale degrees I–V–I (two entries on I and one on V) and the second group the scale degrees V–I–V (two entries on V, and one on I). He thus created a balance between the two scale degrees – each is presented three times – which is the result of the basic complementary relationship between the two groups. (Although Bach's fugues begin as egalitarian societies, a hierarchical order often emerges at a later stage of the working-out process.)

Bach's second step in designing a fugue was to decide where to place the entries within the "tonal space" or registers available to him, and how to distribute the entries among the various voices. He decided to let the entries appear successively on c'', g'' and c', and to assign the entries to voices II, I, and III (I signifying the highest voice.) Bach, after he decided where to place the three entries, no longer had a choice with regard to their order of entry. To assign the entries successively to voices III, I and II was precluded because of the interval of an octave and a half which would result between voices III and I. Bach often made choices which relieved him of further decisions.

When, for the second group of three entries, Bach decided to have the voices enter in the same order as in the first group (II, I, III), it was necessary – since the same two pitches (*c* and *g*) would be used – to choose different entry points for each voice. According to the complementary pattern of scale degrees (V–I–IV), Bach chose an adjacent register (*g*″, *c*‴″ and *g*) for his second group of entries. (In the first group or three entries, described above, the voices entered in the same order – II, I, III – but on different entry-points – *c*″ *g*″ *c*′ – and a different pattern of scale degrees – I–V–I.) When the two groups of three entries are seen as a whole, each voice has two different entry-points: voice I has g″ and c″; voice II has c″ and g′; and voice III has c′ and g. This is a chain, but a chain in which a link is missing. A full complement of entries – that is, for four voices, soprano, alto, tenor and bass – would proceed as follows: *g*″ and *c*″, *c*″ and *g*′, *g*′ and *c*′, *c*′ and *g*; in this case, however, Bach leaves out the tenor entry on *g*′ and *c*′. This solution is only one of several ways by which Bach could have derived a disposition for three voices.

The entry-points, or places of entry, serve only as signposts of the subject and its position within the tonal parameters of the piece. In the case of the present fugue, the subject begins on the octave, extends beyond the octave by a whole step, and descends to the third, omitting the second scale degree and the tonic. In order to show the systematic relationship of the voices to one another, I will describe their range in terms of a standardized octave rather than the actual range of each entry: the voices II, I, III in the first group of three entries have the ranges *c*″–*c*′, *g*″–*g*′, and *c*′–*c*, and, in the second group, ranges of *g*′–*g*, *c*″–*c*′, and *g*–G. Voices II and III, representing the alto and the bass in a normal four-voice disposition, have an authentic range in the first group of entries and a plagal range in the second; voice I, in contrast, has a plagal range in the first group of entries and an authentic range in the second group. (Had a tenor been present, its ranges would have been the same as the soprano.) According to the rules of classical vocal polyphony, the assignment of a piece to the authentic or plagal mode of a key is determined by the range of the tenor; when the tenor is omitted, as it is here, its role is taken by the soprano. The first group of three entries, therefore, can be considered to be in the plagal mode of the key, due to the plagal range of voice I (the soprano); the second group of entries are in the authentic mode because of the authentic range of voice I. Bach thus combines the two possible modal forms in this fugue not by mixing them, but by retaining one separate mode for each group of three entries.[4]

Next, as a third step, Bach had to reach a decision about the number of subjects and their permutations. In this case, Bach designed a fugue with three subjects, or a subject and two countersubjects: the result is less a fugue on a single theme than one on a short thematic unit of three parts – a "theme" – which was capable of being worked out in double counterpoint at the octave. Bach develops the permutation of these three subjects in the simplest way possible: each voice begins at its first entry with the first subject followed by the second and third subjects, and then the sequence begins anew. From this arises the scheme shown in Figure 1. Bach uses only three

First group of entries:				Second group of entries:		
Voice		Subject			Subject	
I		1	2	3	1	2
II	1	2	3	1	2	3
III			1	2	3	1

Figure 1 Permutation scheme of the three subjects

of the six possible permutations of the three subjects, namely, 1–2–3, 2–3–1, and 3–1–2; the other three permutations – 1–3–2, 2–1–3, and 3–2–1 – are missing. That this is the usual practice for a fugue with three subjects is not always acknowledged by the analysts who criticize Bach for not using all six permutations.

Now that the plan of the entries is clear, we can turn to the subject itself. The genesis of the first subject is reconstructed in Example 1. The reconstruction is based on an ostinato pattern of five units, each with four half-measures. The pattern, built on the scale degrees I–IV–I–VII– I, shows the harmonic basis of the first subject, namely, an extended cadential progression in which a tonic chord is inserted between chords with subdominant and dominant functions.

Subject 1 is shown below in the form in which it makes its first complete appearance with the second and third subjects. This combination of sub-

---

[4] For a discussion of the modality of the primary points of entry and the question of functional interpretation, see Ulrich Siegele, "Zu Bachs Fugenkomposition," in *Johann Sebastian Bachs Traditionsraum*, ed. R. Szeskus, *Bach-Studien* 9 (Leipzig, 1986), pp. 19–24.

Example 1 Genesis of the subject 1 reconstruction in five stages

jects as a "theme" or thematic unit in the permutation 2–3–1 (reading from top to bottom) is shown in Example 2a in four half-measures, labelled A, B, C, D. To reduce the first entry of the "theme" to its principle notes (as shown in Example 2b) allows us to clarify its motivic, contrapuntal and harmonic structure, and to observe Bach's use of invertible counterpoint at the octave. In B, subjects 2 and 3, in parallel thirds, move in contrary motion to subject 1. In C, subject 2 and 1 in parallel thirds move in contrary motion to subject 3, the pitches of subject 2 are identical to those of subject 3 in

Example 2a First statement of "Theme" or thematic unit, mm. 7–8
b Reduction of "Theme," mm. 7–8

B but are stated in reverse order, while subject 3 repeats the same pitches as subject 2 in the previous half-measure (B) but one octave lower. Harmonically, the second and fourth eighth-notes of C are part of a diminished seventh chord built on the seventh degree of the scale; the third eighth-note functions as an accented passing-note. The first to third eighth-notes of the fourth half-measure (D) also belong to the same diminished seventh chord: the first eighth-note, the *g′* of subject 3 (opposite the *f* of subject 1), is an unprepared appoggiatura, or an accented upper note between the two *f*s; the second eighth-note, the *c″* of subject 2, is a passing-note between *b″* and *d″*. The voices throughout the passage are completely interchangeable, except for the two last notes of subject 3 (*d′* and *g′*); when subject 3 is stated in the lowest voice, these notes are changed to *g* and *c* and function as the bass of a V–I cadence.

Subject 1, when stated on the dominant in measure 3, is in the form of a tonal answer, as shown in Example 3a; only a single note, however – the fourth note in the upper voice – differs from the original statement of the subject. In contrast to the *dux* form on the tonic (as seen in Example 3b), in

Example 3a Tonal answer of subjects 1 and 2: *Comes* form on V
b Subjects 1 and 2: *Dux* form on I

which the third and fourth pitches emphasize the descending fourth of the authentic mode (*c–g*), the tonal answer outlines the descending fifth of the plagal mode (*g–c*). Modal and tonal elements are intertwined in the use of the two forms. Subject 1 and the 'theme' when stated on the tonic – in the *dux* form – are based on the harmonic C minor scale, and when stated on the dominant – in the *comes* form – are based on the harmonic G minor scale.[5] Tonally, the change from the harmonic C minor scale to the harmonic G minor scale can be seen as the tonal modulation from the tonic to the dominant. In this way, the modal shift of the tonal answer is given a

[5] Only the sixteenth-note figure with which subject 2 begins deviates from this pattern: it is based on the descending melodic C minor scale at its entry on I, and on the ascending melodic C minor scale at its entry on V – as a descending scale pattern.

functional significance, since the fourth note of subject 1 preserves the tonic as the harmonic basis of the first half-measure of the *comes* form and prevents the immediate modulation to the dominant implied by the *f♯* as the lower appoggiatura of *g*. In the absence of a minor third, the *g* continues to be functionally related to the tonic. This explains the unusual use of the ascending C minor melodic scale – in place of the descending melodic G minor scale – in the *comes* form of the second subject (m. 7). The functional significance of the modal shift in the tonal answer also prepares the first half-measure of the *comes* form for its harmonic role – that is, to mediate between the tonic and the dominant, or, in general, between a given scale degree and its upper fifth. (Generally the *comes* form, to the extent it is used, exists only when a new thematic entry is related to the preceding entry, or the preceding harmony, by the interval of the fifth above.)

Subject 1 uses every note of the harmonic minor scale. The number of times each pitch is used appears to follow a predetermined order: in the twenty notes of subject 1 in the *dux* form, *c* is used six times, *g* four times, *b* three times, *d*, *f* and *ab* twice, and *eb* once. (The original plan for the subject may have included six statements of the tonic, four of the dominant, and two of every additional note.) Subject 2 also has twenty notes. The twenty notes of subject 1 are divided into ten and ten, and those of subject 2 into twelve and eight; subject 3 adds twelve notes, divided into three and nine. A perfect numerical balance, 26 notes and 26 notes, would be achieved between the two parts of the "theme," or thematic unit, if subject 3 were to divide its twelve notes into four and eight.

Bach's conceptual plan for the first stage is summarized in diagram form in Figure 2. Line 1 shows the scale degrees of the entries and the *dux* and *comes* forms, abbreviated as Dx and Cs. Line 2 shows the entry-points of the first subject, and the normal range of its entrances. Line 3 shows the disposition of the voices. Line 4 shows the permutations of the three subjects within the "theme" or thematic unit. Line 5 is relevant only to the second stage.

The execution of the first stage is shown in Example 4. Each of the entries – two groups of three – takes up four half-measures, which means 24 half-measures or twelve whole measures in all. But the fugue cannot close with the sixth entry, and a cadence is added, which takes up two half-measures or one whole measure. As a fugue, the piece is quite regular, purely thematic – apart from the closing cadence – and rather pedestrian. But we must recall that such fugues existed, and that Bach knew of them. The fugues and fugal gigues in *Hortus Musicus* (a collection of trio sonatas by his teacher in Hamburg, Jan Adams Reinken) follow precisely this format. In his keyboard transcriptions from the collection – including three fugues and a

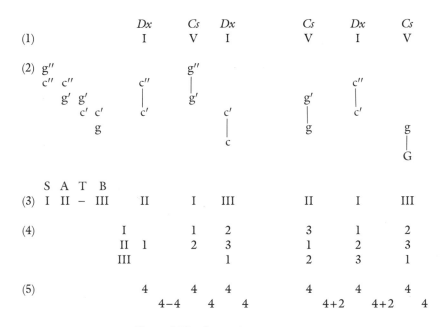

Figure 2 The first and second stages

Example 4 Execution of the First Stage

Example 4 (*cont.*)

gigue – Bach inserted several non-thematic sections. A similar process can be seen at work in the second stage of the C minor fugue.

The second stage

When Bach decided to add non-thematic sections, he had to determine how long they should be. To begin with, he made them the same length as the thematic entries. An equal balance between thematic and non-thematic sections is typical of the basic plan of Bach's fugues, and seldom in the *Well-Tempered Clavier* does he begin with an imbalance or entirely omit non-thematic sections. Since it is essential in fugal writing that the non-thematic sections are harmonically and tonally related to their corresponding thematic sections, it should not be surprising that the two are also related in terms of proportion and dimension.

Bach balances each thematic entry in stage two with a non-thematic section of equal duration, which means that he gives as much time to the non-thematic sections as to the theme. He could have accomplished this in the manner shown in Figure 3 by following each thematic entry with a

Figure 3 Distribution of thematic and non-thematic sections in units of equal duration (in half measures)

non-thematic section identical in length: the number 4 in Figure 3 represents the duration of four half-measures. Something is obviously wrong with this distribution, however, since it would be unlikely, or even impossible, to find a fugue with a non-thematic section immediately after the first entry, at least not a section equal in length to the subject. According to general fugal procedures, therefore, the first non-thematic section must be deleted and a unit of four be removed. But this amount of time – these four half-measures – must be made up somewhere else. Bach had various ways in which he could do this. In this case he singled out the non-thematic sections after the first and second entries in the second group (hereafter referred to as Part II) and added half the deleted portion – that is, two half-measures to each entry, as shown in Figure 4 and in line 5 in Figure 2.

Figure 4 Bach's distribution of thematic and non-thematic sections
(in half measures)

The execution of the second stage is shown in Example 5. It begins with the first and second entries (mm. 1–2 and mm. 3–4) followed by the first non-thematic section of four half-measures (mm. 5–6) which lead from V to I. The upper voice of the non-thematic section is derived from the

Example 5 Execution of the Second Stage

beginning of subject 1; the lower voice fills in with continuous sixteenth-note motion until the fourth beat of measure 6, as shown in Example 6a. The upper voice has a plagal range, the lower voice an authentic range. The contrapuntal movement of the lower voice, (as shown in reduced form in Example 6b) forms tenths, thirds and sixths with the upper voice, and, on the last eighth-note of measure 6, a diminished fifth; continuous sixteenth-note movement is the result of minor rhythmic and melodic adjustments (including an appoggiatura on the last eighth note of m. 6 and rhythmic displacement in m. 5,2 and 4, and m. 6,2).

Example 6a First non-thematic section, mm. 5–6
b Reduction of mm. 5–6

The harmonic movement of this passage also deserves our attention: the V on the downbeat of measure 5 is immediately changed to III in the upper voice by the second eighth-note, eb. The harmony then rises sequentially upward by step in half measure units: IV–V–VI. If we look at the harmonic relationships in more detail, we find that a dominant is placed before each of these scale degrees – I–IV, II–V, III–VI – with VI as the scale degree of the deceptive cadence. It is important to note that this harmonic progression is determined by the movement of the lower voice, and not by the upper voice. If the upper voice from the first beat of measure 5, to the third beat of measure 6 is considered by itself, the succession of scale degrees reads: V–VI–VIII–I; or, with the insertion of the dominants: V, III–VI, IV–VII, V–I. It is the addition of the lower voice that creates the deceptive cadence, which then requires the addition of a second "corrective" cadence, as shown in completed form in Example 7, to lead back to the tonic. (The

Example 7 Reconstruction of "corrective cadence" in mm. 6–7

penultimate eighth-note of measure 6 needs to be seen as a subdominant with an added sixth, and the last eighth-note of the measure as a dominant with an added seventh and 4–3 suspension. With the resolution of the 4–3 suspension on the first eighth-note of measure 7, a statement of subject 2 begins in the soprano while subject 1 enters in the bass.)

The second and last non-thematic section of part I of the second stage consists of a descending harmonic sequence by fifths (mm. 9–10). The two upper voices (I and II) are derived from the beginning of subject 1; the lower voice (III) is derived from the beginning of subject 2. The initial motive of subject 1 is stated alternately in half-measure units between the two upper voices, so that each voice by itself forms a descending sequential pattern an entire measure in length. The sweeping gesture of the bass, in contrast to the upper voices, is created by a sequence of sixteenth-note scalar passages, which descend in octave patterns through the circle of fifths. A reduction of the above passage, shown in Example 8, reveals the inner rich-

Example 8 Second non-thematic section: reduction of mm. 9–11

ness of Bach's contrapuntal writing for the upper two voices; the lower voice – in a reconstructed form – merely outlines the basic harmonic progression. Proceeding by half-measure units from the beginning of measure 9, we find the following scale degrees: I–I–IV–VII–III. Instead of completing the cycle of descending fifths – which, for comparative purposes, can be reconstructed from the above progression as VI–II–V–I – the bass descends a third, from III to I, as shown by the movement in the lower voice at the beginning of measure 11 – that is, by a leap from E♭ to *c′* with the entry of subject 2. After the tonic is reached in this manner, the first entry of part II, in the *comes* form (mm. 11–12), follows on the dominant.

The first non-thematic section of part II of the second stage – as a result of the two-measure insertion described above (see Figure 4) – is six half-measures long (mm. 13–15) and is directly related to the first non-thematic section of part I (mm. 5–6). The relationship can be seen most clearly by comparing the middle and bottom voices of the second half of the above section (the sixth eighth-note of m. 14 to m. 16,1) with the two upper voices of the corresponding section in part I (the second eighth-note of m. 5 to m. 6,3): the middle voice restates the upper voice of the earlier section an octave lower, while the bottom voice restates the second voice not just an octave, but an octave and a fourth, lower (see voices II and III in mm. 14,3–16). The use of double counterpoint at the twelfth (here stated a fourth lower) leads on the downbeat of measure 16 to I, instead of VI, as the scale degree of the next entry. The nature of the basic harmonic progression thus remains unaltered by the lower voice: V–VI–VII–I.

In contrast, the first half of the non-thematic section stands a fifth higher than the second half as described above, and closes on V, the same scale degree as the preceding thematic entry. From a harmonic standpoint no progress has been made, since the first half of the non-thematic section ends on the same scale degree as that of the thematic entry which immediately preceded it. Movement from V to I does not actually occur, therefore, until the measures which follow – that is, the second group of three half-measures.

The section as a whole includes two complete groups of three half-measures (six half-measures or three measures) since – through the use of double counterpoint at the twelfth – the deceptive cadence is avoided and there is no need of a half-measure "corrective" cadence to lead back to the tonic. The two three-half-measure groups are joined together on V, which serves as the arrival of the first group and the point of departure for the second. The continuous sixteenth-note motion ceases momentarily at the point where the two groups come together – in the middle of measure 14. It is also at this point that a change of register occurs: first, the thematic material stated in the lower voice in the first three half measures, which corresponds to the upper voice in mm. 5–6, is now shifted to the middle voice; similarly, the material in voice II (corresponding to the lower voice in mm. 5–6) is shifted to voice III. In contrast to mm. 5–6, a third voice is added. Its accompanimental figure – in parallel thirds with the principal voice (II) – forms a sequential pattern, which, as it moves to a lower register for the second group, gives the impression of leading directly to the next entry of subject 1. In measure 16, at the entry of subject 1, the first three notes of subject 3 are stated in the lower octave, preceded by two eighth-notes, e and f; these two notes may be seen as a remainder of the preceding sequence (see Example 9). In addition, the raising of the leading-tone ($e♮$) provides the I with a dominant function in relation to the IV which follows.

The second non-thematic section of part II is also six half-measures long (mm. 18–20), and corresponds to the second non-thematic section of part I (mm. 9–11). The tonic, however, is not repeated in the second half of

Example 9 Entry of subject 1, m. 16

measure 18 as it was in measure 9. Rather, the progression leads directly from the I on the downbeat of measure 18 through the circle of fifths (I–IV–VII–III–VI–II–V) to the V on the downbeat of measure 21 and the next entrance of the subject (mm. 21–2). The harmonic sequence in measure 18 thus begins a fifth lower than its counterpart in the corresponding section in measure 9. This is true not only with regard to scale degree, but also – at least for the two upper voices – with regard to register. The lower voice – in its entirety – cannot be stated a fifth lower, however, because of the limited range of the keyboard. Its range, therefore, alternates between the lower fifth and the upper fourth, while the position of the upper two voices remains the same as in the earlier section until the last eighth-note of measure 20. As a result, the overall range of the section is contracted by nearly an octave, compared with the corresponding section of part I.

The purpose of the third non-thematic section of part II is to lead in four half-measure units (mm. 23–4) from the dominant scale degree of the previous entry to a final cadence on the tonic. This is the same function performed – and in the same amount of time – by the first non-thematic section of part I (mm. 5–6). In measures 23–4, the two upper voices from measures 5–6 are interchanged in double counterpoint at the octave, and given to the middle and lower voices. The same succession of scale degrees is retained: V–IV–V–VI, or, with the insertion of the dominants, V, I–IV, II–V, III–VI. The upper voice again accompanies the sixteenth-note figure of the principal motive, this time in sixths. The deceptive cadence on VI is again "corrected" or resolved by a second cadence: IV–V–V–I.

Bach's conceptual plan for the second stage is exactly twice as long as for the first one, minus the two half-measures required to form a cadence. The 24 measures are divided as follows: half for thematic entries and half for non-thematic sections. Twelve measures are taken up by the two-times-three thematic entries in the first stage, and twelve measures by the non-thematic sections new to the second stage. The non-thematic sections are divided into two types according to the scale degrees of the thematic sections which precede and follow them: between an entry on V and an entry – or a conclusion – on I, we find a sequence which ascends in half-measures by step in conjunction with almost continual eighth-note motion (labelled A in Figure 4); between an entry on I and one on V, we find a sequence which descends in half-measures through the circle of fifths with a continuous sixteenth-note movement in the lower voice (labelled B in Figure 4). Even though each type of sequence preserves the modulatory function of the non-thematic section, Bach found two different ways with two different durations as acceptable.

The thematic and non-thematic sections are structurally differentiated from one another in several ways. The "theme," comprised of the three subjects in the manner defined above, remains intact in the thematic entries, and in a similar manner is absent, as a unit, in the non-thematic sections. The thematic entries take place on one of two scale degrees (I and V); the non-thematic sections take place between the same two scale degrees. The thematic entries are restricted to a specific duration; the non-thematic sections may vary in duration. This structural differentiation – according to the presence or absence of the thematic material as a whole, and the degree of harmonic and periodic stability and variability – is on the one hand sharply drawn, and, on the other hand, blurred by contrapuntal elaboration; on the one hand, the thematic entries are characterized by predominantly eighth-note motion, and the non-thematic sections by a continuous sixteenth-note motion; on the other hand, the beginning of each non-thematic section includes the initial motive of subject 1, which allows it to be combined with the initial motive of subject 2 to form the beginning of the "theme." The contrapuntal procedures used to differentiate the thematic from the non-thematic sections are, nevertheless, unified by their overall use of the same thematic material.

The third stage

The third stage is concerned only with the last seven measures of the second stage, (mm. 18–24) and takes as its point of departure the final entry in this stage (mm. 21–2). (Figure 5 includes a diagram of both the third and fourth stages.) In the first and second stages, the final entry was placed on V; in the third, the entry is shifted to I – from the *comes* to the *dux* form – altering not only the range of subject 1 by the interval of a fifth (from *g–G* to *c–C* in standardized octaves) but also creating the possibility of a new entry-point

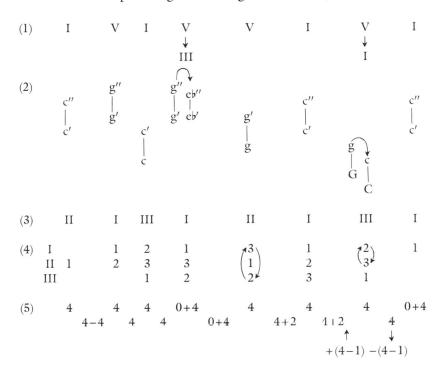

Figure 5 The third and fourth stages

and a new register for the "theme". As a result of this transposition, the non-thematic section which follows the entry no longer needs to lead from V to I, and therefore can now be placed before the final entry rather than after it. One of the four half-measures, however, is needed for a final cadence, since the entry of subject 1 in the bass voice – which ends on the third degree of the scale – cannot conclude the piece. Only the three remaining half-measures, therefore, can be placed before the final entry.

As a result of the new ordering, two non-thematic sections – one of six half-measures, and one of three half-measures – now are placed between the penultimate and the final thematic entries. The first of the two sections remains basically unchanged from the second stage; for the second section, however – in keeping with its new function – new material is needed. In order to provide a link between the six half-measures of the first non-thematic section (which lead from I to V) and the entry which follows on I,

a V pedal, complete with raised third, is introduced. Since the pedal begins
at the point where we expect a thematic entry on V, it serves to delay, as well
as to prepare for, the final entry of the subject on the tonic (see Example
10a). The pedal continues as much as possible the double-layered texture of
the preceding non-thematic section. The reduction to a single layer, as
shown in Example 10b, reveals that the number of voices above the pedal-
point increase from half-measure to half-measure, beginning with two
voices and increasing to four. The scale degrees above the pedal-point, moving by half-measures, include V (with the minor seventh) I–IV (with the
sixth), and again V (with the minor seventh).

Example 10a Non-thematic section with pedal point, mm. 21–2
b Reduction of mm. 21–2

The re-positioning of a non-thematic section and the introduction of new
material – as the result of a new function – open up new possibilities for the
arrangement of the material in the non-thematic sections as a whole. Bach's
conceptual plan for the second stage included one type of sequence (type A),
ascending in step-wise motion, which is found in the first non-thematic
section of part I and the first and third sections of part II; a second type
(type B), descending by fifths, is found in the second non-thematic section
of part I and the second section of part II (see Figure 6).

	I			II				
Thematic entries:	4	4	4	4	4		4	
Non-thematic sections:		4	4	4+2	4+2	+(4−1)	−(4−1)	
Scale degree:	I	V	I	V	I	(V)	I	(I)
Type of sequence:		A	B	A	B	(pedal)	(cadence)	

Figure 6 Bach's revised distribution of thematic and non-thematic sections
(in half-measures)

Type A thus occurs once in part I and twice in part II; type B occurs once in each part. The placement of the sequences was dependent on their relation to the scale degrees of the entries which preceded or followed them. With the change in the nature of the third non-thematic section in part II (shown as (pedal) in Figure 6), each of the two types A and B is now found once in each part, while the final section has its own material corresponding to its new function – that is, the pedal-point (see Example 10). As Figure 6 makes clear, the sequences which rise by step (type A) now occur between an entry on V and an entry on I in the first non-thematic section of each part; the sequences which descend by fifths (type B) occur between an entry on I and an entry (or the pedal point) on V, in the second non-thematic section of each part. This arrangement is possible only because of the deletion of the non-thematic section originally called for after the first entry of part I.

An execution of this plan for the third stage is shown in Example 11 (upper system, mm. 18–24). A non-thematic section – unchanged from the second

Example 11 Execution of the Third Stage

Example 11 (*cont.*)

stage – leads in a six half-measure unit from I to V, while the repositioned non-thematic section forms three new half-measures above a pedal-point on the dominant, followed by the last thematic entry, now on I, and the closing cadence (IV–V–V– I) of one half-measure. The final entry, however, in its new register a fifth lower (see Example 11, upper system, end of m. 22,3 to m. 24,3) sounds dull when compared with the corresponding measures in the second stage (see Example 5, m. 21,1–m. 23); this effect is created primarily by the upper and middle voices, which move beyond their lower limits (c' and f). Bach therefore decided to make a change in the register of the entry. But he did not do this simply by moving voices I and II up an octave, since this would create too large an interval between the two upper voices and the bass voice. Rather, he transposed the middle voice up an octave (in m. 23) but left the upper voice in its original register; thus, what previously was stated in the middle voice is now stated in the new upper voice, and *vice versa*. In this way he changed the permutation of the "theme" or thematic unit from 2–3–1 to 3–2–1.

As a result of these changes, several further adjustments were required to prepare for the new position of the middle voice in measure 23. As preparation for the change of register, Bach transposed parts of the upper voice in measure 21 and the first half of measure 22 up an octave (see Example 11, lower system), and, at the entry of the thematic unit or "theme" in the last half of measure 22, transposed the descending scale passage up an octave as well. As a result, subject 2 begins in the upper octave in the first voice and then continues in the middle voice, a peculiarity that can be explained only by the need for registral balance. Further additions and alterations are required by the octave transposition in measure 22: the upper voice moves to c'' instead of f' in the first eighth-note of measure 23, followed in the scale passage in measure 22 by *b′* and *a′* in place of *bb′* and *ab′*. On the last eighth-note of measure 22, *f′* is added to the middle voice which moves to *eb* on the first eighth-note of measure 23. The effect of these changes on the harmonic progression of the first half-measure of the entry (m. 22,3–4) is as follows: the last eighth-note of measure 22 is now on V rather than I, and the first eighth-note of measure 23 is on VI (the deceptive cadence) rather than IV, with the result that the last eighth-note of the entry in measure 22 refers back to the pedal-point not only through the thematic note *G*, but also through its harmonic reference to V.

Adjustments are also needed in measure 20, the final two half-measures of the non-thematic section leading to the V pedal. Changing the figuration in the upper voice in the first half of measure 20 (see Example 11, lower system) prepares for the change of register by introducing the *c″* in pre-paration for the entrance of the *d″* above the pedal-point in the first half of measure 21. A half-measure later, the same sixteenth-note figuration is in-troduced a fifth lower in the middle voice, creating the only moment in the piece where successive sixteenth-notes are stated simultaneously in two voices. This moment occurs immediately before the first half-measure of the pedal point, where – unusually for a non-thematic section – eighth-note motion prevails.

I believe a balance of register was in general more important to Bach than contrapuntal purity. We can observe the subtle changes he made to main-tain this balance if we compare the upper and lower systems in Example 11. A comparison of the beginning of the non-thematic section in measure 18 with the corresponding non-thematic section of part I shows that the former is contracted by about an octave. Seen as whole, however, the range of the passage is gradually expanded. In combination with the added pedal-point, a dynamic drive or intensification is introduced, which is the most striking characteristic of Bach's conceptual plan for the third stage.

The fourth stage

The fourth stage – the version of the fugue with which we all are familiar – is the only stage supported by source evidence. Instead of citing examples, therefore, I will refer to the fugue as it is known in modern editions and as it is summarized in Figure 5.

In the fourth stage, Bach extends the form by adding a thematic entry and a non-thematic section at the end of part I, and another entry at the end of part II. That the two new entries, planned for the dominant (V) at the end of part I, and the tonic (I) at the end of part II, are intended to function as extra entries can be seen by the fact that subject 1 is assigned to voice I in both entries: the entry points of voice I (*g″* in part I and *c″* in part II) – as well as its register – are now doubled in each part of the form. The entry added at the end of part I, however, is transposed: it enters in a related key rather than the dominant, and in the *dux* rather than the *comes* form. The entry is on III, a third lower than the dominant, with *eb″* as the point of entry for subject 1. (I hesitate to call the III the relative major of C minor, since it is derived not from I but from V, and is not accompanied by Bb major, the relative major of V.) Although there are instances in Bach's music when he transposes the entries on I and V up or down a third and the relationship to a relative key – whether major or minor – is clearly recognizable, such is not the case here: Bach transposes only one entry, not two. III, therefore, functions as the third scale degree – or as the third of the tonic triad – and can be seen as the mediant. In this case I consider the shift to be a modal one.

The new entry on III immediately follows the second non-thematic section of part I (mm. 9–10), and begins as a direct continuation of the preceding two measures, and continues the melodic sequence and descending circle of fifths of the preceding two measures – which accounts for the presence of the *g′* and *ab′* in the middle voice in measure 11 on beats 2 and 3. A new permutation of the "theme" – 1–3–2 – results from extending the sequence to the first half-measure of the entry, *eb*.

The shift to major, however, requires an adjustment in the use of the seventh chord – based on the leading-tone of the scale – which functions as an intermediate harmony or "bridge" between the basic harmonies. In the original key of C minor, this seventh chord is diminished and its disposition for three voices, rather than four, may be derived in one of the four ways outlined in Example 12a; of the four voicings, the second and third (b and c) are preferable since they include both the leading-tone and the interval of a diminished seventh. Since, however, the seventh in a major key is minor (see Example 12b), the role of the diminished seventh must now be assumed by the interval of a diminished fifth. Example 12c shows the "theme" with the seventh chord in major voiced as in B (see Example 12b) – its usual disposition with the diminished fifth omitted. Example 12d shows subject 3 in measure 12 (fourth stage) altered (that is, voiced as in A) to include the diminished fifth above the leading tone of the scale – or, in this case, the augmented fourth plus an octave below the leading-tone. In measure 12, the pitches of subject 3 are stated in reverse order, on the second to the fourth eighth-notes, and are followed by a rest on the first eighth-note of the second half of the measure.

Example 12a Possible dispositions of diminished seventh chord

b Possible dispositions of minor seventh chord

c Reconstruction of subject 3, with seventh chord voiced as in B

d Entry on III, m. 11, with seventh chord voiced as in A

The nature of the non-thematic section (mm. 13–14) which is added after the above entry is in direct contrast to the non-thematic section which was already in place before the entry (mm. 9–10). The succession of scale degrees in the first section – including I–I–IV–VII–III – are stated in reverse order in measures 13–14 as III–III–VII–IV–I. In the first section, the sixteenth-note scale passages derived from the beginning of the second subject descend in the left hand; in the second section, they ascend in the right hand while the contrapuntal line in the left hand consists of parallel thirds in eighth-notes.

The first entry of part II now follows. To link the entry in its original permutation (3–1–2) – as it appeared in mm. 11–12 of the second stage (see Example 5) – directly with the new non-thematic section described above results in a registral imbalance, even though the arrival of the subject on the tonic in the *comes* form in measure 11 is in keeping with normal practice.

In addition, a break now occurs in the upper voice between the end of the ascending passage in measure 14 – the new non-thematic section – and the entrance of subject 3 in measure 15 (as it appears in the second stage, m. 11). Subject 2, consequently, is shifted to the upper voice and subject 3 to the lowest voice, and an added sixteenth-note passage is inserted at the end of measure 14. The new position of subjects 2 and 3 now avoids the break in the line of the upper voice and results in new permutation, 2–1–3, which is not among the normal three cited above and which replaces the original permutation, 3–1–2. Further adjustments in measure 15 (the second half-measure) include a shift of subject 2 to the lower octave, due to the upper limit of the instrument's range (c'''), and the transposition of the first three notes of subject 3 down an octave.

The principle of extension is seen not only in the formal nature of the additions described above but also in the working out of the thematic material. The new thematic entry added at the end of part I, for example, is the only entry in the entire piece on a scale degree other than I or V, and the only one in a major key; it is an entry with its own permutation of the subject. (The entry begins in measure 11 and continues through measure 12.) The non-thematic section which follows (mm. 13 and 14) is the only one to use a harmonic sequence in ascending – rather than descending – fifths, as well as inverted sixteenth-note passages derived from the beginning of subject 2, and parallel thirds in eighth-notes; none of these compositional devices is found elsewhere in the fugue, except for the ascending sixteenth-note passage used in conjunction with the pedal-point. In addition, this is the only non-thematic section which does not include a figure derived from the initial motive of subject 1. The entry added at the end of the work is also unique since it introduces only the first subject, stated above an octave pedal-point on the tonic. The other two subjects are omitted – in part because neither hand is free to play them – and in their place supplementary notes are added above the middle voice and in the final chord.

The connection between the new entry (beginning on the third beat of m. 29 of the fourth stage) and the end of measure 24 of the third stage (lower system of Example 11) now also requires an adjustment. Bach adds a non-thematic half-measure to correct the registral imbalance caused by the abrupt change of register when subject 1 enters on c'' after the cadence on c' (an octave lower). His first step is to prepare for the entry of subject 1 on c'' by introducing a' and b' in the upper voice – beginning with the upbeat to measure 29 – with the bass moving in contrary motion (eb, d and c), and the middle voice, in reduced form, moving from c' to f' and eb'. Harmonically, the passage moves from VI to VII to I, with the sixth and the seventh scale degrees raised, and each implying a dominant function in relation to the following scale degree. (The dominant relationship of VI to VII becomes clear if we think of the VII as initially lowered.) In the final portion of the cadential sequence V–V–I (m. 29, third to fifth eighth-notes), voice I does not continue, as one might expect, in the upper part of the octave, moving from c'' to b' to c'', or from c'' to b' to a rest, and followed on the next eighth-note by the entry of subject 1; nor does voice II – reduced to eighth notes – move from eb' to d' and c'. Instead, Bach returns to the lower part of the octave – which he used in the preceding thematic passage – in order to complete the cadence: voice I takes over the notes which normally would belong to the middle voice if stated in a higher position – that is, eb', d' and c'; voice II states the pitches (c', b and c') which normally would belong to voice I, but now are stated an octave lower. On the next eighth-note, subject 1 enters on c'', prepared as described above and fulfilling the expectation which was raised at the beginning of measure 29, but momentarily thwarted by the return to a lower register for the cadence.

Bach uses the remaining two eighth-notes of the added half-measure to insert a rest, and to lengthen the eighth-note preceding the rest, in order to create a short dramatic pause – a time when all three voices have a chance to catch their breath. Bach accentuates the lengthened note in the middle of measure 28 by double appoggiaturas moving in contrary motion – on the last note of the entry of subject 1 in the lower voice, immediately before the upbeat to the cadence in measure 29. This rhetorical gesture is closely connected to the dynamic intensification introduced at the end of the third stage, and Bach might have emphasized it even more by the addition of a short fermata placed over the third beat, or over the rest itself. The insertion of the half-measure shifts the cadence which precedes the new entry – and subsequently the conclusion of the section and of the entire piece – from the downbeat to the third beat of the measure.

An objection could be raised at this point that the insertion of a single non-thematic half-measure destroys all the carefully established relationships of the parts to one another, including the relationship of the thematic entries and the non-thematic sections. Such an objection, however, confuses the means with the end. If the finished work were a means of realizing the proportional relationship, such an objection would be correct. But the opposite is true: the proportional relationship is one of the means by which Bach composed and realized the work. When the end has been achieved, the means can then be set aside. At certain points in realizing the work, other concerns – such as maintaining registral balance, establishing a sense of expectation or creating a rhetorical gesture – must take precedence.

In the final entry, we find the basic harmonies of the "theme" coming as expected on the downbeats of the half-measures, beginning on the third beat of measure 29 (m. 29,3, and mm. 30–1, 1 and 3.) The progression of scale degrees is I–IV–I (the fourth is initially suspended in the middle voice)–VII–I. The eighth-notes which precede the downbeats on IV, I and VII introduce "linking" or "bridge" harmonies: before IV, the third of I is raised to become a leading-tone and provide a dominant function; before the I which follows, we find the seventh chord also assuming a dominant function; before the VII, in contrast, the IV includes an added sixth, and thus functions as a subdominant. The metrical placement of these linking and fundamental harmonies – on the last eighth-note of one half-measure, and the downbeat of the next – continues the rhythmic design established by the sequences in descending fifths over the pedal-point. The harmonic and rhythmic design postulates the absence of subjects 2 and 3 – that is, of the "theme" in its entirety. The VII, placed in the first half of the final measure, provides no space for a linking harmony before the final chord, which, as is typical for the time, includes the major third.

From the first stage to the fourth stage

Over the course of the four stages, the range of the voices – the bass in particular – and their general disposition have been altered. In the first stage, the voices of both groups of three entries, seen as a whole, were based on the projected range implied by subject 1: *g″–c′* for voice I, *c″–g* for voice II, *c′–G* for voice III – that is, a disposition of the four normal voices in which the soprano, alto and bass are present, but the tenor is missing. The use of two additional subjects extends the normal range of the three voices upward by a fourth or a fifth to the next *c* or *g*; each voice, in the same disposition, now has a range of two octaves: *c‴–c′* for voice I, *g″–g* for voice II, *g′–G* for voice III. (In contrast to the standardized range described above, the actual range of the entries in stage one, not including the added cadence, are as follows: *c‴–c′* for voice I, *f″–f* for voice II, *f′–B* for voice III.)

The lowest voice is altered until the fourth stage when a fifth is removed from the top and added to the bottom of its range. Not only is the penultimate entry of the fugue (m. 26) transposed a fifth lower, but the voice as a whole is shifted downward; its range is still two octaves, but at a lower pitch level. In contrast, the normal range of the other two voices remains unchanged: *c‴–c′* for voice I, *g″–g* for voice II, *c′–C* for voice III. As a result, two voices, the third and fourth of a five-voiced disposition – one with the range of *c″–c* and the other with the range of *g′–G* – are missing, rather than just one voice with a two-octave range between the second and third voice. The voices which remain are the first, second and fifth. (In contrast to the normal range, the actual range of the voices is as follows: c'''–c' for voice I, f''–f for voice II – with one eb in m. 13 – and d'–C for voice III.) The voices now cover the entire four-octave range of the keyboard: the upper limit, c''', is found at the end of part I, and the lower limit, C, at the end of part II. The shift of subject 3 to the lower octave in the second entry of part II (mm. 20–1) belongs to a later development of the fourth stage.[6]

Figures 7–9 provide an overview of the changes which occur in the proportional relationships between form (in the sense described at the beginning of this essay – that is, as the arrangement of the work's sections in time) and the thematic structure. (The number 1 in the three figures indicates a four half-measure unit; number 2 indicates a section twice as long. The placement of the entries in groups of 2 and 1, is possible only after considering of the fugues in the *Well-Tempered Clavier*.)

The basic distribution of the two types of sections as shown in Figure 7 is

Thematic:	2	1	2	1		6
Non-thematic:	2	1	2	1		6
Total:	4	2	4	2		12

1 = 4 half measures
2 = 8 half measures

Figure 7 Basic distribution of thematic and non-thematic sections

subject to two alterations over the course of the four stages. First, the non-thematic section between the first and second thematic entries of part I is assigned to the first and second non-thematic sections of part II, with half added to each section. This means that in Figure 8 a non-thematic unit is subtracted from the first sub-section of part I, and a non-thematic unit is added to the first sub-section of part II. This changes the durations of the first sub-section of each part, and thus of the parts themselves; the duration of the non-thematic time and of the work as a whole, however, is not altered.

---

[6] See A. Dürr, *Zur Frühgeschichte des Wohltemperierten Klaviers I von Johann Sebastian Bach*, in Nachrichten der Akademie der Wissenschaften in Göttingen, I. Philologisch-historische Klasse (Göttingen, 1984) p. 19.

Thematic:	2	1	2	1		6
Non-thematic:	2–1	1	2+1	1		6
Total:	4–1	2	4+1	2		12

1 = 4 half measures
2 = 8 half measures

Figure 8 Revised distribution of thematic and non-thematic sections

Secondly, as shown in Figure 9, a thematic unit and a non-thematic unit are added at the end of the second sub-section of part I, and a thematic unit is added at the end of the second sub-section of part II as well. This extends the duration of the second sub-section of each part, and thus of both parts I and II; it also extends the length of the thematic and non-thematic time, and the length of the work as a whole. In conclusion: the form (in the sense defined above) and the thematic structure are in direct proportion to one another: the length of part I is equal to that of the non-thematic sections taken as a whole; the length of part II is equal to that of the thematic entries. Finally, the proportion of part I to part II is the same as the proportion of the non-thematic sections to the thematic entries.

Thematic:	2	1+1	2	1+1		6+2
Non-thematic:	2–1	1+1	2+1	1		6+1
Total:	4–1	2+2	4+1	2+1		12+3
		6+1		6+2		

1 = 4 half measures
2 = 8 half measures

Figure 9 Final distribution of thematic and non-thematic sections

The genesis of the
Prelude in C Major, BWV 870

JAMES A. BROKAW II

The rubric "Compositional Studies" actually contains several very differ-ent modes of inquiry: "biographical" questions that concern the composer's working methods, and "musical" questions that concern the genesis of individual works. This distinction is particularly significant in the case of J. S. Bach, where the vocal and instrumental works call for very different kinds of investigation, not only because the available source materials are so different but also because such different questions arise.

Composing and revising scores are most plentiful among the vocal works, and these allow us a detailed view of Bach's working methods.[1] Here, indeed, the question of how Bach usually composed vocal music is generally more interesting than the genesis of individual pieces since Bach relied for the most part on relatively "streamlined" composing methods,[2] due in part to the near-impossible demands of time under which he worked. On the other hand, it is usually impossible to know anything about Bach's working methods in the instrumental works because so many holographs of all kinds (to say nothing of revealing composing scores) are missing. But the key-board and organ works were composed in a more "spontaneous," "organic" fashion than the vocal works.[3] In general, one can actually speak of a higher level of "originality" among the keyboard and organ works.

Hence, questions of individual genesis are of much greater interest here.

---

[1] Robert L. Marshall, *The Compositional Process of J. S. Bach* (Princeton, 1972).

[2] "the rationalistic mechanics of the period – the preexistent modulation plans, the widespread use of static transposition as a modulation technique, sequential repetition, permutation and combination of constituent elements, large-scale repetition of sections via the technique of 'ritornello quotation'. . . seemingly enabled the arias and choruses to be spun out 'automatically'" (Marshall, p. 239).

[3] *Ibid.*, p. 240.

Additionally, knowledge gained by investigating a work's genesis can be an important adjunct to analysis. While studies of this kind are popular in Beethoven sketch research, few Bach scholars have attempted to couple analysis and genesis investigation in a similar fashion. In the realm of Bach's keyboard works, one can pursue questions of genesis by comparing the various versions of keyboard pieces, which survive abundantly (though often in near-bewildering array). An effective means of focusing such study is to concentrate on cases of expansion in the preludes and fugues, which are the genres in which expansion is most common.[4]

The preludes in C major and D minor from the *Well-Tempered Clavier II* are exceptional cases.[5] Not only do these preludes exist in versions of different lengths, but, in these rare instances, we have Bach's composing scores for the expanded preludes. These composing scores survive in the so-called "London Autograph" (BL),[6] that compilation of the *Well-Tempered Clavier II* prepared by J. S. Bach and his wife Anna Magdalena.[7] This manuscript provides us with quite singular views of Bach's self-critical action in composing for the keyboard.

The present discussion will deal with the C major prelude. There are three stages in the work's evolution: its earliest, seventeen-measure ancestor (BWV 870a) is found in P 804 and P 1089, the two most important sources for the works that pre-date the British Library manuscript. The "London Autograph" itself presents the prelude doubled in length, but still at an intermediate level of maturity (BWV 870b). As the prelude stands in the British Library manuscript, the last quarter of the fourteenth measure and the four subsequent measures (mm. 15–19) are crossed out, and a revised passage has been entered on the two staff systems that follow the prelude's conclusion. The prelude's final form (BWV 870) is found in a copy (P 430) made by Bach's student and (afterward) son-in-law, Johann Christian Altnikol.

---

[4] See James A. Brokaw, II, "Techniques of Expansion in the Preludes and Fugues of J. S. Bach" (unpublished Ph.D. dissertation, University of Chicago, 1986).

[5] Both of these cases are described elsewhere in the literature. See George Stauffer, "Bach as Reviser of his own Keyboard Works," *Early Music*, 13 (1985), pp. 185–98; Werner Breckoff, "Zur Entstehungsgeschichte des zweiten Wohltemperierten Klaviers von Johann Sebastian Bach" (unpublished Ph.D. dissertation, University of Tübingen, 1965), pp. 66–73; and Hermann Keller, *Das Wohltemperierte Klavier von J. S. Bach* (Kassel, 1965).

[6] Johann Sebastian Bach, *Das Wohltemperierte Klavier II*, ed. Don Franklin and Stephen Daw, No. 1 in the series British Music Facsimiles (London, 1980).

[7] See Walter Emery, "The London Autograph of the Forty-Eight," *Music and Letters*, 34 (1953), pp. 106–23, and Breckoff, pp. 24–37.

The earliest version is part of a corpus of five brief preludes and fughettas (BWV 870a, 899–902), upon which Bach drew heavily as he compiled the *Well-Tempered Clavier II*. In addition to the C major prelude, four other *WTC* II pieces have their origins in this small, apparently informal collection: the prelude in D minor, and the fugues in C major, G major and A flat major (transposed from F major). Neither P 804, fasc. 38 (copied by J. P. Kellner)[8] nor P 1089 (copied by J. C. Vogler)[9] contain all five works.[10]

The various versions, together with the autograph corrections in the BL provide an unusually wide variety of evidence to illuminate the prelude's evolution. The present discussion will concentrate on the process of expansion *per se* – that is, on the relationship between the early prelude found in P 804 and P 1089, and the preliminary versions of the *WTC* II prelude found in the BL. Here we have an unusually wide variety of evidence at our disposal. Not only can we compare the brief and expanded preludes, but we can probe the more immediate evidence of the compositional act itself at crucial stages of the work's evolution. Thus, as will be seen, an unusually detailed and vivid record emerges of the composer in dialogue with his material.

Nature and style of the early version

The C major prelude (BWV 870) is often cited as evidence of Bach's emulation of J. K. F. Fischer,[11] for the prelude's continuation bears strong resemblance to the themes of Fischer's Preludes I and V from the *Musikalische Blumenbüchlein* (1696).

[8] See Breckoff, pp. 17–18 and Russell Stinson, "The Bach Manuscripts of Johann Peter Kellner" (unpublished Ph.D. dissertation, University of Chicago, 1985).

[9] See Hans-Joachim Schulze, *Studien zur Bach-Überlieferung im 18. Jahrhundert* (Leipzig-Dresden, 1984), pp. 60–7.

[10] A late eighteenth-century manuscript in the hand of C. P. E. Bach's scribe Michel contains all five works, organized by key, and with consistent titles. The manuscript, N. Mus. MS 10490, acquired by the Staatsbibliothek Preussischer Kulturbesitz (West Berlin) in 1981, was described by Klaus Hofmann at the 1985 Bach Conference at Leipzig; he suggested that it represents the final stage of the brief collection's evolution. But the manuscript contains a startling corruption of the C major fughetta; and other indications, such as the consistent title "Preludio" – uncharacteristic for Bach's keyboard works – make it seem unlikely that the manuscript was copied from a Bach holograph.

[11] Reinhard Oppel, "Über Joh. Kasp. Ferd. Fischers Einfluss auf Joh. Seb. Bach," *Bach-Jahrbuch*, 7 (1910), pp. 63–9; and Siegfried Hermelink, "Das Präludium in Bach's Klaviermusik," *Jahrbuch des Staatlichen Instituts für Musikforschung Preussischer Kulturbesitz* (1976), pp. 7–80.

Hermann Keller, however, looks to the beginning of the Baroque era for the prelude's ancestry. He identifies the work as a *Toccata di durreze e ligature*[12] – a work whose texture is heavily colored by dissonance and suspension. By characterizing the prelude thus, Keller links the work with that small but well-known body of experimental, dissonant keyboard music composed at Naples during the early seventeenth century by such men as Frescobaldi, Macque and Trabaci.

Margaret Murata notes that such pieces are highly improvisatory and are characterized by a strong sense of spontaneity and formlessness, even by comparison with contemporary vocal works that also explore distant tonalities:[13]

Whereas vocal pieces such as Marenzio's *O voi che sospirate* or Guillamo Costeley's chanson *O Seigneur* move smoothly through remote keys based on the circle of fifths, the *durreze* and *stravaganti* use a variety of chords and chord progressions, seemingly chosen by caprice and deliberately not going anywhere.

The predominance of third-related chords and the dilution of common tones go hand in hand with the elimination of cadences as an organizing principle. . . . Constant deceptive resolution heightens the sense of formlessness.

In the C major prelude, Bach of course achieves the sense of "formless improvisation" by means better suited to the more highly developed tonal style of the eighteenth century. Here, chords are chosen not at all by caprice (progressions tend to follow the circle-of-fifths), but the composer has taken care to dilute the music's harmonic direction. Deceptive resolutions are frequent, a feature which the prelude has in common with its Neapolitan forbears. Motivic connections, which on first hearing seem to pervade the work, are on closer listening found to be only approximate. Indeed, strict imitation is used only sparingly, and then only under special circumstances, as will be seen at the end of this discussion.

Another feature of the prelude's style, presumably derived from the tradition established by the Neapolitans, is the fact that authentic cadences are often inverted, and are nearly always marked by a strong dissonance, usually prepared by a suspension (hence the generic title "toccata of dissonances and suspensions"). These devices serve to suspend musical tension just at the moment of resolution, so that the music continues smoothly and with minimal interruption, obscuring what would otherwise have been a point

---

[12] Hermann Keller, *Das Wohltemperierte Klavier von J. S. Bach* (Kassel, 1965), pp. 136–7.

[13] Margaret Murata, "Extravagant Harmony and Dissonance in Early *Seicento* Keyboard Music: *Stravaganze* and *Durreze e ligature*," (unpublished M.A. dissertation, University of Chicago, 1971), pp. 65–6.

of clear articulation. In general, Bach emphasizes the most important cadences by sustaining the root of the "goal harmony" in the bass while continuing the harmonic motion above, so that the "goal tone" becomes a pedal-point, and musical tension remains unresolved. Finally, the prelude is characterized by an elastic, fluidly shifting metric scheme.

All these elements are already present in the prelude's earliest form: the approximate motivic structure, the dilution of harmonic direction, and the fluid metric scheme. Note, in the Vogler copy of the early prelude (see Plate 1), that the scribe has mistakenly entered and then crossed out a bar-line at the middle of measure 5, perhaps because of the strong arrival on the third beat of that measure. (The previous cadence occurred on the downbeat of measure 2.)

In expanding the prelude for inclusion in the *Well-Tempered Clavier* II, Bach added an element of paradox. Beneath this guise of formless improvisation, the composer introduced a feature basic to closed musical form: the literal return. Indeed, the music in measures 20 to the third beat of bar 28 is a virtually literal restatement at the upper fourth of the material beginning in measure 5,3 through to the downbeat of measure 14.

Although the expanded prelude's first thirteen measures, as they stand in the British Library manuscript, are largely similar to the first preliminary version found in P 804 and P 1089, Bach made a number of changes as he wrote out the prelude in this source, several of which are of no little significance (see Example 1). He enriched the texture at several points, most

Example 1 Variants between BWV 870a (P 804/P 1089) and the initial scribing of BWV 870b in BL Add. MS 35021

Measure/Beats	P 1089/P 804	BL 35021
1 mm. 1–3	Pedal at c.	Pedal at c, C.
2 m. 1/3–4	*(musical notation)*	*(musical notation)*
3 m. 2/2	*(musical notation)*	*(musical notation)*
4 m. 3/3–4	*(musical notation)*	*(musical notation)*
5 m. 5/3–4	*(musical notation)*	*(musical notation)*
6 m. 6/4	*(musical notation)*	*(musical notation)*

Example 1 (*cont.*)

Measure/Beats	P 1089/P 804	BL 35021

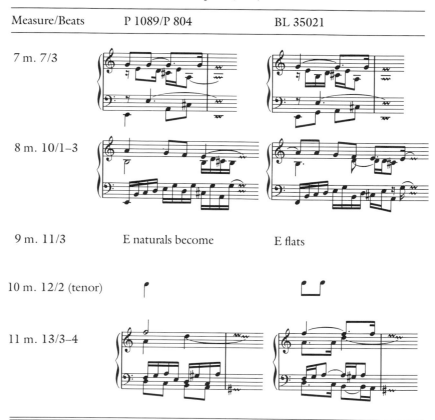

	P 1089/P 804	BL 35021
9 m. 11/3	E naturals become	E flats

notably at the very beginning, where he fortified the tonic pedal-point by adding the lower octave C.

As if keeping the free, "improvisatory" style in mind, he eliminated the sequential link between measures 1 and 2 by replacing the conjunct melodic motion in the second half of measure 1 with descending broken-chord motion. He adorned the cadence in measures 12–13 by adding a passing F♯ between the G and F♮. And he changed the supertonic-six chord with which the cadence begins to a Neapolitan by lowering the E♮s to E♭s in the soprano in the second half of measure 11. Bach added a written-out mordant to the fourth beat of measure 6, and he sharpened the rhythm of the bass in measure 12, by replacing the single whole-note with a dotted half-note and quarter-note.

Plate 1   BWV 870a, P 1089, fo. 4v (copy by J. C. Vogler)

The BL composing score: the order of events

Like nearly all of the pieces in the British Library manuscript, the C major prelude is written entirely on one side of a single bifolio (see Plate 2). The bifolio is ruled – again, like nearly all the others in the manuscript – in two columns of fourteen staves (or seven systems) each.[14]

Bach copied the first fourteen measures of his early version, with the alterations mentioned above, into the first five systems of the first column. In the last two systems in the first column he composed the passage that moves between the already-existing material, and the restatement at the subdominant. Beginning at the top of the second column, Bach began entering the restatement, and he finished at the beginning of the fourth system. In the rest of the fourth system, Bach added a three-measure tonic pedal-point to the original cadence; and he completed the expanded prelude in the fifth system of the second column, leaving two systems blank.

Some time after he finished writing the piece out, Bach entered a revised reading of the four-measure transition (mm. 14,4–19,4) on the two blank systems in the second column. It is clear that he revised the transition only later because he had already entered the note *V.S.* [*verte sequitur*] *volti* at the right side of the sixth system before he wrote down the revision.

Curiously, traces of three erased bar-lines may be seen in the first system in the second column. Werner Breckoff supposed that as Bach began entering the restatement, he inadvertently entered the bar-lines as they had fallen at the beginning of the movement, not noticing the half-measure shift.[15] Indeed, the note heads, stems and beams are carefully spaced around the erased bar-lines, but the existing bar-lines are crowded in between.

But in his preface to the facsimile edition, Don Franklin pointed out that the last of the erased "bar-lines" is in fact a double bar – perhaps indicating, as Franklin suggests, that Bach had at first intended to copy the seventeen-measure early version as it stood, and had ruled the page accordingly, but decided to expand the work only after he had begun to copy it out.[16]

---

[14] The bifolio on which the G♯ minor pair is written has columns of eight systems each.

[15] Breckoff, pp. 65–6.

[16] At seventeen measures, the work would have been by far the shortest prelude in the second cycle. Only the 21-measure G minor prelude approaches BWV 870a in brevity – but the G minor prelude is the *only* work marked *Largo* by the composer in the *Well-Tempered Clavier* II. It is well known that Bach expanded twelve preludes in the *Well-Tempered Clavier* I. Alfred Dürr has recently suggested that these expanded preludes may reflect Bach's systematic effort (interrupted, perhaps, by the move from Cöthen to Leipzig) to enlarge all the preludes in the *WTC* I in response to a new conception of the balance between prelude and fugue. See Alfred Dürr, *Zur Frühgeschichte des Wohltemperierten Klaviers I von Johann Sebastian*

Plate 2 BWV 870b, composing score (Add. MS 35021, fo. 1r)

There are problems with this view. First of all, the early version would seem to be inappropriate for the *Well-Tempered Clavier* II simply because of its length.[17] Second, the manuscript itself is not entirely consistent with the notion that Bach at first intended simply to copy the early version. Bach could have fit the seventeen-measure piece on the first column of the page with ease. If he really intended to put the final three measures of his unexpanded early version at the top of the second column, where traces of the erased bar-lines remain, then he must have drawn only five systems in the first column, instead of the seven found everywhere else in the manuscript. That Bach would use only five systems where he had space for seven seems particularly unlikely in view of the composer's well-known efforts to conserve paper.

Bach, (Göttingen, 1984), pp. 64–7. If Bach were already enlarging his preludes in relation to fugues as early as 1722, then it would seem extremely unlikely for him to include a seventeen-measure prelude in the *WTC* II whose accompanying fugue (that is, BWV 870a, 2) is 34 measures long.

[17] Bach, *Das Wohltemperirte Klavier II*, p. vi.

It may be that Bach began with a completely different notion of how to expand the seventeen-measure prelude,[18] one that he abandoned during the course of his work. Perhaps he did not at first intend so substantial a restatement of material; or perhaps he meant only to rely on an extended pedal-point, a component of so many expansions of preludes in the *WTC* I.[19]

The composition and revision of measures 14–19

We have several indications of how Bach composed the transitional passage. In the last system in the first column, the composer was forced to write a dotted-eighth/sixteenth rhythm in such a way that the beam straddles a bar-line. This suggests that Bach, in composing the five and a half measures of new material, first wrote out the bass, then supplied the bar-lines, and finally filled in the upper parts. As he completed the upper parts, he ran into spacing problems in the fourth quarter of measure 18, where his notation of the soprano crosses the bar-line.

If Bach's attention was drawn from matters of calligraphy as he entered the new passage in the BL bifolio, it was surely with good reason. The five and a half bars, after all, precede the work's most important point of internal articulation. At measure 20, the recapitulation at the subdominant level begins. If Bach is to preserve the mien of continuous improvisation he has cultivated so carefully in the first thirteen measures, then the seam at which the restatement begins must be handled with great care indeed.

Now, the transition is a prolonged approach to the F major cadence at measure 20, where the restatement begins (see Plate 2). The structure of the external voices gives the passage a very strong contrapuntal focus. The approach really begins in measure 15, where the bass achieves its highest register in the prelude, *B*♭, and from that point descends in gradual, mostly stepwise motion through the interval of an eleventh to *F* at measure 20.

---

[18] In any case, Bach cannot have laid out all the bar-lines in advance. The first erased bar-line at the top of the second column is placed at the half-measure; yet there is no corresponding half-measure at the bottom of the first column. The manuscript's appearance suggests that he laid out bar-lines in advance only for the coda, which, like the first fourteen measures, already existded in the early version. According to this hypothesis, Bach would have simply copied out the first fourteen measures, bar-lines and text together (with some alteration), but would have left blank the staves on which he planned to compose the new material (according to the later-abandoned expansion scheme). The composer would then have supplied the bar-lines for the coda at the top of the facing page.

[19] Cf. the preludes in F♯ minor, G♯ minor, A minor, B♭ major and B major. Dürr, p. 66.

This linear descent is complemented by a similar stepwise descent in the soprano, from *a″* on the third beat of measure 14 to the pitch *a′* in measure 20. The original passage, Bach's revision and the further changes in Altnikol's copy are compared in Example 2. Bach's improvements render the passage more fluid; harmonic progressions become more chromatic as the contrapuntal motion becomes more focused.

Example 2 BWV 870b, mm. 14–19, comparison of initial scribing and revision

Let us look closely at the cadence itself at the passage's close. Here, Bach rendered the uppermost part chromatic; more importantly, he created a brief parenthesis at G minor, just before the arrival at F major. In the final quarter of measure 18 and in the second quarter of 19, Bach replaced E♮s with E♭s; and throughout the passage he replaced F♮s with F♯s. This harmonic transformation is depicted in Figure 1. The parenthesis robs the

Measure: 18   19   20
Initial scribing: F: V⁷/iii–vi–IV–vii–iii–vi–ii–V–I
        Revision: F: V⁷/iii–vi–IV
                                 G: III–vi–V⁷/V–V⁷–i
                                         F: ii–V–I

Figure 1 BWV 870b: analysis of harmonic changes in mm. 18–19

central F major cadence of its harmonic emphasis. Surely we may see Bach's action as an effort to minimize the impact of tonal arrival at one of the work's most important points of articulation, in service of the prelude's "improvisatory, formless" style.

Bach altered the bass significantly. He replaced the steady eighth-note motion with a dotted rhythm that changes to steady eighth-notes only two beats before the F major arrival, emphasizing the conclusive ii–V–I motion at the cadence. In the prelude's final version (as copied out by Altnikol in P 430), Bach changed the bass again. As shown in the *ossia* to Example 2, he replaced eighth-note anacruses with sixteenth-notes. The revised upbeats match those in the soprano. Bach did more than sharpen the rhythm when he revised the bass. He replaced the *D* in measure 19,2 with an *F♯*; and he replaced the *C* in measure 19,4 with an *E*. In doing so, Bach removed the roots of the submediant and dominant harmonies, reducing even further the harmonic component of the prelude's most important internal cadence, while strengthening its contrapuntal shape with the rhythmic changes just mentioned.

All of Bach's revisions to this passage seem intended to obscure, at least locally, the crucial medial cadence. This observation helps to clarify an important problem in performing the C major prelude. Should one maintain a relatively strict tempo, driving toward the arrival at F major, which is one of the work's most important structural junctures? Or should one allow the passage the greater flexibility of rhythm that the abundant chromaticism would seem to call for? In view of the way Bach worked to skew the passage's harmonic direction by injecting the chromaticism (while honing its contrapuntal focus, as if in compensation), it seems clear that the performer should join in the effort to hide this central articulation from all but the most careful listener. It is as though Bach wished to conceal so far as possible the paradox essential to the expanded prelude: that although it feigns continuous improvisation it incorporates a near literal return.

The coda

While the seven measures that precede the restatement are the most crucial newly-composed group on the BL bifolio, Bach still needed to deal with the expanded work's conclusion. The coda effectively begins with the C major arrival on the downbeat of measure 30. Bach found he was able to work in the early version's final measures, from measure 30,3 to measure 32,1.

Instead of allowing the cadential material to close the work, however, Bach added a two-measure pedal-point that resolves at measure 34. Newly composed, then, is the material from measure 28,3, where the restated music leaves off, through the C major cadence at measure 30,1 to 30,3 (see Example 3). This newly-composed group is quite remarkable, for the

Example 3 BWV 870b, mm. 28–30

first two half-measures (mm. 28,3–29,2) are quite closely sequential. The only deviation in the otherwise strictly sequential progression is the chromatic passing-tone Ab in the soprano of the first half-measure.

By making the two half-measures nearly strictly sequential, Bach imbued his composition with yet another element of paradox. Despite the prelude's motivic economy, this is the only instance that approaches strict sequence in the prelude. The two half-measures stand in subtle yet distinct contrast to the approximate, slightly varying imitation that pervades the rest of the prelude and is so important an aspect of its style. In the BL bifolio, the close imitation is heavily marked by erasure, especially the alto, measure 28, fourth beat; alto and bass, measure 29, first beat, and the alto in the second beat of measure 29 (see Plate 3). We will return to these erasures shortly.

Plate 3   BWV 870b, mm. 28–30,1. BL MS 35021, fo. 1r, second column,
fourth system

The object of this discussion has not been to present a thoroughgoing and
"objective" account of Bach's expansion and revision of the C major prelude,
but to attempt to illuminate his concerns though an analysis of the work
and his revisions. Now, while "an understanding of the compositional
process is not equivalent to insight into the work of art as such,"[20] the steps
an artist takes to refine and clarify the image are surely important clues to
his conceptin of the work, and even to his intentions. While an understanding of the genesis of a work of art is not a surrogate for analysis, it
is clear that these two concerns – investigation of genesis, and analysis –
inform one another to considerable profit.

In this case, Bach's efforts to balance and coordinate various musical
parameters at the medial cadence are telling indeed, for they underscore for
us the main problem of the prelude's composition, and even its stylistic
"point." The medial cadence at measure 20, where the transposed restatement begins, is the prelude's most important internal juncture. And yet
the cadence must for that very reason be understated almost to the point of
imperceptibility in the service of the prelude's outward "improvisatory,
formless" style. Hence, when Bach revised the crucial passage on the BL
bifolio, he inserted a G minor parenthesis in the final cadential motion but
compensated for the weakening of tonal direction by honing and focusing
the passage's contrapuntal motion. And, in changes seen in the Altnikol

[20] Joseph Kerman, "Beethoven Sketchbooks in the British Museum," *Publication of the Royal
Music Association*, 93 (1966–7), p. 93, cited in Philip Gossett, "Beethoven's Sixth Symphony: Sketches for the First Movement," *Journal of the American Musicological Society*, 27
(1974), pp. 248–84.

copy, he eliminated the incisive rising-fourth-falling-fifth motion in the bass to make the moment of arrival at the subdominant as subtle as possible.

Finally, the erasures in measures 28–9 seem to imply that the idea of an episode of strict sequential imitation did not at first occur to the composer. They perhaps suggest the composer's assessment of his creation, and his sense of assurance that it indeed meets the exacting and contradictory demands of its genre: that it appear formless, and yet be highly structured; that it be rigorously cogent while feigning an improvisatory mien. Perhaps the erasures suggest Bach's sense of assurance that the balance between motivic economy and melodic freedom had been so surely struck that he could risk this final aesthetic contradiction.

Reconstructing the *Urpartitur* for *WTC* II: a study of the "London autograph" (BL Add. MS 35021)

DON O. FRANKLIN

No complete copy of *The Well-Tempered Clavier* (*WTC* II) in Bach's hand survives. The primary autograph source, Add. MS 35021 – also known as the "London autograph" or the BL – is a collection of 22 folios, seventeen of which are autograph; the remaining five include the hand of Anna Magdalena. (The only other autograph source, a single folio in P 274, contains a second copy of the fugue in A flat, BWV 886,2.) The "London autograph" originally may have been complete, but in its present state contains the text for only 21 of the 24 preludes and fugues: the three missing pairs include the preludes and fugues in C♯ minor, D major and F minor (BWV 873, 874 and 881).[1] Although a large number of the folios are written out in a calligraphic hand, the manuscript as a whole is not a *Reinschrift*: the folios do not include a dated title page or a "Soli Deo Gloria" ("S.D.G."), Bach's usual indications that a work is in a completed form. Along with several fair copies, the folios include one composing score and several revising or intermediate copies.

---

[1] The "London autograph" was lacking four of the 24 preludes and fugues when it was acquired by the British Museum in 1896. The E major prelude and fugue, numbered as folio 21, was subsequently purchased by the museum, but the remaining three folios have been missing since at least 1879, when Miss Sara Emmett received the folios from her father, who had purchased them from Clementi's estate in 1832. (See Walter Emery, "The London Autograph of 'The Forty-eight'," *Music and Letters*, 34 (1953), pp. 107–13.) The fact that Clementi printed the BL text of the C sharp minor fugue (one of the three missing portions) in his "Introduction to the Art of playing the Pianoforte," published in 1820, suggests that the book was complete when it came into his possession. He may have received the manuscript from his father-in-law, the Berlin cantor Johann Gottfried Lehmann, who, as a member of the Berlin Bach circle, had close ties with Agricola, and perhaps with Wilhelm Friedemann as well. (For a discussion of Lehmann's role in the transmission of Bach sources, see Hans-Joachim Schulze, *Studien zur Bach-Überlieferung im 18. Jahrhundert* (Leipzig-Dresden, 1984), pp. 59, 150–1.)

Scholars, because of the composite nature of the manuscript, have viewed the BL as an intermediate copy and not a final one, and have assigned the role of *Primärquelle* to the two earliest complete scores of *WTC* II, both copied out by members of the Bach circle: P 430, known as the Altnikol copy, written out by Bach's son-in-law in 1744, and Am.B. 57.2, known as the Kirnberger copy, written out by a Kirnberger scribe in Berlin in the 1750s (see Table 1). Both copies, however, transmit readings of the text widely divergent from one another and from the BL; in the case of the Altnikol copy, the readings often appear to pre-date the "London autograph." Although recent scholarship has attempted to account for these discrepancies and to define the relationship among the three sources, the role of the BL in the genesis and the early transmission of *WTC* II, as the summary below will show, has not yet been fully clarified. To define and clarify that role – including to what extent the BL may represent a final copy of Book II – is the aim of the present study.

The "London autograph" remained largely unknown by Bach scholars until the mid-twentieth century.[2] In 1953, Walter Emery, the first scholar to examine the handwriting in the manuscript, verified it as an autograph – specifically as an apograph, since he identified the hand of Anna Magdalena in five of the folios. Emery also identified two basic groups of folios, one with "Praeludium" titles, and the second with "Prelude" titles.[3] A decade later, Werner Breckoff undertook a more extensive study of the BL as part of his 1965 dissertation, "Zur Entstehungsgeschichte des zweiten Wohltemperiertes Claviers."[4] Breckoff's study, which laid the foundation for further research, includes a comprehensive list of sources for *WTC* II, along with a detailed comparative study of the two manuscript groups stemming from the Altnikol and Kirnberger copies. Breckoff describes the "Praeludium group" (whose watermark he identified) as a *Niederschrift*, or first copy,

---

[2] The first scholar to examine the manuscript in any detail was Frederick Westlake, who in his article on "Das Wohltemperirte Klavier," in *A Dictionary of Music and Musicians*, ed. G. Grove (London, 1893), Vol. 4, pp. 482–5, presents the results of a brief comparative study with Kroll's *Bach-Gesellschaft* edition. Ebenezer Prout, in "The Autograph of Bach's Wohltemperirtes Clavier, Pt. 2," in *Monthly Musical Record*, 26 (1896), pp. 49–52, and 73–6, gives a more detailed description of each individual folio. Prout may have examined the manuscript at the request of Alfred Dörffel, the editor of Vol. 45 of the *BG*, a supplementary volume published in 1897. In the appendix to the volume, pp. 243–50, Dörffel prints the BL text of the C major prelude, BWV 870b, and provides a list of variants for each movement, based on Prout's description of the 22 folios.

[3] Walter Emery, "The 'London Autograph,'" pp. 113–23.

[4] Werner Breckoff, *Zur Entstehungsgeschichte des zweiten Wohltemperiertes Claviers* (unpublished Ph.D. dissertation, Tübingen, 1965).

written out in 1738/9, and the "Prelude group" (whose watermarks he was unable to identify) as a *Reinschrift*, written out between 1740 and 1742. Breckoff concludes that the "Prelude group" includes a later or more final version of the text than the "Praeludium group." Taken as whole, Breckoff considers the BL to be an "intermediate copy" which served as the basis for the Kirnberger manuscript; the Altnikol manuscript he believes to be based on a second copy in Bach's possession containing his corrected scores.

Walter Dehnhard, the editor of the Wiener Urtext Edition of Book II, published in 1983,[5] also viewed the BL as an intermediate manuscript. His edition is the first to appear in almost a century and the first to include the BL as one of the primary sources. (The Steingräber edition of Hans Bischoff appeared in 1894 and the *Bach-Gesellschaft* edition of Franz Kroll, Vol. 14, was published in 1853; the BL was not known to either editor.) Dehnhard, in the stemma which he provides for each movement, assumes that Bach, wrote out an additional score for the majority of the preludes and fugues, and that a copy of his later scores is transmitted in P 430, the Altnikol copy.[6] He acknowledges, however, that for almost half of the preludes and fugues, it is difficult, if not impossible, to derive a final text directly from his stemmata. For at least 22 of the 48 movements, he is forced to present a composite version, incorporating details of both texts, as in the D# minor and B♭ minor pairs, or to base the prelude and fugue on separate sources, as in the D major and E major pairs. For the movements, such as the A minor fugue (to be discussed later in the study), where the Altnikol copy clearly transmits an earlier version of the text, Dehnhard is unclear about which reading to choose. Even though for eleven of the 48 movements he chooses the BL reading as the final one, at no point does he consider the possibility that the BL in any systematic way may transmit a later reading of the text. And, in contrast to his edition of *WTC* I, Dehnhard does not provide a chronological summary of Bach's revisions for Book II. (For Book I, Dehnhard identifies four different readings of the text, based on stages of correction and revision in the autograph score.[7]) Like Kroll and Bischoff

[5] *J. S. Bach: Das Wohltemperierte Klavier II*, ed. W. Dehnhard (Vienna, 1983).

[6] Dehnard's stemmata for 36 of the 48 movements posits a second copy of the score (ß, or A2) as the basis for the Altnikol copy. For several of the 36 movements, however, including the preludes and fugues in C sharp minor, F minor and B major, Dehnhard bases his text on the BL or the Kirnberger copy. (It will become clear in the course of this study that the Altnikol readings, except for a few specific cases, cannot be seen as representing a *Fassung letzter Hand*.)

[7] *J. S. Bach: Das Wohltemperierte Klavier I*, ed. W. Dehnhard (Vienna, 1977). The stages A 1 to 4 are described by Dehnhard on pp. x–xxi. That at least two of these stages have a direct relationship to Book II is shown in the reconstructed chronology at the end of this essay.

100 years earlier, Dehnhard, therefore, must determine Bach's final text for almost half of the volume primarily on the basis of "taste" and an innate sense of style.[8]

This paper approaches the problem of a final text for *WTC* II from another perspective. Rather than constructing a stemma by positing a series of lost composing or revising scores, I propose to identify a set of working procedures which will provide a basis for reconstructing Bach's "copying-out process" for Book II. An understanding of this process will, in turn, allow us to define the nature and scope of the *Urpartitur* – used in a broad sense to encompass Bach's working text[9] – and eventually to consider the question of a *Fassung letzter Hand*. Rather than limiting myself to the traditional philological approach (which in the case of *WTC* II produces questionable results) I draw on three basic types of evidence: diplomatic (paper, hand and lineal), notational (title, clef and placement of fermatas), and style-critical. (The latter category includes observations about Bach's formal and stylistic procedures, including his use of distinctive key schemata, or groups of keys, as a part of the compilation process.) The diplomatic and notational evidence will be considered first, followed by a discussion of Bach's key schema for Book II. Comparisons will be drawn with the key schemata and notational practice in the autograph and early manuscript copies of the Inventions and Sinfonias, and *WTC* I, Bach's two other primary collections for "clavier" (I use the term "clavier" as defined by Robert Marshall in his terminological study of the keyboard works.[10]) The paper concludes with a description of Bach's copying-out procedures for the BL and the implications of this

---

[8] Bischoff prefers the Kirnberger copy over the two Altnikol copies, and bases 28 of the 48 movements on Kirnberger, and 20 on Altnikol. (His choice, as he states in the preface, is often made on the basis of which reading the finds the "most beautiful" – that is, on taste.) Of the 48 pieces, Kroll bases eighteen on the Fürstenau copy, eighteen on the Altnikol and twelve on the Kirnberger.

[9] *Urpartitur* traditionally is defined as a "complete but not final score." Since Bach copied out Book II over a period of several years and in several stages, a complete score for the entire work may not have existed until the BL was completed *c.* 1740. I use the term, therefore, to denote Bach's working scores (based directly on the *Konzeptpartitur*), which include portions of his composing scores or preliminary drafts, and represent the initial stages of the compilation process.

[10] Robert L. Marshall, "Organ or 'Klavier'? Instrumental Prescriptions in the Sources of Bach's Keyboard Works," in *J. S. Bach as Organist: His Instruments, Music and Performance Practices*, ed. G. Stauffer and E. May (Bloomington, 1986), pp. 212–39. Marshall defines four categories of Bach keyboard works, based on the designations found in the primary sources: "manualiter," "pedaliter," "clavier" and "cembalo." According to Marshall, pp. 232–4, Bach uses "clavier" to denote composition which could be played on a single manual instrument, and which were restricted to a four range compass, from C–c'''. (See note 41 for a discussion of the exceptions found in Book II.)

process for the reconstruction of the *Urpartitur* and the early transmission of *WTC* II. Rather than including illustrations from the BL in the body of the paper, I will refer the reader to the folios as they are reproduced in a facsimile edition published by the British Library.[11]

My discussion, while focusing on BL, draws on the five source-groups described in Table 1. (The list is selective, but includes all primary sources copied out before *c*. 1760.)[12] Source-group A includes the two autograph sources cited above, and source-group B the primary non-autograph sources: the Altnikol and Kirnberger copies, along with a second copy written out by Altnikol in 1755, P 402 (which will be referred to by manuscript number), and the Hamburg MS, with a title page dated 1742 and additions in a later hand. Several additional manuscript copies (source-group C 1–3) preserve portions of the BL text at various stages of its compilation and revision. Of particular importance is the Fürstenau manuscript, which, as an early and exact copy of Add. MS 35021, can be used to provide the text to the three missing preludes and fugues. Further evidence about Bach's working methods, as well as his *Urpartitur*, is provided by the individual preludes and fugues (source-group D 1–2) copied out in the late 1730s by Anna Magdalena and Agricola. Another source-group (E 1–2), recently described by James A. Brokaw,[13] includes manuscript copies of an earlier group of preludes and fugues which Bach composed in the 1720s and 1730s and on which he drew in compiling Book II.

Diplomatic evidence

A close examination of the BL reveals that it is a compilation of three distinct layers or groups. Layer 1, with one type of paper and one lineal, or staff-liner, includes the twelve preludes and fugues with the "Praeludium" title (Emery's Group A) in an ascending primarily diatonic key schema: c d E♭ E e F f♯ G g A a b. Layers 2 and 3 include the nine movement-pairs with the "Prelude" title. (Emery's Group B is based on the titles for all nine "Prelude" pairs, but two distinct layers can be differentiated on the basis of

[11] *Johann Sebastian Bach: Das Wohltemperierten Klavier II*, ed. D. Franklin and S. Daw (London, 1980). The facsimile edition reproduces the present format of the BL in which the original bifolios were unfolded, mounted and bound as full sheets, numbered as fo. 1r to 22v.

[12] The only primary source not consulted is the Konwitschny copy in the Bach-Archiv in Leipzig, which has recently come to light. The manuscript is based on P 430, the Altnikol copy.

[13] See James A. Brokaw II, "Recent Research on the Sources and Genesis of Bach's *Well-Tempered Clavier*, Book II," *Bach*, 16 (1985), pp. 17–35.

Table 1 *Description of primary manuscript sources for WTC II*

Group	Shelf no.	Scribe	Date	Titles
A	Autograph scores			
1	Add. MS 35021 (BL) BWV 870–93 (BWV 873874 and 881 missing)	JSB	*c*. 1738/9–40	[Titles shown in Table 2 and in Plates 2–6]
2	P 274 (SPK) BWV 886,2	JSB	*c*. 1738?	"Fuga ex Gis dur"
B	Complete manuscript copies			[Title pages cited in chronology]
1	P 430 (SPK) BWV 870–93	Altnikol	1744	"Prelude [Key]" "Fuga à 3, à 4" "Fugetta à 3" (889,2)
2	Am.B. 57,2 (SPK) BWV 870–93	Kirnberger scribe	1750s	"Preludio [Nr]" "Fuga [Nr.]" "Fuga à 3, à 4"
3	Hamburg. Hand 1/ BWV 873–85 887–93	Gestiwitz?		Identical to BL except: "Praeludium [Nr] di. J. S. Bach," "Fuga," "Fuga à 4" (881 891 and 892).
	Hand 2/ BWV 870–2 886			"Prelude," "Fuga, Fuga à 3, à 4" (870–2 and 886)
4	P 402 (SPK) BWV 870–93	Altnikol	1755	"Prelude" "Fugue à 3, à 4"
5	Hering copy Location unknown	Michel?	1750s?	unknown
C	Incomplete manuscript copies			
1	[Fürstenau] P 416, Adnex 3 (SPK) BWV 872–5 881 885 886,2 887,1 888 890,1 891,1 892,1	Anon12 (Ur)?	*c*. 1740	Identical to BL. In addition: "Prelude 4 di J. S. Bach," "Fuga" (873) "Prelude 5 di J. S. Bach," "Fuga à 4" (874) "Prelude ex 12 F," "Fuga" (881)
	876,1 (frag.) Add. 38068 (BL) BWV 884 Newberry Lib, Chg. (Cn) BWV 892,2			"Prelude ex Es+" "Praeludium 15," "Fuga 15" "Fuga à 4"

Table 1 (*cont.*)

Group	Shelf no.	Scribe	Date	Titles
2	Gorke S. 312 (Bach-Archiv) BWV 870–92 (BWV 876 893 886,1 887,1 891,1 892,1 missing)	Lpz.copyist	*c.* 1750s	Identical to BL and Fürstenau except: "Praeludium [Nr] di J. S. Bach," "Fuga à 3, Fuga" (870 and 890); "Praelude [Nr] di J. S. Bach," "Fuga, Fuga à 3" (880 and 881)
3	P 209 (SPK) BWV 872 874 877 880 883 886 887 890	Kirnberger	1750s	"Praeludium [Nr] J. S. Bach," "Fuga, Fuga à 4"
D	Manuscript copies of individual movements			
1	P 595, Adnex 4 (SPK) BWV 875,2 872b,2 (in C) 871,2 876,2 (in D)	Agricola	*c.* 1738/9	"Fughetta"
2	P 226 (DSB) BWV 872a,1 875,1 and 2	Anna Mag	*c.* 1738–41	Hand of JSB: "Praeludium," "Fuga"
E	Manuscript copies of earlier collections of preludes and fugues			
1	P 1089 (SPK) BWV 870a 901,2 875a,1	Vogler	*c.* 1728	"Praelude composeè par J. S. Bach," "Fughetta" (870a); "Fughetta" (901,2); "Praeambulum" (875a,1)
2	P 804 (SPK) BWV 870a 902,2 873,2	Kellner Unknown	1730s	"Praelude et Fughetta" (870a); "Fughetta" (902,2); "Fuga à 3" (873,2)

　* Paper ruled with 16 staves instead of 14
　** Last page of folio ruled only to end of fugue

paper and lineal.) Layer 2, copied out on three types of paper with two lineals, includes seven pairs in an ascending chromatic order: C♯ d♯ F♯ g♯ B♭ b♭ B; layer 3 includes two of the remaining preludes and fugues (C and A♭) written out on two types of paper and with two different lineals or staff-liners. The diplomatic evidence is summarized in Table 2. (The watermark numbers and dates are taken from the recently published watermark cata-

Table 2 *The BL (Add. MS 35021): diplomatic evidence*

Layer	Scribe	WM no. and date	Lineal	Other Bach mss with same paper and lineal
1 Praeludium c d E F G	Anna Mag (Titles JSB)	105 1738–40	B	
E♭ e F f♯ g A a b	JSB		B	St 129, (BWV 1057) cemb St 154, fi and vla (BWV 1067) P 28 (BWV 245), pp. 9–24, [paper only]
2 Prelude C♯ d♯ F♯ B♭ b♭*	JSB	72 [1739–40];	C	P 226 (BWV 872a, 1; 875, 1&2) pp. 19–29: St 76, (BWV 210) 1 and 7 P 202 (BWV 866–9), PP. 65–75 lineal only] PP 28 (BWV 245), pp. 25–92 [paper only]
g♯*		70	C	
B		60	B?	
A♭				
Prelude A♭	JSB	17	D	
3 Praelude C Fuga**	JSB	67 1739–42	A	P 226 (BWV 1037), p. 5–17

* Paper ruled with 16 staves instead of 14
** Last page of folio ruled only to end of fugue

logue by Wisso Weiss and Yoshitake Kobayashi;[14] the lineals are numbered as in the facsimile edition.)

Taken as a whole, the evidence indicates that the three layers were compiled in a basic chronological sequence and that the majority of the folios were written out in 1739 and 1740. Although only two of the six types of paper can be dated (layer 1, Nr. 105, 1738–40, and layer 3, Nr. 67, 1739–42), it can be shown that the remaining papers were used by Bach during the late 1730s. Bach's hand reflects the same basic chronological sequence as the paper. The forms of the C clef, as described by Dadelsen in

---

[14] Wisso Weiss and Yoshitake Kobayashi, *Katalog der Wasserzeichen in Bachs Originalhand-schriften*, NBA IX/1–2, (Kassel, 1985).

his *Schriftchronologie*,[15] include the simple "hook" form, typical of the mid to late 1730s, as well as later variant forms. The shape of the half-notes also reflects a basic progression from the oval and tear-shaped noteheads, with stems on the left, to the more rounded noteheads, often open on top, with the stem close to the middle of the notehead. (The quarter-note rests show a comparable progression from a small curved form – a reverse Z with tails – to a simpler and less calligraphic form without tails.) The handwriting in the three layers, however, does not reflect as strict or continuous a chronological progression as seen in P 271, the autograph copy of the eighteen chorales, also copied out during this period.[16] Rather, the presence of several clef forms and differences in script suggests that Bach went back and forth between the various layers over a period of several months and perhaps several years, filling in missing preludes or fugues, or substituting an entire folio. The lineals, when compared with other manuscripts of the same period, serve as a further tool in dating each layer.

Layer 1 may have been begun as early as 1738, but was likely written out by Bach in 1739. The paper (Hammer and Anvil, Nr. 105) is the same as that found in the parts for two instrumental works, St 129 (BWV 1057) and St 154 (BWV 1067);[17] the lineal (lineal B) is also identical (see Table 2). That Bach intended to copy out layer 1 as a complete group of preludes and fugues is seen by the fact that all twelve folios are lined with the same staff-liner; however, evidence presented later in the essay will show that he did not copy out the entire layer at one sitting but over an extended period of time.

Layer 2, as both hand and paper indicate, was copied out slightly later than layer 1. The paper for five of the pairs (C♯, d♯, F♯, B♭ and b♭, folios 3, 6, 9, 18 and 19) was in use by Bach and his copyists in the late 1730s and at least until

---

[15] Georg von Dadelsen, *Beiträge zur Chronologie der Werke Johann Sebastian Bachs*, Tübinger Bach-Studien (Trossingen, 1958), Vols. 4/5, pp. 107–13.

[16] The early portions of the eighteen chorales (BWV 651–63), copied out in P 271, reflect more closely the *Schriftchronologie* established by Dadelsen and described above: the clefs become increasingly smaller and less hook-shaped and the noteheads are of the latter two types found in the BL. Although Dadelsen concluded that P 271 was written out after the BL (*Beiträge*, p. 109), the similarity in handwriting suggests that Bach was working on both manuscripts during the same time period – that is, beginning in the late 1730s.

[17] See Weiss, *NBA* IX/1, p. 86. The form of the watermark found in St 129 is reproduced in *NBA* IX/2, p. 195. The characteristics of Bach's hand, including the form of the C clef and the shape of the half-notes in both St 129 and 154, indicate a relatively early date for the parts and for the BL (*c.* 1738–9); the parts presumably were intended for performance by the Collegium Musicum in the fall of 1739.

1740. Several of the sources which use the same paper (Schönburg coat of folios: portions of P 226, in the hand of Anna Magdalena (source D 2) are directly linked to the BL, as later discussion will show, and can be dated 1738–41;[19] the lineal is identical with that of the above five folios (lineal C). Two autograph parts for Cantata 210 (St 76, 1 and 7), dated 1738–40 by Dadelsen,[20] also use the same lineal and show the same handwriting characteristics. (The parts belong to a set of seven written out by Bach and Agricola, another scribe – see source D 1 – who appears to have assisted Bach in compiling Book II.) Finally, autograph portions of the score for the St John Passion, P 28, believed to date from 1739, use the same type of paper and also show similarities in handwriting; particularly striking is the shape of Bach's initial "P" on the first folio of P 28 and in the titles of the preludes in layer 2 (see folios 15r and 18r).[21]

The other two papers in layer 2 are more difficult to date. The paper for the G sharp minor prelude and fugue, folio 15 (two-headed eagle with scepter, Nr. 70), is singular; its similarity to other two-headed eagle papers (Nrs. 65–9) may imply a *c.* 1739–40 date, but the evidence is inconclusive. (It is lined with the same staff-liner as the five folios described above.) The paper for the B major prelude and fugue, folio 20 (two-headed eagle with letters HR, Nr. 60) is also of a singular type. Bach's handwriting in the two folios exhibits many of the same characteristics seen in layer 3, and the two preludes and fugues may have been copied out in conjunction with the folios described below.

Bach copied out layer 3 on three separate bifolios, rather than two, using two types of paper. The C major prelude and fugue, folio 1, and the A flat

---

[18] See Weiss, *NBA* IX/1, pp. 62–3 for a description of the watermark and a list of the Bach manuscripts which use the Schonburg paper.

[19] Agricola assisted Anna Magdalena in copying out this portion of the manuscript. On the basis of Agricola's handwriting in P 226 (pp. 30–1), Alfred Dürr concludes that the manuscript (along with P 202, see note 29) was copied out early during Agricola's time in Leipzig, 1738–41. See Alfred Dürr "Zur Chronologie der Handschrift Joh. Christ. Altnikols u. Joh. Friedr. Agricolas," *Bach-Jahrbuch*, 56 (1970), pp. 49–56.

[20] See Dadelsen, *Beiträge*, p. 110. (The cantata is available in facsimile as Band 8 of the series published by the VEB Deutsche Verlag für Musik. Werner Neumann, in his preface, argues that the presentation copy was intended for the 1744 wedding of the daughter of the Graf family in Leipzig, close acquaintances of Bach and his wife. The diplomatic evidence, however, does not support Neumann's hypothesis.)

[21] The title of P 28, folio 1r, is reproduced in facsimile in the appendix to *NBA* II/4. Note the shape of the "P" in the title and the same letter in the final titles for both layers 1 and 2, as shown in Plates 1 and 3. (Arthur Mendel was the first to attribute a date of 1739 to P 28; see his commentary in *NBA*, II/IV, *KB*, pp. 75–6.)

fugue, folio 14, use paper which can be dated 1739–42 (two-headed eagle, Nr. 67). The paper is of the same type used for both P 416, an early copy of the BL (source C 1), and P 200, which contains the earliest portions of the *Art of Fugue*. In the first case, the similarity of paper is another form of evidence to suggest that the copy was made immediately after Bach completed the BL;[22] in the second case, the similarity confirms a close chronological relationship between *WTC* II and the *Art of Fugue*.[23] The A flat prelude, in contrast, is copied out separately from the fugue on a second type of paper, smaller in size (three lilies with unicorn, Nr. 17).[24] The final page of the prelude, folio 13v, is almost illegible, since at some point, perhaps in the late nineteenth century, the prelude and fugue were glued together to avoid being lost or separated. Bach's hand in layer 3, as in the final portions of layer 2, suggests a date of 1740 at the earliest.[25]

That Bach drew on a variety of papers in compiling the BL is not surprising in light of his working methods in the late 1730s and early 1740s. That he drew, however, on the same sequence of papers as he did for two of the manuscripts mentioned above (P 28 and P 226, see Table 2), can be seen as further evidence that Bach was copying out the "London autograph" in the late 1730s. For the score of the St John Passion, P 28, begun but not completed by Bach, the sequence of Hammer and Anvil and Schönburg papers (Nrs. 105 and 72) is the same as in the BL.[26] Another manuscript, P 226, a collection of several gatherings, also includes a sequence of papers and lineals identical to the BL, proceeding from the middle fascicles to the top

---

[22] Several factors suggest that the Fürstenau manuscript is a direct copy of the BL. Not only does the general layout of the folios closely follow that of the BL, but the attempt to duplicate such details as the form of clefs, accidentals, fermatas and rests, indicates that the scribe was trying to reproduce the BL folios as literally as possible. Further evidence of a direct connection between the two manuscripts is seen in the fact that the watermark (Nr. 67) of the extant portions of the MS (including the single folios in the BL and the Newberry Library) is the same as in layer 3 of the BL. That the scribe is probably not Anon. 12 (Anon. 5r), to whom P 416 has previously been attributed, is clear from a comparison of the handwriting on p. 106 of P 271 (in the hand of Anon. 12) and pp. 63–112 of P 416.

[23] That the opening portion of the manuscript, p. 1–24, is written out on the same paper (Watermark Nr. 67, see Weiss, p. 60) and therefore may date from the early 1740s suggests that Bach began work on the *Art of Fugue* immediately after compiling the BL.

[24] Weiss, *NBA* IX/1, p. 36.

[25] Bach's hand is a more helpful tool than paper or lineal in dating the two folios: the form of the half-notes (with open noteheads and stems in the middle) and quarter-note rests are increasingly of the later type described above.

[26] In P 28, the Hammer and Anvil paper (Nr. 105) is used for pp. 9–24 and the Schönburg paper (Nr. 72) for pp. 25–92; the text of the latter portion of the score is in the hand of a scribe.

bifolio; first, keyboard pieces (including duplicates of movements in layer 1 of the BL) in the hand of Anna Magdalena and Agricola with Schönburg paper and the same lineal (C) as layer 2: then the Sonata for gamba and obbligato cembalo (BWV 1027) in Bach's hand with the same form of two-headed eagle paper (Nr. 67) and the same lineal (A) as in layer 3 of the BL.[27]

That Bach was drawing together a second book of preludes and fugues during this period is one more sign that these years were a time of intense compiling and "copying-out activity", as well as a period when he was focusing on the composition and compilation of works for the clavier and cembalo.[28] The impetus for beginning Book II in the late 1730s may have stemmed directly from his continued interest in *WTC* I. We know that he returned to his autograph copy of Book I several times after it was completed in 1722 to enter revisions and corrections. One of the layers of corrections, dating from the early to mid-1730s, is the basis of the text for a second copy of Book I, P 202, begun by Anna Magdalena and Wilhelm Friedemann. The copy was completed by Agricola during his first years as a Leipzig copyist (*c.* 1738/9),[29] a time when he was also helping Anna Magdalena copy out portions of P 226 and writing out the four fughettas in P 595 (source D 1). If, as Hans-Joachim Schulze suggests,[30] Book II, like Book I, originated in a time of crisis – that is, during the period of Bach's controversy with Ernesti in 1736 – it would have been possible for a group of composing scores and preliminary drafts to have been completed by 1738–9 when Bach instructed Anna Magdalena to copy out the first pairs

---

[27] P 226 includes a collection of several fascicles placed on top of one another and later bound together. The earliest include the Overture in the French style (C minor version, BWV 831a) in the hand of Anna Magdalena; the top bifolio contains an autograph keyboard score of the three-voiced ricercar from the *Musical Offering* (BWV 1079,5).

[28] Bach's collaboration with Zacharius Hildebrandt around 1740 in the design and construction of a *lautencembalo* is well known and demonstrates his interest in expanding the expressive range of the keyboard. He also was experimenting with new forms and styles of keyboard pieces: the "Prelude pour la Luth. ò Cebal. par J. S. Bach," BWV 988, dates from the early 1740s, as does the "Fantasia per il Cembalo," BWV 908. In addition, in the late 1730s Bach began to use a greater variety of time-signs and articulation markings. (For a discussion of Bach's articulation signs during this period, see my paper, "Articulation in the Cembalo Works of J. S. Bach: A Notational Study", in *Alte Musik als ästhetische Gegenwart: Kongreßbericht Stuttgart 1985*, ed. D. Berke and D. Hanemann, Bd. 2 (Kassel, 1987), pp. 451–66.)

[29] When Agricola begins as copyist on p. 65, there is also a change of paper and a new lineal; the paper, pp. 65–72, was in use in 1739 (Watermark Nr. 23, see Weiss p. 38). The lineal, which continues to the end of the manuscript, is the same one found in layer 2 of the BL (lineal C) and also in P 226 (see Table 2).

[30] Hans-Joachim Schulze, *Studien*, pp. 10–11.

of the "Praeludium" layer in the BL and directed Agricola, perhaps at the same time, to finish P 202, a second "house-copy" of Book I.

Notational evidence

A survey of Bach's notational practice (summarized in Table 3) sheds further light on the composite nature of the BL. Several factors indicate that Bach intended the folios which comprise layer 1 to be a final score, even if not a fair copy. First, the physical layout or format for each folio, with two exceptions,[31] consists of a single prelude copied on the recto side of a folio

Table 3 *The BL (Add. MS 35021): description of notational evidence*

Layer:	1	2	3
BWV	871 875–6 878–80 883–5 888–9 893	872 877 882 887 890–2	870 886
Key:	c d E♭ E e F f♯ G g A a b	C♯ d♯ F♯ g♯ B♭ b♭ B	C and A♭
Title:	"Praeludium [Nr] di J. S. Bach" "Fuga [Nr]"	"Prelude [Nr] di J. S. Bach" "Fuga, Fuga à 3, à 4"	"Praelude et Fugue 1 par J. S. Bach," "Fuga à 3" (870) "Prelude 17 è Fugue par J. S. Bach," "Fuga ex Gis dur" (886)
Score:	Fair copies and revising scores	Revising scores and intermediate copies	Composing score and copies of drafts
Scribe:	AMB and JSB	JSB	JSB
Clef:	Soprano (C)	Soprano (C)	Treble (G)
Format:	12 bifolios	7 bifolios	3 bifolios
Fermatas:	23 of 24 mvts	8 of 14 mvts*	None
Fine:	1 of 24 mvts	4 of 14 mvts	1 of 4 mvts
✓	6 of 24 mvts	1 of 7 mvts	None

* P 416 includes fermatas after 5 of the 6 missing movements (BWV 873,2, 874 and 881), a "Fine" after two pairs (873 and 874) and a ✓ after the F minor prelude (881,1). (Placement of marks for the remainder of the movements is identical to the BL.)

31 The two exceptions are the F major and G minor pairs, folios 8 and 12. Emery, in "The London Autograph," p. 119, was the first to observe that Bach took over as scribe in the middle of the F major prelude in order to fit both movements in the allotted space; he needed to return to the recto side of the folio, however, to complete the fugue. For the G minor pair, Bach began the fugue on the verso side, leaving room for the prelude on the right hand portion of the recto side of the folio.

and a fugue on the verso. The folios originally were folded in half to form bifolios, a format characteristic of many of Bach's fair copies. Secondly, the majority of the pairs are written out in a calligraphic hand, as seen in folios 10, 17 and 21. Of the folios which include revisions (folio 4r, 5r and 12v), only one (folio 5r, the E flat major prelude) is a revising score. (Folio 12 includes minor revisions for the G minor prelude and fugue; the additions to the D minor fugue (folio 4r) were entered after the BL was completed, as later discussion will show.) Thirdly, the layer contains many of the notational conventions typical of Bach's fair copies: both prelude and fugue titles follow a consistent format ("Praeludium [Nr] di J. S. Bach" and "Fuga [Nr]"); fermatas appear with great regularity at the end of each movement, and Bach's characteristic sign of completion, ⌄ , is found at the six of the 24 movements. A "Fine" is placed only at the end of the B minor fugue on the final folio to denote the end of the layer and of the entire collection.

Bach does not copy out the seven preludes and fugues in layer 2 in as prescribed and careful a format as in the "Praeludium" layer. Although the shorter preludes and fugues (see folios 3 and 6) were easily copied out on two sides of a bifolio, longer movements such as the B flat major and minor fugues (folios 18 and 19) required additional space at the bottom of the recto sides of the folio – even with the addition, as on folio 19v, of two extra staves (sixteen rather than the usual fourteen). Since Bach does not copy out the longer movements in as systematic a fashion as in layer 1 (see folio 10v), he may for the first time be copying out each pair from two separate sheets on to a single bifolio.

Nor is Bach's notational practice as consistent in layer 2 as in layer 1. Although several of the folios in layer 2 appear at first glance to suggest a calligraphic *Reinschrift*, as Breckoff concluded, a closer examination reveals that they are revising copies. In the case of the D sharp minor fugue, folio 6r, Bach may have been transposing and revising as he copied, as seen in the placement of accidentals in measures 12–14, and in the character of the handwriting in general. The C sharp major fugue, folio 3r, is another case in point. Bach, perhaps again transposing as he copied, began to change the character of the running sixteenth-note figures on beats 2 and 4 in measures 8 and 9. Still copying and revising simultaneously, he incorporated the new form of the figure into the textural fabric of the movement. (Bach's revising hand can also be seen in the change from quarter-note to eighth-note stems on the bottom staff of the left-hand side of the folio, measure 20.)

Other aspects of Bach's notational practice in the second layer also contrast with layer 1: the fugues are designated simply as "Fuga" or by the number of voices, "Fuga à 4," "Fuga à 3," rather than by numerical order. Fermatas occur less frequently and often are placed over the final notes of a piece rather than over the final bar-lines; the characteristic mark, $\curlyvee$, is found only once in layer 2, at the end of the C sharp minor fugue, folio 3r. Finally, the placement of the "Fine" at the end of individual movement-pairs (four of the fourteen) is more typical of Bach's composing and revising scores than of his fair copies, and seems in this case to indicate that an individual movement or pair have reached a certain stage of completion – and perhaps are now ready to be copied out in a more final form. (In P 271, also not a *Reinschrift*, a "Fine" is written at the end of all but two of the chorales; in the prints of the keyboard works, in contrast, a "Fine" is placed only at the end of an entire group or collection.)[32]

Bach's notational practice in layer 3 differs in several respects from layers 1 and 2. All four movements are notated in the treble (G) clef rather than the soprano (C) clef, and the titles for the two preludes include the unusual description, "par J. S. Bach," and, in one case, the "Praelude" spelling. (Both will be discussed later in this essay.) No fermatas are notated at the end of any of the four movements, but Bach, as in layer 2, places a "Fine" at the end of the C major fugue to denote that the pair is now complete. Layer 3 also provides an example, rare in Bach's keyboard works, of a composing score – the C major prelude (BWV 870,1), folio 1r – discussed in detail by James A. Brokaw in the preceding essay. Also unusual is the fact that the A flat prelude and fugue are written out on separate bifolios.

In summary: each of the three layers reflects – in addition to different watermarks and lineals – a different set of notational characteristics, including title, clef and fermatas. Layer 1, even though the earliest to be copied out (begun in 1738–9), is the most calligraphic; striking is the consistent use of "Praeludium" titles in conjunction with fair copy conventions. The two "Prelude" layers display a greater range of notational practices than layer 1: the first (layer 2) includes primarily revising scores, a less careful format, and varied fugue titles. Layer 3, a second "Prelude" group, is the last to be copied out (1740 at the earliest) and its titles are the most varied ("Praelude et Fugue" and "Fuga ex Gis dur"). In addition, it includes the only extant composing score for Book II, and the least complete set of notational markings.

---

[32] In P 271, Bach places a "Fine" at the end of all but two of the chorales. In *Clavier-Übung* I, III and IV, a "Fine" or "Finis" is printed only on the final page, while in *Clavier-Übung* II an "Il Fine" is printed at the end of the Italian concerto and a "Fin" after the Overture in the French style. (In his fair copies of *WTC* I and the Inventions and Sinfonias, as shown in Tables 4 and 5, Bach places a "Fine" only on the last page of each volume.)

Key schema

A comparative study of the role of a key schema, or ordered group of keys, in the Inventions and *WTC* I provides additional evidence about the nature of the process by which Bach copied out his works for clavier. The three stages reconstructed in Tables 4 and 5, based on evidence drawn from the autograph and early manuscript copies of the two collections, reveals that Bach, for each of the collections, begins with a group of pieces in the "primary" keys. Bach's original schema for each work, as shown in Stage I, is based on fifteen of the sixteen keys described by Mattheson in *Das neue-eröffnete Orchester* of 1713:[33] d g a e C F D G c f Bb Eb A E b f♯. (Niedt, in his *Musikalische Handleitung* of 1710, also cites sixteen primary keys but includes the keys of B major and Bb minor, and omits Eb major and F♯ minor. In contrast to the modal order of Mattheson, he pairs the minor and parallel major keys in ascending diatonic order: c C d D e E f F g G a A bb Bb b B.[34])

For the Inventions and Sinfonias (see Table 4), Bach (leaving out the key of F♯ minor), first copies out each of the two groups with the titles "Praeambulum" and "Fantasia" in an ascending "diatonic" sequence, followed by a descending "chromatic" order. For the "Praeambulum," Wilhelm Friedemann writes out the group of ascending keys (C–b), and Bach then takes over as scribe for the second group, which includes copies of drafts as well as revising scores. (No such differentiation by group is found in the Fantasias; all are in Bach's hand.) A second copy, in the hand of Anon 5 and representing an intermediate stage in the copying-out process (Stage II), alters both the titles and the key schema. (Inventions and Sinfonias in the same key are now paired in a successive order.) For his fair copy, (Stage III), Bach retains the new titles, "Inventio and Sinfonia," but copies out each collection separately in the traditional ascending chromatic order, and with notational conventions similar to those seen in layer 1 of the BL.

For *WTC* I, Bach's use of a key schema is similar (see Table 5). The initial preludes from Book I to appear in the 1720 *Clavierbüchlein*, are also based on Mattheson's list of keys. Seven preludes in successive primary keys (each numbered) are copied out by Wilhelm Friedemann – once again assisting Bach – abruptly followed by a series of four preludes in the "chromatic keys (unnumbered) – F minor is placed with the secondary group of keys: C c d

---

[33] Johannes Mattheson, *Das neue-eröffnete Orchester* (Hamburg, 1713), Pt. III, Cap. 1, pp. 231–53.

[34] Friderich Erhard Niedt, *Musikalische Handleitung; oder Gründlicher Unterricht*. Erster Theil (Hamburg, 1710), Cap. XII. Reprint of the original edition (Netherlands, 1976).

Table 4 *Inventions and Sinfonias: notational evidence and key schemata*

I Notational evidence

Stage:	I	II	III
Source:	*Clavierbüchlein (WF)*	P 219	P 610
Score:	Revising scores and copies of drafts	Intermediate score [Based on lost auto.]	Fair copy
Scribe:	JSB and WF	Anon. 5 (1724)	JSB
Title page:	Dated 1720	(1723)	Dated 1723
Titles:	"Praeambulum"	"Inventio"	"Inventio"
	"Fantasia"	"Sinfonia"	"Sinfonia"
Clef:	Soprano (C)	Soprano (C)	Soprano (C)
Fine:	Prae: 5 of 7 (WF)		Final folio
S.D.G.:	None	None	Final folio
*	Prae: 2 of 7 (WF)	None	Inv: 12 of 15
	Fant: 1 of 14 (JSB)		Sinf: 9 of 15

II Key Schema

Key and Nr:	C d e F G a b/Bb	CC dd ee FF GG aa	C c D d Eb E e F
	1 2 3 4 5 6 7/8	11 22 33 44 55 66	1 2 3 4 5 6 7 8
	A g f E Eb D c		f G g A a Bb b
	9 10 11 12 13 14 15		9 10 11 12 13 14 15

* Fermatas placed at end of all remaining movements, except Prae. 6 and Fant. 1

D e E F/C♯ c♯ eb f. Originally, Bach may have planned to copy out an entire group of preludes in the primary keys, since, as Plath points out in his critical commentary to *NBA* V/5,[35] the layout of the book allotted 45 pages for copying-out a group of pieces-enough room for fifteen, possibly sixteen preludes. An intermediary ordering for Book I (Stage II) is preserved in P 401, in which the key schema and numbering is conventional (C c C♯ c♯/ 1 2 3 4), except for the following pairs – d D e E a A/9 10 15 16 19 20 – where the keys with non-raised or natural thirds, as opposed to the keys which require chromatically raised thirds, are given precedence. (P 401 and the unnumbered preludes from the *Clavierbüchlein*, according to a recent philological study by Alfred Dürr, transmit the third of three pre-fair copy – P 415 – readings of the text.[36]) Another manuscript which reflects this intermediate key order is the copy of Book I in the hand of Walther:

---

[35] Wolfgang Plath, *Klavierbüchlein für Wilhelm Friedemann Bach*, NBA V/5 KB, pp. 22–34.

[36] Alfred Dürr, *Zur Frühgeschichte des Wohltemperierten Klaviers I von Johann Sebastian Bach*. (Göttingen, 1984), p. 14. The unnumbered preludes, in secondary keys, were entered after preludes 1–7, and represent a later stage in the copying-out process.

Table 5 *WTC I: notational evidence and key schemata*

I Notational evidence			
Stage:	I	II	III
Source:	*Clavierbüchlein (WF)*	P 401	P 410
Score:	Intermediate copies and copies of drafts	Intermediate score [Based on lost auto.]	Fair copy
Scribe:	WF and JSB	Anon. 5 (1722/3)	JSB
Title page:	Dated 1720	[1722]+	Dated 1722
Titles:	"Praeludium [Nr]" "Praeludium"	Praeludium [Nr] di Sig^re Joh. Sebast. Bach" "Fuga [Nr] à 3, à 4"	"Praeludium [Nr]" "Fuga [Nr] à 3, à 4"
Clef:	Soprano (C)	Soprano (C)	Soprano (C)
Format:	Folio vol	Bifolios	Folio vol.
Fine:	None	11 of 24 pairs	Final folio
S.D.G.:	None	Final bifolio	Final folio
*	2 of 11 prel (JSB)	10 of 48 mvts	28 of 48 mvts
II Key schema			
Key and Nr:	C c d D e E F/ 1 2 3 4 5 6 7 C♯ c♯ e♭ f (unnumbered)	C c C♯ c♯ d D 1 2 3 4 5 6 E♭ d♯ e E F f 7 8 9 10 11 12 G g a A 13 14 15 16	CcC♯c♯Dd. . . 1 24

* Fermatas placed at end of all remaining movements, except: C♯-major prelude in Clvrb. and preludes 3, 4, 11 and 20 and fugue 2 (?) in P 415

+ Individual title pages: "Praeludium [Nr] et Fuga in [Key]/ manualiter/ composees par J. S. Bach

P 1074.[37] For the *Reinschrift* of *WTC* I (Stage III), Bach includes both a dated title page and an "S.D.G."; in addition, he employs a consistent format for the titles, and a chromatically ascending key order.

To return to *WTC* II: the key schema of the BL in its present state is incomplete (see Table 6a). Each of the first two layers includes only portions of a group of primary keys (layer 1) and a group of secondary keys (layer 2);

---

[37] P 1074 is copied out as a folio volume, even though it may have been based on a loose collection of composing scores. Unlike Anon. 5, the scribe of P 401, Walther reverses the G minor and G major pairs, as well as the A minor and major pairs, but places the E major before the E minor pairs. Also unlike Anon. 5, Walther uses "Prelude" titles.

Table 6a *Key schema of BL in its present state*

Layer

1 "Preludium": 12 preludes and fugues

	c		d Eb	E e F		f# G g		A a			b
	2		6 7	9 10 11		14 15 16		19 20			24

2 "Prelude": 7 preludes and fugues

	C#	d#	F#		g#		Bb bb B	
	3	8	13		18		21 22 23	

3 "Prelude" ("Praelude"): 2 preludes and fugues

C		Ab
1		17

Total of 12 pairs with "Praeludium" title and 9 pairs with "Prelude" title.

6b *Key schema of BL, in reconstructed form, as complete
collection of 24 preludes and fugues*

Layer

1 "Preludium": 12 preludes and fugues

	c		d Eb	E e F		f# G g		A a			b
	2		6 7	9 10 11		14 15 16		19 20			24

2 "Prelude": 10 preludes and fugues

	C# [c#] [D]	d#	[f] F#		g#		Bb bb B	
	3 4 5	8	12 13		18		21 22 23	

3 "Prelude" ("Praelude"): 2 preludes and fugues

C		Ab
1		17

Total of 12 pairs with "Praeludium" title and 12 pairs with "Prelude" title. Titles of three missing pairs [c# D and f/4 5 and 12] taken from P 416 (see Plate 1).

layer 3 fills in two of the missing pairs. The key schema of the BL in its original state can be reconstructed if the three missing preludes and fugues are added to layer 2 of the schema; all three are copied out in P 416 (source C 1) in the soprano clef with "Prelude" titles. (The titles are the first three shown in Plate 1.) The format of the schema for all 24 pairs, however – as shown in Table 6b – is not in keeping with Bach's practice in his two earlier collections. Based on the procedures described above, we would have

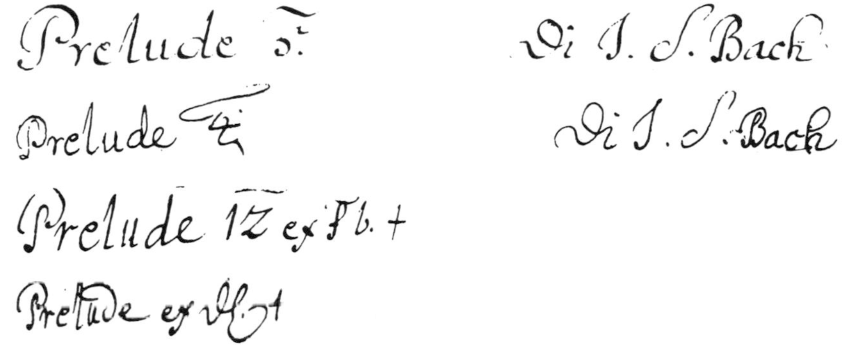

Plate 1   Prelude titles of BWV 871, 874, 881 and 876
(fragment) as copied out in P 416

expected the pair in C major, as well as the D major and B flat major pairs
from P 416, to be part of the group of primary keys – that is, to be included
with layer 1. If, however, the three preludes and fugues originally were
intended to be part of a group of fifteen primary keys (as defined by both
Mattheson and Niedt), but, for reasons yet unexplained, were removed or
omitted from the primary group – and if, as in Book I, Bach intended the
F minor pair to be grouped with a secondary group of keys – his key schemata for the compilation of Book II would then be similar to those identified for the Inventions and *WTC* I. (An early, intermediate and final stage
are reconstructed in Table 7.)

It now remains to describe in greater detail the nature of Bach's "working
procedures" for *WTC* II and to reconstruct the *Urpartitur* for each layer of
the BL. In the discussion which follows, the non-autograph sources cited
in Table I play an important role. Traces of Bach's "working scores" can be
found in the text of individual movements, or groups of movements, in
sources A–E, as well as in the notational practice of individual copyists.
Further evidence about the compilation process is provided by the script of
the titles for the 21 extant preludes and fugues, all written in Bach's hand
and shown in Plates 2–6. By observing the shape of the initial letters of the
titles for each prelude and fugue, along with Bach's signature on the recto of
each folio, it is possible to reconstruct a *Schriftchronologie*, or chronology of
handwriting, for each of the three layers of the BL. (The chronology is based
on the assumption that Bach followed his usual procedure of writing out
the titles at the same time as he notated the text, and takes into account the
general character of the handwriting in each of the folios, including the type
of clefs, rests, and accidentals.) My aim is not to reconstruct a successive
sequence for all 42 extant movements, but to establish a copying-out order

Table 7 *Key schemata, in reconstructed form, for Book II:*
early, intermediate and final stages

I Early stage:
  15 Primary keys
  1a: C c d D e E F G g a   A b   Eb f# Bb
      1 2 3 4 5 6 7 8 9 10 11 12 13 14 15

  1b: C c D d Eb E e F f# G g   A a   Bb b
      1 2 3 4 5   6 7 8 9   10 11 12 13 14 15

  9 Secondary keys
  2: C# c# d# f   F# Ab g# bb B
      16 17 18 19 20 21 22 23 24

II Intermediate stage:
  C c C# c# d D Eb d# e E F f   F# f# g G Ab g# a   A   Bb bb B   b
  1 2 3   4   5 6 7   8   9 10 11 12 13 14 15 16 17 18 19 20 21 22 23 24

III Final stage:
  C c C# c# D d Eb d# E e F f   F# f# G g Ab g# A   a   Bb bb B   b
  1 2 3   4   5 6 7   8   9 10 11 12 13 14 15 16 17 18 19 20 21 22 23 24

Table 8 *Copying-out order of preludes and fugues within each layer of the BL*

Layer 1
        Preludium: c d G   E F   A   e   b   a   f# g   Eb
        Nr: 2 6 15 9 11 19 10 24 20 14 16 7
        Fuga: c d G   E e   A   f# b   Eb g   a   F
        Nr: 2 6 15 9 10 19 14 24 7   16 20 11

Layer 2
        Prelude   F# bb d# B   C# g# Bb
                    13 22 8   23 3   18 21

                    C# F# g# Bb d# bb B
                    3   13 18 21 8   22 23

Layer 3
        Prelude   C   Fuga C   Fuga Ab   Prelude Ab
                    1   1   17   17

for each of the three layers of preludes and fugues, and, where possible, to
point out the implications for the compositional plan – and compositional
procedures – of Book II as a whole. (The reconstructed order for each layer
is presented in Table 8 with key symbols and numbers, and reproduced in
Plates 2–16 by title.)

Reconstructing the *Urpartitur*: layer 1

The first group of preludes and fugues to be copied out in layer 1 of the BL (see Table 8) is based on a sequence of five primary keys, c d G E F, similar but not identical to the key schema which provided the basis for the collection of preludes and fugues Bach compiled in the mid-1720s.[38] (Although the copying-out order for the preludes as shown in Plate 2 places the G major pair, number 15, ahead of the E major and F major pairs, numbers 9 and 11, the similarity in script and ink indicates that all five pairs, except for the F major fugue, were copied out as a group.) Bach, as in Stage II of the earlier collections for clavier, entrusts the five preludes and fugues to a scribe, an indication that he had brought the group to some sort of complete, even if not final, state. In this case, Anna Magdalena writes out the text and Bach the titles. A close look at Plate 2 shows that "Praeludium 6" was first copied out as "Praeludium 5," numbered on the basis of the key schema (in which D minor precedes D major) seen above in P 401, the intermediate copy of Book I (see Table 5). Originally, Bach may have intended the first group in layer 1 (which likely included portions of the C major and D major pairs as well) to fulfill a similar intermediate role in the copying out process for Book II, as shown in Table 7, II. At some point in the compiling process, however, he decided to retain the five pairs as part of a final copy, changing the "5" to a "6" in order to avoid the necessity of recopying the entire group. He may not have made the change until he returned to the group to finish copying the F major prelude and fugue begun by Anna Magdalena (see folio 8r). That this did not occur until after the remainder of the layer was complete, and possibly portions of the other two layers had also been copied out, is indicated by the position of the F major fugue, "Fuga 11," in the reconstructed order for layer 1, as shown in Table 8 and Plate 3. (Bach's handwriting in folio 8, and the shape of the half-notes in particular, is relatively late.)

An initial group of fugues in the primary keys – C c d D – may have formed the core of the sequence described above (see Table 7, I, 1a). Copies of "fughettas" in these four keys[39] are found in P 595 in the hand of Agri-

---

[38] Manuscripts in which portions of this early collection are copied out are listed in Table 1, source-group E. Evidence from a manuscript recently acquired by the Staatsbibliothek Preußischer Kulturbesitz, Berlin, and described by Klaus Hofmann in a paper read at the 1985 Bach Conference in Leipzig, "'Fünf Präludien und fünf Fugen.' Über ein unbeachtetes Sammelwerk Johann Sebastian Bach," indicates that Bach's early collection may have been based on an ascending hexachord of keys with "natural" or unaltered thirds: C d e F G a. For a description of other manuscript copies of the movements listed in Table 1, as well as for a summary of Hofmann's paper, see Brokaw, "Recent Researches," pp. 24–32.

[39] The key order of the four fughettas, now found as pp. 41–4 in P 595, is: d C c D. As a single bifolio, folded in half – presumably Agricola's format – the order then would be: C c D d.

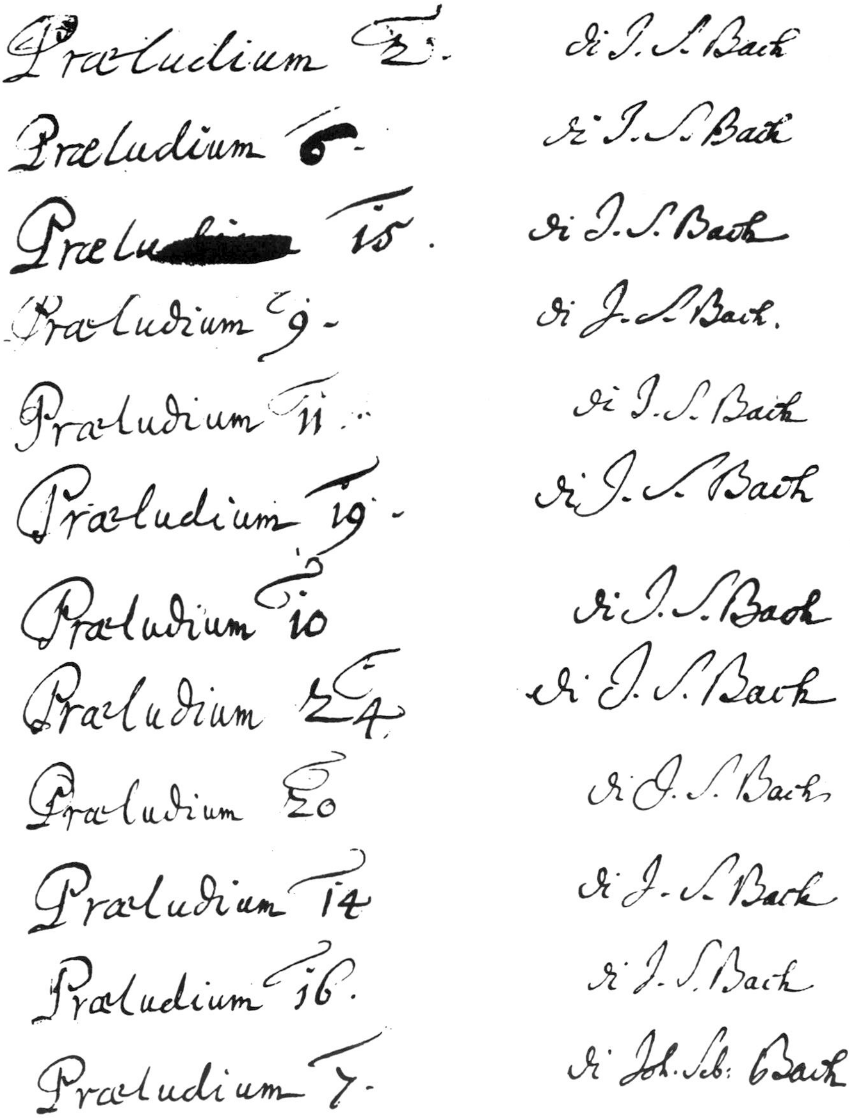

Præludium 5.   di J. S. Bach

Præludium 6.   di J. S. Bach

Prælu~~dium~~ 15.   di J. S. Bach

Præludium 9 –   di J. S. Bach.

Præludium 11 ..   di J. S. Bach

Præludium 19 –   di J. S. Bach

Præludium 10   di J. S. Bach

Præludium 24   di J. S. Bach

Præludium 20   di J. S. Bach

Præludium 14   di J. S. Bach

Præludium 16.   di J. S. Bach

Præludium 7.   di Joh. Seb: Bach

Plate 2   Reconstructed chronology of the prelude titles in layer 1

cola (see Table 1, source D 1), and Bach may have added (or intended to add) a prelude to each of the fugues. In the process of compiling layer 1 of the BL, he included only two of the pairs in their original key (C minor and D minor) and reserved the two pairs in a major key (C major and D major) for use later in C sharp major and E flat major. Evidence to support this hypothesis is found in P 226 (source D 2), which contains copies, in Anna Magdalena's hand, of movements from two of the above pairs: the C major prelude (BWV 872a,1) and the D minor prelude and fugue (BWV 895b). The C major prelude is likely to have been paired with the C major fughetta as the opening prelude and fugue in the sequence; both were later included in *WTC* II, in a transposed and elaborated form, as the C sharp major pair. The D minor pair in P 226 is identical to that copied into the BL by Anna Magdalena – that is, before Bach's revisions were added. (The D minor prelude is a revised version of an earlier work, BWV 875a,1; see Table 1, source E 1).

For the remainder of layer 1 (see Table 8), Bach continued to copy out the preludes and fugues in groups of two or three pairs; the reconstructed order for the copying-out of the fugues (e A f♯ b E♭ g a F) varies slightly from that of the preludes (A e b a f♯ g E♭). Additional evidence that the E♭ prelude was the last to be entered in layer 1, is provided by a single folio in the Fürstenau copy of the BL, P 416 (source C 1). The folio contains several crossed out segments from various pieces in Book II, beginning with a five and a half measure fragment entitled "Prelude ex Es+". (The title is shown in Plate 1.) That the scribe of P 416 had access to the draft or composing score of the earlier version means that it was among the papers still attached to the BL in the final stages of the compilation process.[40]

Further traces of the "working scores" for layer 1 can be found in the two Altnikol copies. First, the titles represent an early stage in the copying-out process: Altnikol writes "Prelude" and "Fugue" in P 402, and "Prelude [Key]" and "Fuga à 3, à 4" in P 430. Secondly, the limited range of the bass voice in the Altnikol texts for layer 1 (P 402 in particular), in contrast to a more extended range (down to AA) in the BL, implies an earlier reading of the text;[41] and, finally, the motivic figures in P 430 and P 402 are often simplified versions of the BL text, and, as Dadelsen pointed out in his discussion of Bach's revising process in "*Die Fassung letzter Hand*," are therefore

---

[40] The fragment of the E flat prelude may have been a copy of a preliminary draft for the movement and can be seen as supporting evidence that the prelude was one of the last to be copied out: that is, that Bach was working on it in the final stages of the compilation process. The single sheet, with several fragments, remained among the folios because it contained the final three measures of the B flat minor prelude, BWV 891,1.

[41] See Alfred Dürr, "Tastenumfang und Chronologie in Bachs Klavierwerken," in *Festschrift Georg von Dadelsen zum 60. Geburtstag*, ed. T. Kohlhase and V. Scherliess (Stuttgart, 1978), for a discussion of the chronological implications of the range of Bach's keyboard works. As

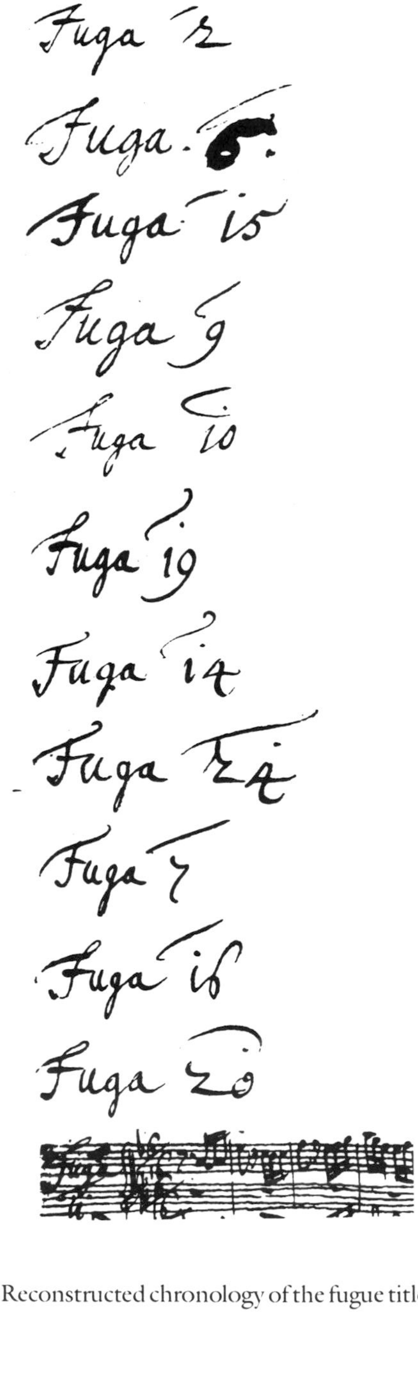

Plate 3 Reconstructed chronology of the fugue titles in layer 1

more likely to represent an earlier stage in the copying-out process.[42] The A minor fugue is a case in point. The eighth-note figuration in measures 6 and 17 in both of the Altnikol copies (as compared with the sixteenth-note figuration found in the BL, folio 17v), combined with a limited range in the bass in measure 15 (P 430 and 402) and measure 29 (P 402 only), are indications that the text is earlier than the BL: confirmation is provided by Altnikol's title in P 430, "Fughetta à 3." (The "Fughetta" title is also found in P 212, the Forkel copy, which transmits early readings of several preludes and fugues from layer 2.[43]) A comparative study of the texts of the BL and Altnikol copies reveals that Bach revised several of the movements in layer 1 in similar fashion, including the F sharp minor prelude and the G minor fugue, as he copied them into the BL from his composing scores.[44] A more detailed study of P 402, which contains slightly different readings from P 430, may reveal that the second Altnikol manuscript is based almost exclusively on Bach's composing scores for layer 1.[45]

Dürr points out on p. 83, the four-octave range, C–c''', is surpassed in Book II in at least five movements, only two of which concern us here: the final bass notes of the A minor and B minor fugues, are notated as *A* and *B* in P 402; in the BL and P 430, the lower octave (*AA* and *BB*) is added. In measure 15 of the A minor fugue, however, both Altnikol copies notate the sixteenth-note figure an octave higher than in the BL; for the final cadence, Altnikol adds a lower *AA* to his 1744 copy (P 430), perhaps based on the reading in the BL.

[42] See Georg von Dadelsen, "Die 'Fassung letzter Hand' in der Musick," *Acta Musicologica*, 33 (1961), pp. 1–44. Reprinted in *Georg von Dadelsen: Über Bach und anderes. Aufsätze und Vorträge*, 1957–82, ed. A. Feil and T. Kohlhase (Laaber-Verlag, 1983), pp. 55–67.

[43] P 212 includes eight pairs from Book II in Forkel's hand: BWV 875, 878, 879, 882, 883, 884 and 889. As in the Altnikol copy, BWV 889,2 is titled "Fughetta à 3." (For Book I, P 212 transmits early versions of the text, with "Prelude" and "Fughetta" titles. See Dürr, *Zur Frühgeschichte*, pp. 8–10.)

[44] The Altnikol copies include a simpler figuration, for example in m. 16 of the G minor fugue, in mm. 7, 8, 13 and 17 of the F sharp minor prelude, and m. 50 of the E major prelude. In m. 4 of the C sharp minor prelude, the longer and simpler appoggiatura figure (which continues throughout the piece) is found only in the Altnikol copies. (Most of these variants, as well as those mentioned in the notes which follow, are printed either in *BG*, XIV, or the Steingräber edition, reprinted by Kalmus.)

[45] The B minor prelude, notated in basic sixteenth-note motion and with a time-signature of C in P 402, is a clear example of an earlier text. In the BL and P 430, as well as in the other primary manuscripts, the basic notational level was changed to eighth-notes and the time signature to *alla breve*. (A similar example is found in the gigue from the E minor partita (BWV 830); the early version, notated in *alla breve* with dotted eighth-note figures, is found in P 225, written out in 1725; the later version, notated in ϕ with dotted quarter-note figures, is printed in *Clavier-Übung* I.) Other earlier readings in P 402, which may be based directly on Bach's composing scores, include: D sharp prelude, m. 20; E major fugue, m. 8; G sharp minor prelude, m. 20; and the B flat minor prelude, m. 15. (Examples of the restricted range of the bass voice were cited in note 41, and the absence of slur marks for the opening measures of the F major prelude may also indicate an earlier version of the text.)

The copying-out process for layer 1, as described above, has implications for our understanding of Bach's compositional process – or, more precisely, Bach's music writing procedures. In the two- and three-voiced preludes which form the following sequence of ascending diatonic keys – c d G e a – Bach experimented with various patterns of invertible counterpoint, one measure to four measures in length; the A minor prelude, the last in the ascending sequence, shows Bach's most systematic use of the procedure. In addition, each of the preludes is written in a basic two-part form.[46] Of the remaining preludes (E F A b f# g Eb), all, except G minor, are also imitative in nature, and include the full or partial use of a reprise.[47] Looking at the entire group of preludes in the order shown in Table 8, and taking into account the number of voices for each, we see that Bach first copied out two preludes in two voices (c and d/2 and 6), then four preludes in three voices (G, E, F and A/15, 9, 11 and 19), followed by three in two voices (e, b and a; 10, 24 and 20) and concluding with three preludes in a basic three-voiced texture (f#, g and Eb/14, 16 and 7).

No similar grouping can be reconstructed for the fugues in layer 1 since the majority (eight of the twelve) are three-voiced. If we look more closely at the original group of four fughettas (C c d D), however, we find it consists of two three-voiced and two four-voiced fugues, each approximately the same in length (28–30 measures). For each of the movements, Bach devised a short motivic subject, capable of being combined with itself in a variety of ways: in inversion (C[C#] and d), in augmentation (c), and in stretto (D[Eb]). In contrast, two of the fugues from the final portion of the group are composed on a larger scale: the F sharp minor fugue, as the only triple fugue in Book II, is the second Bach composed in *c.* 1738/9, the other being the well-known E flat fugue for organ, the "St Anne" fugue from *Clavierübung* III; and the G minor fugue, with its harmonically-based contrapuntal writing – a characteristic of several of the fugues in layer 2.[48] (That the G major fugue is drawn from Bach's earlier collection of preludes

---

[46] Four of the preludes (c G e and a) are written in bipartite form. The D minor prelude, a written out two-part form, is a revision of an earlier piece (BWV 875a,1), which is extended by seventeen measures, with several measures of invertible counterpoint added to balance the form.

[47] A full reprise is found in four of the preludes (F A f# and Eb); a partial reprise in two (E and b). The fact that the G minor prelude (without a reprise) is considerably shorter – only twenty measures – and stylistically reminiscent of many of the preludes in Book II might indicate that it is an earlier composition or modeled on an earlier piece.

[48] Other examples from layer 2 include the F minor fugue, the B flat major and B flat minor fugues, and the F sharp major and B major fugues.

and fugues is well-known; further style-critical study is needed to determine which of the remaining fugues in layer 1 are newly-composed and which may be based on earlier models.)

Layer 2

The reconstructed order for layer 2 confirms that Bach did not write out the seven folios with a "Prelude" title in as systematic a fashion as he did the "Praeludium" group. The differences between the order of the preludes – F♯ b♭ d♯ B C♯ g♯ B♭ – and that of the fugues – C♯ F♯ g♯ B♭ d♯ b♭ B (as shown in Table 8) – indicate that the individual movements were copied out separately from one another far more frequently than in the "Praeludium" group. The script of the titles (see Plates 4 and 5), and Bach's hand in general, are also more varied than in layer 1, and, for several of the movements (the D sharp minor fugue, "Fuga. a 4"/number 8, the B major prelude, "Prelude 23," and the F sharp major prelude and fugue, number 13) the placement within the copying-out order is problematic due to the unusual character of Bach's script, or due to a discrepancy between the script of the titles and Bach's scribing hand in the folios. (The position of the F sharp major prelude and fugue, number 13, for example, was determined more on the basis of Bach's handwriting than on the script of the titles.) Further, the similarity of the titles in the following two groups of preludes suggests that portions of layer 2 were written out at the same time as parts of layer 1 (see Plates 2 and 4): group one includes preludes 19, 10 and 24 in layer 1 and preludes 8 and 23 in layer 2; group two includes the final three preludes in layer 1 (14, 16 and 7) and the final two in layer 2 (18 and 21). Significantly, the preludes in the first group in both layers are two-voiced, the preludes in the second group are three voiced. Finally, the numbers in larger script attached to the titles of four of the fugues in layer 2, as shown in Plate 5, are in the hand of Wilhelm Friedemann.[49]

[49] Since the numbers are not found in the Fürstenau copy – as can be seen by the form of the title, "Fuga à 4," on the folio which survives in the Newberry Library – they were probably added when the BL came into Friedemann's possession, presumably after Bach's death in 1750. According to a note attached to the B major fugue described above, the Newberry folio was part of the estate of Friedemann's pupil, Sarah Levy; see Richard S. Hill, "A Mistempered Bach Manuscript" *Notes*, 7 (1949–50), pp. 377–86. Did Friedemann perhaps have two copies of Book II in his possession – selling or giving away both of them? (An example of Friedemann's hand can be seen in the illustration of Dok. 805, placed before p. 240, in *Bach Dokumente, Bd. III: Dokumente zum Nachwirken J. S. Bachs, 1750–1800*, ed. Hans-Joachim Schulze (Kassel, 1972) See also Gerhard Herz, *Bach Sources in America* (New York, 1984), pp. 215–19.

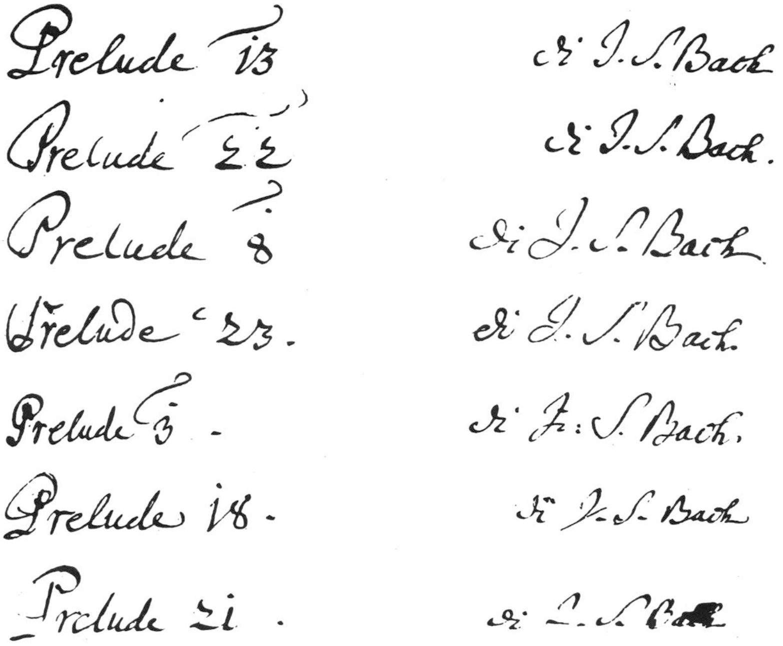

Prelude 13   di J. S. Bach

Prelude 22   di J. S. Bach.

Prelude 8   di J. S. Bach

Prelude 23.   di J. S. Bach.

Prelude 3 .   di J: S. Bach.

Prelude 18.   di J. S. Bach

Prelude 21 .   di J. S. Bach

Plate 4   Reconstructed chronology of the prelude titles in layer 2

Fuga

Fuga à 3 . 13.

Fuga

Fuga . r.

Fuga . à 4

Fuga à 4 . 22.

Fuga à 4 . 23.

Plate 5   Reconstructed chronology of the fugue titles in layer 2

Further evidence that layer 2 was a "working stage" and included individual movements and pairs in differing states of completion is found in the titles of the manuscript copies in source-group C. The title for the F minor prelude and fugue, "Prelude 12 ex Fb," as copied out in P 416 (see Plate 1), indicates that this pair was in an "intermediate" stage when copied into the BL.[50] (In similar fashion, the Gorke manuscript (source C 2) – which preserves traces of a "pre-final" stage of layer 2, and perhaps of the manuscript as a whole[51] – includes the title "Praelude" for both the F minor and F sharp major preludes; each of the pairs transmits an earlier version than is found in P 416 and the BL.) For layer 2, as with layer 1, traces of Bach's working scores can also be seen in the titles of the Altnikol copies, such as the "Prelude [Key]" and "Fuga à 3, à 4" in P 430. A comparative study of the text of the BL and the Altnikol scores again suggests that Bach revised several of the movements as he copied them into the BL. The Altnikol copies may provide the earliest readings for at least four of the seven pairs in the layer (d♯, g♯, F♯, B), as well as for two of the three missing pairs, as transmitted in P 416 (c♯ and f); the case of the C sharp major pair deserves further study.[52]

Style-critical study of layer 2 shows that Bach once again may have been addressing particular compositional issues, often in a group of movements. Seen as whole, the ten newly-composed preludes for layer 2 (including the three transmitted in P 416 – c♯, D and f – as shown in Table 6b), all include the use of a reprise: for five of the ten (D d♯ f g♯ B♭), a large three-part struc-

---

[50] See note 61.

[51] Missing from the Gorke manuscript are two movement-pairs, E flat major and B minor, and four preludes: g♯ A♭ b♭ and B. If Gorke were based on a manuscript which reflects the BL in its final stages of compilation, it would confirm that the four last pieces to have been copied out were the preludes to the four double fugues (b♭ g♯ B and A♭), precisely the final preludes shown in Plates 3 and 5. It would also confirm, as discussed above, that Bach was in the process of composing and copying out the E flat prelude, and revising the B minor prelude (from its earlier version transmitted in P 402). Another possible explanation is that the Gorke is based on a loose but complete set of folios, dating from *c.* 1740–2, several of which (C, F♯ and f, for example) represent different stages in the copying-out process, and several of which were lost.

[52] The BL text of the C sharp major pair appears to be a revising copy, perhaps transposed directly from Bach's composing score or draft of the C major prelude (BWV 872a,1). Although the Altnikol copies for the prelude include variants, as in m. 24, which suggest they transmit an earlier version, the added thirty-second-note figuration in the fugue, on the other hand, is the sign of a revised or later version. Style-critical study may eventually provide the basis for determining which represents Bach's final text. Meanwhile, most editors, except for Kroll (*BG*, Vol. 14), have based their texts on the Altnikol version.

ture is realized within a bipartite form.[53] Although Bach, in the preludes, continues to focus on imitative procedure (d♯ and B♭), including the use of the three-voiced sinfonia style in two of the preludes (c♯ and b♭), his interest turns increasingly to fugues with multiple subjects and more elaborate contrapuntal devices, as seen in the final three fugues to be copied out: g♯ b♭ and B. Bach, as with the preludes in layer 1, may have copied out the fugues according to their number of voices, beginning with the three-voiced ones (C♯ F♯ g♯ and B♭), each notated with a "Fine" – and then proceeding to the four-voiced ones (d♯ b♭ B). Gregory Butler observed, in another context, that the fugues in G sharp minor, B flat minor and B major, along with the F sharp minor fugue from layer 1, were part of a group of contrapuntal works in which Bach employed several of the contrapuntal *oblighi* discussed by Mattheson in Chapter 22 of *Der Volkommende Kapellmeister.* (Mattheson published his treatise in 1739 but Butler suggests Bach may have known it somewhat earlier.) The reconstructed chronology of layer 2 can be seen as further support for Butler's hypothesis that the group of fugues was composed *c*. 1739–40.[54]

Layer 3

Bach, in order to complete his second book of preludes and fugues (assuming that the missing three pairs were copied into layer 2 as transmitted in P 416), needed to fill in two gaps in the key schema reconstructed in Table 7 III: the C major prelude and fugue and the A flat prelude and fugue. (By this time in the compilation process, Bach's original C major pair with the prelude BWV 872 had been removed from the original group of primary keys and transposed to C sharp major; it is also possible, as discussed below, that the A flat fugue had already been transposed and revised from its earlier

---

[53] The preludes appear to be of three different types: one, a through-composed form, with the reprise occurring in the last quarter of the prelude (c♯ b♭ A♭ F♯ B); two, a bipartite form, in which the reprise occurs at approximately the same place – that is, the last ten to twenty measures of the piece (d♯, f and g♯); and, three, a larger structure, also bipartite, in which the reprise takes up a greater proportion of the total form (B♭ and D). (In this context, another work of the second type should be mentioned, the Fantasia in C minor, BWV 906. Of the two autograph copies, the earlier is written out in treble clef and dates from the mid-1730s; the second is notated in the soprano clef and dates from the early 1740s. See *Johann Sebastian Bach. Fantasia per il Cembalo, BWV 906*, ed. Robert L. Marshall, Published for its Members by the New Bach Society, Leipzig, 1976).

[54] See Gregory Butler, "'Der vollkommene Capellmeister' as a Stimulus to J. S. Bach's Late Fugal Writing," in *New Mattheson Studies*, ed. G. Buelow and H. Marx (Cambridge, 1983), pp. 293–305, for a discussion of various types of *oblighi* which Bach used for the four fugues.

version in F major, and that only a prelude was needed to complete the pair.)
Bach drew the new C major pair from his earlier collection of preludes and
fugues, as he had previously done with individual movements in layers 1
and 2 (see P 1089, source E 1). The similarity of titles (see Plate 6) suggests
that he had his earlier scores directly in front of him as he wrote out (and
revised) the two movements: the title "Praelude par J. S. Bach" is almost
identical to that of P 1089, based on a copy of the lost autograph.[55] The
titles in the BL, however, are written out in several stages: first "Praelude,"
possibly at the same time as "par J. S. Bach" (the "par" may be in the hand of
Wilhelm Friedemann), then "et Fugue" followed by the number "1"; for
the fugue, first the "Fuga" was written and then the "à 3." For the Ab pair,
Bach composed a new prelude, and copied out the Ab fugue ("Fuga ex Gis
dur") from a second autograph copy in P 274 (source A 2), also entitled
"Fuga ex Gis dur" and notated in the treble clef.[56]

The stylistic implications of the copying-out order for layer 3 are as
follows: first, the C major prelude, with its newly-created four-voiced texture – the only such example in Book II – can be seen as the culmination of
the sequence of two- and three-voiced preludes begun in layers 1 and 2;
secondly, the A flat fugue completes the series of double fugues begun in
layer 2; and finally, the A flat prelude, a newly-composed movement, is
similar in style to the F sharp major prelude from layer 2. (The two preludes,
equal in length and written in a two-voiced concerto style with identical
final cadences, are cast from the same mold.)

In summary: Bach's "working-procedures" for *WTC* II closely resemble
those seen in his earlier collections for clavier. He begins with a group of
pieces in the primary keys, and brings them to some sort of completion
before proceeding to compile a group of pairs in the secondary keys; he then
fills in the missing pairs from each group. (It is likely that Bach followed
certain compositional schemata in compiling these two groups, some of
which have been suggested in this essay: to what extent all 24 pairs reflect
an overall compositional plan awaits further study.) For layer 3, the last to
be copied out, Bach's "working-scores" are transmitted in the BL itself: each
movement (with "Prelude" and "Fuga" titles which in one case refer to key)
is written in the treble clef – two of the four movements on separate bifolios.
For layers 2 and 3, Bach's "working-scores" (as will be seen) are to found

---

[55] The C major prelude and portion of the fugue are reproduced as Plate 1 in the preceding
essay. (See James A. Brokaw, "The Genesis of the Prelude in C major, BWV 870", p. 231.)

[56] The autograph copy is a single sheet containing no watermark; the hand suggests a date from
the late 1730s (see Dadelsen, *Beiträge*, p. 113), and the presence of a "Fine". Bach, in the BL
copy, makes minor alterations in voicing (m. 8, 16 and 23), and clef (m. 6), but makes no
revisions in the text until II:A 2.

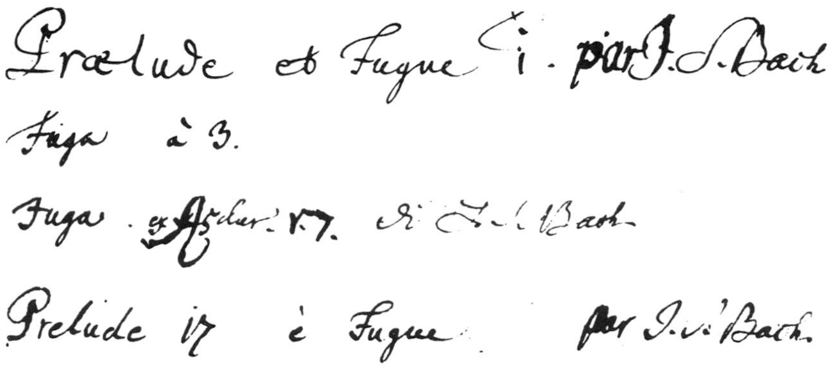

Plate 6   Reconstructed chronology of the prelude and fugue titles in layer 3

outside of the BL, since the two layers represent a later stage in the copying-out process. The procedures for layer 2 are less systematic: the "intermediate" nature of the key schema (compare Tables 6a and b with Table 7 I 2) and the varying titles of the individual pairs may indicate the haste in which Bach was trying to complete the layer and the entire collection. Layer 1, reflecting Bach's final titles for Book II ("Praeludium") is in a "pre-*Reinschrift*" stage, perhaps intended by Bach to play a role analogous to the autograph score of Book I on which P 401 was based (see Table 5).

Rather than recording a sequence of events in which the first layer to be copied out represents the earliest stage of the process – as seen in the genetic stages reconstructed in Tables 4 and 5 – the BL preserves the stages of the copying-out process in reverse order: for layer 1 (a group of primary keys), the process was complete; for layer two (a group of secondary keys), the process was not yet finished; and, in layer 3 (filling out each of the two groups of keys), the process had just begun.

To write out layers 2 and 3 in a format characteristic of a final text – that is, including the use of soprano clef, "Praeludium" titles and consistent fermata markings – would complete Bach's copying-out process for Book II. To what extent a final copy of each of the layers can be identified, and to what extent the process was continued after the BL was completed, is demonstrated in the final portion of this essay.

A Fassung letzter Hand

A comparative study of the texts of the BL and sources B 1–4 reveals that none of the manuscript copies reflects the format of a *Reinschrift* – that is, all 24 pairs with the "Praeludium" title, complete with title page and "S.D.G." Rather, two stages of revision (post-BL) can be identified and are labelled as II:A 1–2.

Bach's revisions for the first stage (II:A 1) include the following: for layer 1, expanding and revising two pairs (D minor and E minor), in addition to making minor changes in the text of individual movements; for layer 2, writing out the majority of the pairs in a more final format with "Praeludium" titles; and, for layer 3, writing out the C major pair in the soprano (C) clef and with a "Praeludium" title. That these revisions were notated and transmitted on single bifolios can be seen in the examples cited below. At some point the folios were collected together to provide the basis for a second score, probably compiled by 1742, since we know of at least one copy of Book II with a title page dated in that year – the Hering copy, source B 5, whose location is now unknown.[57] (Hilgenfeldt cites a 1740 copy, which also fits this description.)[58]

For layer 1, Bach made substantial revisions in only two movements – the D minor prelude and the E minor fugue. To each, Bach adds several measures: eight for the prelude and seventeen for the fugue. He writes out the revisions for the prelude at the bottom of folio 4v of the BL; a separate fragment or folio, however, was needed for the new conclusion of the fugue and further revisions in the prelude.[59] For only a few of the remaining 22 move-

---

[57] For a description of the Hering copy, see Georg von Dadelsen, "Originale Daten auf den Handschriften J. S. Bachs," in *Hans Albrecht in memoriam*, ed. W. Brennecke and H. Haase (Kassel, 1962), reprinted in *Georg von Dadelsen: Über Bach und anderes. Aufsätze und Vorträge, 1957–82*, ed. A. Feil and T. Kohlhase, (Laaber-Verlag, 1983) pp. 75–9.

[58] C. L. Hilgenfeldt, *Johann Sebastian Bach's Leben, Wirken und Werke* (Leipzig, 1850; reprinted by Hilversum, 1965), pp. 123–4. Hilgenfeldt, in describing "autograph" copies of Book I and II, states that the copy of Book II (the title is given in the chronology) originally belonged to Philipp Emanuel Bach and included a date of 1740 – whether on the title page or not is not specified. He further states that both copies (Books I and II) contained copious changes, in black and red ink, entered over an extended period of time. Even though it is unlikely that Hilgenfeldt was looking at autographs, his description confirms that a copy of Book II, with a date of 1740, existed, with revisions and additions. Either Hilgenfeldt cites the incorrect title page for Book II, however, or he is in error in stating that the copy once belonged to C. P. E. Bach, since the title of Philipp Emanuel's copy, as printed in the 1790 *Nachlass* (see Schulze, *Bach Dokumente*, Bd. 3, Nr. 957), is identical to that of the Hamburg copy. The title page which Hilgenfeldt cites is similar to that of the Hering copy; see notes 57 and 67 and the chronology.

[59] The D minor prelude was revised at least twice before 1742: the first revision, entered by Bach at the bottom of the BL folio, is transmitted in the two Altnikol copies, as well as the Hamburg. (P 226, P 416, and the Gorke manuscript transmit the BL text without the revisions.) The second stage, including a more elaborate figuration on the first beat of mm.

ments, Bach, as he did with Book I, continued to make minor revisions or to add "finishing touches"; these changes, found primarily in the Kirnberger copy, (with a few included in the Altnikol copy as well),[60] were entered in the 1742 score or on substitute folios.

For layers 2 and 3 Bach continued the copying-out process. For layer 2, the non-autograph sources, several of the "Prelude" pairs shown in Table 6b were copied out with a "Praeludium" title and/or in a revised form. Hamburg/ 1 contains the F minor prelude and fugue in a revised version as a "Praeludium 12" and "Fuga," and an additional two pairs (b♭ and B) copied out with "Praeludium" titles but an unrevised text.[61] Single folios in Kirnberger's hand, contained in P 209 (source C 3), transmit further pairs in layer 2 (C♯ d♯ F♯ g♯ B and B♭) with "Praeludium" titles; as with the Hamburg copies, the majority of the texts are not revised. Even though Hamburg and P 209 may include a final text for portions of the layer (in some cases identical with the text of the BL), a *Fassung letzter Hand* is more likely to be found in the Kirnberger copy, with its generic "Preludio" and "Fuga à 3, à 4" titles, to be discussed in greater detail below. For layer 3, Bach wrote out the C major prelude and fugue in the soprano (C) clef with a "Praeludium" title, as transmitted in both the Gorke manuscript and the Kirnberger copy.[62] These changes appear to have been made immediately after the BL was completed,

---

22 and 24, is found only in the Kirnberger copy, and is added to the BL folio in a later hand. The E minor prelude and fugue also may have undergone several minor revisions. In P 402, for example, the voicing of the lower voices in m. 83 of the fugue suggests an early reading, possibly based on Bach's first draft of the added measures. On the other hand, Altnikol, in P 430, copies out the thirty-second-note additions to the initial figure of mm. 3–4 as if he were squeezing them into a figure already in place – that is, the sixteenth-note figure as notated in the composing scores. In contrast to both of the above, the final version of the prelude and fugue, as transmitted in the Kirnberger copy, is based on a substitute folio or a later autograph score.

[60] These revisions include the following (in addition to mm. 22–4 of the D minor prelude cited in note 59): C minor fugue, soprano, m. 26, and the E major prelude, bass, m. 50. Of these two, only the first is found in P 430, and neither is found in P 402. Several of the twelve pairs in layer 1 (F f♯ G g A a b) include no sign of revision or of "finishing touches."

[61] It is not surprising, based on the title found in P 416 ("Prelude 12 ex F") that Bach revised and copied out the F minor pair in a more final format, and with minor revisions. In contrast to Dehnhard, I would conclude, on the basis of the evidence presented in this study, that the readings in the Hamburg and Kirnberger copies represent Bach's final text of BWV 881, rather than the Altnikol reading (identical to P 416 and the Gorke MS). (This means that in m. 53, Bach, in the end, chose to continue the melodic sequence of the previous two measures rather than avoid the parallel augmented fourths.)

[62] Although the Gorke scribe enters the "Praeludium" title, the Kirnberger scribe gives the generic "Preludio" title (equivalent to "Praeludium"?) which he uses for the entire manuscript.

perhaps in conjunction with the first revisions of the D minor prelude cited above.

The second and final stage of Bach's revisions for Book II (II:A 2) is transmitted only in the Altnikol copies, or in scores based on the Altnikol, such as the Hamburg/2. For layer 3, Bach wrote out the A flat major pair with a change of clef and title, and revised the C major and A flat major preludes.[63] Bach's revisions, including a new folio for the A flat pair – the last to be written out in the soprano clef – were added to his composing scores, rather than to the 1742 score, thereby providing the basis for the text (but not the titles) of the two Altnikol copies. (Seen in this context, the second copy of the A flat fugue, written out in treble clef and titled "Fuga ex Gis dur" was not originally part of a second complete copy of Book II, as Christoph Wolff has suggested, but represents an earlier stage in the copying-out process described above.[64]) For layer 2, the B major fugue and possibly the C sharp major prelude were revised; for layer 1, additional "finishing touches" may have been added to individual movements.[65] The A 2 revisions were complete by 1744 when Altnikol made his first copy of Book II.

Finally, the relationship between the BL and P 430 is now clear: for layer 3, the Altnikol contains a *Fassung letzter Hand*, and the BL the *Urpartitur*; for layers 1 and all but two of the pairs in layer 2 (Bb and possibly C#), the BL contains a later reading of the text, and the Altnikol copy transmits the text of Bach's working scores, the *Urpartitur* – in some cases with revisions

[63] A final version of both pairs, with a revised text, as well as a change in clef, is found in the two Altnikol copies, along with the Hamburg copy and P 209. A "Prelude" title is found in the Altnikol copies, however, since both preserve the titles of Bach's composing scores, even when copying out revised texts. (The "Prelude" titles in the Hamburg are based on the Altnikol scores.) For the two pairs, however, Kirnberger and his scribe appear to have had access to Bach's revisions or final scores, perhaps through Philipp Emanuel, since both P 209 and the Kirnberger copy, Source B 2, transmit revised readings of the BL text. Kirnberger's "Praeludium" title for the later version of the A flat pair in P 209, therefore, may stem from a copy in Philipp Emanuel's possession, in which "Praeludium" titles were given to Bach's final scores.

[64] See Christoph Wolff's review of *Johann Sebastian Bach: Das Wohltemperierten Klavier II*, ed. D. Franklin and S. Daw (London, 1980), in *Bach-Jahrbuch*, 69 (1983), pp. 123–4. There is no evidence to suggest that the P 274 autograph was based on (or derived from) a second complete copy of Book II – other than Bach's own composing scores. As a transposition and expansion of BWV 901,2, in F major (the earlier fugue is doubled in length), the second autograph copy may well represent a draft or a copy from a group of double fugues which Bach was compiling *c*. 1738. (See note 56.)

[65] Bach, in the additive process described by Dadelsen (see note 42), revised mm. 5–6 and altered the voice leading in mm. 88–90 in the B flat major fugue. The following minor touches may have been added as well: D major prelude, bass, m. 12; E flat major prelude, soprano, m. 46; B flat minor fugue, soprano, m. 81; and B major prelude, ornament in soprano, m. 23.

added later, based on the BL or the 1742 score. (Further study is needed to determine if any of these revisions stem from Altnikol, as Dehnhard suggests.)

The relationship of the BL to the Hamburg and Kirnberger copies can also now be clarified. Both manuscripts include the scores for Book I, as well as for Book II. Since each of the two copies of Book I transmits a slightly different version of the text – the Hamburg copy is based on P 202 (I:A 2), and the Kirnberger on Bach's last set of revisions in P 415 (I:A 4) – it is likely that the Kirnberger and Hamburg texts for Book II are also based on two different, but closely related, manuscripts. For the Hamburg copy, the scribe may have tried to draw together the final texts for each layer:[66] layer 1 is based on the BL, with only a portion of the A 2 revisions inserted: layer two is based in part on the BL and in part on loose folios (or portions of the 1742 score) which contain several pairs written out with "Praeludium" titles (II:A 1); and layer 3 is based on the final texts of the C major and A flat major pairs (II:A 2), as transmitted in the Altnikol copy. The composite nature of the Hamburg manuscript corresponds to Hilgenfeldt's description of the 1740 copy, and its title page is identical to that cited in the 1790 *Nachlass* of Philipp Emanuel. (Could Philipp Emanuel have owned a second copy of Book II *c.* 1740, based on the BL, with layers of corrections for individual movements and substitute folios for selected pairs, primarily those in layers 2 and 3?) The Kirnberger copy, in contrast, includes all of the A 1 revisions for both layers 1 and 2, with proportionately fewer texts based directly on the BL. Its title page is an abbreviated form of the 1742 title given in the Hering copy and the text of the two manuscripts may be identical.[67] (A study of the titles offers no new evidence, since the Kirnberger scribe wrote out the entire volume with a "Preludio [Nr]" title

---

[66] Although the major portion of the Hamburg copy is written in hand 1, the first folios of the volume appear to have been removed to allow a second hand (perhaps the same scribe) to enter the revised versions of the C major prelude and fugue and the A flat major prelude and fugue (II:A 2); the remainder of the revisions in A 2 are not inserted. In addition, the second hand copied in the revisions of the E minor fugue, crossing out the final measures of the BL text. (The first set of revisions for the D minor prelude had been entered earlier by scribe 1, who again crossed out the BL reading.) As a result of these insertions, the folio structure was slightly altered and the scribe needed to recopy the prelude and fugue in C minor and C sharp major, still basing his text on the BL readings (presumably contained in the discarded folios.) It was perhaps at this point that the two title pages were exchanged (they are now reversed).

[67] Dadelsen, in "Originale Daten," p. 119, concludes, on the basis of the information given in the auction catalogue, that the Hering copy transmits early readings of the text, similar to those in the BL. In light of the above discussion, it seems likely that the Hering, as the Kirnberger, may contain readings similar but not based directly on the BL. If so, the two copies may be based on a 1742 score, either a composite of several layers, or a complete score copied

and "Fuga" or "Fuga à 3, à 4.") In summary, the Kirnberger copy, based on a 1742 score (A 1), represents the completion of the copying-out process for layers 2 and 3, except for the A 2 revisions described above; the Hamburg manuscript, which includes only portions of the A 1 text for layer 2 but the majority of the A 2 changes, is based primarily on the BL.

Finally, the year 1742 may represent not only the date of a final score for Book II, but also the last time Bach focused his attention on the *WTC* in any systematic way. The date on the Hamburg title page for Book I (considered by Breckoff to be an error) may be an indication that Bach's final set of corrections for Book I also date from this year, and that Bach changed the date on the final folio of his autograph score to 1742, rather than 1732 as previously thought.[68] That Bach not only compiled and revised the two books in a similar manner, but also intended the two works to be transmitted together as *WTC* I and II, is shown in the chronology which ends this chapter.

Chronology for *WTC* II

1736–8/9 Bach began to compile Book II according to the key schema reconstructed in Table 7.

Completion of second layer of corrections of Book I (I:A 2).

1738/9–40, (1739–42?)[69] Compilation of the BL as reconstructed in Table 6b.

Completion of P 202, copy of Book I by Anna Magdalena and Agricola.

Fürstenau manuscript based directly on BL (pre-II:A 1).

Gorke MS 312 may preserve a final stage of the copying-out process (includes portions of A 1).

1740 title page, cited by Hilgenfeldt (possibly incorrect): "XXIV Preludien und Fugen durch alle Ton-Arten sowohl mit der grossen als kleinen Terz; verfertiget von Johann Sebastian Bach."

Title of copy of Book II in C. P. E. Bach *Nachlass* of 1790: "Das wohl temperirten Claviers zweyter Theil bestehend in 24 Präludien und 24 Fugen durch alle Töne und *Semiton*. Eingebunden."

[Completion of third layer of corrections of Book I (I: A 3)?]

out by Bach or a member of the Bach circle; the title, as Dadelsen states, would then be derived directly from Bach, rather than adapted, as in the case of the Altnikol and Hamburg copies, from the title page of Book I.

68 The date on the final folio of P 415 cannot be seen in the facsimile edition, published by the Deutscher Verlag für Musik, Leipzig, since the number now lies flush against a new binding. In examining the manuscript, however, I was able to determine that the number in question (17[ ]2) could possibly have been a "4" because of the presence of a tail, ⌁, often found in the number as written by Bach; I saw no clear evidence of the upper portion of the letter 3. (See Dadelsen, *Beiträge*, p. 106, for a discussion of the problem.)

1742 Completion of first stage of revisions (II:A 1).

1742 title page, as preserved in Hering copy: "XXIV/Preludium und Fugen/Durch alle Ton Arten/sowohl mit der kleinen als grossen Terz/ verfertigt/von Johann Sebastian Bach/ zweiter Theil: Anno 1742."

1742 title page of Hamburg MS for Books I and II: "Das Wohltemperir-ten Claviers/Zweiter Theil/bestehend in/Preludien und Fugen/ durch alle/Töne und Semitonien/verfertigt/von /Johann Sebastian Bach/ Anno 1742." (Based on BL and portions of A 1 and A 2.)

[Completion of final layer of corrections for Book I (I:A 4)?]

1744 Completion of second stage of revisions (II: A 2).

P 430, Altnikol copy. Title page: "Das Wohltemperirten Claviers/Zweiter Theil/bestehend in/Preludien und Fugen/durch alle/Töne und Semi-tonien/verfertigt/von /Johann Sebastian Bach."

(Based on composing scores and A 2.)

1755 P 402, Altnikol copy, Books I and II. No title page.

(Based on composing scores and A 2.)

1750s Am. B. 57. Books I and II copied out by Kirnberger scribe.

Title: "24 Clavier Preludien und Fugen/Zweiter Theil/ von Joh. Seb. Bach" (Based on 1742 score with A 1 revisions: identical to Hering?)

---

[69] These are the dates assigned to the BL by Yoshitake Kobayashi in "Zur Chronologie der Spätwerke Johann Sebastian Bachs Kompositions- und Aufführungstätigkeit von 1736 bis 1750," *Bach-Jahrbuch*, 74 (1988), pp. 7–72, a study which appeared while my paper was in press. Kobayashi sets forth a revised chronology of the late works based on paper and *Schrift-chronologie*, and his dates for *WTC* II are determined primarily by two criteria: first, dated Bach documents (letters and other non-musical sources) written out on the same paper as portions of the BL (since the paper itself cannot be precisely dated); and second, a handwriting chronology in which the form of the half-note with the stem in the middle (category "g" cited on p. 35) – and found in layer 3 of the BL – is dated 1742. My reading of the same evidence, in conjunction with a comparative study of the lineals, led to a slightly earlier dating of the three layers of the BL. The differences can be explained as follows: first, the dated Bach documents often used a type of paper a year or two after it was used for copying out a musical score, as Kobayashi's chronology itself attests. (See his discussion of Weiss 133 on p. 12, and the dating of BWV 245 on p. 44) Second, the change in Bach's scribing described above ("g") is found in Bach's scores as early as 1738 (in P 234, for example) and more frequently in 1739–40 (in St 76, and, in a similar form, in P 28); a definitive date of 1742 for the change seems arbitrary, especially when the date of the paper for layer 3 was determined by a Bach document (see the description of Weiss 67, p. 11). In the case of the manuscripts ancillary to the BL (such as P 271) our conclusions are similar. Only in the case of P 274, the second autograph copy of the A flat fugue do we differ significantly: Kobayashi, on p. 53, places it considerably later. In addition to finding the notation of the half-notes ("g") to be typical of the late 1730s, I find no evidence, as Kobayashi states (p. 46) that the copy transmits a later reading of the text (see notes 56 and 64 above). Finally, I continue to question that the scribe of source C 1 is Anon. 12 (Vr) because of the many differences in notational practice, and the almost ten-year gap, between P 416 and the remainder of the sources listed on pp. 29–30. (A summary of my earlier argument appears in Brokaw, "Recent Research," pp. 20–2.)

Part 4
Transmission and Reception

Bach in the eighteenth century

LUDWIG FINSCHER

In 1955, Heinrich Besseler published an article, the title of which has become something like a musicological catch-word: "Bach als Wegbereiter."[1] Had he known Arnold Schoenberg's now famous Brahms article, he would have perhaps called his own paper "Bach the Progressive" – although the author who twenty years later did use this title maintains that progressiveness and trail-blazing are quite different attitudes.[2] Besseler clearly saw Bach's historical role as that of a path-finder, the path leading towards the musical language of Viennese Classicism, and he summed up his article in six theses:

Seit 1716 wurde das Gefühlshafte in Gestalt "inneren Singens" die Grundlage der Bachschen Polyphonie. Zum kantablen Orgelstil trat um 1720 der expressive Klavierstil, der vor allem durch Philipp Emanuel Bach in die Sprache der Empfindsamkeit einging.

Seit etwa 1720 war die Expressivpolyphonie des von Bach geschaffenen "feierlichen Klavierstücks" mit einer Ausdrucksdynamik verbunden, obwohl Bach am Kielflügel festhielt. 1756 forderte der Bachschüler Johann Gottfried Müthel als erster für Sonaten das Hammerklavier.

Um 1720 schuf Bach sowohl für Konzerte wie für Klavier- und Orgelfugen das auf Gliederung und Kontrast beruhende "Charakterthema." Die Bachschüler bringen es vor allem im 1. Satz ihrer Klaviersonate. Philipp Emanuel Bach hat mit diesem Vorbild auf Joseph Haydn gewirkt.

Ausgehend von der Chromatischen Fantasie 1719, bringt Bach auch in geschlossenen Formen öfters eine auf Überraschung beruhende "erlebnishafte" Harmonik.

[1] Heinrich Besseler, "Bach als Wegbereiter," *Archiv für Musikwissenschaft*, 12 (1955), pp. 1–39.
[2] Robert L. Marshall, "Bach the Progressive: Observations on his Later Works," *The Musical Quarterly*, 62 (1976), pp. 313–57.

Der hier neu auftretende Zug des "Originellen," von Philipp Emanuel Bach fortgeführt, gipfelt in der freien Fantasie der Geniezeit.

Das individuell-persönliche Musikerlebnis, von Bach in der Chromatischen Fantasie herangezogen, führte zur Umwandlung der bisherigen Strukturform in die neue "Erlebnisform." Besondere Bedeutung hat hierbei seit etwa 1720 der langsame Satz in der Klaviermusik, bei Johann Gottfried Müthel 1756 der Sonaten-Mittelsatz, später bei Philipp Emanuel Bach außerdem die Fantasie.

Um 1720 drang Bach, vom Charakterthema ausgehend, in Konzertsätzen zur "thematischen Arbeit" vor. Das Prinzip der Einheitsgestaltung des Satzes, um 1730 auch im Klavierkonzert angewandt, lebt in der Klaviermusik der Bachschule fort. Philipp Emanuel Bach hat an ihm stets festgehalten und hierdurch auf Joseph Haydn gewirkt, bis zur "klassischen" Wende von 1781.

From 1716 on, emotionality in the form of "inward singing" became the basis of Bach's polyphony. Around 1720 the cantabile organ style was joined by the expressive keyboard style, which was introduced into the musical language of the *Empfindsamkeit* primarily by Philipp Emanuel Bach.

From about 1720, the expressive polyphony of the "solemn keyboard piece" – a genre created by Bach – became linked with expressive dynamics, although Bach [continued to compose] for the harpsichord. Only in 1756 did his pupil Johann Gottfried Müthel write sonatas which expressly required the fortepiano.

Around 1720, Bach, in his concertos as well as in his harpsichord and organ fugues, created the "character subject" (Charakterthema); his pupils used it especially in the first movements of their piano sonatas. Haydn was influenced by it through Philipp Emanuel Bach.

Starting from the Chromatic Fantasy (which Besseler dates 1719), Bach frequently, even in closed forms, introduces an individual harmonic language based on the principle of surprise. This tendency towards demonstrative originality, developed even further by Philipp Emanuel Bach, leads to the free (keyboard) fantasy of the "Geniezeit" (vulgo Sturm und Drang).

The new way of experiencing and expressing individual experience through music – as first witnessed in the Chromatic Fantasy – leads to a shift from predominantly structural to predominantly expressive and individual ways of composing. Of special significance from about 1720 was the slow movement in keyboard music; later, with Johann Gottfried Müthel, 1756, the middle movement of a sonata, and later still, with Philipp Emanuel Bach, the fantasy.

Around 1720, and arising from the concept of the "character subject," Bach established in his concertos the principle of thematic development, using it as a means of ensuring the structural unity of a movement (Einheitsgestaltung). This principle, which also appears around 1730 in the keyboard concertos, is taken over by Bach's pupils, and through Philipp Emanuel Bach it influenced Haydn – up to the beginning of the "classical" era in 1781.

From a methodological point of view, this approach obviously is highly problematic, and shows at best that Bach's music – as, indeed, with any great music (and just because it is great music) – must be interpreted by every generation anew, and that it can be, more or less convincingly, interpreted in many different ways – even, as in this case, in completely ahistoric terms like "inneres Singen," "Expressivpolyphonie," "feierliches Klavierstück," "Ausdrucksdynamik", "Charakterthema," "erlebnishafte Harmonik," "individuellpersönliches Musikerlebnis", and "Erlebnisform." Aesthetic and highly idiosyncratic terms like these – useful and even enlightening as they may be for an aesthetic evaluation of music – cannot serve the historical interpretation which is promised by the title of the paper. Consequently, the above interpretation fails most obviously where Philipp Emanuel, again and again, must serve as the missing link between his father and Haydn and where, therefore, the fundamental differences between Bach *père* and Bach *fils* must be explained away with the help of these very generalized aesthetic categories.

Reaction to Besseler was not slow to set in. Two years later Hans Heinrich Eggebrecht published his article "Über Bachs geschichtlichen Ort,"[3] in which he viewed Bach's historical role from a position diametrically opposite to that of Besseler: Bach (in the words of Wilibald Gurlitt) as a manifestation of the German Middle Ages in a modern world, the last and greatest example of a specifically German and Protestant tradition – a tradition exemplified by the rhetorical aspects of his music, and fundamentally opposed to the "New Music" originating in Italy in the 1730s (and the tradition from which this music springs). Besseler's attempt to link Bach and Haydn *via* Philipp Emanuel was rejected – following earlier studies by Hermann Beck, Reinhold Hammerstein und Jacques Handschin – in favor of a dialectic relationship between Bach and Mozart: Mozart's mature style as the end of a stylistic development to which Bach essentially did not belong; Bach's style as the end of a development of which Mozart was not part, and to which he could relate only by conscious rediscovery and reinterpretation. The methodological basis for this interpretation is (as expressly stated by the author) Eggebrecht's view of the relation between historical and historiographical terminology, as developed in his terminological studies.[4]

---

[3] Hans Heinrich Eggebrecht, "Über Bachs geschichtlichen Ort," *Deutsche Vierteljahrsschrift für Literaturwissenschaft und Geistesgeschichte*, 31 (1957), pp. 527–56.

[4] Hans Heinrich Eggebrecht, *Studien zur musikalischen Terminologie* (Mainz, 1955; 2nd ed. 1968).

Although a number of more recent studies have dealt anew with the issues raised by Besseler and Eggebrecht, Eggebrecht's methodological and historiographical position has been more or less confirmed, at least insofar as most authors have attempted to define Bach's position by analyzing his music with the most modern and historically appropriate tools available. But this approach, admittedly a normal one in the writing of music history, implies a definition of music history as being primarily the history of composition, and this history of composition as the result of processes which involve virtually the complete compositional output of the century. If this is a necessary stylization of history – necessary for writing history at all – it is a fundamental stylization nevertheless; that is, the history of music as written in the imaginary museum. Only in passing do Besseler and Eggebrecht mention what we would now call the history of taste, intellectual history, and *Rezeptionsgeschichte* – citing (predictably) the Scheibe–Birnbaum controversy.

Rezeptionsgeschichte with regard to Bach, however, had started much earlier, with Gerhard Herz's path-breaking doctoral dissertation of 1935[5] – which, for well-known political reasons, could not make the impact upon Bach scholarship that it rightfully should have – and with Leo Schrade's important article, "Johann Sebastian Bach und die Deutsche Nation,"[6] published in 1937 when Schrade was on the point of leaving this very nation for the very same reasons. *Rezeptionsgeschichte* has grown ever since, especially in the country where this term was coined, and has become fashionable during the last decade. A number of pertinent studies have been published, one of the most recent, most comprehensive and most interesting being Martin Zenck's "Stadien der Bach-Deutung."[7] But whereas here and in similar studies dealing with the reception of other composers' music, emphasis is laid upon writings on music – and to this extent Schrade's approach is being repeated – a new branch of *Rezeptionsgeschichte* has developed, which in its emphasis on the transmission of Bach's works in the eighteenth century (and, consequently, its emphasis on source research) is characteristic of the current state of international Bach research. Witness to this development are, above all, Hans-Joachim Schulze's studies, the third volume of *Bach*

---

[5] Gerhard Herz, *Joh. Seb. Bach im Zeitalter des Rationalismus und der Frühromantik* (Kassel, 1935).

[6] Leo Schrade, "Johann Sebastian Bach und die deutsche Nation. Versuch einer Deutung der frühen Bachbewegung," *Deutsche Vierteljahrsschrift für Literaturwissenschaft und Geistesgeschichte*, 15 (1937), pp. 220–52.

[7] Martin Zenck, "Stadien der Bach-Deutung in der Musikkritik, Musikaesthetik und Musikgeschichtsschreibung zwischen 1750 und 1800," *Bach-Jahrbuch*, 68 (1982), pp. 7–32.

Dokumente and his *Studien zur Bach-Überlieferung im 18. Jahrhundert.*[8] Only now, I think, and only due to Schulze's monumental achievement, can we start to ask the questions that should have been asked in the beginning: what did Bach's contemporaries know about the composer and his music? Which of his works did they know? Who were the people who knew this music at all, and what was their position in European music culture? How, where, why and by whom were Bach's works studied after the composer's death? Which works were kept alive – in theoretical studies or practical performances – and which were forgotten? How, if at all, did the reception among writers on music relate to the reception of Bach's music among composers? How important were theoretical and aesthetic statements for the history of theory and aesthetics, and how important was the "Bach-Reception" by individual composers for the history of composition – for example, Clementi's and Mozart's Bach studies for Beethoven?

With regard to these questions, I obviously can make only a few observations here. Let me begin with that *locus classicus* of Bach literature, "Eine bedenckliche Stelle in dem sechsten Stück des *Critischen Musicus*", by Johann Adolph Scheibe, as Scheibe's opponent Johann Abraham Birnbaum called it. Günther Wagner, in his article in the *Bach-Jahrbuch* of 1982,[9] has convincingly demonstrated that nearly everyone, that is, nearly every musicologist (except George Buelow)[10] has read into Scheibe's Bach criticism a general condemnation of Bach's works and style which simply is not there. Slightly reshaping and expanding Wagner's argument, one could say that Scheibe – far from being a supporter of the then growing fashion of simple and harmonic music based on models from song and dance – mainly aims his comments at Bach's treatment of text in his church music, and this kind of criticism is easily understandable not only from a follower of Gottsched and his literary doctrines. (Scheibe's well-known comparison of Bach and Lohenstein is not only a diatribe against Bach but at the same time a compliment to Gottsched for his reform of German poetry and language.) Moreover, exactly this type of criticism seems to have been common in Leipzig around 1738. Surely it is no coincidence that Bach's staunchest

[8] *Bach-Dokumente*, Hrsg. vom Bach-Archiv Leipzig unter der Leitung von Werner Neumann, Vol. 3, *Dokumente zum Nachwirken Johann Sebastian Bachs 1750–1800*. Vorgelegt und erläutert von Hans-Joachim Schulze (Kassel–Basel–London, 1972); Hans-Joachim Schulze, *Studien zur Bach-Überlieferung im 18. Jahrhundert* (Leipzig–Dresden, 1984).

[9] Günther Wagner, "J. A. Scheibe – J. S. Bach: Versuch einer Bewertung," *Bach-Jahrbuch*, 68 (1982), pp. 33–49.

[10] George J. Buelow, "In Defence of J. A. Scheibe against J. S. Bach," *Proceedings of the Royal Musical Association*, 101 (1974/5), pp. 85–100.

supporters, Mizler and Birnbaum, use the same arguments – and even draw on the same composition – in their defense of Bach's part-writing and harmony. To quote Mizler, in the translation given in *The Bach Reader*:

If Mr. Bach at times writes inner parts more fully than other composers, he has taken as his model the music of 20 or 25 years ago. He can write otherwise, however, when he wishes to. Anyone who has heard the music that was performed . . . at the Easter Fair in Leipzig last year . . . must admit that it was written entirely in accordance with the latest taste and was approved by everyone. So well does the Kapellmeister know how to suit himself to his listeners.

The cantata in question was "Willkommen, ihr herrschended Götter der Erden" with the text (predictably) by Gottsched. The work is lost, but judging from the fact that Mizler, writing in 1739 and Birnbaum (in his "Vertheidigung seiner unparteyischen Ammerkungen über eine bedenkliche Stelle. . ."), writing in 1745, could name only one and the same cantata when looking for an example of Bach's vocal style at its simplest, not many works of this kind can have been available. If Bach's supporters could not do better, his enemies surely were not far off the mark.

But the case of the "bedenckliche Stelle" is interesting beyond the fact that around 1740 Bach's cantata style was regarded as old-fashioned even by his supporters ("he has taken as his model the music of 20 or 25 years ago"), and that he deliberately kept to this style, knowing very well how to write modern music when the occasion called for it. (Robert Marshall, in the article mentioned above, has reminded us of some of these occasions and the works related to them.) The case is interesting because it shows some of the leading "motifs" of Bach-reception throughout the century: the discussion of a single work or one group of works alone – to the detriment of other groups and other aspects of Bach's œuvre – and the focus of the discussion on a very small group of people, who are in one way or another biographically linked to the composer and who have a predominantly theoretical and aesthetic interest. If these observations are correct, the importance of research on the transmission of Bach's music and even on the genealogy of the people who transmitted and discussed this music – that is, the importance of Hans-Joachim Schulze's recent studies – then becomes obvious.[11]

A search for the "leitmotifs" of the "Bach-Reception" reveals that, as in Wagner's later music dramas, some of them undergo subtle variations in the course of the century without losing their "leitmotivic" shape and function. Most of them are well-known, albeit not always in their function as "leitmo-

---

[11] The following details and quotations are after *Bach-Dokumente*, Vol. 3, if not otherwise stated.

tifs." We may call them (without trying to give a comprehensive list): Bach the organ virtuoso, Bach the father of harmony, Bach's chamber music as *Musica reservata* for connoisseurs, Bach's chorales and fugues as examples for the teaching of composition and for keyboard exercise, Bach's music as ancient music, Bach as the German composer. But let us start with the transmission of certain works and the non-transmission of others, and with the groups of people involved in this process, because these are the motifs from which all others can be developed.

Obviously, much of the transmission of Bach's works depends on the simple fact that Bach had an unusual number of extremely gifted and energetic pupils, including his sons, and that most of these pupils became church musicians and organists like their teacher. (Apparently no other composer in the eighteenth century raised a comparable band of musicians; this tradition, seen in terms of social history, was already somewhat archaic in Bach's time.) Together with the overwhelming greatness of the music with which these pupils were continually confronted – and against which only the strongest talents like Philipp Emanuel and Johann Christian rebelled – and with the natural inclination of church musicians towards a conservative taste, this situation proved to be fruitful for the transmission of Bach's music during and shortly after his lifetime, and – since these pupils frequently trained their own students – one or two generations later. This set of circumstances was also responsible for two other phenomena: the concentration of the "Bach-Reception" in one region – Middle Germany, in two cities, Leipzig and Berlin – and on only a few groups of works. Of course, there were also differences, due to the different reasons for which the tradition was kept alive. The tradition in central Germany, Thuringia and Saxony, was dependent on church musicians, and hence the organ works were prominent. The local tradition in Leipzig seems to have been strong in performances of some of Bach's motets and even – if Rochlitz's report is to be trusted – the performance of three(!) passions. The Berlin tradition, as is well known and well documented, tended towards scholarly study, appraisal and criticism, and towards the collection of mainly instrumental works. Nowhere in Germany were there as many pupils and admirers of Bach gathered together in one city: Marpurg since his youth, Philipp Emanuel since 1738, Christoph Nichelmann in 1739 and again from 1745 to 1755, Johannes Ringk (pupil of Johann Peter Kellner) since 1740, Johann Friedrich Agricola since 1741, Kirnberger (probably) since 1751, Karl Volkmar Bertuch since 1764, Friedemann Bach from 1774 until his death in 1784, and, of course, the social focus of this circle, the Princess Anna Amalia.

The provincial Bach tradition, dependent upon the activities of little-known, conservative and isolated church musicians in smaller towns, can be reconstructed tentatively and only with difficulty; even Hans-Joachim Schulze's vast knowledge of the sources has so far resulted in a rather sketchy picture. But an idea of its scope can be gained from some of its stranger ramifications: as, for example, when we learn that the original parts of the C major harpsichord concerto BWV 1061 in Forkel's collection came from the composer and organist Carl Christoph Hachmeister in Hamburg, whose nephew was none other than August Friedrich Christoph, or Augustus Frederick Christopher Kollman, who was the first writer on music in England to quote extensively from Bach's works in his treatises, and who planned an edition of the *Well-Tempered Clavier* in 1799 and published an edition of the Chromatic Fantasy in 1806. Or, when we learn that Johann Gottlieb Preller, one of the founders of the so-called Mempell-Preller Collection, lived and worked in Dortmund well into the 1780s as a church musician. Or – to name a more amusing than significant connection – when we learn that the so-called "Sebastian Bach's Choral-Buch" (now in Rochester) was perhaps transmitted to its later owner, Karl Constantin Kraukling, by two former pupils of the Thomas School in Leipzig – and that the two pupils were none other than Johann August Apel, co-author of the "Gespensterbuch" in which Weber found the Freischutz story, and Friedrich Kind, who wrote the Freischutz libretto.

We know much more, of course, though not nearly enough, about the Bach tradition in Leipzig, the continuity of which was established by Bach's successor Johann Friedrich Doles, by Johann Adam Hiller who succeeded Doles, and (further into the nineteenth century) by August Eberhard Müller and Johann Gottfried Schicht, who each in turn served as Thomaskantor. Müller, who had studied with Johann Christoph Friedrich Bach in Bückeburg, came to Leipzig on the recommendation by Reichardt, who played an important role in the Berlin Bach tradition. There is at least some evidence that from Doles's early years until Schicht's edition of five motets by Bach (1802/3) there was an unbroken tradition of singing Bach's motets in the Thomas Church – well-known, and frequently over-rated as to its importance, is the putative performance of *Singet dem Herrn* during Mozart's visit in 1789[12] – and that at least the St Luke Passion and one of

---

[12] Rochlitz's famous report appeared in the first volume of the *Allgemeine Musikalische Zeitung* (Leipzig). In Rochlitz's autobiography (in Ernst Ludwig Gerber, *Neues historisch–biographisches Lexikon der Tonkünstler* (Leipzig, 1812/14)), the motet performance is not mentioned but Rochlitz claims to have been very close to Mozart during the composer's visit to Leipzig. If this were true, one wonders how Rochlitz, in his report in the *AMZ*, could write that Mozart, before coming to Leipzig, had known Bach "more by hearsay than from his

the choral cantatas were also performed. (Rochlitz, who was to become such an important literary proponent of Bach, received his first impressions of Bach's music as a pupil of Doles.) Without any break, the Leipzig tradition seems to have changed from a conservative tradition proper into a consciously historicist renewal of Bach in the time of Schicht.

The principal difference between the Leipzig and the Berlin Bach traditions was obviously the theoretical, aesthetic and literary bias of the latter, in addition to the fundamental social difference between a Lutheran church and choir school on the one hand, and an enlightened court (or rather, a court faction in opposition to the musical taste of the monarch) on the other. In Berlin there were apparently few public performances of Bach's music beyond occasional organ recitals, the tradition of the public organ recital in church having been imported to North Germany during the seventeenth century from the Netherlands *via* seaports such as Hamburg and Lübeck. But there must have been an endless series of private concerts and discussions in the manner of a French aristocratic salon. The discussions, at least, left their literary traces in the writings of Kirnberger and Agricola as well as in Sulzer's *Allgemeine Theorie der schönen Künste*, and, on a different level, in Reichardt's fragment of a novel of 1779, in which the young hero grows up with "the most difficult pieces" by Bach and Handel. Direct testimony of a courtly conversation about the living Bach tradition is given in van Swieten's report of a talk with Frederick the Great after an organ recital by Wilhelm Friedemann Bach in 1774, and we all know how important van Swieten's connection with this tradition became when he returned to Vienna three years later.

The few examples given may suffice to give us an idea of the central Bach tradition in the eighteenth century. Comparatively small groups of musicians in Leipzig, musicians and writers in Berlin, and a larger but scattered group of church musicians in central Germany knew some of Bach's music, performed it and studied it. The core of this repertory was the keyboard music. The Leipzig motet (and perhaps passion and cantata) performances were local events, little known beyond the boundaries of the city, and became more widely known only by Rochlitz's publications – that is, in a new stage of "Bach-Reception." Concentration on the keyboard music, together with the tradition of Lutheran organ music led – one is tempted to

works" – a statement which would have been quite absurd in 1789. A better clue as to the reality of Mozart's interest in *Singet dem Herrn* could be the manuscript score from Mozart's estate – if the provenance of this score could be established. See, as still the best study of the whole problem, Ernst Fritz Schmid, "Zu Mozarts Leipziger Bach-Erlebnis," *Zeitschrift für Musik*, 111 (1950), pp. 297–303; also Konrad Ameln, *Kritischer Bericht* of the *Neue Bach-Ausgabe*, 3/1 (1967).

say by necessity – to a restricted understanding of the music itself, with an emphasis on its technical difficulties and its "learnedness." Performances of organ works by Philipp Emanuel or Friedemann were seen as sensational technical achievements, perpetuating the tradition that their father had been the greatest organ player of all times. The *Well-Tempered Clavier* was used primarily as a collection of fugues from which budding musicians could learn the technique of fugue composition and the fingering of difficult keyboard conterpoint. A direct tradition leads from Hiller (who had succeeded Doles as Thomaskantor), to Neefe, who was proud to have raised Beethoven in Bonn with the *Well-Tempered Clavier* and who made this fact publicly known. A different aspect of the tradition – to see it only as a collection of fugues – led to the copying out of the manuscript which van Swieten took with him to Vienna; since the manuscript contained no preludes, Mozart and others were obliged to compose new preludes for their string trio and string quartet transcriptions. The view that Bach's music was above all teaching material grew and spread together with the practical concentration on the keyboard works. The Birnstiel choral collection of 1765 was recommended by Sulzer as a model of four-part counterpoint, and by Agricola for the practice of organists who should play the upper voice on the first manual, the two inner voices on the second, and the bass on the pedal. The Breitkopf edition of 1784/8 was advertised as the first "authentic" publication of "the unique models of pure counterpoint" ("die einzigen Muster des reinen Satzes"), but was printed on two staves for the convenience of keyboard players ("den Liebhabern der Orgel und des Claviers zu Gefallen auf zwey Systeme gebracht").

The view of Bach as a composer of fiendishly difficult fugues likewise grew, the more so as counterpoint in general became obsolete for practical purposes and a mere teaching subject at best. Already in 1756, Marpurg called "Ockenheim" the Bach of his time because he had composed "all kinds of fugues" ("allerley Arten von Fugen"), a comparison Forkel mentions nearly 50 years later – a good example of how even "secondary leitmotifs" were kept alive, especially in the discourse among theorists and writers on music, up to the moment when the severely selective tradition gave way to a more comprehensive and objective historical understanding. Finally, Reichardt's novel of 1779 came to life: the idea of Bach's keyboard works as the epitome of musical and technical difficulties brought up the first "Bach freak," Wilhelm Christoph Bernhard, who (as Cramer's *Magazin* reports in 1785) lived as a recluse in Göttingen, playing nothing but Bach, the works of the "greatest harmonist," a formula which strongly suggests that the report came from Forkel, who probably had the greatest influence on the unfortunate young man who died a few years later. Three years before, in 1781/2, Forkel had inspired another young man, Prince Karl Lichnowsky, who studied at Göttingen University, to play Bach on the harpsichord, and had furnished him with manuscripts of the French and English suites and two-part inventions. Later, when back in Vienna, Lichnowsky accompanied his music teacher and Masonic brother Mozart to Berlin, *via* Leipzig.[13]

There is, of course, a rather close relationship between the practical and theoretical concentration on Bach's keyboard works and the repertory of the music publishers and sellers of Bach's works. But there is also a development between the 1760s and 1770s which suggests (although the evidence is slight) that the publishers did not set but rather followed the trend. From the beginning there was an emphasis on keyboard works because these were the few Bach works published in print: in 1761, Breitkopf offered (apart from the printed keyboard works) motets, a number of cantatas, five masses and two sanctuses (albeit spurious ones) and the St Luke Passion, and, in 1764, the Christmas Oratorio and the *Well-Tempered Clavier*. But in 1774, Westphal in Hamburg offered only one cantata, a number of printed works, and, in manuscript, the *Well-Tempered Clavier*, the partitas and suites, the sinfonias and inventions; while in 1794, Haehne in Moscow also offered the *Well-Tempered Clavier*. The last catalogue from the eighteenth century – and the one farthest away from the central region of Bach tradition (apart from Haehne) – is from Traeg in Vienna, dated 1799, and offers the C major overture, three sonatas for violin alone and all six solo cello suites, the complete *Clavierübung* and the *Well-Tempered Clavier*, the organ trios, Goldberg variations, *Art of the Fugue*, inventions and sinfonias, canonic variations, *Musical Offering*, and the Breitkopf edition of the chorales. Traeg was apparently not much interested in Bach's vocal music since he saw no market for it. The copy of the St Matthew Passion in the collection of the Emperor Franz II, and the copy of the B minor mass in Haydn's library came to Vienna through unknown channels and were never used for performances. It is significant in this connection that the Bach and Handel activities of van Swieten and his circle were strictly divided between private performances and discussions of instrumental music with emphasis on Bach – as van

---

[13] See Ernst Fritz Schmid, *op. cit.* The manuscripts bought by Lichnowsky are dated "Göttingen 1782"; they later became the property of Gottfried van Swieten. Lichnowsky returned from Göttingen to Vienna in 1782, took lessons from Mozart, whose Masonic brother he became, and gained access to Baron van Swieten and his musical salon. Mozart's voyage of 1789, with the visit to Leipzig, was arranged and financed by Lichnowsky, who after Mozart's death became one of the most important patrons of Beethoven.

Swieten had learned it at the Prussian court – and public performances of music by Handel, after the model of the first Handel performances on the continent.

The concentration of the Bach tradition (north and south) on counterpoint, learnedness, extremely complicated texture and virtuosity as exemplified in the keyboard works, strengthened the idea of Bach as the "father of harmony," the "greatest master of harmony," as Forkel called him, "the greatest master of harmony of all ages and nations," as Reichardt had it in 1781. The term "father of harmony" was no longer appropriate, however, when one had to admit that the melodic invention – in the chorale settings, for example – was not "up to date." Agricola in his review of the 1765 edition of the chorales admired the "ever-full harmony" ("unterm Zwange der immervollen Harmonie"), although the melodies seemed to be not always as charming and moving ("reitzend und rührend") as those of other composers. Agricola's qualification was taken over nearly literally by Hiller in his famous Bach biography of 1784 – "the master of harmony and the master of serious and profound music," but writer of "strange" ("zwar sonderbar") melodies – and later by Ernst Ludwig Gerber, who, by the way, was the son of Bach's pupil Heinrich Nicolaus Gerber, and exemplifies the genealogical connections and inter-relations which occur wherever one turns within a small and (so to speak) static circle of connoisseurs.

Burney, in acknowledging the well known learnedness of the fugues, turned the argument on its head in his attack on "the trammels of fugues and crowded parts in which his [Philipp Emanuel's] father so excelled" (1771), or when he writes, "unequalled in learning and contrivance, [he] thought it so necessary to crowd into both hands all the harmony he could grasp, that he must inevitably have sacrificed melody and expression" (1773). The argument worked both ways, and only when the unfortunate and not very well-informed Burney went on to compare Bach's and Handel's art of playing the organ – to Bach's disadvantage – did the defenders arise. The traditional argument of Bach as the greatest organ player of all times – a conviction which started to grow in Bach's lifetime, apparently from Birnbaum's over-reaction against Scheibe's dictum that there was only one keyboard player comparable to Bach, namely Handel – was linked with another idea, which too was traditional, but which now, in the last third of the century, grew rich in nationalistic overtones: "Bach the German." In the various defenses against Burney's attacks, especially in the long anonymous article (possibly by Philipp Emanuel), this idea was cleverly combined with another which at this moment was gaining in popularity, namely, that Handel was, after all, also a "German" composer, and the second greatest after Bach – an argument which must have considerably pained Burney because he himself had repeatedly stated that Handel had never quite succeeded in becoming an Englishman.

The combination of Bach and Handel, and the definition of both composers as German (a double "leitmotif," so to speak) seem to have been linked from the beginning, and, as with other "motifs," to have originated more in literary than in musical circles – specifically, in Gottsched's circle in Leipzig. Mizler, in 1737, asked where the keyboard virtuosos of other nations were, who were comparable to Handel and "our Herr Bach here," and Gottsched in 1740 talked of the "German Handel who was adored in England." Scheibe, in his essay on national styles in music (second version, 1745), called Handel and Bach "the two great men now among the Germans" – but with regard not to keyboard virtuosity, but to keyboard composition. Marpurg in 1749 maintained that German music was by now equal to, if not better than, Italian music, and boasted (wrongly) that Handel "and the learned Bachs" ("die gelehrten Bachen") were well-known on the shores of the Tiber. The first hints of aggressiveness against foreign music appear around this time, and sometimes in connection with other musical issues: as, for example, when in 1750 Finazzi's complaint that Bach's music was too difficult for amateurs is answered by Agricola with a nasty attack on Italian castrati. On the other hand, there are writers who simply state that Handel lives in England – Bellerman, in 1743, calls Bach *"Lipsiae miraculum, sicut Haendelius apud Anglos"* – and Mizler, in 1747, proclaims that without any possible doubt the two greatest organ players in the world are Handel in England and Bach in Leipzig.

The decisive and general change of attitude (general at least in the realm of literature and music criticism) seems to have occurred in the 1760s, again originating in a literary circle – the group around Klopstock in Hamburg, including Voss, Eschenburg, Ebeling and Philipp Emanuel Bach. But Handel, not Bach, was the center of interest.[14] Klopstock's patriotic "Wir und Sie," aimed against proud Albion unabashedly claimed Handel as a German musician whom the English had to import because they had no

---

[14] The documentary evidence on early Handel oratorio performances is assembled in Walther Siegmund-Schultze, "Über die ersten Messias-Aufführungen in Deutschland," *Händel-Jahrbuch*, 6 (1960), pp. 51–72, and Theophil Antonicek, *Zur Pflege Händelscher Musik in der 2. Hälfte des 18. Jahrhunderts* (Österreichische Akademie der Wissenschaften, Phil.-Hist. Klasse, Sitzungsberichte, 250. Band, 1. Abhandlung (Wien, 1966). See also my paper "'Gleichsam ein kanonisirter Tonmeister': Zur deutschen Händel-Rezeption im 18. Jahrhundert," in *Kanon und Zensur*, ed. Aleida and Jan Assmann (München, 1987), pp. 271–83.

one like him, and the first Hamburg performance of the *Messiah* with German text (1775) was sung in Klopstock's and Ebeling's translation. Handel performances flourished for a short time in German cities and courts – Schwerin, Braunschweig, Mannheim, Berlin, Leipzig, Weimar – and in Kopenhagen and Stockholm, and, at the same time (probably inspired by the earlier activities in Florence) in Vienna. The works performed, translated and rescored usually included *The Messiah*, the most Christian of the oratorios; *Alexander's Feast* and *Ode to St Cecilia's Day*, the two philosophical works with texts written by a great poet; and *Acis and Galatea*, a moving and sentimental story. Only a few performances of other works are recorded – *Judas Maccabaeus* in Braunschweig and Vienna, for example.

It is noteworthy that Philipp Emanuel's public performances of works by his father (and even of Johann Christoph Bach's motet *Lieber Herr Gott, wecke uns auf* in the arrangement by Johann Sebastian) came along after the Handel performances in Hamburg. And Philipp Emanuel's pasticcio versions of works by his father (with emphasis on the choral settings and choirs) were written after the arias in the Handel performances had met with criticism, whereas the choruses were unanimously praised. It is equally noteworthy that Christoph Daniel Ebeling, who had arranged the two *Messiah* performances in Hamburg in 1772, was one of the very few people who at that time still had a word of praise for Bach's church music. In 1770, he praised Bach not only (as usual) as one of the greatest masters of harmony of all times, but as the master of church music which was not only "learned," but – and this seems to be a unique statement in the 1770s – "sublime and full of fire."

The concept of Bach and Handel as the two greatest masters of German music was fully developed around 1800, up to the point that even the famous Marchand anecdote developed nationalistic overtones: Hiller in his 1784 biography wrote that Bach did himself proud in this contest, and Gerber emphatically stated that he "saved the honour of his nation" by forcing the Frenchman into ignominious flight. The concept of not one but a pair of great composers was first of all a rhetorical concept (a figure of speech well-known in the history of all arts), and as a rhetorical concept – a way of thinking in "related opposites" – it helped to define the realms of music for which each of the two stood: Bach as the timeless composer of profound and intimate chamber music for the connoisseur, and Handel as the master of large-scale choral works, performed in public concerts, whose music moved the hearts of the populace at large. The generation of Forkel and Gerber, accordingly, discovered and sought to preserve what they seemingly had lost in the music of their own time: learned counterpoint and monumental simplicity. They regarded as obsolete Bach's and Handel's contributions to those genres which had or seemed to have withstood the revolution of style which took place in the 1730s. Forkel could thus write that Bach's harpsichord concertos (the only Bach concertos he knew) were obsolete, and Forkel and Gerber alike could propose to combine the choruses of the *Messiah* (in Mozart's arrangement) with newly-composed arias, because Handel's arias were hopelessly out of date.

However, we should not forget that this model of "related opposites" was only the last result of a development which had already started in Bach and Handel's lifetime. After 1759, no one in England, Germany or Italy seems to have had a reasonably accurate or comprehensive view of either of the two composers, or even a reasonably comprehensive knowledge of their works. And for Bach the situation was even worse: apart from the provincial performances of his organ works by an active "subculture" – along with the activities of isolated specialists and the local Leipzig performance tradition – his fame was kept alive by discussion, controversy, and private performances among professionals and connoisseurs. Hence, he was forgotten by the general public and the amateur, and his fame rested more and more on professional qualities: "learnedness," counterpoint and harmony. Handel's oratorios were performed in an unbroken tradition in England, and exported to the continent, where a tradition was established in Germany and Austria (and for a very short time in Florence in Austrian Tuscany). But it was only a handful of non-typical works which were performed; hence, his fame was kept alive by musicians and ideologists. Bach was famous on a theoretical–professional level, Handel on a practical–ideological level.

There is one exception, of course: the purely fortuitous fact that Mozart, at the most critical moment in his life, came into contact with van Swieten, who introduced him to Bach and Handel – namely, Bach's fugues and Handel's oratorios, as it turned out, due to Mozart's process of selective assimilation. In Mozart's most symbolic work these two forces, which changed his style from 1782 onwards, are presented in symbolic juxtaposition: the learned and sublime counterpoint of the chorale arrangement in the C minor "Gesang der Geharnischten" and the monumental simplicity of the C major march in the "Feuer-und Wasserprobe." In the history of eighteenth-century music – seen as history of taste and ideas – Bach had consistently played a major, although continuously changing, part. In the history of eighteenth-century music – seen as history of composition – he started to play his part only in 1782; but from the beginning it was a decisive, although "instrumental," part (and remained 'instrumental' well into the nineteenth century). Bach as the incomparable aesthetic event of the first half of the eighteenth century – the role in which we see him today – was a discovery of the twentieth century.

Tradition as authority and provocation: Anton Webern's confrontation with Johann Sebastian Bach

MARTIN ZENCK

A comprehensive study of Anton Webern's relationship to Bach has not yet been carried out. Scholars to date have limited their attention to Webern's "arrangement" of the six-part Ricercar from the *Musical Offering*,[1] viewing the work as an isolated and autonomous phenomenon, rather than in relation to other works of Webern, such as Opus 27 and 28, or the "arrangements" of other composers, especially those of Feruccio Busoni. Recently, the opportunity for a more comprehensive study of Webern's "creative confrontation" with Bach was greatly enhanced by the purchase of the Moldenhauer Webern-Archive by the Paul Sacher Stiftung in Basel and the availability of new source materials. Particularly relevant for the present study are: first, Webern's arrangements of eighteen chorales of J. S. Bach;[2] second, his letters to the Swiss painter Franz Rederer[3] and to the conductor Hermann Scherchen[4] – which include materials relating to the genesis of Webern's Bach "Ricercar-transcription"; and third, the sketches to Opus 27 and 28 which, in association with the newly orchestrated Bach Ricercar

---

[1] See Carl Dahlhaus, "Analytische Instrumentation. Bachs sechsstimmiges Ricercar in der Orchestrierung Anton Weberns," in *Bach-Interpretation*, ed. M. Geck (Göttingen, 1969), pp. 197ff; H. J. Bauer, "Interpretation durch Instrumentation: Bachs sechsstimmiges Ricercar in der Orchestrierung Anton von Weberns," in *NZM* [*Neue Zeitschrift für Musik*], 135 (1974), pp. 3ff: T. W. Adorno, "Über einige Arbeiten Anton Werberns," in *Anton Webern (I)*, ed. H. K. Metzger and R. Riehn, *Musik-Konzepte* (Sonderband), (Munich, 1983), pp. 272ff; G. Zacher, "Zu Anton Weberns Bachverständnis. Die Instrumentation des Ricercars", *ibid*. pp. 209ff. E. Budde, "Webern und Bach," in *Alte Musik als ästhetische Gegenwart: Kongressbericht Stuttgart 1985*, ed. D. Berke and D. Hanemann, Bd. I (Kassel, 1987), pp. 198ff.
[2] Paul Sacher Foundation, Basel, Mo 84–101. (Archive listing according to Moldenhauer's Webern biography, London, 1978.)
[3] Paul Sacher Foundation, Basel.
[4] Hermann-Scherchen-Archive, Akademie der Künste, West Berlin.

of 1935, provide further evidence of a "Bach-Reception" in Webern's late compositional period.[5] Recent publications dealing with Webern's activities as a conductor in the "Verein für musikalische Privataufführungen"[6] (Society for Private Concerts) as well as in publications of the correspondences between Webern and Eduard Steuermann[7] and conversations between Hansjörg Pauli and Rudolph Kolisch,[8] shed further light on Webern's continuous and intensive preoccupation with Bach, a preoccupation seen today as important not only in relation to the reception of Bach in the Second Viennese School by Schoenberg, Berg and Webern, but also to the post-dodecaphonic school of Leibowitz,[9] Krenek[10] and Kahn,[11] and the serial music of Nono,[12] Schnebel,[13] and Boulez.[14] In order to map out as extensively as possible the context of "Bach-Reception" in the twentieth century, reference must also be made to Webern's musical interpretations of Bach. As far as we know, no taped recording exists of his arrangement of the Bach Ricercar, even though he conducted this work in 1935 in both London and Vienna. Nevertheless, a recent "technically reconstructed" performance of the Berg Violin Concerto with the Bach chorale *Es ist genug*, and, in addition, the recordings of the Bach Ricercar by Bruno Maderna and Hermann Scherchen – both of which realize Webern's expressive ideal –

---

[5] The sketch-book IV was previously not accessible (since 1985 in the possession of the Paul Sacher Foundation, Basel).

[6] R. Busch, "Verzeichnis der von Webern dirigierten und einstudierten Werke," in *Anton Webern (II)*, ed. H. K. Metzger and R. Riehn, *Musik Konzepte* (Sonderband), (Munich, 1984), pp. 308ff.

[7] "Aus dem Briefweschel Webern–Steuermann," transcribed, with commentary, by R. Busch, in *Anton Webern (I)*, pp. 23ff.

[8] H. Pauli and R. Kolisch, "Aus Gesprächen über Webern," in *Anton Webern (II)*, pp. 252ff.

[9] R. Leibowitz, *L'Evolution de la musique. De Bach à Schönberg* (Paris, 1952); R. Leibowitz, "Die strukturelle Dialektik im Werk J. S. Bachs" (1950), in *Johann Sebastian Bach*, ed. W. Blankenburg, Wege der Forschung, Vol. 170 (Darmstadt, 1970), pp. 85ff; and Johann Sebastian Bach, Toccata and Fugue D minor (BWV 565), orchestrated by René Leibowitz (UE 1958).

[10] Concerning the relationship of Krenek to Bach, see my article, "'Wenn Bach Bienen gezüchter hätte' – Zur Bedeutung Bachs in der Interpretations- und Kompositionsgeschichte des 20. Jahrhunderts," in *Bach im 20. Jahrhundert, 59. Bachfest der Neuen Bachgesellschaft* (Kassel, 1984), pp. 102ff.

[11] E. I. Kahn, "Actus Tragicus" (1947) for 10 instruments; R. Leibowitz and Konrad Wolff, *Erich Itor Kahn – un grand représentant de la musique contemporaine* (Editions Buchet/Chastel, Paris, 1958).

[12] L. Nono, "Text – Musik – Gesang," in J. Stenzel, ed., *Luigi Nono, Texte. Studien zu seiner Musik* (Zurich/Freiburg, 1975), pp. 50ff.

[13] D. Schnebel, "Contrapuncti für Stimmen" (1972–6); arrangements of the fugues Nos. I, VI and XI from the *Art of Fugue*.

[14] P. Boulez, "Moment de Jean-Sebastien Bach," in *Pierre Boulez, Relevés d'apprenti* (Paris, 1956).

allow us to assess and reexperience Webern's aural conception of Bach's music. It is possible in the present study to consider only some of these aspects.

There are two phases in Webern's biography and compositional development in which a confrontation with J. S. Bach is particularly evident. The first of these occurred – after his initial training in Graz, where his teacher Komauer familiarized him with Bach's polyphony (the B Minor Mass and the solo suites for cello)[15] – during the period of his musicological studies under Guido Adler and his subsequent compositional apprenticeship with Arnold Schoenberg. These studies provided the foundation by which later, in his creative work, he sought to legitimize himself through recourse to Bach as an historical model, and also provided him with the technical skill to execute not just strict canons but also to realize the ideal, adopted by Schoenberg, of a synthesis of the horizontal and vertical aspects of music[16] – that is, of combining fugue and sonata, Bach and Beethoven – by means of the twelve-tone technique.

The first phase, which lies before Opus 1 and during which he, together with Karl Horwitz,[17] harmonized and figured Bach chorales under Schoenberg's supervision, was followed by an interval of almost 22 years (after 1906). In 1928, Webern again – at the beginning of the second phase – began to establish connections between his own works and those of Bach (in particular, as a result of his activities as a Bach conductor) in order to place himself in the context of an established tradition, and, at the same time, make himself more comprehensible to friends, interpreters and publishers, as well as to the "musical public" – often with the paradoxical result that the "newness" of his music was accentuated rather than diminished by its reference to Bach. Thus, on 20 August 1928, for example, he wrote to his teacher and friend Arnold Schoenberg that certain two-movement sonatas of Beethoven and also two-movement orchestral works of Bach had served as models for his Symphony Opus 21.[18] Further, in a letter to the director of the Universal Edition, Emil Hertzka, on 19 September 1928, he refers to being occupied with the composition of a new work, a concerto (it was Opus 24) for violin, clarinet, horn, piano and string orchestra – reminiscent

---

[15] Cf. H. and R. Moldenhauer, *Anton von Webern: A Chronicle of his Life and Work* (London, 1978). References are to the German edition, *Anton von Webern. Chronik seines Lebens und Werkes* (Zürich/Freiburg, 1980), pp. 27, hereafter abbreviated as Mo.

[16] R. Busch, "Über horizontale und vertikale Darstellung musikalischer Gedanken und den musikalischen Raum," in *Anton Webern (I)*, pp. 225ff.

[17] Mo 76.

[18] Mo 294.

of certain Brandenburg concertos of Bach.[19] Finally, according to Peter
Stadlen, he pointed out in reference to the Scherzo of the Variations for
Piano, Opus 27, a connection to the Badinerie in the Bach Suite in
B Minor,[20] and emphasized in his own analysis of the String Quartet, Opus
28, composed two years later, not only the B–A–C–H motive but, in particular, his "sought-after synthesis" in the Finale of a combination of scherzo,
sonata and fugue in the manner of Beethoven and Bach.[21]

With the first cantata, a change occurred in Webern's relationship to the
music of Bach. In a letter to the poetess Hildegard Jone, Webern refers – in
relation to the concept of the text of the cantata – to "choral works of Bach"
in which "a large section is built out of a few words – a single movement"
("ein Riesenstück aus ein paar Worten – einem einzigen Satz – aufgebaut
ist"), and also mentions in this context the "Kyrie eleison, Christe eleison –
of the masses." In contrast to his earlier explanations, he expressly qualifies
his reference to the Bach works as "only a general orientation" ("nur zur
allgemeinen Orientierung").[22] Moreover, he also makes reference to music
of earlier eras, composed before the time of Bach: to the Netherlands
composers,[23] to whom he had devoted his doctoral dissertation,[24] and who
marked for him a decisive stage in the history of music[25] – along with the
Gregorian chant repertory, and the music of J. S. Bach, Beethoven and
Brahms.

A clear departure from Bach is implied in Webern's letter of 4 September
1942, to the Humplicks: "The chorale referred to – 'Freundselig ist das
Wort' – should not be thought of in a Bachian sense, in purely musical
terms, I mean. It is something quite different" ("Den erwähnten Choral –
'Freundselig ist das Wort' – dürft Ihr Euch nicht im Bachischen Sinne
denken, rein *musikalisch* meine ich. Es ist ganz anders").[26] The abandon-
ment of Bach as a source of authority (and legitimacy) and the search for
earlier historical models had nothing to do with a sense of tradition. Rather,
there is, in Webern's late compositional period, as in that of J. S. Bach,

---

[19] Mo 382.
[20] See evidence in Mo 440, note 6.
[21] Anton von Webern, "Analyse des Streichquartetts op. 28," quoted from Mo 671.
[22] Mo 508.
[23] Mo 519.
[24] Anton von Webern, "Heinrich Isaac, 'Choralis Constantinus'. Zweiter Teil. Graduale in
      mehrstimmiger Bearbeitung (a cappella), bearbeitet von Anton von Webern," *Denkmäler der
      Tonkunst in Österreich*, 14/1 (Vienna, 1909).
[25] Anton Webern, *Der Weg zur Neuen Musik*, ed. Willi Reich (Vienna, 1960).
[26] Mo 525.

Beethoven and Mahler, a historical dimension, a traversing of historical distance, in which the archaic[27] assumes the appearance of the modern.[28] It is therefore not surprising that Webern offers fewer explanatory comments or statements about the works before Opus 21, since in these works (as for instance in the Bagatelles Opus 9) the new is not sought in the past but in the future. That the confrontation with tradition did not result in Traditionalism, nor in either New Classicism ("Neue Klassizität" or "Junge Klassizität")[29] – in the sense of Busoni – or Neo-Classicism, was probably related to the non-continuous nature of Webern's relationship to the music of Bach. Webern, in his works between Opus 5 and Opus 11, and after his musicological studies and compositional apprenticeship with Schoenberg, reached a point in his stylistic development as a composer which was not a direct outgrowth of his earlier compositional style. Nothing in these works is reminiscent of the Bach tradition as it had been taught by Schoenberg. The tradition in fact was so broken by the new elements in Webern's compositional style, that it is impossible to pick up the threads of a familiar Bach tradition again 29 years later. Webern's harmonization and figuring of Bach chorales in 1906, and the Fugue (Ricercata) No. 2 of 1935 and the String Quartet Opus 28 of 1937 are thus worlds apart.

Before I go on to speak about the second phase of Webern's confrontation with Bach in the Fugue (Ricercata) No. 2 from the *Musical Offering*, I would like briefly to discuss the works from Webern's first Bach phase. (The material to which I will be referring has been placed at my disposal by Mr Han Jörg Jans of the Paul Sacher Foundation in Basel.) According to Moldenhauer's biography, Schoenberg, during the summer holidays of 1906, set Webern the task of harmonizing German chorales. On 29 July 1906, Webern questioned Schoenberg in a letter:

Soll ich die Choräle einfach harmonisieren oder auch kontrapunktisch bearbeiten? Ich habe Sie so verstanden, daß ich die Choralmelodien in der Weise, wie etwa die Choräle der "Matthäuspassion" sind, bearbeiten soll; vierstimmig mit ein paar Durchgangsnoten. Was aber Horwitz meint ist im Sinne von Bachs Choralvorspielen: in einer Stimme den Choral, in den anderen Canones oder Durchführungen eines oder mehrerer Themen.

---

[27] See Mo 194 with regard to Webern's rejection of the "archaic" as being something "preexistent." (See Barbara Zuber, "Erforschung eines Bildes. Der VI. Satz aus Webern Kantate op. 31," in *Anton Webern (I)*, pp. 119ff.)

[28] See W. Benjamin, *Ursprung des deutschen Trauerspiels* (Frankfurt am Main, 1963), pp. 209ff, for a discussion of this concept in reference to Baroque allegory.

[29] See F. Busoni, *Wesen der Einheit der Musik* (Berlin, 1956), pp. 34ff.

Am I simply to harmonize the chorales or also to arrange the work contrapuntally? I understood that I should arrange the chorale melodies in a manner similar to the chorales in the "St Matthew Passion" – four-voiced with a few passing notes. Horwitz maintains, however, [that they should be arranged] in the manner of Bach's Chorale-preludes – the chorale in one voice and canons or elaborations of one or more themes in the other voices.[30]

Eighteen chorales resulted, "arranged" in both harmonic and contrapuntal styles. An example of each of these styles, not always wholly legible in the original, is reproduced here for the first time: "Herr Jesu Christ, du höchstes Gut" and "O Ewigkeit, du Donnerwort" (see Examples 1 and 2 and Plate 1). Webern's harmonization of the choral melody "Herr Jesu Christ, du höchstes Gut"[31] shows, when compared with Bach's own harmonization, BWV 334, a more intensive chromaticism and the use of unprepared suspensions, which at times may be understood as independent harmonies. The idea that dissonances are not non-harmonic tones but exist at a more distant relationship to the consonant, may, according to Rudolf Stephan, in an important article about Schoenberg and Bach,[32] be traced back to Schoenberg's *Harmonielehre* (*Theory of Harmony*) of 1911. It is probable that Schoenberg already held this view in 1904, at the time he was teaching Berg, Webern and Horwitz. In Webern's harmonization, the primary tonal points of reference are still preserved at the fermatas, which mark off the phrases of the chorale. The intervening chords which occur between these points either stand as independent entities or appear not to demand resolution to the primary harmonies marked by the fermatas.

In the figured choral "O Ewigkeit, du Donnerwort," based on the Bach chorale BWV 397, Webern first seeks an appropriate harmonization, before he finds, as illustrated in the sketch reproduced in Plate 2,[33] a suitable counter-subject to the cantus firmus, which is then imitated in the alto, tenor and bass voices before being paraphrased in toccata-like figuration – as is common in certain Bach chorale settings for organ (see Example 3).

It does not appear to be purely coincidental that approximately 30 years later in the Bach Year of 1935 both Webern and Berg, who harmonized and figured Bach chorales under Schoenberg's guidance, based – each in his own way – a movement or a composition on a theme of Bach, compositions

---

[30] Mo 76.

[31] Paul Sacher Foundation (Basel), Mo 97 (XIV); Webern's numbering of the Bach chorales is based on Kirnberger's edition. Due to copyright difficulties, it is not possible to reproduce Webern's sketch of "Herr Jesu Christ, du höchstes Gut."

[32] R. Stephan, "Zum Thema 'Schönberg und Bach,'" *Bach-Jahrbuch* 58 (1978), p. 233.

[33] Paul Sacher Foundation, Basel, Mo 88 (V).

Example 1 Transcription of Webern's arrangement of "Herr Jesu Christ, du höchstes Gut" based on BWV 334: four-voiced chorale score on two staves

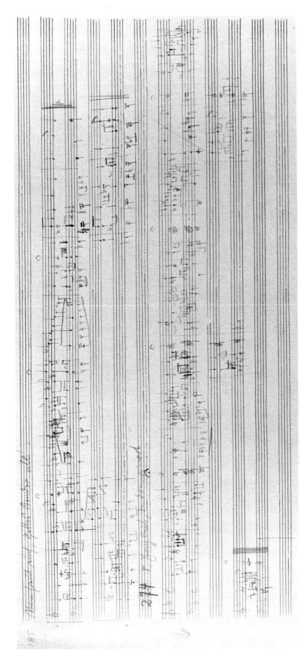

Plate 1 Webern's arrangement of "O Ewigkeit, du Donnerwort," based on BWV 397: four-voiced chorale on two staves

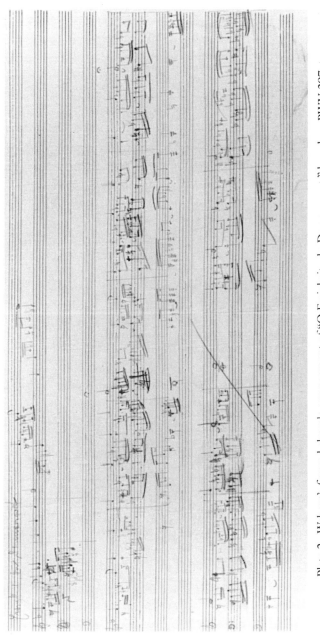

Plate 2   Webern's figured chorale arrangement of "O Ewigkeit, du Donnerwort," based on BWV 397;
a three-voiced figured chorale with the melody in the upper voice, notated on three staves

Example 2 Transcription of Webern's arrangement of
"O Ewigkeit, du Donnerwort," based on BWV 397: four-voiced chorale score on
two staves

Example 3 Transcription of Webern's figured chorale setting of "O Ewigkeit, du Donnerwort," based on BWV 397

Example 3 (*cont.*)

which stood in stark contrast to the contemporary practice of idolizing Bach. Berg, in his violin concerto, composed variations on "Es ist genug," the final chorale from Bach's cantata, "O Ewigkeit, du Donnerwort," and Webern orchestrated (and recomposed) Bach's six-voiced Ricercar from the *Musical Offering*.

Significant for Webern's second phase of intensive preoccupation with Bach is the close connection, already mentioned, between his compositional interest in Bach, as seen in Opus 21–9,[34] and his activities as a conductor of Bach's music. This connection is manifest in Webern's score of the six-voiced Ricercar from the *Musical Offering* completed in 1935, which represents – as will be shown – not only an effective use, in his later period, of the compositional procedures gleaned from his earlier Bach "arrangements," but which also drew on his experience as a Bach conductor. Regarding Webern's sonorous transformation of Bach's musical score, a factor of crucial importance to the piece, Schoenberg, in his reply to Webern on 27 August 1936, writes:

Es ist sehr anstrengend, sich das vorzustellen und außerordentlich schwer, den Faden der einzelnen Stimmen zu finden und wenn man ihn hat, ihn nicht zu verlieren. Das ist sicher nur fürs Spielen und fast nichts fürs Lesen. Und vielleicht ist das auch das Wichtigste: was herauskommt. Gerne würde ich es hören und ersuchte Klemperer, es einmal durchzuspielen.

It is very hard to form a mental picture of this music and extraordinarily difficult to find the thread of the individual voices – and once one has it, not to lose it. The piece is certainly [intended] only for playing and hardly for reading. That is the most important thing, in any case – how it sounds. I would like to hear it, and have requested Klemperer to play through it sometime.[35]

---

[34] Mo 76, with regard to Berg's Bach exercises with Schoenberg. See also *Die Werke von Alban Berg. Handschriftenkatalog, Alban Berg Studien*, ed. Fr. Grasberger and R. Stephan, ed. (Vienna, 1980), Vol. 1, pp. 78–9, in particular No. 278.

[35] Mo 403.

Two of Schoenberg's observations are important for an understanding of Webern's transcriptions. First, Schoenberg, in his remark about it being "difficult to find the thread," draws attention to the extensive filigree-work in the polyphony. Secondly, Schoenberg perceives that the full impact of Webern's reworking is only accessible when one hears the work from a sonorous point of view – a surprising remark for the theoretician Schoenberg, who preferred the silent meditative reading of a score. I would like first to explore this "sounding exterior" and then look at the "compositional interior."

The extraordinary importance of the "sonorous exterior" – exceptional for a composer oriented to structural thinking can be traced back to Webern's increasingly intensive activities as a conductor from the year 1928. From the time when he began to explain his own works in terms of the historical monument "Bach," he repeatedly performed works of Bach with such great interpreters as Rudolph Kolisch and Eduard Steuermann: the Concerto for Four Pianos, BWV 1065, on 8 January 1927; the Concerto in A Minor for Violin, Flute, Piano and String Orchestra, BWV 1044, on 17 April 1928; the Prelude and Fugue in E Flat Major, BWV 552, in Schoenberg's instrumentation (it was the first performance) on 10 and 11 November 1929; the "Kreuzstab Cantata," BWV 56, in the edition of Ferrucio Busoni on 14 December of the same year; the third Brandenburg Concerto on 4 March 1930; and the Concerto for Two Pianos in C major, BWV 1061, on 1 May, also 1930. On 1 November 1931 he directed all of the rehearsals, including the dress rehearsal, for the "Actus Tragicus," BWV 106, and similarly in 1933 the rehearsals for the St John Passion. Finally, he conducted the first performance of his own Fuga (Ricercata) No. 2 from the *Musical Offering*, together with Schubert's Unfinished Symphony and his own Opus 1 and 6, at the BBC, London on 25 April 1935, along with the first Austrian performance of the Bach Ricercar-transcription on 13 July of that same year. Eduard Steuermann, to whom the Variations for Piano Opus 27 were dedicated, and with whom Webern prepared several works of Bach for performance, reported the following in relation to his work with Webern:

Nach meiner Ansicht dirigierte er [Webern] Bach am besten. Er verband eine Projektion der motivischen Struktur, die Musik mit innerem Leben vibrieren ließ, mit einem Gespür für die grosse Linie, stets gestützt auf einfache und klare Dynamik.

In my opinion he [Webern] conducted Bach best of all. He combined a projection of the motivic structure, which set the music vibrating with inner life, with a sense for over all line, always supported by simple and clear dynamics.[36]

---

[36] Mo 418.

An insight into Webern's rehearsal technique is given by Johann Humpelstetter in his diary on 10 January 1928. According to the entry, Webern
complained during rehearsals of the "Actus Tragicus" about the unclear
dynamics in the edition being used, prepared by Robert Franz, and spoke
about "how difficult if often was for him [Webern] to specify exactly the
right expression in writing" ("wie schwer es ihm oft gelingt, den richtigen
Ausdruck[37] schriftlich niederzulegen").[38]

It was exactly this quest for "the right expression" – the sounding realization of the musical thought – which aptly describes Webern's recomposition
of the Bach Ricercar. Timbre, articulation, dynamics and agogics become
the musical means through which Bach's composition was to be freed for
the first time in its history from an abstract, purely ideal presentation. The
unspecified scoring of its pure six-voiced structure was the prime motivation
for Webern's "instrumentation" of the Bach Ricercar. It was also the basis
for the movement, prominent since the mid twenties, to give the two late
works of Bach, the *Musical Offering* and the *Art of Fugue*, concrete musical
realizations. In this context, Hermann Scherchen, a friend of Webern,
writes to his son on 6 February 1928:

> Ich habe in diesem Monat hier eine große Arbeit vor mir: die Erstaufführung der
> *Kunst der Fuge* von Bach. Schon jetzt probiere ich, instrumentiere einiges um und
> versuche, eine reifere Form für die Wiedergabe dieses Werkes zu finden, als es dem
> jetzigen Bearbeiter Graeser gelungen ist. Bach hat dieses letzte, riesenhafteste Werk
> seiner Phantasie überhaupt nicht mehr für Instrumente fixiert, sondern nur nieder-
> geschrieben in vier gänzlich neutralen Stimmen. Man hielt deshalb dieses Werk
> immer für ein blosses Studienwerk. In Wirklichkeit ist es die vielleicht grossartigste
> Schöpfung des Meisters.

> In this month I have a most important task before me: the first performance of
> Bach's *Art of Fugue*. I am already trying it out, reorchestrating certain things and am
> attempting to find a more mature form for its performance than the present editor,
> Graeser, has achieved. Bach did not specify the instrumentation for this last most
> gigantic work of his fantasy, but notated it in four purely neutral voices. For this rea-
> son one always considered it to be a work for study only. But it is in truth perhaps the
> greatest creation of the master.[39]

The question of the appropriate scoring for the *Art of Fugue*, as evident in
the arrangements, settings, transcriptions and adaptations of Graeser, Hans

---

[37] See M. Zenck, "Weberns Wiener Espressivo," *Anton Webern (I)*, pp. 179ff.

[38] Johann Humpelstetter, "Anton Webern als nachschaffender Künstler, als Chorleiter und
Dirigent," in *Anton Webern (I)*, p. 58.

[39] Hermann Scherchen, . . . *alles hörbar machen. Briefe eines Dirigenten, 1920–1939* (Berlin,
1976), p. 128.

Theodor David,[40] Scherchen's corrected version of Graeser's,[41] and further that of Roger Vuataz[42] – carried out at Scherchen's behest – was posed again in the thirties, forties and fifties in relation to the *Musical Offering*. Among the various settings of the work is one by Heinrich Besseler in 1933 for the Institute of Musicology in Heidelberg (the performance of which was directed by Wolfgang Fortner) and, two years after the publication of Webern's recomposed version of the Ricercar, a complete instrumentation of the full work by Roger Vuataz,[43] published in 1937 by Scherchen's Ars Viva-Verlag. In the same year a further setting of the *Musical Offering* by Ludwig Landshoff[44] for strings, woodwinds and harpsichord was published by Peters, and, finally, complete arrangements by Hans Theodor David[45] and Igor Markevich[46] were published respectively by Schirmer in New York in 1945 and by Boosey and Hawkes in 1952. In this context, it is interesting to note that it was Webern who declared that the neutral notation of the voices (as referred to by Scherchen, his close friend, in regard to the *Art of Fugue*) was decisive in motivating him to carry out his so-called "arrangement" of the Ricercar. This is revealed in a letter to the Swiss painter Franz Rederer, published here in it entirety for the first time (and reproduced in Plate 3) in which he writes:

Endlich komme ich dazu, Ihren lieben Brief zu beantworten. Sind Sie mir bitte, nicht böse, daß es so spät geschieht. Ich hatte mich sehr über Ihre lieben Zeilen gefreut und wollte gleich antworten. Aber ich kam nicht dazu! Ich hatte, als Ihr Brief eintraf, über u. über mit der Durchführung eines Chorkonzertes zu tun u. mußte mich auch schon auf mein Konzert in London vorbereiten, wohin ich bald nach dem Wiener Konzert reisen mußte. In London dirigierte ich im Rundfunk drei eigene Werke u. dazu eine Schubert-Symphonie. Unter jenen war auch die Uraufführung meiner Orchesterbearbeitung einer Fuge von Johann Sebastian Bach, eines völlig unbekannten, wundervollen Werkes. Im Original rein abstrakt notiert [wie dann später die Fugen in der "Kunst der Fuge"]. Da steht nicht, ob das zum Singen oder zum Spielen ist, ob das schnell oder langsam sein soll. Das heißt ohne

---

[40] H. Th. David, ed., *Joh. Seb. Bach, Die Kunst der Fuge* (Leipzig, 1928).

[41] See W. Kolneder, *Die Kunst der Fuge. Mythen des 20. Jahrhunderts, Teil III, Spezialuntersuchungen* (Wilhelmshaven, 1977), p. 424.

[42] J. S. Bach, *Die Kunst der Fuge*, Instrumentierung Roger Vuataz/(Seinem Freunde Hermann Scherchen gewidmet), Ars Viva-Verlag (Zürich, 1950).

[43] *Musikalisches Opfer. Johann Sebastian Bach*, Version Roger Vuataz pour quatuor à cordes solo, flûte, hautbois, cor anglais, basson et clavecin (Ars Viva-Verlag, Brussels, 1937).

[44] See commentary of Christoph Wolff, *NBA*, VIII/1 (Kassel, 1976), *Kritischer Bericht*, pp. 126ff.

[45] *Ibid.*, pp. 126ff.

[46] J. S. Bach *Das Musikalische Opfer*, orchestrated by Igor Markevich (London, 1952).

Mein lieber Herr Rederer,

endlich komme ich dazu Ihren lieben Brief zu
beantworten. Sind Sie mir, bitte, nicht böse,
dass es so spät geschieht. Ich hatte mich zu so
über Ihre lieben Zeilen gefreut u. wollte
gleich antworten. Aber ich kam nicht dazu!
Ich hatte, als Ihr Brief ankam, über u. über
mit der Durchführung eines Chorkonzertes
zu tun u. musste mich erst schon auf
ein Konzert in <u>London</u> vorbereiten, wohin
ich bald nach dem Wiener Konzert reisen
musste. In London dirigierte ich im
Rundfunk 3 eigene Werke u. dazu eine
Schubert-Symphonie. Unter ihnen auch
die Uraufführung meiner Orchesterbearbeitung
einer Fuge von J. S. Bach, eines
völlig unbekannten, wundervollen
Stückes. Im Original wie abgestellt
notiert (wie denn später die Fugen in der
„Kunst der Fuge"). Da steht nicht, ob das
zu singen oder zu spielen ist, nicht ob's
schnell oder langsam sein soll [d.f. ohne
Tempobezeichnung], nichts von dynamischer
Bezeichnung, also ob laut oder leise, kurz
nichts von dem, was man sonst hinzufügt,
um anzudeuten, wie man den Gedanken
verstehen soll oder verstehen hätte.

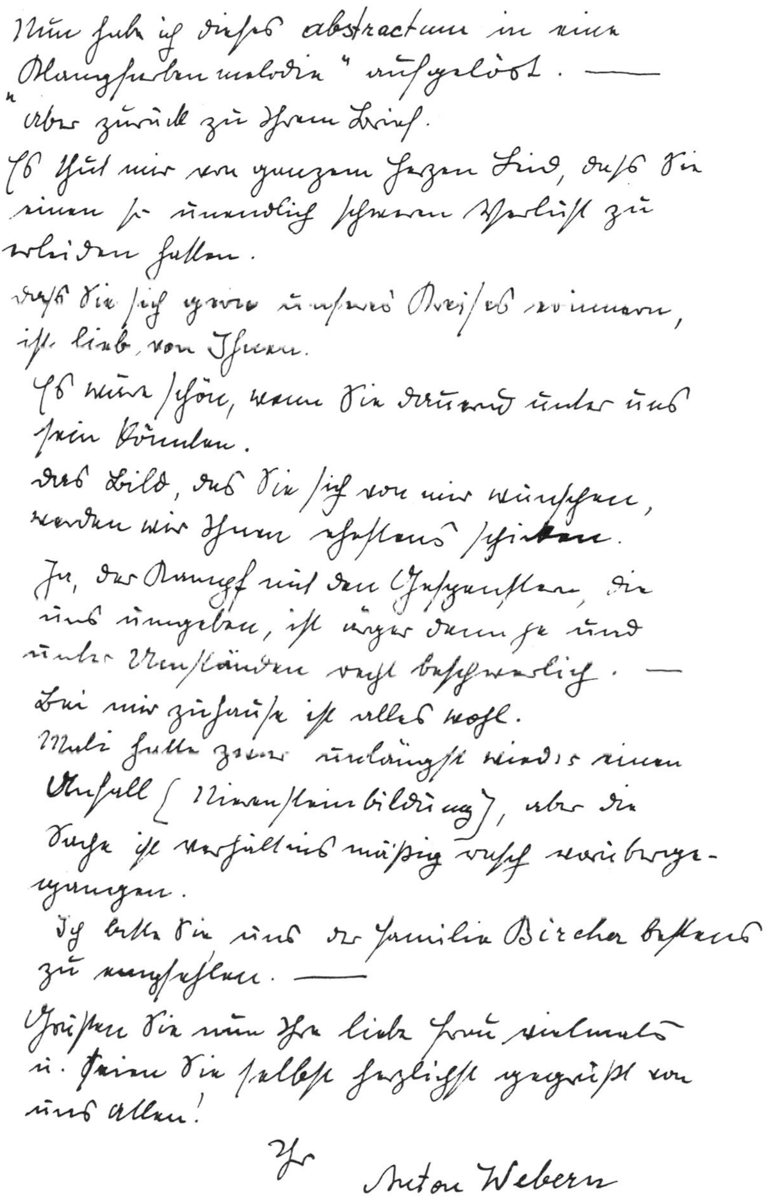

[handwritten letter in German]

Anton Webern

Plate 3   Anton Webern's letter to Franz Rederer, 16 May 1935

Tempobezeichnung, nichts von dynamischer Bezeichnung, also ob laut oder leise, Kurz nichts von dem, was man sonst hinzufügt, um auzudenken, wie man den Gedanken verstehen soll oder aufzuführen hätte. Nun habe ich dieses abstractum in eine "Klangfarbenmelodien" aufgelöst.

At last I am able to answer your kind letter. Please don't be angry with me for replying so late. I was very happy to receive your thoughtful lines and intended to answer them immediately, but I wasn't able to! I was busy when your letter arrived, involved in a choral concert, and I also had to prepare myself for my concert in London, where I had to go soon after the concert in Vienna. In London I conducted three of my own works and also a symphony of Schubert on the radio. Among the works was the first performance of my orchestral arrangement of a fugue of Johann Sebastian Bach, a totally unknown and wonderful work. Abstractly notated in the original, as are later the fugues in the Art of Fugue, it is unspecified as to whether it should be sung or played, whether it should be performed fast or slow. It is without tempo markings, includes no dynamics, in short, nothing by which one normally indicates how things are to be understood or performed. And now I have transformed this abstract conception into a "Klangfarbenmelodie."[47]

In this letter of Webern's from 16 May 1935, and in a later letter to Hermann Scherchen (to which I will refer in detail), Bach's completely free musical notation, or open scoring, is indicated as being the essential reason for Webern's specific concern with "expression" in his Bach arrangement. Webern may also have been strengthened in his purpose by hearing Scherchen's many performances of the *Art of Fugue* and by the critical tradition which viewed the *Art of Fugue* and *Musical Offering* as purely abstract works. Either there existed, for Webern, a contradiction between the ideal notation of a musical text and its sonorous realization, or he drew a principal distinction between construction (structure) and expression. When one considers that Webern composed the Variations for Piano Opus 27 – which Ernst Krenek maintains to be one of the most abstract of all Webern's works[48] – only nine months after completing the Bach arrangement, the question then arises: why did Webern, in taking away from the Bach Ricercar all form of abstraction by in fact overloading it with expression markings, issue at approximately the same time a published form of Opus 27 which contained very few performance directions, was un-pianistic, and was quite "absolute" in its conception? Would it not have been more logical to have left Bach's Ricercar in a form similar to Opus 27, as a "Kunstbuch" (Book of Art), as a "Livre" in the sense of Mallarmé?[49] Can the seeming contradiction be

[47] Paul Sacher Foundation (Basel); Webern's letter of 16 May 1935 to Franz Rederer (partly in facsimile): *Anton von Webern: Perspectives*, ed. H. Moldenhauer (Seattle and London, 1966), p. 38.

[48] Anton Webern, *Variationen für Klavier op. 27*, edition of Peter Stadlen (Vienna, 1979).

[49] As, for example, the "Livre pour Quatour" of P. Boulez.

understood when it is assumed that for Webern a principle difference exists between composition and musical interpretation – as exists between the first edition of Opus 27 in 1937 and the "interpretative" edition of Stadlen in 1977? Or did there exist for Webern an ideal unity of composition and realization, which however could not be realized in a musical performance because the latter had not kept pace with the state of compositional practice? (That a resolution is possible is seen by comparing the edition of Stadlen and the letter of Webern to Rederer.) In the case of the Ricercar, as also in that of Opus 27, Webern had to recognize that the pure musical thought can achieve nothing when no one knows how it is to be "understood and performed." It is still also to be kept in mind (with regard to this apparent contradiction) that while Webern's performance indications for Opus 27 reflect the nature of his own interpretations, he expressly states in the letter to Rederer (and even more in the one to Scherchen) that his aim is to interpret Bach anew, while striving, at the same time, to reveal the motivic structure of the contrapuntal lines.

If the earlier quoted remarks of Webern, regarding Bach, show that tradition for him (Webern) was an historical authority through which he could legitimize himself, it is made unmistakably clear, in the famous letter belonging to the Hermann-Scherchen-Archive of the Akademie der Künste, Berlin – written by Webern to Scherchen on 1 January 1938 – that tradition also is to be understood in the sense of provocation; in specific terms, that Bach's work should be subjected to a new ideal – above and beyond the eighteenth-century concept of music.

I am very glad that you are doing "my" (I think I may call it that) Bach Fugue on the BBC. And more particularly that you have written to tell me so, which, anyway for me, reopens the contact between us that appeared to be broken after the unhappy days in Barcelona. To think that absolutely nobody understood me then, and how I felt right after Berg's passing, and that I was simply not up to the emotions aroused by the task of giving the first performance of his last work – so soon after his death! Right up to the last moment I had hoped to be able to stand it, but I did not succeed.

Now for your question: the "rubato" you ask me about is intended to indicate that I think of these measures of the fugue subject as played with movement – every time, even with all the later additional counterpoints: *accel.*, *rit.*, finally merging into the "poco allargando" of the last notes (of the subject). For I feel this part of the subject, this chromatic progression (*g–b*) to be essentially different from the first five notes, which I think of as being very steady, almost stiff (that is, in strict tempo, since the tempo is set by this phrase) and which in my view I find to be the same character as the last five notes. More precisely, I intend the "rubato" like this: from *g via f♯* to *f* faster, then holding back a little on the *eb* (accent given by the harp) and again rubato on the trombone progression (including the tied *eb* of the horn where the trombone has a quarter-note rest in measure 6). By the way, *g* to *eb* is also five notes if you count the *eb* as a link or a dividing point (to the inner ear this first quarter-note of measure 6, the tied *eb* on the horns plus the quarter rest of the trombone, is heavily stressed, and I have orchestrated it as such); now, if you count the *eb* twice, you again have five notes (from *eb* to *b*). The structure therefore appears to me as follows: 5 notes, then 4+1 and 4+1, which is twice 5, and at the end another five notes!

And the two middle sections of 5 notes, the actual center of the structure, I feel to be quite different in character from the beginning and the end. The latter leads back with the "poco allargando" to the stiffness of the opening – now appearing in the answer. In dynamics this means that you must make a strong difference between the *pp* of the first five notes and the *p* of the central ones! And in the return of the last five notes *molto dim.* (⟩) to *pp.*

I hope I have made myself understood. I must add that (of course) the subject must not appear too disintegrated by all this. My instrumentation is intended (and I speak of the whole work) to reveal the motivic coherence. This was not always easy. Beyond that, of course, it is supposed to set the character of the piece as I feel it. What music it is! To at last make it available, by trying through my orchestration to express my view of it, was the ultimate object of this bold undertaking. Is it not worthwhile to awaken this music, asleep in the seclusion of Bach's own abstract presentation, and thus unknown or unapproachable by most men? Unapproachable as music! Let me know about your impressions and experiences in London. I shall listen! One more important point for the performance of my arrangement; nothing must be allowed to take second place. Not even the softest notes of the muted trumpet must be allowed to be lost. Everything is of primary importance in this work – in this instrumentation. . .[50]

In this letter Webern speaks on the one hand in a reserved manner about his "instrumentation" and "arrangement," but accentuates on the other hand the independent aspect of *his* "Bach Fugue." When, further, the emphasis of the "bold undertaking" ("gewagten Unternehmens") is taken into consideration, which according to Webern consisted of revealing "the motivic coherence" through the instrumentation ("den motivischen Zusammenhang bloss zu legen") and setting "the character of the piece as I feel it. What music it is!" ("anzudeuten, wie ich den Character des Stückes empfinde; dieser Musik!"); then it is only reasonable for the composer to note at the end of the letter: "Everything is of primary importance in this work – in this instrumentation" ("Alles ist Hauptsache in diesem Werk und – in dieser Instrumentation"). The "work" is now no longer Bach's work, but that of Webern; the instrumentation is the means of making its recom-

---

[50] Letter of 1 January 1938 from Webern to Hermann Scherchen (courtesy of Hermann-Scherchen-Archiv, Akademie der Künste, West Berlin).

posed form more understandable. It would be wrong to assume that the "new" here is to be found in the instrumentation. Rather, a specific compositional insight into the "motivic coherence" (as it will be referred to below) leads to an appropriate realization of the "sonorous exterior."

Although Webern does not explain exactly what he means by revealing the "motivic coherence" in the "whole work," it is to be gathered from his description of the subject and the assertion "everything [is] of primary importance in this work" ("Alles [sei] Hauptsache in diesem Werk") that he was reinterpreting Bach's Ricercar on the basis of the idea of thematic process – adapted from the twelve-tone technique. Webern divides the theme or subject into three parts: first, to correspond to the triadic melodic lines at the beginning and the end of the theme, and then to point up the structural significance of the *eb* marked with an * in Example 4 – the note *eb* is the end of the first part after the Lamento bass and at the same time the beginning of the second part. When Webern further, in the context of "motivic coherence," designates this same line to several instruments – with a similar rubato-style tempo articulation at all entrances – it then becomes obvious that he perceives Bach's composition, including its episodes, from the perspective of thematic process. Example 4 shows my analysis of the subject based on Webern's letter to Scherchen.

Example 4 Analysis of J. S. Bach's *Ricercar a sei voci*: mm. 1–4, based on Webern's letter to Hermann Scherchen

* Midpoint of subject

To discuss Bach's Ricercar in terms of the thematic process of the Viennese Classical instrumental style is appropriate (and one can see further evidence of this in Webern's statements in the letter) to the extent that the counterpoint can be seen as thematic derivation. And, what is more important, the expositions of the fugue utilize material derived from the middle part of the subject (the chromaticized Lamento bass) while the normally freely conceived episodes are also thematically linked. In the same manner, the episodes, occurring between the expositions, are based upon a common melodic material, derived from both the subject and the counter-subject.

A further and more detailed analysis of all the expositions and episodes would show that Webern did not perceive Bach's Ricercar as a representation of six independent and flowing voices, but, rather, perceived the continuity (from a thematic point of view) as being constantly disrupted. In his orchestration, therefore, he applied a principle, which I will call *non-lineal* – or better, *dia-lineal* – analogous to his idea of the *fragmentation of lines*. In comparison with the arrangement of the *Musical Offering* by Roger Vuataz, published two years later, it is clear that the latter (see Example 5) was concerned with a direct and consistent assignment of separate polyphonic voices to specific instruments, and Webern (see Example 6) with the distribution of a single line among several instruments, which resulted in the prismatic splintering of several lines throughout the whole orchestra.

At first hearing, the Webern score may initially give the impression of an overblown Romantic or late-Romantic work – the superimposition of a monumental orchestral setting on a simple, clear and firmly outlined six-voiced movement. On the other hand, in its defense, the Fugue (Ricercata) No. 2, along with Opus 27 and 28,[51] can be seen as a radical transformation of the tradition, the same tradition that was accepted by Webern as authoritative. Webern, through his reinterpretation, gave new meaning to the work in the highly-celebrated Bach year of 1935.

[When this chapter was delivered as a paper, it concluded with a recording of the Webern orchestration conducted by Bruno Maderna,[52] a performance which closely conforms to Webern's intentions.]

---

[51] The application of the composition technique of the Opus 27 and 28 to the Bach Ricercar could be stated as follows: Webern treats the complete subject of Bach, which comprises fifteen notes according to his counting, as a twelve-tone row, out of which he selects segments and treats them motivically. This procedure is particularly evident in Opus 28, where Webern develops four-tone segments motivically and in imitation until at a certain point (first movement, mm. 66–7) the B–A–C–H motive is revealed.

[52] Recording with the Kölner Rundfunk-Sinfonieorchester, produced for radio in Cologne, 1961, by the Westdeutscher Rundfunk, Köln.

Example 5 J. S. Bach, *Fuga (Ricercata)* from the *Musical offering*, Vuataz arrangement, opening and closing sections (mm. 1–6 and 94–103) (reprinted by permission of Ars Una-Verlag, Berlin)

Example 5 (*cont.*)

Example 6 (opposite and p. 322) From Fuga (Ricercata) a 6 voci No. 2, from the *Musical Offering* by J. S. Bach, orchestrated by A. Webern, opening and closing sections (mm. 1–5 and 201–5) © 1935 by Universal Edition A G Vienna, © renewed 1963; with permission of Universal Edition A G Vienna

Example 6 (*cont.*)

The human side of the American Bach sources

GERHARD HERZ

In spite of its horrendous financial deficit, the United States of America is somewhat richer than we might think. The autograph music manuscripts that reach from Bach, Mozart and Beethoven to most of the music of Mahler, to Schoenberg's *Gurrelieder* and Berg's *Wozzeck* that America calls her own, constitute a priceless and unique humanistic legacy. To concentrate on Johann Sebastian Bach, as we must, we can state that America owns more original manuscripts and other primary Bach sources than exist anywhere else outside of Bach's homeland, now East and West Germany. America has become the home of fifteen autograph scores,[1] 55 original performing parts, and other autograph writings such as letters, receipts, a signature, as well as a portrait of the master painted from life, and Bach's own Bible. These Bach treasures are dispersed throughout America. They can be found in 30 different locations, from the Library of Congress in the South to Harvard University in the East and to Stanford University in the West.

What is the actual significance, if any, of these American-housed Bach scores? Do any of these compositions or documents hold a special place in Bach's *œuvre* or in his life? Indeed, an astonishing number of them are, in the literal sense of the word, extraordinary. The autograph score of Bach's very first cantata, Cantata 131, *Aus der Tiefen rufe ich, Herr, zu dir*, is the property of a well-known pianist who lives in New York City. It is in fact the earliest autograph of a major composition by Bach that has come down to us (see Plate 1).

The heading at the top of page one of the score is written in amusingly faulty Italian and thus an indication of the very early origin of this cantata:

---

[1] For a complete description of and commentary on the sources, see Gerhard Herz, *Bach-Quellen in Amerika – Bach Sources in America* (Bärenreiter, Kassel, Basel, London, New York, 1984).

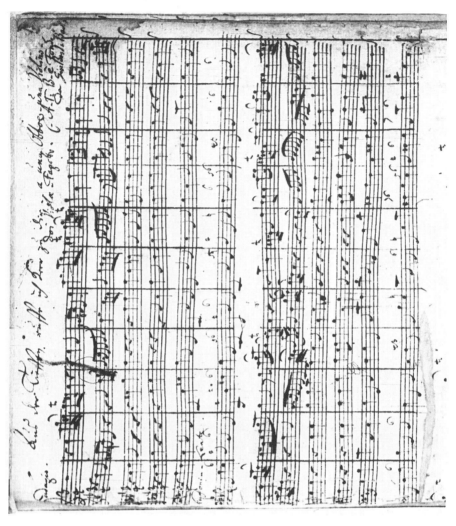

Plate 1 Cantata 131, *Aus der Tiefen rufe ich, Herr, zu dir* (autograph score), fo. 1r

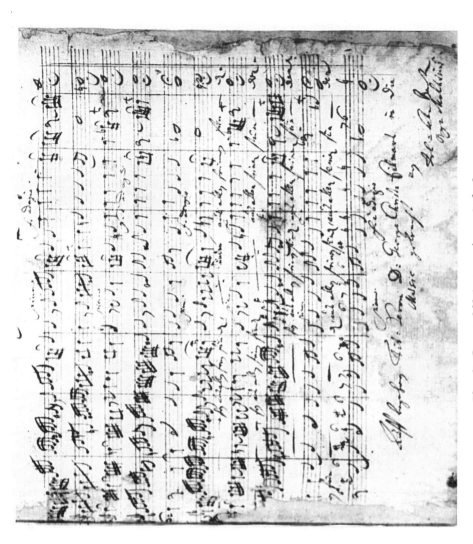

Plate 2 Cantata 131 (autograph score), fo. 8r

"Aus der Tieﬀen ruﬀe ich Herr zu dir" (in German script, as Bach's titles always are), "a una Obboe, una Violino/doi Violae. Fagotto. C. [=Canto] A. T: B.è Fond./da Gio: Bast: Bach" (in Latin script). For instance, the "è" would be much better off without the *accent grave*. (I do not think Bach, at this point, when he was 22 years of age, would have been able to pass a course in Italian.) The early date, 1707, is corroborated by Bach's unique postscript, which translated reads: "At the request of Herr Dr Georg Christian Eilmar set to music by Joh. Seb. Bach/organist in Mühlhausen" (see Plate 2). It thus appears that Eilmar, who was not the minister of Bach's church, was the instigator of Bach's first church cantata. Since Frohne, the minister of Bach's church, was an ardent pietist and thus inimical to the new cantata form, as all pietists were then, the newly appointed organist Bach was not supposed to compose much less to perform cantatas. The intention of Bach's postscript thus seems to have been to shift the responsibility for having composed and performed a cantata in Mühlhausen to Eilmar, the minister of St Mary's Church. As an orthodox Lutheran, and thus musically a liberal, Eilmar supported the new form of the cantata wholeheartedly.

We know that Bach's oldest son Wilhelm Friedemann did not guard his father's musical legacy with the same zeal as did his brother Carl Philipp Emanuel. The circumstances of Friedemann's wayward life forced him eventually to sell the bulk of the manuscripts he had inherited from his father. Since Philipp Emanuel had inherited the scores of the cantatas his father had performed during his first year in Leipzig, we should not expect to find any of them in America; and indeed, none of them is there. But of Bach's second yearly cycle of cantatas, the scores and duplicate parts of which Friedemann had inherited, there is almost an *embarras de richesses* of which several have unfortunately left America during the last three years.[2] It is America's good fortune that this is the year of the chorale cantatas, Bach's most original artistic contribution to the cantata genre.

I was astonished to find a great many traits of Bach's character and other idiosyncrasies of the master reflected in the American Bach documents. A careful selection of some of them will reveal Bach's intuitive sense for a consistently beautiful aesthetic use of the available space on his title pages. But in the writing of the music itself, Bach's well-known economical nature shows itself in a variety of ingenious ways of filling the space of the paper to the utmost. At times, the composer's creative momentum is so intense that he fails to notice the bounds of the available space. The assembly-line type

---

[2] For some scores which have recently left America, see Herz, *Bach-Quellen in Amerika* pp. 60–1.

of production of the performing parts demonstrates the apparently chronic lack of time that lay between Bach's completion of a score and its performance. The beginning and end of a Bach score even give us a sense of Bach's devoutness; another score gives us a new insight into the father–son relationship that was to become so fateful for Wilhelm Friedemann. Bach's very last documents that are in America are marked by obvious signs of writing cramp and one of them is a touching witness to Bach's deteriorating eyesight.

The autograph title page of Cantata 178 (*BS* 354)[3] is particularly beautiful because it is totally unmarred by any library stamp, owner's name or other inscription. It is one of the three Bach items discovered during my five-year pursuit of original Bach sources in America. As late as 1967, Alfred Dürr wrote in his critical report to the publication of this cantata in the *NBA*, "the title page is at present not traceable." But it *is* to be found, and in a place in which one would not likely be inclined to look for a Bach manuscript: at the Metropolitan Opera House in New York. There in the Belmont Room of the Metropolitan Opera Guild, it hangs, a gift of Louisville-born Edwin Franko Goldman, the founder and director of the famous Goldman Band. The beauty of the handwriting and the artistic use Bach made of the available space speak for themselves. Only rarely can one see such a clear contrast between Bach's Latin script and the German script of the title, *Wo Gott der Herr nicht bey uns hält*.

The duplicate flute part of Cantata 9 (*BS* 366) remained unknown even to the world's foremost Bach scholars and manuscript hunters. However, in 1971 it was found on a pile of rubble near Greenwich Village in New York City where some houses had been torn down to make way for new construction or, more likely, for a parking lot. I sought out the proud finder and keeper of this page and persuaded him to let the Pierpont Morgan Library photograph his manuscript. The autograph title page in the possession of the Metropolitan Opera Guild, this flute part and, recently, the discovery by Christoph Wolff of 33 formerly unknown organ chorales in a copy made a generation after Bach's death by an otherwise unknown scribe named Neumeister, show that new Bach sources can still be found in our day.

The "J. J." (Jesu Juva) that preceeds the autograph heading of most of Bach's church compositions is Bach's characteristic prayer for divine assistance during the act of creation, here for the New Year Cantata 171,

---

[3] Numbers in parentheses refer to the page numbers of the plates in Herz, *Bach-Quellen in Amerika*.

Gott, wie dein Name, so ist auch dein Ruhm, which is the Urform of what later was to become the "Patrem omnipotentem" chorus in the Credo of the B Minor Mass (see Plate 3). As can be seen, Bach made the utmost use of the available space on the paper. Since he notated the instruments of the opening movement in the order in which he had listed them in the caption, there was no need for him to name them again at the beginning of the score on the left side of the opening page of the manuscript. On the unused seven lower staves of the first seven pages, that is, below the opening chorus and running parallel with it, he entered the second movement of the cantata, a tenor aria, though using on the first page the bass clef, showing that even J. S. Bach could commit a scribal error.

Bach's economical use of space took a more unusual form for the third movement of Cantata 20 (*BS* 319 and 320). Here, Bach appended the final first violin, tenor and continuo measures before the *da capo* of this tenor aria on the three lowest staves of the page. Lacking additional space, he then notated the final measures for "Violin 2" and "Viola" (which are harmonically filling parts needing less notes) on the two lowest staves of the preceding page. He calls attention to their misplaced position not by his usual insert symbol or by NB (Nota Bene), but by two primitive upward-pointing three-fingered hands. The left hand clarifies what is to be transferred while the right hand shows where it is to be inserted. The opening page of Cantata 10, *Meine Seele erhebt den Herrn*, shows something else again: namely how Bach used the time while he had to wait for the ink to dry before he could turn the page (see Plate 4). On the two lowest staves one can see how his creative momentum simply continued as he sketched the treble and bass of the next three measures which complete the orchestral ritornello of this vigorous movement.

When Bach sat down to compose a cantata, he had before him the text and a stack of folios folded lengthwise. In the case of Bach's first Chorale Cantata, *O Ewigkeit, du Donnerwort* (BWV 20) this meant that the overall layout of this eleven-movement cantata was decided when Bach put pen to paper. The score was written obviously at breakneck speed and constitutes a typical composing score of the master. Bach reached the penultimate movement, a duet for alto, tenor and continuo, at the bottom of page nineteen. When he turned the page, he came to the last page of his fifth folio (see Plate 5). By the time he had filled its seven available braces of three staves each (in alto, tenor and bass clefs), it should have been perfectly clear to him that there was no chance whatsoever of completing the cantata on this page, and that he would simply have to reach for another folio. As it turned out, only the latter's first page was needed to complete the duet and to notate the

Plate 3   Cantata 171, *Gott, wie dein Name, so ist auch dein Ruhm*
(autograph score), fo. 1r, opening of the choral fugue (mvt. 1)

Plate 4 Cantata 10, *Meine Seele erhebt den Herren* (autograph score),
fo. 1r, orchestral ritornello of the opening movement

final chorale. The three remaining pages of this new folio are empty though they are fully lined. That Bach was economical by nature is well known, but the *largesse* shown on the last page (see right side of Plate 5), as well as the fact that Bach did not cut this last folio lengthwise in half, thereby saving one leaf for later use, rules out his economical instinct in this particular case. The reason for the tremendous contrast of these two pages thus must be found elsewhere.

It seems to me that Bach's total involvement in the creative process precluded any practical consideration beyond the moment at hand. When Bach arrived at the empty two last staves of the obviously pre-lined score (see left side of photo) his creative impulse evidently was not to be stopped. His pen simply continued to write the next five measures for the two voices. Since there was no space left to add a hand-drawn staff for the still missing continuo part, he supplied it by making use of the old space-saving device of tablature (that is, of letter notation). Only now did Bach come to realize that another page was needed. His creative involvement thus had only delayed the necessary interruption of the flow of the pen by the few minutes it had taken him to write the final brace on the penultimate page. On the last page (see right side of Plate), he notated the remainder of the duet. After its last brace (the third), he squeezed in the word "Choral," then entered the latter textless on the next two braces of four staves each. The last brace left just enough space for Bach to jot down: "Fine SDG" (Soli Deo Gloria), his thanksgiving for the granting of the divine assistance which his "J. J." (Jesu Juva) had implored at the beginning of the score. Seeing these two pages as we see them today, one wonders whether Bach may belatedly have become aware of the contrast between these two pages and seen that this last page provided him with more than ample space for the completion of the duet and the notation of the final chorale. I personally believe that Bach was totally oblivious to the contrast of these two pages. Bach, who at the very end of the penultimate page had failed to think ahead, as has been shown, probably was now thinking ahead to the task that still lay ahead: namely, the customarily frenzied effort of overseeing the completion of the copying of the parts, lending thereby here and there a helping hand himself and correcting them wherever necessary. Above all, Bach knew how little time there remained for rehearsal before his first chorale cantata was to be performed on the first Sunday after Trinity on 11 June 1724.

The exact date "d:5 Juni 1729" (see Plate 6), at the end of the alto part of Cantata 174, *Ich liebe den Höchsten von ganzem Gemüte*, constitutes a rare phenomenon in Bach manuscripts. That this part and probably most, if not all, parts of this cantata were completed only on the day prior to the can-

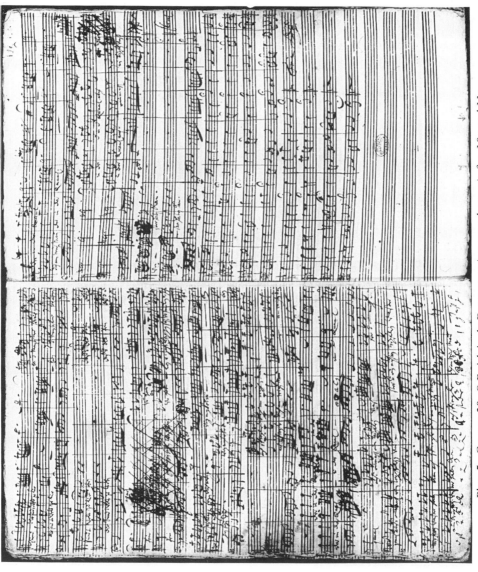

Plate 5 Cantata 20, *O Ewigkeit, du Donnerwort* (autograph score), fos. 10v and 11r, duet and final chorale

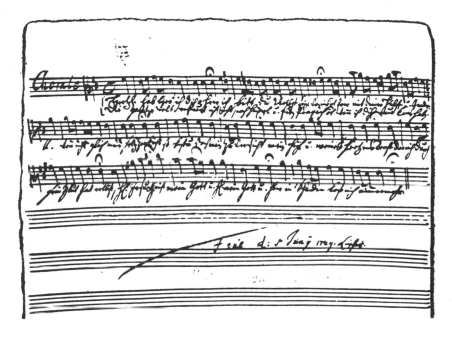

Plate 6   Cantata 174, *Ich liebe den Höchsten von ganzem Gemüte*, the verso page of
the alto part, which shows the final chorale as well as the date

tata's first performance, is for once concrete proof of the general lack of time
and the inadequate preparation from which the first performances of Bach's
cantatas appear to have suffered. Moreover, 5 June was not a free day, but
Pentecost Day, which had to be celebrated by the proper musical services in
the two principal churches of Leipzig. The only rehearsal time available to
all participants seems to have been the evening of the 5th. On the other
hand, Bach could at least rely on the inborn musicianship of his eighteen-
and fifteen-year-old sons, Friedemann and Philipp Emanuel, as well as on
that of his favorite pupil, fifteen-year-old Johann Ludwig Krebs. That time
was, however, of the utmost essence can be deduced also from Bach's
unusually rich participation in the copying of the parts. The basso part, for
instance (see Plate 7), is entirely in Bach's hand, showing the artistic verve
and the harmonious *ductus* of the 44-year-old master's handwriting. On the
last page of the third violin part from the same set of parts, the copyist made
the mistake of entering the hymn tune of the concluding chorale. When

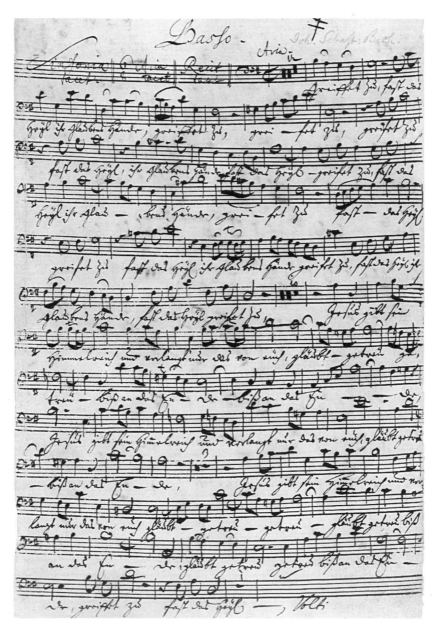

Plate 7   Cantata 174, fo. 1r of the autograph bass part (mvt. 4)

Bach, apparently ever present and watchful, became aware of this, he crossed out the wrong soprano part and entered the correct alto part of the chorale himself, plus the word "Fine."

On the verso page of the second oboe d'amore part of Cantata 168, *Tue Rechnung! Donnerwort*, Bach took the pen from his principal copyist, Johann Andreas Kuhnau, and wrote the *da capo* of the ritornello of this aria himself (see Plate 8). Observe the seven typical violin clefs of J. A. Kuhnau, then Bach's more evenly rounded violin clefs, which resemble the figure 8, and finally the three clefs, the word "Chorale" and the chorale itself as written by Bach's copyist Christian Gottlob Meissner. The participation on this one page of three writers, of Kuhnau as principal copyist, of the composer, apparently as helper in need, and of Meissner as writer of the chorale, indicates something of the frantic pace of production of the performing parts for a Bach cantata.

Plate 9 shows the title page of the third volume of Bach's Bible with vast commentary by the orthodox Lutheran theologian Abraham Calov (1612–86). Unfortunately space does not allow me to relay the remarkable story of how this three-volume Bible came *via* Philadelphia to Frankenmuth in Michigan and finally into the possession of the library of Concordia Seminary in St Louis, Missouri. At the foot of the page on the right Bach entered his name and the date 1733, not only here but on each one of the three title pages of the Bible, intertwining the initial letters JSB to create a harmonious monogram. The same year and monogram also characterize a beautifully preserved autograph signature which I happen to own (see Plate 10).

Let me quote just one of the four marginal remarks Bach entered into his Bible. In the first Book of Chronicles Bach found in the aged King David's order of the music in the temple not only the origin of church music but also that of the profession of the church musician. Bach's remark reads, translated, "N. B. Magnificent proof that besides other functions of the divine service, music has especially been ordered into existence by God's spirit through David." Professor Howard Cox's painstaking chemical analysis of the ink of these unquestionably autograph marginal remarks *and* of the numerous underlining and dots or dashes found in the margins, has recently shown them to be of the same ink, so that the latter too can now be attributed to Bach. A book about this appeared at the end of this Bach anniversary year.[4] After the passage in Matthew (5:24–6) which deals with reconciliation with "thy brother" and "thine adversary," Calov added a com-

---

[4] Howard C. Cox, *The Calov Bible of J. S. Bach* (Ann Arbor, Michigan, 1985).

Plate 8   Cantata 168, *Tue Rechnung! Donnerwort*, fo. 1v of the second oboe
d'amore part, which shows the handwritings of Kuhnau, Bach and Meißner

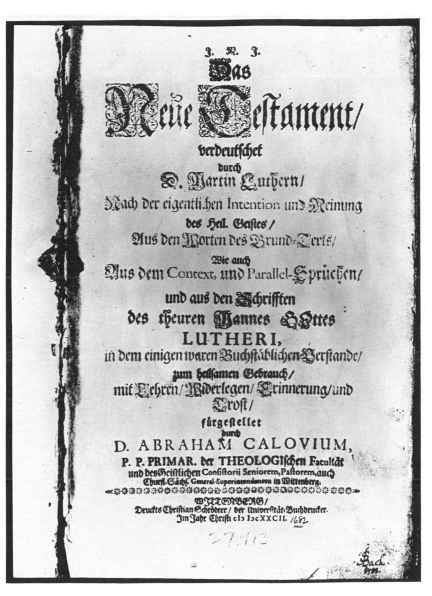

Plate 9   Bach's copy of *Calovii Schrifften*, title page of Vol. 3

Plate 10   Signature of J. S. Bach, 1733

mentary which Bach found so personally meaningful that he underlined
and marked portions of it (see Plate 11). Calov amplified the scriptural text
by saying: "It is true there must be and should be anger." But you "must be
angry not when it concerns you, but when it concerns your professional
service and God. . .As for your person, you shall be angry with no one, no
matter how greatly you have been offended. . .But where your service to
your profession ["dein Ampt"] demands it, there you must be angry, even if
no harm has come to you personally." As Bach's underscoring and marginal
marks show, he found in this passage a God-given justification for his own
pugnacious nature in professional matters. Bach's recurrent and keen disappointments in his professional life were not caused by his faith, but by the
earthly representatives of this faith. With them he fought endless battles. At
them he was, as now we can state, in the literal sense of the word, "angry."

   One of the autograph Bach manuscripts in America adds a new chapter to
the father–son relationship of Johann Sebastian and Wilhelm Friedemann
Bach. It has often been noted that Friedemann, as Bach's oldest son, was
his favorite. Two months after Friedemann's ninth birthday, Johann Sebastian began in Cöthen to compile the first of his three Notebooks. Of
Friedemann's Notebook the Yale University Library is now the proud
owner. Bach's title page – "Clavier-Büchlein/vor/Wilhelm Friedemann

du nicht deinen
o der Richter
anmahnet / und
echsten seine Feh-
VI. 12. c. XIIX. 35.)
Diener / und
worffen. (des
ersöhnliche gehö-
iger Offenb. XXI.
Hader / Neid /
Wercke des Flei-
en das Reich Got-
21. Darumb er-
ir untereinander
en / und vergeben
Ott uns vergeben
die Sonne nicht
hen / v. 26. Son-
hristus uns gelie-

r warlich / du
herauß kom-
ten Heller be-
lle Ewigkeit / denn
hlung. Hier al-
iesem Leben / nicht
icht der geringste
z als einige Hoff-
ällen. Darumb

deinet wegen / sondern von Ampts und Gottes wegen müssest zürnen / und nicht die zwey / deine Person und Ampt in einander mengest. Für deine Person solt du mit niemand zürnen / wie hoch du beleidiget bist / wo es aber dein Ampt fordert / da must du zürnen / ob der wol für deine Person kein Leid geschehen ist. Wenn aber dein Bruder etwas wider dich gethan / und dich erzürnet hat / und bitter bitte abe / und legt das böse Werck abe / so soll auch der Zorn weggehen. Woher kömpt denn der heimliche Groll / den du gleich wol im Hertzen behältest / so doch das Werck und Ursach des Zorns hinweg ist / und er dafür nun ander Werck erzeigt / als der sich bekehrt / und nun gar ein ander Mensch / und ein neuer Baum ist worden mit neuen Früchten / der dich nun liebet und ehret auffs allerhöchste. Damit daß er sich gegen dir beschuldiget / und selbsten strafft / und must für GOtt und aller Welt ein verzweiffelter Mensch seyn / wo du nicht wiederumb dich gegen ihm so erzeigest / und von Hertzen vergiebest / daß dir billich solch Urtheil wiederfähret / wie Christus hier dräuet. Vergleiche auch 1 Tom. IIX. Altenburg. p. 884. da Herr Lutherus saget: GOtt wil keinem gnädig seyn / noch seine Sünde vergeben / er vergebe denn seinem Nechsten auch. So kan auch der Glaube nicht rechtschaffen seyn / er bringe denn diese Frucht / daß er dem Nechsten vergebe / und umb Vergebung bitte. Sonst darff der Mensch für GOtt nicht kommen / ist diese Frucht nicht da / so ist der Glaube und die erste Beichte auch nicht rechtschaffen.)

v. 27. Ihr habt gehöret / daß zu den Alten gesaget ist: du solt nicht Ehebrechen. (2. Mos. XX. 18.)

v. 28. Ich aber sage euch: wer ein Weib ansiehet ihr zu begehren / der hat schon mit ihr die Ehe gebrochen

Plate 11 *Calovii Schrifften, Vol. 3,* passage from Matthew 5

Plate 12   Clavierbüchlein for Wilhelm Friedemann Bach, mostly autograph; title page written by Bach on 22 January 1720

Bach/Angefangen in/Cöthen den/22. Januar/Ao[anno] 1720" – shows not only his inborn sense for an aesthetic use of the available space, but also a loving father's careful and slightly embellished lettering (see Plate 12). Notice the capital letters B, W, F, B and C, as well as the g-like lower case h. The latter, by the way, is characteristic of title and dedicatory pages of the master. Why would eight pieces in this Notebook have been left unfinished?[5] They are in Friedemann's handwriting. Without being able to prove his point, the editor of the *Clavierbüchlein* in the *NBA*, Wolfgang Plath, came to the sensible conclusion that Johann Sebastian simply wanted to teach his son at an early age, as an important lesson of copying, always to be mindful of the available space and not to exceed it by writing the final bars on a new page. Johann Sebastian seems to have given his son a strict model to follow with the first two Praeambula, as the two-part inventions are called here.[6] At least Friedemann wrote each of the next five Praeambula[7] in a much more compact manner, within the prescribed space of two pages. He also indicated, apparently with the justifiable pride of a twelve-year-old boy, that he had shown himself worthy of his father's trust, by adding the word "Fine" in big letters at the end of the next five Praeambula (Nos. 3–7), and then got rid of what ink was left in his pen by a series of scribbly lines with which he filled the end of the staff.[8] In Friedemann's *Clavierbüchlein* the three-part sinfonias are called fantasias. As the F Major Fantasia, for instance, shows,[9] Bach further saw to it that these two-part and three-part pieces were written on the back page of one leaf and the front page of the next, so that each one of them could be played from the opened *Clavierbüchlein* without turning pages.

Between 1726 and 1731 Johann Sebastian started to introduce virtuoso obbligato organ parts into some of his church cantatas, as their most impressive feature. The sudden appearance of these organ concerto movements might suggest, in spite of a one-year absence of Friedemann from home (he was in Merseburg), that they were created with Friedemann's increasingly prodigious technical mastery of the organ in mind. The same is true, with greater certainty, of the six organ trio sonatas which Johann Sebastian

---

[5] See *Johann Sebastian Bach – Clavier-Büchlein vor Wilhelm Friedemann Bach*, edited in facsimile with a preface by Ralph Kirkpatrick (New Haven, Connecticut, 1959). See, for example, pp. 18, 37, 43, 53, 55, etc.

[6] *Ibid.*, pp. 74–7.

[7] *Ibid.*; see, for example, pp. 84–7.

[8] *Ibid.*; see, for example, pp. 79, 81, 85 and 87.

[9] *Ibid.*, pp. 124–5.

compiled in about 1730. It was always Friedemann whom Bach took along on his various journeys to Dresden; and in 1747 it was Friedemann again who accompanied his father on his last major trip to the court of Frederick the Great in Potsdam.

The autograph manuscript of the G Major Prelude and Fugue for organ, BWV 541, which was in New York City from 1945–83,[10] will add perhaps the most astounding evidence of Bach's preferential treatment of his first-born son. This score is a fair copy (*BS 352*) made from one of two earlier autograph manuscripts, which are however no longer extant. The water-mark of the paper occurs in no other composition by Bach, but it appears in two letters which Friedemann wrote on 7 June 1733, to the town council in Dresden and to the influential Council Syndicus, Dr Schröter. However, these letters were written not by Wilhelm Friedemann, but by his father, as can be plainly seen. Friedemann was then 22 years old, and, we may assume, perfectly capable of writing his own letters of application. Yet his father was apparently so anxious for his favorite son to obtain the then vacant position of organist in the Sophienkirche in Dresden that he wrote these letters for him, signing them without any apparent qualms "Wilhelm Friedemann Bach." However, he spells Wilhelm with two l's, Friedemann with one n, and uses a quite unusual C-like B for the B in Bach. Did he, at the point where he signed his son's name, show for a brief moment that he had a bad conscience? Today we would call Bach's action a typical indication of per-missive education. At least, it makes the great Johann Sebastian here a little less of a Saint Sebastian. He certainly had not the faintest notion that some day the truth of this matter would be revealed. The first volume of the *Bach-Dokumente* notes simply "autograph by Johann Sebastian," and then says that he wrote these two letters in the name of his son Wilhelm Friedemann, without adding any additional psychological commentary – which was probably considered to be out of place in the *Bach-Dokumente*. The paper which Johann Sebastian used for his copy of the organ prelude and fugue is also identical in size with that of the two letters of application. We can thus assume that Bach copied this, one of his brightest and most immediately appealing organ compositions, for Friedemann to use as his test piece in Dresden. Although there were seven applicants for the vacant position, of whom three were admitted to the audition, Wilhelm Friedemann was elect-ed unanimously on the day thereafter. Johann Sebastian's solicitude and active help had thus not been in vain.

Can we call Bach's part in this matter a case of paternal over-protection?

[10] It is now in the Staatsbibliothek Preussischer Kulturbesitz in West Berlin.

This much, at least can be said: when two months later the nineteen-year-old Carl Philipp Emanuel applied for the position of organist at St Wenceslas's Church in Naumburg, his father let his younger son write his own letter of application to the Naumburg Town Council, for which he used the same kind of paper. Unlike Friedemann, Philipp Emanuel did not succeed in obtaining the desired position. Apparently he was left to fend for himself, and, as his later positions at the Prussian court in Potsdam and thereafter his position in Hamburg showed, he learned to stand on his own feet. Friedemann, who obviously had received more of Johann Sebastian's love and guidance, apparently became so dependent upon them that life began to play havoc with him when his father died.

It was Friedemann who immediately hurried to Leipzig at the news of Sebastian's death. He returned to his post at the Liebfrauenkirche in Halle only after he had taken care of the affairs of his father's estate, and was rebuked severely for having overstayed the time of his leave. From this point disagreements and squabbles with his employers increased, revealing character traits astonishingly similar to those of his father. But Friedemann did not pursue and resolve these matters with his father's stubborn yet logical single-mindedness of purpose. I might go so far as to suggest that, if Johann Sebastian had still been alive in 1762 to advise his son, Friedemann would have become Graupner's successor as *Kapellmeister* at the Court of Darmstadt. Without his father's guidance, Friedemann vacillated and insisted on curiously inappropriate guarantees that ultimately cost him the coveted position. This position not only would have meant a substantial financial improvement over his Halle post as organist, but also would have represented a marked social advancement in his time. Was Friedemann's curious, self-defeating attitude perhaps caused by a sense of obligation to remain, as the oldest son, loyal to the organ? If so, then Friedemann had to pay dearly for this loyalty, for it was in his lifetime that the Age of Enlightenment was undermining the formerly secure social position and artistic prestige of the organist. Friedemann's instability and the frequent disappointments which he usually brought upon himself eventually led to embitterment and resignation. His father's over-protection was (as Karl Geiringer put it) a "fatal gift" that seems to have left its scars.

In 1764 the 54-year-old Friedemann terminated his position as organist in Halle. In fact, he discontinued his duties so abruptly that the Town Council was not even willing to grant him the requested payment for the remainder of the quarter. Thereafter, Friedemann was unemployed for the remaining twenty years of his life, eking out a meager existence as teacher of gifted students and by highly acclaimed though rare organ recitals, first in Halle, then in Braunschweig and finally in Berlin. Needless to say, Friedemann's unstable social condition was not conducive to a careful preservation of his father's manuscripts. On his abrupt departure from Braunschweig in 1774, apparent need forced him to leave the vast amount of his father's manuscripts behind and ask a friend to auction them off on his behalf.

The autograph score of Cantata 9, *Es ist das Heil uns kommen her*, which is in the Library of Congress, shows at the bottom right in Friedemann's handwriting the inscription "di J. S. Bach/propria manu script" (see Plate 13). Since Johann Sebastian wrote this cantata after Friedemann had left his father's house, Friedemann's authentication of it makes sense only in connection with his intention to sell the manuscript. In the same year (1774) of the planned auction, Carl Philipp Emanuel Bach complained in a letter to Forkel: "It is annoying that the manuscripts of our late father are becoming so dispersed. I am too old and busy to gather them together." Of course that refers not only to Friedemann but, as recently has been surmised, also to Johann Christoph Friedrich Bach. A few years earlier, Friedemann had offered the whole yearly cycle of his father's chorale cantatas to Forkel. But Forkel could not afford the purchase price of twenty Louis d'or at the time and reported in a letter that the whole yearly cycle later was sold out of necessity for twelve thaler. Forkel's letter, which is also in America, closes with the shocking words, "I do not know where they went." But we know that nine of these chorale cantatas eventually found their way to America,[11] as did the original performing parts of another four of Bach's Cantatas.

After this excursion, let me return to Johann Sebastian for the "finale." Unlike Mozart, Bach was not a prolific letter-writer, and of his 29 extant hand-written letters, not counting those where he only signed his name, only two are in America. But these are the last letters of the composer that have survived (*BS* 370 and 371) – those addressed to his cousin Johann Elias Bach. The one of 6 October 1748, about the "Prussian Fugue" (that is, the *Musical Offering*), is in the Scheide Library at Princeton University. The one of 2 November 1748, about the unwelcome gift of a cask of wine, is in the Pierpont Morgan Library in New York City. Although this last extant letter is almost amusingly prosaic in its content, it serves, along with the one-month-older letter, as a poignant reminder of the ageing master's cramped and deteriorating penmanship (see Plate 14). The well-known postscript (*BS* 372) reads:

---

[11] See footnote 1 above.

Plate 13   Cantata 9, *Es ist das Heil uns kommen her* (autograph score),
fo. 1r, opening ritornello of the chorale fantasy (mvt. 1)

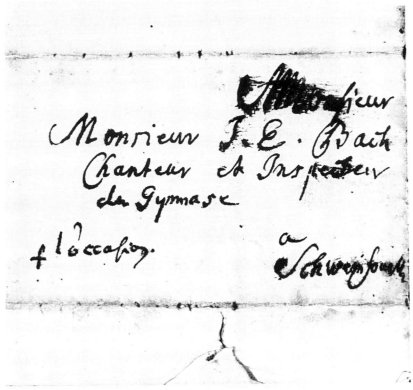

Plate 14   Letter to Johann Elias Bach, dated 6 October 1748

Although my honored cousin offers to oblige me with more of the wine, I must decline his offer on account of the excessive expenses here. For since the carriage-charges cost 16 groschen, the delivery-man 2 groschen, the customs inspector 2 groschen, the inland duty 5 groschen, my honored cousin can judge for himself that each quart [of wine] costs me almost 5 groschen which for a present is really too expensive.

Receipts of payments for usually annually recurring special services are not among the most interesting documents of a genius. Yet here again, out of the twelve in America, all of which of course have their own specific graphological significance, four are of particular interest. Not only do they belong to Bach's last ones, but the very last though incomplete receipt from the annual Nathan bequest from the end of October 1749 is no longer written by Bach himself, but by his fourteen-year-old son Johann Christian Bach (see Plate 15). This moving indication of either failing eyesight or failing general health, or possibly both, appears nine months before the composer's death, midway between Gottlob Harrer's untimely-seeming "trial performance for the future appointment" as Thomascantor "in case the Capellmeister and Cantor Sebastian Bach should die" and the two cataract operations with their ensuing disastrous and eventually fatal result.

The fact that Johann Christian wrote this last receipt is vivid evidence that in the last days of October 1749 his father was no longer able to write. The following leaf with the first receipts of Bach's successor Harrer is no longer in the receipt book (which is likewise in private possession in New York City). Should this leaf still exist, it must show at the top of its front page those six lines in Johann Christian Bach's handwriting that are missing on the surviving leaf (see Plate 15). Should Johann Sebastian have signed his name beneath his son's completed receipt of late October 1749, this signature would constitute the last document from the master's pen.

The superbly preserved oil portrait of Bach that hangs in the music room at the home of William Scheide in Princeton, New Jersey, will conclude my observations (see Plate 16). Painted from life by the Saxon Court painter Elias Gottlieb Haußmann in 1748, it is in all probability the portrait that Philipp Emanuel Bach had owned and which was described carefully in his estate catalogue. It is one Bach source in America which does not go back to Wilhelm Friedemann but to Philipp Emanuel Bach.

The painting shows the 63-year-old master not resigned or embittered, but a still vigorous man who appears to have a sense of humor as well as perspicacity. He looks perfectly conscious of his rank in society, of his dignity and of his identity. He seems to be secure in his knowledge of his abilities without showing any of the grand airs of genius. Self-possessed, he holds out to the viewer a six-part circle canon as a mark of his trade; perhaps a bit bemused, because only he knows the countless solutions to this three-measure miracle he had wrought and by which music, as a member of the old medieval quadrivium – that is, music as a mathematical art – still survived. Bach looks at Haußmann and thus at the beholder as a man who affirmed life, not because society had given him what was his due, but because of an inner knowledge that what he had created in an exceptionally busy life had been good and worth the effort. His seems to be a smile of satisfaction, the unconscious smile of the born artist, who only has to step to his instrument to experience the unspeakable satisfaction of making music, a satisfaction which Bach, as a creative musician and as an unsurpassed keyboard virtuoso, must have enjoyed to the highest degree. This

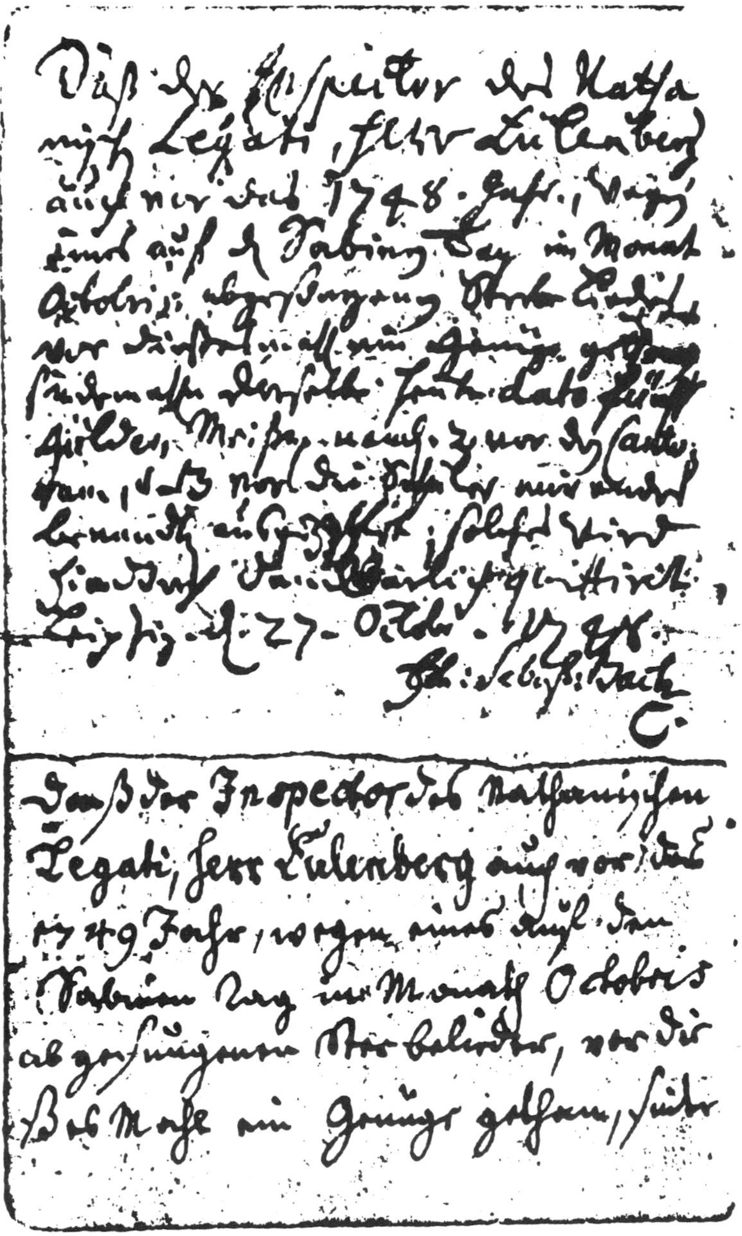

Plate 15   Autograph receipts by Bach; Nathan Bequest 1748 and
first half of non-autograph receipt of 1749

Plate 16 Johann Sebastian Bach; oil portrait,
1748 (?) by Elias Gottlieb Haußmann

painting thus shows the master as he looked in 1748, one year before his health and eyesight began to deteriorate. Another year later, a higher fate stayed his hand, and with it, his pen, through which his creative and daily thoughts had flowed and which we have followed here in some American Bach sources through 42 years of the composer's life.

Index of Bach's works cited

BWV: Wolfgang Schmieder, *Thematisch-systematisches Verzeichnis der musikalischen Werke von Johann Sebastian Bach* (Leipzig, 1950)

1–215 Cantatas

Index of names

This index does not include J. S. Bach

WIDENER UNIVERSITY
WOLFGRAM
LIBRARY
CHESTER, PA.